FAULKNER'S HOLLYWOOD NOVELS

Faulkner's Hollywood Novels

WOMEN BETWEEN PAGE AND SCREEN

Ben Robbins

UNIVERSITY OF VIRGINIA PRESS
Charlottesville and London

The University of Virginia Press is situated on the traditional lands of the Monacan Nation, and the Commonwealth of Virginia was and is home to many other Indigenous people. We pay our respect to all of them, past and present. We also honor the enslaved African and African American people who built the University of Virginia, and we recognize their descendants. We commit to fostering voices from these communities through our publications and to deepening our collective understanding of their histories and contributions.

University of Virginia Press
© 2024 by the Rector and Visitors of the University of Virginia
All rights reserved
Printed in the United States of America on acid-free paper

First published 2024

9 8 7 6 5 4 3 2 1

Library of Congress Cataloging-in-Publication Data
Names: Robbins, Ben, author.
Title: Faulkner's Hollywood novels : women between page and screen / Ben Robbins.
Description: Charlottesville : University of Virginia Press, 2024. | Includes bibliographical references and index.
Identifiers: LCCN 2024004751 (print) | LCCN 2024004752 (ebook) | ISBN 9780813951515 (hardcover ; acid-free paper) | ISBN 9780813951539 (paperback ; acid-free paper) | ISBN 9780813951522 (ebook)
Subjects: LCSH: Faulkner, William, 1897–1962—Criticism and interpretation. | Faulkner, William, 1897–1962—Influence. | Women in literature. | BISAC: LITERARY CRITICISM / American / General | LCGFT: Literary criticism.
Classification: LCC PS3511.A86 Z9613 2024 (print) | LCC PS3511.A86 (ebook) | DDC 813/.52—dc23/eng/20240201
LC record available at https://lccn.loc.gov/2024004751
LC ebook record available at https://lccn.loc.gov/2024004752

Publication of this volume has been supported by New Literary History.

Cover art: Joan Crawford, Robert Young, and Howard Hawks on the set of *Today We Live*, 1933. (©SZ Photo/Scherl/Bridgeman Images)
Cover design: TG Design

For Jake
And in memory of Gary Robbins (1957–2007)

Contents

Acknowledgments — ix
List of Abbreviations — xiii

Introduction: Faulkner's Displaced Hollywood Novels — 1
1. *Sanctuary*, Flapperhood, and the Pre-Code Vice Film — 49
2. Collaborative Labor and the Dialogic Construction of the Hawksian Woman — 83
3. *If I Forget Thee, Jerusalem*, Corporate Artists, and Hack Writers — 132
4. Inscrutable Images and Cultural Migrations: Wartime Noir and the Compson "Appendix" — 167
5. *Requiem for a Nun* and Cold War Hollywood Melodrama — 197
6. "Castrate of Sound": *The Mansion* and the Silence of Cinematic Archetypes — 228

Notes — 249
Works Cited — 265
Index — 281

Acknowledgments

The research for this book began during my doctoral studies within the Graduate School of North American Studies (GSNAS) at the Freie Universität (FU) in Berlin. First of all, my sincerest thanks go to my dissertation supervisors at the FU, Winfried Fluck and Ulla Haselstein. Prof. Fluck was enthusiastic about the project from the very beginning and offered encouragement and support through the doctoral program, and I am grateful to Prof. Haselstein for her insights and input, including helping me to expand the scope of this project. I would like to express my gratitude to the German Excellence Initiative, administered by the German Research Foundation (DFG), for funding my research and making this project possible.

Huge thanks go to Peter Lurie, a leading expert on Faulkner and film studies, who kindly agreed to be an international supervisor for my PhD. Peter has been extremely generous and helpful in nurturing my ideas, giving me feedback on my writing at different stages of revision, and pointing me in the direction of a wide range of resources. I am incredibly grateful for his continuing support and faith in my research.

Within the GSNAS, I benefited hugely from dialogue and lively debate from my doctoral colleagues in the literary and cultural studies programs:

Sonja Longolius, Dietmar Meinel, Ahu Tanrisever, Kathryn Schweishelm, and Lina Tegtmeyer.

This work would not have been possible without the support of the international Faulknerian community. I've had the privilege to present parts of what would become this book at the following conferences in Australia, the United States, and Europe: the Faulkner in the Media Ecology Conference, University of New South Wales, Sydney (organized by Julian Murphet and Stefan Solomon), in 2011; the American Literature Association Conference in San Francisco (as part of a panel titled "Faulkner and Fitzgerald" organized by Maggie Gordon Froehlich and Jay Watson), for which I was lucky to receive a Dahlem Research School travel grant to fund my trip in 2012; the Faulkner and Yoknapatawpha Conferences at the University of Mississippi in 2012, 2013, and 2022 (organized by Jay Watson), for which my most recent presentation was supported by the International Relations Office of the University of Innsbruck; the Reframing and Performing Faulkner symposium at the Center for Transnational American Studies, University of Copenhagen, at the kind invitation of Martyn Bone in 2013; and the Faulkner Studies in the UK Colloquium (organized by Ahmed Honeini) and the Faulkner's Fetishized Words International Symposium (co-organized by Peter Lurie and Frédérique Spill) in 2021. At all these events, I have benefited from invaluable conversations and exchanges with scholars of Faulkner and modernism, including Martyn Bone, Elizabeth Rodriguez Fielder, Sarah Gleeson-White, Robert Jackson, Mary Knighton, John T. Matthews, Owen Robinson, Carl Rollyson, Melanie Masterton Sherazi, Jay Watson, and Michael Zeitlin.

Special thanks go to Steve Railton, who invited me to be a collaborating editor on University of Virginia's Digital Yoknapatawpha (DY) project in 2014. My work within the digital humanities through DY has shaped many of my insights into Faulkner's work over the past years, and I present some of these findings in the book's introduction. And thank you to the international team of collaborating editors on DY for making data entry surprisingly fun!

There is a strong archival component to this research, as I analyze a large body of Faulkner's screenwriting that still remains out of print. In 2012, I was honored to receive a Lillian Gary Taylor Visiting Fellowship in American Literature from the Harrison Institute of the University of Virginia to work with the Faulkner materials in the Special Collections. I would like to thank Hoke Perkins, then director of the Harrison Institute, for coordinating my fellowship and making me feel so welcome in Charlottesville, and all the archivists for their assistance in finding my way through the collections. I also wish to acknowledge my co–Taylor Fellows, Amanda Johnson and Lorie Leavell, for being my archive pals! Additionally, I completed a research trip to the archives at the University of Southeast Missouri (SEMO) to work with the Brodsky Collection. I owe much to Robert W. Hamblin and Christopher Rieger for helping me to use the collections and welcoming me to Cape Girardeau. I also received generous help from the following people to clarify a number of details for the Faulkner holdings at SEMO: Tyson M. Koenig (associate archivist at the Special Collections), Hannah M. Houston, and Stephanie Whanger. Thank you for your diligence in untangling the complexities of the files for *To Have and Have Not!*

I am indebted to my colleagues in the Department of American Studies at the University of Innsbruck for providing me with a stimulating and collegial academic environment in which to complete my work on this book. I am especially grateful to Christian Quendler and Cornelia Klecker for their help and encouragement in producing the book proposal. I also wish to acknowledge my students in both Berlin and Innsbruck for their lively contributions to our discussions over the years about US modernist writing.

Parts of this book have appeared in previous publications and have been revised for republication. The full credits from Intellect Books, Johns Hopkins University Press, and Duke University Press appear below. In relation to these publications, I have been fortunate to have the support and instructive editorial feedback of Jill Nelmes from the *Journal of Screenwriting*; Erik Dussere, editor of a special issue of the *Faulkner Journal*, "Faulkner and noir"; and James Zeigler, academic editor of *Genre*. I am also thankful for Kathryn Schweishelm's generous comments on various drafts of the article on *Requiem for a Nun* that appeared in *Genre*.

In the latter stages of this book's development, I was fortunate to receive the support of Faulknerian colleagues who read a number of chapters, and the manuscript was greatly improved by the feedback of Peter Lurie, Stefan Solomon, and Theresa M. Towner.

At the University of Virginia Press, I would like to express my immense gratitude to the director and editor in chief, Eric Brandt, for his enthusiasm for the book on receiving my proposal and his untiring support in guiding the manuscript towards publication. I would like to acknowledge the helpful feedback of the anonymous reviewers for the Press on both my proposal and sample chapters and the full manuscript. I would also like to thank

Fernando Campos, acquisitions coordinator, and Wren Morgan Myers, project editor, for all their help in the final stages of the book's development.

Last but by no means least, I want to thank Jake Schneider for his energetic engagement with my writing and thoughts over the past decade and whose love has been a constant source of support. And to my parents, Gary and Julie, who indulged their young son's watching of 1940s melodramas on sunny summer days and whose love of reading led me to discover that, in the words of Cat Stevens, "there's a million things to be."

The last section of chapter 2 ("Sexual competition in 'To Have and Have Not'") was originally published as part of Ben Robbins, "The Pragmatic Modernist: William Faulkner's Craft and Hollywood's Networks of Production," in the *Journal of Screenwriting* 5, no. 2 (Winter 2014), 239–57. Published with permission of Intellect Books.

Chapter 4 was originally published as Ben Robbins, "Inscrutable Images and Cultural Migrations: Wartime Noir and the Compson Appendix," Copyright © 2014 Johns Hopkins University Press. It first appeared in the *Faulkner Journal* 28, no. 1, Spring 2014, 55–77. Published with permission by Johns Hopkins University Press.

Chapter 5 was originally published as Ben Robbins, "William Faulkner's *Requiem for a Nun* and Cold War Hollywood Melodrama," in *Genre: Forms of Discourse and Culture* 50, no. 3, Dec. 2017, 343–70. Copyright 2017, University of Oklahoma. All rights reserved. Republished by permission of the publisher, Duke University Press.

Abbreviations

Works by William Faulkner and major archival holdings for the author are abbreviated in the citations and endnotes as follows:

LDBC	Louis Daniel Brodsky Collection of William Faulkner Materials, Special Collections and Archives, Kent Library, Southeast Missouri State University, Cape Girardeau
CL	*Country Lawyer and Other Stories for the Screen*
CS	*Collected Stories of William Faulkner*
ESPL	*Essays, Speeches and Public Letters*
FBC	*Faulkner: A Comprehensive Guide to the Brodsky Collection*, 5 volumes
LG	*Lion in the Garden: Interviews with William Faulkner, 1926–1962*
MGM	*Faulkner's MGM Screenplays*
N	*Novels*, 5 volumes
SL	*Selected Letters of William Faulkner*
SR	*Stallion Road: A Screenplay*
TCF	*William Faulkner at Twentieth Century-Fox: The Annotated Screenplays*
US	*Uncollected Stories of William Faulkner*
WFFC	William Faulkner Foundation Collection 1918–1958, accession number 6074–6074-d, series IV: Writing for Television and

Movies, Albert and Shirley Small Special Collections Library, University of Virginia, Charlottesville, box 10

An additional primary text by Meta Carpenter Wilde and Orin Borsten is abbreviated in the citations and endnotes as follows:

ALG   *A Loving Gentleman: The Love Story of William Faulkner and Meta Carpenter*

FAULKNER'S HOLLYWOOD NOVELS

INTRODUCTION

Faulkner's Displaced Hollywood Novels

WILLIAM FAULKNER INSISTED IN 1958 that he was "not a moving picture man" (Faulkner, "Undergraduate Writing Class"), but he had been a successful Hollywood screenwriter for a considerable length of time prior to making this statement. Between 1932 and 1954, Faulkner worked intermittently for five of the major studios of the Golden Age of Hollywood for a total of around four years: Metro-Goldwyn-Mayer (MGM), Universal, Twentieth Century–Fox, Radio-Keith-Orpheum (RKO), and Warner Brothers. He produced scripts for two of the leading directors of the period, Howard Hawks and John Ford, and developed a long-standing, fruitful collaboration with the former that would last for over twenty years. Although Faulkner only earned a total of six screen credits for his labors in Hollywood, he worked on around fifty film projects at various stages of development and wrote scripts across the diverse genres of romance, horror, melodrama, screwball comedy, the detective film, war and adventure films, and the historical epic. His contributions to these movies helped cement the popular images of leading stars of the studio system, including Joan Crawford in *Today We Live* (1933) and *Mildred Pierce* (1945) and Lauren Bacall and Humphrey Bogart in *To Have and Have Not* (1944) and *The Big Sleep* (1946). Yet, despite this large body of work and his considerable achievements within the profession,

Faulkner would repeatedly distance himself from his time in Hollywood and the screenplays he authored there, insisting, metaphorically, that he had "movie work locked off into another room" (*SL* 186). This language of exclusion is, in a sense, not surprising, since Faulkner was effectively an economic migrant; struggling to support himself from the publication of the experimental, modernist fiction for which he was known, he was among a number of fiction writers who made the journey west to write for the movies to supplement their income with more lucrative studio contracts in the 1920s and 1930s, part of an illustrious group that included F. Scott Fitzgerald, John Dos Passos, and Nathanael West.

Reading against such statements, this book works to reveal cross-media exchanges between Faulkner's fiction and screenwriting across the breadth of his Hollywood career from the early 1930s to the 1950s. Distinct from previous work on Faulkner and film, it takes a thematic approach to this large body of work to show how the author used gender relations to meditate on the intersections, conflicts, and intimacies of the relationship between modernism and popular culture. My work is indebted to pioneering scholarship on Faulkner and women that has demonstrated how the author explores his sense of his own craft through female characters who are symbolic of creativity (procreative and artistic). Minrose C. Gwin argues that Faulkner is "the creator of female subjects who, in powerful and creative ways, disrupt and sometimes even destroy patriarchal structures" borne out of Faulkner's "peculiar bisexuality" as an author who "decenters our notions of the relationship between male creator and female created" (*Feminine and Faulkner* 4). Deborah Clarke sees the disruptive presence of women as "a mysterious, often threatening power, which is aligned with his own creativity and the grounds of his own fiction . . . both the source of and the threat to figurative creativity" (6–7). However, existing studies of Faulkner's female characters have not yet appraised how his distinctive gender portrayals emerged alongside those he created for film, which extend his focus on women as both threat and spur to masculine creativity. In this regard, Judith L. Sensibar, in a ground-breaking feminist biography of Faulkner, has revealed how the author's work and imagination was shaped by his relationships with his Black nurse, Caroline Barr, his mother, Maud Falkner, and his wife, Estelle Oldham (Sensibar, *Faulkner and Love*). In contrast, this book considers the previously overlooked influence on Faulkner's writing of women he encountered in Hollywood, which includes actors (Tallulah

Bankhead, Joan Crawford, Lauren Bacall, and Ruth Ford), screenwriters (Leigh Brackett and Kathryn Scola), and script editors (Meta Carpenter).

In what follows, I aim to move beyond the reductive antagonism Faulkner professed in his public statements and correspondence, to emphasize the contact points between literature and film across his work in terms of collaboration, visual mediation, and genre, paying particular attention to the following: Faulkner's collaborations with women in the production of screenplays and fiction, his meditations on the framing of women within visual culture, and his engagement with and reinvention of female character types within Hollywood genres, which frequently lay outside the Southern imaginary.[1] As we will see, Faulkner's attempts to distance himself rhetorically from his commercial work for film were often expressed in gendered terms. However, this belies the continual dialogue between his screenwriting and fiction throughout his career, which led to the creation of a series of distinctive and formally experimental "Hollywood novels" that incorporated features of his scripts and elements of his experiences within the studio system into his prose. These texts challenge traditional understandings of the Hollywood novel as a regional genre penned by disgruntled screenwriters, since they engage with the genres and creative practices of the studio system in "displaced," non-Californian settings. My work specifically shows how the female filmic archetypes Faulkner wrote for the screen were absorbed into his Hollywood-inspired fictions and reworked again in his screenwriting. The traffic of these archetypes produced representations of filmic womanhood, in which Faulkner's images of women within his modernist prose became increasingly mediated by the techniques, language, conventions, and working methods of Hollywood. This book will demonstrate that for Faulkner, as screenwriter and author, to engage with Hollywood genre was also always to engage with gender.

Given the scale of Faulkner's achievements in Hollywood, despite his primarily economic motivation for moving there, we should consider his attempts to dismiss his work for the studios as somewhat performative. Faulkner's correspondence and statements about Hollywood frequently draw on the themes of contagion, commodification, and illusion to describe the film industry. In his letters, Faulkner presents Hollywood as a disease that, when returning to Mississippi from California, he needs time "to get ... out of [his] system" or "out of [his] lungs," as well as the practice of screenwriting "out of [his] reflexes" (*SL* 187, 205, 248). Faulkner's evocative statement that southern Hollywood was, "artistically" speaking, the "plastic asshole of the world" distills the attributes of commodification and illusion into a single vivid image (Brodsky, "Glimpses" xxvi).

These themes are also sustained in Faulkner's allusions to Hollywood in his fiction, which traffic in the same language of squalid commodification or sinister illusion. We can assess these allusions both qualitatively and quantitatively using new tools from the digital humanities. The Digital Yoknapatawpha (DY) resource contains a comprehensive database of locations, characters, and events for the sixty-eight fictions Faulkner set in Yoknapatawpha, his fictional Mississippi county, and can therefore give us a quantifiable sense of how references to Hollywood spread across Faulkner's work throughout his career. It is possible to use DY's keyword search feature to call up allusions to Hollywood as a cultural signifier in Faulkner's prose. The feature generates three entries from Faulkner's 1950s fictions: one each respectively for *Requiem for a Nun* (1951), *The Town* (1957), and *The Mansion* (1959).[2] In the scene from *Requiem,* the lawyer Gavin Stevens describes his nephew Gowan's vanity using the simile of "the Virginia-trained aristocrat caught with his gentility around his knees like the guest in the trick Hollywood bathroom" (*N* 4: 578). The implication here is that surface appearances are a mere illusion, and Hollywood is synonymous with entrapment. In the reference from *The Town,* Melisandre Backus, a member of a wealthy, plantation-owning family, cannot accept the rumors about her murdered husband's criminal activities. According to the text, "Hollywood itself, let alone Al Capone, wouldn't have been ashamed of" the "limousines" (*N* 5: 157) that turn up at the dead gangster's funeral, the Californian film industry appearing to be representative of an illusory glamor that conceals darker realities. Finally, in *The Mansion* Gavin Stevens is again connected to Hollywood through his failed performance of social status after his marriage to Backus. While Stevens can be found "acting the squire," a figure the narrator associates with relative youth, the image is undermined by his "shock of premature white hair like a concert pianist or a Hollywood Cadillac agent" (*N* 5: 650). Hollywood here is again associated with appearances that confuse the viewer through their polished marketability.

Faulkner's letters, statements, and fictional allusions consistently reinforce the idea that the influence of Hollywood has to be repressed. Such language would, taken at face value, seem to support the "great divide" between high art and popular culture, in which "modernism constituted itself through a conscious strategy of exclusion, an anxiety of contamination by its other: an increasingly consuming and engulfing mass culture" (Huyssen vii). Indeed, Faulkner's words neatly dovetail with many of the objections to popular culture and Hollywood propounded by philosophers such as Max Horkheimer and Theodor W. Adorno, who were members of the Frankfurt School of critical theory and belonged to a group of German émigrés in mid-century California; their work provided a detailed critical definition of mass culture contemporary to the modernist cultural movement. Adorno and Horkheimer's jointly authored book *Dialectic of Enlightenment* (1944) marks a key moment in the critical program to divide modernism from mass culture in order to maintain a position of cultural resistance against the forces of instrumental rationality. This has particular relevance to Faulkner's career, as they position Hollywood film as the epitome of the betrayal of the arts, particularly in the chapter titled "The Culture Industry: Enlightenment as Mass Deception," where they elaborate a series of charges against commercial film, such as the use of formula and its pseudo-intellectualism, which threaten to lull mass audiences into a state of compliant passivity. The essay attacks the formal properties of the movies, ironizing, for example, the transparent predictability of the romance plot, where "the rough treatment which the beloved gets from the male star, the latter's rugged defiance of the spoilt heiress, are, like all the other details, ready-made clichés to be slotted in anywhere" (125). Faulkner too found sufficient ground for ridicule in the mere superficial tinkering of the romance formula that was required to produce a new movie whilst adhering to the overall conventions of a genre; the Hollywood producer Jerry Wald "found in Faulkner's abandoned desk a yellow legal pad bearing the familiar miniscule pen strokes. They formed a series of formulas: 'Boy meets girl . . . Boy gets girl . . . Boy loses girl . . . Boy sues girl. . . .' And so on, for pages" (Blotner, "Faulkner in Hollywood" 293).

Horkheimer and Adorno also wished to protect "high art" from a shallow need to entertain and titillate, since serious work, and works of formal difficulty, should aim to subvert social norms, not succumb to the mass cultural trend of "an intellectualization of amusement," in which entertainment is instrumentalized and its effects are programmed (143). The pseudo-intellectual elevation of mass culture, for Adorno, is echoed by the infantilizing effect mass art has on the subject, who is exposed to cultural products that "would very much like to make adults into eleven-year-olds" ("Culture Industry Reconsidered" 105). Faulkner similarly attacked the phoniness of Hollywood as a place in which appearances do not correspond with reality and gloss belies hollow content. On the social makeup of Tinseltown, Faulkner stated that "this is a nice town full of very rich middle class people who have not yet discovered the cerebrum" (*SL* 313), and in Faulkner's only fictional work set in Los Angeles, the short story "Golden Land" (1935), California appears as a location of pure surface, where intellectual depth has been sacrificed in the pursuit of a timeless, static beauty that implies complexity but is pure image, the foundation of "a new race not yet seen on the earth: of men and women without age, beautiful as gods and goddesses, and with the minds of infants" (*CS* 721). The despair expressed here is that this abstract beauty, in all its surreal perfection, signals an abandonment of the values of depth that allow one to fight against processes of commodification. The fact that these statements on Hollywood (or its milieu) align so well with the language of Adorno and Horkheimer makes it tempting to accept a vision of Faulkner as an author who is uncompromising in his desire to negate the influence of mass culture, since these remarks function to conceal the many contact points between the author's fiction and screenwriting.

If one delves beneath the surface of the fictions Faulkner produced after his work for the studios, his allusions to Hollywood are in fact undercut by the structures of the texts themselves. These works unabashedly borrow from the techniques and genre conventions of commercial cinema, frequently with the intention of configuring gender relations. Another of *The Mansion*'s references to Hollywood neatly illustrates how Faulkner's prose absorbed aspects of his screenwriting, despite the restricted range of language through which he would overtly address Hollywood elsewhere. In a scene of tentative courtship from the novel, Charles Mallison Jr. (or Chick) drives Linda Snopes Kohl home. Linda leaps out of the car to make her way to her front door, without expecting Chick's chivalry. The prose describes the pair's actions, and how Linda can be seen

> already opening the door on her side so that Charles would have to get out on his to get around the car in time. Though no matter how fast that was, she would be already out, already turning up the walk toward the portico . . . Charles would have to overtake, in effect outrun her already halfway to the house; whereupon she would check, almost pause in fact, to glance back at him, startled—not alarmed: just startled; merely what Hollywood called a double-take, still not so far dis-severed from her Southern heritage to recall that he, Charles, dared not risk some casual passerby reporting to his uncle

that his nephew permitted the female he was seeing home to walk at least forty feet unaccompanied to her front door. (*N* 5: 651–52)³

Through the allusion, Faulkner indicates that gendered interactions could be translated to the screen through the rapid and dynamic editing of shots. The scene reveals its awareness of two dominant conventions of Hollywood cinema: first, we sense Faulkner bearing in mind the 180-degree rule, which establishes the position of characters in relation to the camera within a given space, as he creates a clear line of action, between the car and the house, along which Chick and Linda move; and we can also perceive the author considering the structuring of shot/reverse shots here, which establish the characters' positions in relation to one another by cutting between shots, when he describes the exchange of glances between Linda and Chick, of which Linda's "double-take" is a part. Such techniques are used to document characters' movements and interactions in film seamlessly, and within the "classical" Hollywood style they worked to preserve continuity editing by reinforcing "spatial orientation" and aiding the smooth transition between shots (Bordwell et al. 56).

The scene from *The Mansion* provides but one example of the underlying debt of Faulkner's fictions to the conventions of commercial film after his work in Hollywood, and it also demonstrates the author's awareness that cinematic techniques could be used to structure gendered exchanges within his prose. Despite such correspondences between forms in popular culture and constructions of identity within his fiction, Faulkner also drew on gendered language to divorce himself from his Hollywood work. The most intimate account we have of Faulkner's time in Hollywood is a memoir authored by Meta Carpenter and published in 1976, in which she describes her romance with the writer. Carpenter was Howard Hawks's secretary and script editor, and she would have a long-lasting affair with Faulkner after they met while they were both working on the war film *The Road to Glory* (1936) for Hawks at Fox. In the memoir, titled *A Loving Gentleman*, Carpenter describes Faulkner's resolute will not to sacrifice his modernist fictions for his Hollywood work, since "even in his relatively short time as a wage earner in Hollywood, he had seen the system so corrupt novelists of great promise that their new books, if they wrote them at all, were little better than pot-boilers, scarcely recognizable as the work of the same authors. There were even writers who became so habituated to turning out pages only when the first check was in their hot, greedy hands that they could never again write on speculation. 'Whores,' Bill said of them" (*ALG* 185). In this exchange, Faulkner clearly wishes to disentangle himself from the persona of the "hack" writer, who only produces work under commission, since he instead wants to assert the value of his fiction beyond commercial imperatives. The term through which Faulkner expresses this creative distinction is highly suggestive, branding his fellow screenwriters "whores." It appears that hack writing is a process of artistic degradation that Faulkner associates with feminization, as the author metaphorically invokes the figure of the "promiscuous" or "immoral" woman to describe this activity.

This statement could perhaps be overlooked if it were an isolated incident, but Faulkner consistently allied forms of popular culture in which he had a hand—whether screenwriting, magazine writing, or pulp fiction—with feminization in order to detach himself from them through the use of sexist discourse. In the winter of 1932, a few months after he first started working for Hollywood, Faulkner wrote to his publisher, Harrison Smith, that, due to financial difficulties, he may have to put aside work on his novel *Light in August* (1932) and "go whoring again with short stories" (*SL* 59). It was a statement he would reiterate in the autumn of 1934 in a letter to his agent, Morton Goldman, in relation to placing short stories with periodicals, describing that "I like to help all these earnest magazines, but I have too goddamn many demands on me requiring and necessitating orthodox prostitution to have time to give it away" (*SL* 85). Apparently forms of writing with a clear commercial intention, and which distracted from labor on his modernist novels, could be associated with feminization and sexual exploitation. Faulkner even described one of his modernist novels, *Sanctuary* (1931), using a dissociative gendered binary due to its debt to popular culture and pulp writing (since the text explicitly draws on the mass-market genres of the detective story and gangster fiction). In his introduction to the 1932 Modern Library edition of *Sanctuary*, Faulkner draws a distinction between the novels that were crafted without an eye to the market and those that were intentionally composed for financial gain. On the one hand, *The Sound and the Fury* (1929) and *As I Lay Dying* (1930) were produced when he was "young" and "hard-bellied" and "had never lived among nor known people who wrote novels and stories," so as such he "did not know that people got money for them" (*ESPL* 176). On the other hand, *Sanctuary* was allegedly composed in a state of weakness, as he had become "a little soft" (*ESPL* 176) after an awareness of the market pervaded the writing that he pitched to magazine editors, leading to his own self-commodification, in which he "began to think of [himself] again as a printed object . . . to think of books in terms of possible money" (*ESPL* 177).[4] Though the *Sanctuary* introduction is of course performative in nature, the essay draws on a similar gendered opposition in which Faulkner associates his apparently "autonomous" modernist novels with tough masculinity, while the pulp-inflected "potboiler" *Sanctuary* is related to feminine dependency.[5] In fact, in a literal reflection of his metaphors for pulp fiction, Faulkner told Carpenter that he had written the novel based on "what whores in Memphis told" him (*ALG* 52), a statement that we should not take at face value but is nevertheless suggestive.

Faulkner was playing a common modernist discursive trick here, in which mass cultural forms were Othered as feminine in order to dominate them and control their influence. Gender conflicts have always been at the center of modernism, and developments in feminist criticism have shown how the cultural movement was "shaped by a host of exclusions and embattlements pertaining to gender" (Mao and Walkowitz, *Bad Modernisms* 8) as part of an enduring gender bias against popular culture.[6] Andreas Huyssen has demonstrated how mass culture became synonymous with the large-scale political movements of the late nineteenth and early twentieth centuries that threatened the dominant culture, as "in the age of nascent socialism *and* the first major women's movement in Europe, the masses knocking at the gate were also women, knocking at a gate of a male-dominated culture" (47). Cultural discourses absorbed this conflict within a hierarchical structure, polarizing feminine mass culture with high culture, which, within this framework, "whether traditional or modern, clearly remains the privileged realm of male activities" (47). This led to the gendering of specific modes of artistic expression; as John T. Matthews summarizes, "the expression of liberatory aspirations in mass cultural forms like popular romance, short fiction, theater, and ultimately the movies leads high culture to associate mass culture with the feminine, to try to subordinate it as woman" ("Culture Industry" 70). Faulkner was, then, following a pattern in which popular culture was connected to negatively coded "feminine" qualities to maintain a clear opposition between zones of creative activity.

Allusions to Hollywood in Faulkner's fictions also maintain these cultural associations, in which popular culture is associated with feminization and "whoring." DY's cumulative location entry for Hollywood gives more information about Faulkner's Yoknapatawpha fictions that use the West Coast film community as a location for an event or a character's residence.

The two texts listed in the entry are "Appendix Compson: 1699–1945" (1946) and *The Mansion*. Hollywood is only once given as the site of an event in the Yoknapatawpha fictions: it is where Caddy Compson, a central figure from Faulkner's novel *The Sound and the Fury* (1929), meets her second husband, "a minor movingpicture magnate" (*N* 1: 1133), which is described in Faulkner's "Appendix" to the original novel, a character development I analyze in detail in chapter 4. In *The Mansion*, Hollywood is linked to the financial ambitions of the Snopes family as the residence of Montgomery Ward Snopes, a former brothel owner and the man who brought French pornography to Yoknapatawpha, who is last seen in Los Angeles "engaged in some quite lucrative adjunct or correlant to the motion picture industry or anyway colony" (*N* 5: 660). Ward Snopes is therefore potentially active in the production of pornographic film there. From these examples alone, Hollywood again becomes associated with the exploitation of female sexuality, since Compson's short-lived marriage is presented as a key stage in her degradation, as she apparently moves between partners for financial gain, and Ward Snopes's career implies that commercial film and pornography are essentially interchangeable in their seedy objectification of the female image.

On a superficial level of reference, then, the presence of Hollywood in Faulkner's fictional worlds would appear limited and a mere reinforcement of the negative associations of contagion, commodification, illusion, and feminization that the author maintained in his statements elsewhere. However, as Maria DiBattista challenged in the mid-1990s, "neither of the cultural models currently available—the theory of contagion, which presumes the necessary, often predatory encroachments of high and low on each other's domain, and the theory of exclusion, which pictures high modernist males slamming the door in the face of the low moderns variously characterized as 'feminine,' populist, commercially savvy, or sunk in a materialist bog—captures the suppleness, inventiveness, erotic ambivalence, misunderstandings, estrangements, and even the occasional tenderness of the relation" (18). Reading against these models of contagion and exclusion, and the gendered language that has often underpinned them, this book attends to the multiple ways in which Faulkner's fictions, produced after and alongside his work in Hollywood, reveal their debt to the tropes and conventions of commercial cinema by paying close attention to instances of cross-pollination between Faulkner's screenplays and fiction from the early 1930s to the late 1950s.

In labeling a series of Faulkner's works of fiction "Hollywood novels," I am adapting existing definitions of the literary genre. These texts are not Hollywood novels in the traditional sense, since none of them are principally set within the Californian film industry. The action central to the novels on which the subsequent chapters focus principally takes place in the states of Mississippi, Tennessee, Louisiana, Illinois, Wisconsin, and Utah, only ever briefly referencing California. Although a number of Faulkner's fellow modernists who tried their hands at screenwriting would progress and cement the genre of the Hollywood novel, such as West in *The Day of the Locust* (1939) or Fitzgerald in his unfinished, posthumously published *The Last Tycoon* (1941), Faulkner would never himself write a novel-length work about California, only ever producing a single short story set in the Hollywood area: "Golden Land." However, it is productive to reframe a number of texts Faulkner produced after his work for the studios as displaced Hollywood novels. Although these works are geographically distanced from California, they share some of the thematic concerns of the Hollywood novel, and, most importantly, they repeatedly demonstrate their debt to the genre conventions of commercial film through their dialogic relationship to Faulkner's screenwriting.

The Hollywood novel is a regional genre that emerged in tandem with the development and growth of the film industry in the 1910s, and it reached its apotheosis in the 1930s and 1940s, part of the classical era of Hollywood, through the publication of canonical works such as Budd Schulberg's *What Makes Sammy Run?* (1941) and Evelyn Waugh's *The Loved One* (1948), in addition to the novels by West and Fitzgerald previously mentioned. These texts were predominantly written by screenwriters and communicated alternative stories about the industry, in other words stories that Hollywood would not choose to tell about itself (Rhodes 2). This ability to talk about Hollywood from the perspective of an insider without having to conform to its conventions and ideological stances produces a form of displaced critique within the genre. Often this would take the form of a lament about the working structures of Hollywood, opening a window on what K. Edington summarizes as "the nightmarish aspects of a highly competitive culture in which career success determines one's sense of self and self worth" (64). As Justin Gautreau argues, "the Hollywood novel opened up the space for cultural critique of the film industry at a time when the industry lacked the capacity to critique itself" (3), and, for Gautreau, these works exposed the hidden workings of classical Hollywood, specifically the industry's construction of technical artifice and creation of seductive promotional discourses that bolstered its image.

Two of the novels I discuss in this book, *Sanctuary* and *If I Forget Thee, Jerusalem* (1939), have previously been described as Hollywood novels by other scholars, but their justifications for attributing them to this genre differ substantially to mine.[7] Alan Spiegel calls *Sanctuary* Faulkner's "Hollywood novel" by virtue of its critical reception, its circulation in popular media, and its effect on his career, since it was "his first best-seller, the only one of his works to be filmed twice, and the book that first brought him to the studios" (156). While it is true that popular awareness of *Sanctuary* played a key role in Faulkner securing his first contract with a Hollywood studio, the elements Spiegel introduces are largely external to the work itself as contingencies emerging from its publication. In contrast, as I show in chapter 1, Faulkner himself put *Sanctuary* directly in dialogue with Hollywood cinema by both incorporating vocabularies of popular cinema into the novel (such as those from the flapper film) and by adapting aspects of the text in his early treatments for MGM within the genre of the pre-Code vice film.[8]

If I Forget Thee, Jerusalem has also been framed as an indirect Hollywood novel by virtue of its exploration of the fraught relationship between art and commerce, particularly in "The Wild Palms" sections of the novel, which focus on the creative labors of two characters: Charlotte Rittenmeyer, a visual artist, and Harry Wilbourne, a magazine writer. Michael Grimwood asserts that this text adheres to the favored subject of the Hollywood novel, namely "the artist's temptation to compromise his art for the sake of money, fame, or power" (115), since "The Wild Palms" considers the struggles of Charlotte and Harry to produce their work under market conditions. Karl F. Zender suggests that in "The Wild Palms" Faulkner indirectly engages with his Hollywood experiences "in a parabolic fashion" through a consideration of the influence of "the world of wage labor and commercial art" (*Crossing* 43) on his fiction and life. Similarly, Richard Godden and Pamela Knights contend that Faulkner's work in Hollywood queued him to the commodification inherent within mass culture and that this knowledge supplied him with the material to launch a critique of "the condition of a world where a man appears just as an instrument for the circulation of commodities" (203) in the novel.[9] These critics claim this text as a Hollywood novel on the basis of its exploration of the uneasy relationship between money and artistic practice or human interactions more broadly, which follows the literary generic template by providing a displaced critique of Hollywood working practices. However, such an approach inadvertently obscures the novel's more intimate debt to Hollywood. As I show in chapters 2 and 3, *If I Forget Thee, Jerusalem* is in fact heavily bound up with the systems of characterization and genre conventions central to the films of Hawks, Faulkner's most long-standing collaborator in Hollywood, since it presents Charlotte as a prototypical Hawksian heroine by borrowing from aspects of the screwball comedy and the adventure film, the genres in which this figure typically appeared. Faulkner would himself go on to adapt the "Old Man" sections of *If I Forget Thee, Jerusalem* as a teleplay in the early 1950s, a cross-media translation I analyze in depth in chapter 3.

Indeed, it has been argued that the focus on art and commerce as the dominant conflict in the Hollywood novel is something of a misrepresentative cliché, since, as Chip Rhodes asserts, Hollywood itself reflected on this association through its cinematic output, within "Hollywood on Hollywood" pictures such as *Sunset Boulevard* (1950) and *In a Lonely Place* (1950), meaning a literary interrogation of these themes would not offer a clear alternative narrative (2). Instead, he sees the recurring thematic preoccupation of the genre in its diverse incarnations as the relationship between "sexuality and aesthetics" (Rhodes 2), specifically the ways in which sex is sublimated into art to shape and control the desires of mass audiences. Perhaps more than art and commerce, this is an aspect that unites Faulkner's wide-ranging work within the genre in which the sexualities of cultural laborers are expressed through spectacles of mass entertainment (such as the aerial stunts of the barnstorming fliers in his novel *Pylon* from 1935) or through products intended for the mass market in ways that cultivate the desires of audiences and consumers (such as the sculptures Charlotte creates for a department store window in Chicago). Near the beginning of "The Wild Palms," for example, a text in which references to popular culture abound, the commercial artist Charlotte neatly sums up this close relation between erotic drives and creative labor in mass-market art when she proclaims the following to her new lover: "I like bitching, and making things with my hands" (*N* 3: 555), "bitching" being a euphemism for sex in the narrative. I consider the close relationship between commercial art and female sexuality within Faulkner's Hollywood novels in detail in chapters 2 and 3.

Most significantly, though, I believe these works should be incorporated into the Hollywood novel genre neither on account of their exploration of economic selling out nor the bastardization of art but rather through their close dialogue with the conventions, tropes, and working practices of commercial film that were generated through direct exchanges with Faulkner's screenwriting, a dialogue from which these works derive a great deal of their communicative power. In fact, it is arguably these texts' debt to Hollywood that has led to their relative marginalization within critical appraisals of the Faulkner canon. These novels have sometimes been overlooked for being set outside Faulkner's fictional county of Yoknapatawpha (in the case of *Pylon* and *If I Forget Thee, Jerusalem*), as well as either for their generic hybridity (*Requiem* fuses drama and prose) or relative lack of formal experimentalism (*The Mansion* employs a largely linear, exteriorized narrative style). However, Faulkner's shift of focus away from Mississippi, his dynamic fusion of genres, and the increased attention he pays to the objective, visual plane in these works can all, in part, be attributed to his time in Hollywood, tasked as he was with working far from home in California across a diverse range of projects for the medium of film.

Faulkner and Film: Resemblance, Critique, and Dialogue

My examination of transmedial exchanges between modernist fiction and cinema builds upon and is indebted to three related, and roughly chronological, strands of scholarship on Faulkner and film, which, in broad terms, have approached this relationship in terms of resemblance, mass cultural critique, or productive dialogue. This book makes a series of new contributions to this scholarship. First, studies that have emphasized a formal resemblance between Faulkner's experimental fiction and film have paid disproportionate attention to early or avant-garde cinema rather than the Hollywood projects Faulkner himself had a hand in. Second, critics that have identified a subversive critique of mass culture, including commercial film, within Faulkner's fiction have not yet taken into account the diverse ways in which the author incorporated aspects of his screenwriting into his prose *without* trying to undermine these conventions and types. Finally, dialogic approaches have identified an array of fascinating exchanges between Faulkner's fiction and screenwriting, but this book provides the first thematic critical approach to Faulkner and Hollywood by focusing on the author's evolving exploration of gender across his work for page and screen. It thereby generates new insights into Faulkner's developing understanding of the gendered dynamics of collaboration, visual culture, and genre over a period of almost three decades.

The first major assessment of Faulkner's achievement as a screenwriter was Bruce F. Kawin's book *Faulkner and Film* (1977), which brought the large amount of scripts Faulkner wrote for the screen to scholarly attention—work that was further supported by Kawin's annotated edition of *Faulkner's MGM Screenplays* (1980)—and showed how features of Faulkner's fiction approximate cinematic techniques. *Faulkner and Film* fuses biographical information with detailed genetic criticism of the compositional process through a focus on the writer's screenplays, treatments, and scenarios, and Kawin reveals a wide range of parallels between Faulkner's novels and screenplays in terms of theme and characterization. However, the book struggles to reconcile the experimental modernism of Faulkner's fiction with the film projects he actually worked on in Hollywood. Kawin emphasizes the skill of Faulkner's filmic craft and demonstrates how Faulkner's novels themselves are cinematic in character, but he does not view the two bodies of work as formally compatible. For Kawin, Faulkner's modernism is inclusive of cinematic forms, singling out montage in Faulkner's fiction as being particularly noteworthy (*Faulkner and Film* 6), through which seemingly disconnected elements are juxtaposed and the reader is invested with the task of fusing together a coherent whole through the power of the imagination to visualize unity.[10] In Kawin's description, what Faulkner was doing through montage, tessellating formally diverse first-person monologues in novels like *The Sound and the Fury* and *As I Lay Dying*, for example, resembled the techniques of montage used by a modernist filmmaker like Sergei Eisenstein, in whose works the constituent components "ought not to build on each other but to *collide*" (*Faulkner and Film* 8), which was defined in general terms by Eisenstein in *The Film Sense* as the process through which "two film pieces of any kind, placed together, inevitably combine into a new concept, a new quality, arising out of that juxtaposition" (14). A similar approach on the basis of formal resemblance has been pursued by Doug Baldwin, who views Faulkner's modernist novels as cinematic through their use of experimental techniques derived from film (42). However, both Kawin and Baldwin find it difficult to align Faulkner the "cinematic" novelist with the film projects Faulkner was involved in. As Kawin observes, these movies were not formally experimental in an Eisensteinian sense, since "the coming of sound had rendered montage unfashionable" (Kawin, *Faulkner and Film* 148).

Faulkner's longest collaboration in Hollywood was with the film director Hawks, a director who steered away from montage, preferring a smooth, linear style (Kawin, *Faulkner and Film* 12) typical of the rise of continuity editing in American commercial film, which favored nonfragmentary (and often chronological) film narratives that "bare the central principle of causal linearity" (Bordwell et al. 22). Similarly, Baldwin argues that Faulkner borrowed from early film, as opposed to the cinema of his own era, which he sees as symptomatic of Faulkner's "disdain for the commercial Hollywood production system of the 1930s" (39).[11]

Existing approaches that have highlighted the formal resemblance between Faulkner's experimental modernist writing and the visually innovative features of cinema have thus far not appreciated how much the author's fictions mimic the commercial film projects he himself worked on. For example, recent work on Faulkner's screenwriting has shown that the author did in fact directly interact with the projects of modernist filmmakers who had experimented with montage in Hollywood. Sarah Gleeson-White describes how Faulkner built on Eisenstein's 1930 scenario for a film project, "Sutter's Gold," to write his own film treatment in July 1934 and that Faulkner demonstrated his familiarity with the director's film praxis within his screenwriting, for example in his use of Eisensteinian "montage, visual and sonic," and the harsh overlaying of images through the technique of double exposure ("Auditory Exposures" 89, 90). Although this is a rare example of this particular technique in Faulkner's scripts, if one takes a more heterogenous definition of visual and literary modernism, moving beyond the disjuncture of montage, it is apparent that Faulkner was on occasion able to advance aspects of his formal experimentalism *within* his Hollywood screenplays when working for directors and within genres that incorporated nontraditional features, such as economical abstraction and indeterminacy.

For example, in his screenplays Faulkner came to inhabit the distilled, architectural style of Hawks, which has been labeled modernist. Henri Langlois recognizes that Hawks's films "are stripped bare almost to the point of abstraction—but it is as if they are made of concrete" (73). Langlois sees Hawks as the first director to bring a vision of American modernism to the cinema through what Peter Wollen summarizes as a "streamlined economy of means and a rationalized functionalism" ("Introduction" 7), based on Hawks's belief that "a film should work like a piece of precise engineering" (*Signs* 216). While such aesthetic reduction in literature would appear closer to the modernism of Ernest Hemingway than the verbal excesses of

Faulkner's fiction, one can observe this experimental style in Faulkner's screenplays that are concerned with aviation, particularly his war films, which share Hawks's "fascination with speed" (Wollen, "Introduction" 8) as a feature of modernity.[12] In Faulkner's screenplay for the World War I–era romantic drama "Turn About," directed by Hawks as *Today We Live*, features of technological modernity interact with one another and provide the underlying structure for the transition between shots, the individual unit of the moving picture; in a cut between a scene in the aerodrome and at sea, Faulkner shifts between aerial and naval warfare through the economical use of sound in the directions: "The engines begin to turn over. the [sic] sound mounting through dissolve and continuing. The sound of exploding bombs enter and cease, but the sound of the engines continue into and through . . . Ronnie and Claude at sea, approaching Zeebrugge. The boat is going fast" (*MGM* 250–51). The layered sounds of the plane and ship engines and the bombing raid create an aural landscape of speed that propels the narrative forward through a form of "streamlined functionalism." The technology of flight and the structuring of shots work in tandem here, a unity that reflects the shared histories of aviation and cinema. The first powered flight by the Wright Brothers in 1903 occurred contemporary to the very beginnings of the development of narrative cinema in the early years of the twentieth century (the first motion pictures had been screened to a public audience in the United States at the end of the nineteenth century). Indeed, Faulkner's aviation fictions more broadly conceived, both literary and filmic, are concerned with what Michael Zeitlin calls "the new aesthetic epistemologies of airplane speed and flight" (*Faulkner, Aviation, and Modern War* 14), and Jay Watson has suggested that it is particularly in his early 1930s fictions that Faulkner "was most fully committed to exploring the representational strategies and expressive possibilities of both speed and literary modernism" at the same time that the author came to work for the "influential twentieth-century speed medium" of cinema (*William Faulkner* 100–101). In Hollywood, Hawks and Faulkner fused their apprehension of these twin features of modernity in the flight films on which they collaborated.

Faulkner also encountered experimental Hollywood features through his work within the genres of the pre-Code vice film and film noir. In the pre-Code era of Hollywood cinema, before the strict enforcement of the Motion Picture Production Code guidelines in 1934, taboo topics related to sexuality and violence could be more directly explored onscreen in the first few years of talking pictures. Among these were a series of films that focused on sex and the actions of transgressive female characters, known as "vice" pictures, which I study in relation to Faulkner's novel *Sanctuary* in chapter 1. In order to keep these films within acceptable moral boundaries, they had to maintain a degree of ambiguity through what Richard Maltby calls "a textual indeterminacy that shifted the responsibility for determining what the movie's content was away from the producer to the individual spectator" ("Production Code" 40). Faulkner incorporated this form of indeterminacy into his early pre-Code scripts, such as his 1932 treatment for MGM, titled "The College Widow," in which a young Southern woman in a college town named Mary Lee Blair has an extramarital affair with a dangerous man. In order to leave the sexual nature of this relationship ambiguous, Faulkner introduces an abrupt scene shift between the hotel where the assignation takes place and the railway station the morning after:

25. A ROOM DOOR
The porter opens the door and goes in. Mary Lee holds back, terrified, pleading.
The man is cold, masterful. He leads her in.
The porter emerges. The door closes behind him.

26. RAILWAY STATION—THE NEXT MORNING
Mary Lee enters, buys a ticket hurriedly—frightened, looking back over her shoulder. She runs into the train. She shows extreme fear until the train begins to move. (MGM 47)

Here the viewer is required to fill in the causal gap between the two scenes, namely that the sexual encounter she experienced the night before is the source of her anxiety the morning after. The burden of interpretation is thereby shifted from the producers of the film to the spectator in the movie theatre, part of a system of encoding "in which 'innocence' was inscribed into the text while 'sophisticated' viewers were able to 'read into' movies whatever meanings they were pleased to find" (Maltby, "Production Code" 41). This technique, which Thomas Doherty calls "figurative literalness," is used to activate the desires of both male and female audiences simultaneously, since "just as the edge of the film frame served as a beckoning 'No Trespassing' sign (for the male gaze), a timely detour into offscreen space could infuse the onscreen narrative with otherwise censorable material for the female imagination" (*Pre-Code Hollywood* 119).

Faulkner extended his use of strategies of indeterminacy in his 1940s screenplays for the films *To Have and Have Not, Mildred Pierce,* and *The Big Sleep*. James Naremore has commented on how noir shared thematic and formal territory with high modernist literature and art, including psychological complexity, the prevalence of horror, an exploration of irrationality, as well as the use of "subjective narration" and "nonlinear plots" (40, 45). While we should not generalize modernist literature on the basis of these categories of comparison alone, noir's preference for convoluted plots, interiorized narratives, and enigmatic characterization could nevertheless create interpretative burdens on the viewer akin to the difficulties the spatial and temporal disruptions of modernist narrative can create for readers. The plot of a noir film like *The Big Sleep*, on which Faulkner worked, was so complicated that Raymond Chandler, the author of the 1939 novel on which the screenplay was based, could not say who had murdered one of the text's key characters (McCarthy 381). Although Faulkner and his collaborator Leigh Brackett tried to clarify a number of ambiguous plot points in their jointly authored screenplay adaptation of the novel, Hawks said of the work in the 1970s that he couldn't "follow the story" but nevertheless asserted that "you don't really have to have any explanation for things" (McCarthy 383) to achieve an overall aesthetic effect. This statement can be read as a Hollywood modernist commitment to irresolution and perspectival ambiguity that Faulkner also demonstrated in his fiction.

A second body of scholarship on Faulkner and film has explored the author's profound engagement with mass culture as one of subversive critique. Matthews was the first to provide a more reflexive appreciation of Faulkner's work in Hollywood, suggesting that the author's screenplays may themselves be able to call attention to the limitations of the conventions of popular culture. He argues that Faulkner's short story and film work has the ability to resist market prescriptions, commenting that "even works aimed at the mass market possess reflective and resistant features that make their relation to the culture industry and the social order it endorses the very heart of the problem" ("Culture Industry" 60), rightly asserting that "to segregate any writer's serious art fiction totally from his or her writing for commercial uses, or even from an awareness of market pressures, is to participate uncritically in a myth advanced by modernist aesthetics" ("Culture Industry" 69–70). While this approach asserts the value of Faulkner's screenwriting in terms of its critical capacity, it still perpetuates a divide in which Hollywood formulas and modes of writing are presented as something to be resisted.

Peter Lurie's *Vision's Immanence: Faulkner, Film and the Popular Imagination* (2004) pursues the inverse approach to Matthews, reconciling Faulkner the modernist's engagement with Hollywood by suggesting that the author's experimental novels demonstrate a deep awareness of mass culture in the service of a wider critique. Lurie revealed how the high modernist experiments of Faulkner's 1930s novels were consistently infused with the "methods, types, and formulae" (1) of popular culture. He argues that it is the novels, rather than the screenplays, where Faulkner is able to express his vision of Hollywood, since when at a remove from the center of commercial film production he was no longer required to subordinate his experimental impulses to "accessibility or narrative coherence," and so consequently displaced his critique of film into his fiction (Lurie 21). Lurie advances that in these modernist works Faulkner "co-opted the practices of mass culture for the purposes of exposing and questioning them" (31) rather than negating them and demonstrates how many of Faulkner's novels reflected the "manner of impression and visual activity" (6) of the cinema through strategies of allusion and technical innovation. Julian Murphet's recent book *Faulkner Media Romance* (2017) is also an important contribution to this critical tradition, as he shows how Faulkner's modernist writing was indebted to the tropes of the romance genre in its diverse transmedial incarnations. Murphet argues that Faulkner would indulge in the features of romance "under the masking device of one or other of the various media technologies of his day" (43) through a mode that simultaneously exhibits and obscures popular cultural features, allowing the author "to cast a withering glance sideways at the contemporary culture industry" and to launch an "ironic critique of the contemporary source of romance" (44). Similar to Lurie, Murphet argues that mass cultural media, including commercial film, were absorbed into Faulkner's fictions in order to be critiqued; however, Murphet only briefly analyzes one of Faulkner's screenplays ("War Birds" from 1932) to illuminate such exchanges, even though Faulkner would repeatedly return to the romance genre in his Hollywood work on films from *Today We Live* to *To Have and Have Not*. Such approaches, which have exposed a mass cultural critique in either Faulkner's screenplays or prose, have largely not considered how the author may have incorporated popular cultural formulas into his writing without striving to subvert them. This scholarship also still largely privileges the experimental novel as the primary locus of meaning in interactions between modernism and popular culture. By contrast, I consider the popular cultural products Faulkner produced alongside his fiction, rather than reappraising how the author's formally difficult works can be seen to incorporate an awareness of modern ideas of cultural heteronomy or technological mediation at a remove from Hollywood.

In this way, *Faulkner's Hollywood Novels* pursues a much more transactional analysis of Faulkner's relationship with film through his own participation in it. My work here builds on the recent dialogic turn in studies of Faulkner and film, which has been borne out of broader shifts in modernist studies. This wave of scholarship has emerged in tandem with the reshaping of modernist studies within the past fifteen years. Douglas Mao and Rebecca L. Walkowitz's essay "The New Modernist Studies" from 2008, for example, suggested moving beyond the hierarchical high/low axis of modernism and mass culture, since they argue that the modernist focus on commodification may previously have obscured our vision of the alliances between modernism and popular culture that occur in the modern writer's search for a voice and style that encompasses new media. They reflected on the vertical expansion of the field, which had begun to take into account how much modernists may have "absorbed and remade forms of mass culture rather than merely disparaging them" (Mao and Walkowitz, "Modernist Studies" 744); this activity is echoed in Faulkner's own statements, as he once said to Hawks, "I have no qualms at all about stealing from you; I think it's good stuff" (Kawin, "Faulkner's Film Career" 176), a stark contrast to modernist discourses of exclusion. A scholarly emphasis on a beneficial dialogic relationship between Faulkner's novels and screenplays is a relatively recent development in the field. The innovative work of Gleeson-White and Stefan Solomon, in particular, has paid increased attention to the impact of Faulkner's screenwriting on his fiction, thereby emphasizing the permeable relationship between the two bodies of work. Gleeson-White has illuminated the exchange of techniques and themes across Faulkner's prose and screenplays,[13] and she has also significantly advanced the field by bringing Faulkner's screenplays for Fox into the public domain through her publication of an annotated edition of his scripts for the studio in 2017 (*TCF*), material which I analyse in depth in chapters 2 and 5. In her introduction, she highlights a series of common practices that animate Faulkner's entire oeuvre across literature and film, showing how Faulkner's prose and Hollywood cinema are both marked by patterns of structure-giving repetition, the revisiting and rewriting of source texts "as an equal partner in the redaction process" ("Introduction" 35), and collective processes of creation. In addition, Solomon's comprehensive *William Faulkner in Hollywood: Screenwriting for the Studios* (2017) offers a chronological survey of the majority of Faulkner's roughly fifty screenplays, assessing their relation to his fiction; he shows how these two bodies of work are "porous and intertwined" by "offering an empirical analysis of [Faulkner's] debt not only to Hollywood but even more to the craft of screenwriting" (7) and reveals many examples of fascinating dialogue between the related textual mediums. This is an approach that has now also been pursued in biography too, as Carl Rollyson's recent two-volume *The Life of William Faulkner* (2020) has worked to integrate "Faulkner's screenplays, fiction, and life into one narrative" (*Past* xi).[14]

Building on the work of these scholars, who have collectively pioneered the dialogic turn in the field, *Faulkner's Hollywood Novels* is the first book to offer a thematic critical analysis of the relationship between Faulkner's fiction and screenwriting through a focus on gender. While a number of productive cycles of influence have been established between Faulkner's fiction and screenplays, these instances of exchange have not yet been gathered into an overall narrative of the relationship between modernist literature and Hollywood film across the author's vast oeuvre. The following chapters consider Faulkner's exchange of tropes for the representation of female characters, and the commercial genre conventions in which they are situated, between his fiction and screenplays from the early 1930s to the late 1950s, including the "bad girl" of the pre-Code vice film (between his novel *Sanctuary* and his MGM screenplays), the "Hawksian" woman of the adventure film and the screwball comedy (in his novels *Pylon* and *If I Forget Thee, Jerusalem*), the femme fatale of film noir and the secret agent of the war film (in his genealogical short story "Appendix Compson: 1699–1945"), and the suffering mother of the woman's film (in his novel *Requiem for a Nun*).[15] Near the end of his career, Faulkner would revisit all these tropes, which he had derived from his screenwriting, through the characterization of Linda Snopes Kohl in a single novel, *The Mansion*. As these case studies will demonstrate, rather than keeping his fiction separate from his screenwriting, Faulkner was able to reimagine his literary characters outside the bounds of his novels and adapt them for the particular formal demands of cinema, just as he reworked his filmic characters in his modernist prose. These exchanges are, however, not simply dialogic, since they contributed towards the creation of new generic forms and character archetypes that spoke to a range of social anxieties, developments, and shifts pertaining to gender throughout the period Faulkner worked for the studios. Faulkner used his portrayal of women in his writing to explore the relationship between literature and film, modernism and popular culture in three key areas, thereby revealing the cross-gender collaborative networks that underpinned and connected these two spheres of production, the close relationship between visual media and structures of sexual difference, and the ways in which generic conventions have the potential to revise dominant cultural ideologies that pertain to gender.

Collaboration

Attending to the relationship between Faulkner's fiction and screenwriting in terms of gender helps to reveal how both textual forms were animated by previously underappreciated collaborative networks that brought together men and women in shared artistic endeavors. By tracing these connections, one can expose the complex and dynamic relationship between power, sexuality, and authority that occurs in acts of collective creation. Collaboration as a practice has historically been disparaged by modernist writers, who associated communal artistic processes with a betrayal of values of autonomous creativity. Fitzgerald called Hollywood films "a mechanical and communal art . . . in which words were subordinate to images, where personality was worn down to the inevitable low gear of collaboration" (78), objecting to the elevation of film over literature, a medium that he deemed inferior in conveying thought and emotion. Faulkner too stated that "any collaboration is compromise" (*LG* 240), since it dilutes the individual author's "intent," and that Hollywood work was antithetical to the "true" task of the writer, since "it is a matter of a lot of people working together, when the . . . writer has to get off into solitude and isolation to do the work" ("At Washington & Lee University"). Faulkner's work on collectively authored screenplays—and his diverse collaborations with co-screenwriters, editors, producers, directors, and actors in Hollywood to compose these texts—would seem to undermine this modernist imperative of autonomy. His resistance is, in itself, highly gendered. Vera John-Steiner has considered how gender differently affects attitudes towards artistic collaboration and "the ownership of . . . ideas" (8); she reaches the conclusion that women are more comfortable than men with collaborative modes of work, since men are socialized to "experience a powerful push toward independence, competition, and autonomy" (122), whereas woman are socialized to be more widely engaged in relational practices that foreground mutuality and interdependence. It is interesting to consider how the dominance of men within the modernist movement may have contributed to its investment in masculinized values of creative independence that belittled collaboration.

In the case of Faulkner, the author's circulation of masculine values of autonomy was a bid to generate alternative forms of capital for his modernist art by obscuring its relationality. The sociologist Pierre Bourdieu has examined this phenomenon in his studies of the literary and artistic field. He showed how the distribution of power and authority within societies is not solely structured around economic capital but that prestige—or symbolic capital—is also a defining tool in the hierarchization of society. When Fitzgerald and Faulkner assert the autonomy of their "serious" literary work, they are garnering symbolic capital, part of a tactic to assert modernist practice's independence from economic structures and to defend the charismatic image of literary activity as "pure, disinterested creation by an isolated artist" (Bourdieu 34). However, the work of art cannot be separated from the wider structures that inform its ideologies of cultural negation and autonomy; as Bourdieu states, "whatever its degree of independence, [the literary and artistic field] continues to be affected by the laws of the field which encompasses it, those of economic and political profit" (39). In reality, "no cultural product exists by itself . . . outside the relations of interdependence which link it to other products" (Bourdieu 32–33), meaning that, as Fitzgerald's and Faulkner's careers evidence, the relationship between the modernist novels and the Hollywood films on which they both worked is, of course, permeable. As Gleeson-White states, Faulkner's work for the studios "invites us to reconsider this high modernist in an alternative artistic guise as a networked, industrial laborer" ("Introduction" 41). Robert Jackson also comments, in relation to Faulkner's career as a novelist and screenwriter, that "thinking about collaboration means considering networks and processes rather than merely the individual authors and auteurs whose long shadows so often obscure their contexts" ("Images" 41). These networks often created surprising connections, since members of Faulkner's Hollywood community were also, on occasion, themselves modernist artists. In a letter from 1945, Faulkner tells Malcolm Cowley how he had "become aware of [his] European reputation"—referring to the early positive reception his writing received in France—at a party in Hollywood in which he encountered the British modernist writer and screenwriter, Christopher Isherwood, and the surrealist artist, Jean Hélion, whose early work had been strongly identified with modernist abstraction, "squatting on their heels and knees in a kind of circle in front of me" (*SL*, 203), closely listening to his words in the position of acolytes. By considering the networked intersections of Faulkner's fiction and screenwriting, we can better appreciate how the author's creative contacts in Hollywood, Mississippi, and beyond frequently traversed artistic distinctions between modernism and mass culture, as his collaborators were themselves invested in and produced diverse cultural forms.

Studies of Faulkner's literary collaborations have shown how a number of the author's works of fiction were embedded in collaborative processes of editing, writing, and mentoring, but we are just beginning to recognize how these communal creative acts established connections between literature and film. Jack Stillinger, in his wider deconstruction of "the romantic notion of single authorship" (183), has discussed the sizeable influence one of Faulkner's editors at Random House, Saxe Commins, had on the author's craft, particularly in the "marathon sessions" (151) Commins carried out with his authors to work over their manuscripts line by line, often at his home in Princeton, New Jersey. Commins edited Faulkner's work from 1936 until 1958, and his wife, Dorothy Berliner Commins, observed one of these sessions, enjoying the sight of Faulkner and her husband "on their knees, moving from one page to another, marking, deleting, transferring passages here and there" (Commins 225), as the editor encouraged Faulkner to iron out inconsistencies in *The Town*. Evidently Faulkner permitted a considerable amount of intervention from trusted collaborators in the revision of his texts. Noel Polk similarly asserts that Faulkner accepted significant editorial input, particularly in the process of revising his late-career works; for novels such as *The Mansion* and *The Reivers* (1962), Faulkner would send typescripts to his editors at Random House, Commins and later Albert Erskine, and then travel to the publisher's offices in New York to work over the text together, once his editors had had time to review everything (Polk, *Dark House* 11). As Polk summarizes, "there seems to have been not only delegated (negotiated, at any rate) intention, but absolute collaboration on certain details of the text of the late novels" (*Dark House* 11).

In some cases, Faulkner's collaborations on his fiction moved beyond editing to instances of potential co-authorship. Faulkner, for example, drew on tales he had developed alongside the Southern writer Sherwood Anderson in New Orleans during his composition of his 1927 novel *Mosquitoes* (Rideout and Meriwether). Faulkner also worked with women on a number of his short stories and novels, collaborations that spanned practically the entire duration of his career and were imbued with pronounced gendered power imbalances. Sensibar argues that within the context of the South, where Faulkner learned his craft, artistic pursuits in general were viewed as "sissified," or feminizing, and that the young author "really had no significant male models: the *living* storytellers and the visual artists in his family were all women" (7). In terms of active collaboration, Sensibar argues that Estelle Oldham's fiction stimulated Faulkner's turn to writing prose in 1924 before he married her in 1929. When Faulkner typed out Oldham's short story "Star Spangled Banner Stuff," Sensibar believes that Faulkner was enriched by Oldham's imagination, particularly her exploration of "racialized gender confusion and its dismantling of iconic figures like the Southern belle and the New Woman" (425), which he drew on for his first novels, *Soldier's Pay* (1926) and *Mosquitoes*. In addition, Faulkner's short story "Elly" (1931) had originally been Oldham's work, titled "Selvage." During the time he was writing *The Sound and the Fury*, the couple revised it together, along with several other short stories that were originally hers, and Faulkner submitted it to *Scribner's* in December 1928 with a joint byline (Sensibar 458–59). The rejection letter from *Scribner's* is, however, the only known public record of their literary collaboration (Sensibar 471), since Faulkner went on to resubmit and publish "Elly" as his own. Activities such as these clearly show that Faulkner, as Sensibar comments, "merged his erotic and creative life . . . in mutual collaborations" (454) and used his power within the relationship to take credit for and exert authority over his partner's work. As Holly A. Laird suggests, this dynamic is typical of "collaborative desire," which is characterized by "reciprocally operating power exchanges between two desiring subjects who are attracted as much (or more) by their affinities and contiguity as by what they may have to gain from each other" (14), although in the case of Oldham and Faulkner, it remains unclear what reciprocal material benefit she derived from these collaborations.

Such a charged power dynamic across a gendered divide was perhaps even more pronounced in Faulkner's late-career collaboration with the twenty-one-year-old aspiring author Joan Williams, who was thirty years his junior. Coming down to New York from Bard College, where she was an undergraduate, Williams met Faulkner at the Biltmore Hotel in February 1950, where an exchange between them apparently led him to develop the dramatic sections of his novel *Requiem for a Nun* (Hickman 43). During his courtship of Williams, Faulkner invited her to participate in the composition of the play sections of *Requiem for a Nun* by first sending her a three-page draft of the opening dialogue from the work in early 1950 (Hickman 195), at which point he asked her to produce material for a "first draft" and insisted that they should "let it change itself in either your hands or mine while we are getting it on paper" (*SL* 299). Williams would respond by providing detailed suggestions on character development, tone, staging, physical movement, and temporal structure. By the summer of 1950, he set Williams to work extracting a "workable play script" (*SL* 305) from his first complete draft, and Williams was involved in the work's composition right up until its publication in October 1951. However, collaboration on *Requiem*, as Lisa C. Hickman acknowledges in her biography of the two writers' romance, was "more of a ruse" (66), since it strongly intersected with Faulkner's desire to continue the affair with Williams.

In the most explicit example of this ulterior motive, Faulkner suggested to Williams that they should have sex through the title page of *Requiem for a Nun* before it was bound (Hickman 94). Collaboration is framed by Faulkner here as an erotic act, and he would repeatedly talk of both his and Williams's writing as their joint progeny. In a letter to Williams from 3 March 1950, Faulkner insists that *Requiem for a Nun* "is yours too. If you refuse to accept it, I will throw it away too. . . . it is so much yours too as if we had got a child together" (Letter to Joan Williams). Faulkner also provided feedback on Williams's work in progress, and in a letter from 6 November 1952 he spoke of her character Jake Darby, from what would become her novel *The Morning and the Evening* (1961), as a product of their sexual intimacy, arguing that "Jake came from that time or time when I touched your flesh and you accepted me, just like a child comes. It had to be more the cold relation between teacher and pupil; that way I could have taught you only the cold mechanics of words and style. The passion came from the other, the flesh's, the bodies' intimacy; that too, to be an artist, you must not be afraid of" (Letter to Joan Williams). Although such statements should be read for their obvious sexual intentions, Faulkner espouses a vision of creativity and collaborative activity in which formal and erotic concerns overlap and energize another.

Such collaborations in the world of fiction can be latent, obscured, suppressed, or pursued in bad faith, but within Hollywood they are a fundamental creative requirement of a collective medium. In terms of gender, Jackson has explored how Faulkner's screenwriting extended and reflected the power exchanges that shaped the author's prose, since both creative contexts emphasized the shared link between intimate aesthetic experiences and sexual energy (33). By opening up Faulkner's vast oeuvre to collaborative processes of creation, the complex relationships with women that animated and inspired many of his works of fiction and screenwriting become apparent.

These collaborations should not simply be considered as "context" for the material production of these works, since they determine the structures, themes, style, narrative structure, and systems of characterization of Faulkner's texts themselves, as well as establishing intimate links between literature and film. Faulkner, for example, would write *both* screenplays and prose in homage to Hollywood actresses of the Golden Age across the breadth of his Hollywood career. Faulkner originally secured a contract at MGM in 1932 at the suggestion of his friend, the Paramount actress Tallulah Bankhead, and one of his first screenwriting projects was to adapt a story he had written for Bankhead into the treatment titled "The College Widow." The work drew on characteristics of the flapper figure Faulkner had explored in his novel *Sanctuary*, but it also was clearly shaped by his knowledge of Bankhead's Hollywood film roles in a series of early 1930s vice films, where she was presented as a "fallen heroine" or "bad girl," as I discuss in chapter 1. Faulkner could, therefore, adapt aspects of his writing to suit the screen image of a particular Hollywood star. Almost twenty years later, *Requiem for a Nun* was also inspired by Faulkner's encounter with a Hollywood actress, Ruth Ford, who, like Faulkner, was a Southern migrant to California who hailed from Mississippi. Ford probably first met Faulkner around 1933 when she was a graduate student in philosophy at the University of Mississippi dating Faulkner's youngest brother, Dean (Rollyson, *Alarming Paradox* 357). By chance Ford and Faulkner met again ten years later in 1943 when she was an actress under contract at Warner Brothers, where Faulkner was also working. As Orson Welles's goddaughter, Ford was well connected to the Hollywood cultural elite, and after she appeared in a production of Welles's Mercury Theatre group, he assisted in her transition to movies. Working for Columbia Pictures and Warner Brothers in the 1940s, Ford appeared in a slew of B–movie pictures: horrors, crime dramas, and Westerns among them. Ford's ambitions lay more in theatre than in Hollywood films; sensing an opportunity, she asked the famous Southern author to write a play for her even though Faulkner had not written a dramatic work since his early symbolist play *The Marionettes* (1920). The author was resolute in the face of some opposition from his agents that the piece was to remain her play and her play alone, in effect a "star vehicle," reassuring Ford in one letter that "the play, part, was written for you, so no contract is needed . . . It will be pretty fine if we can make a good vehicle for you. I would like to see that title in lights, myself" (*SL* 318). Elsewhere in his letters, Faulkner asserted that his sketching of the part of Temple Drake in *Requiem for a Nun* was born out of his admiration for Ford's "rather terrifying determination to be an actress" and that he "wrote [the] play for her to abet it" (*SL* 324).[16] Just as Estelle Oldham arguably stimulated Faulkner's turn from poetry to prose in the mid-1920s, Ruth Ford appears to have inspired his temporary shift from prose to drama in the 1950s. Both "The College Widow" and *Requiem for a Nun* can be seen as "commissions" for Hollywood actresses, drawing on diverse popular genre conventions to further the careers of women who had cultivated distinctive onscreen personas.

In Hollywood, too, female agents had the power to significantly rework and reshape Faulkner's writing. While Faulkner was adapting his short story "Turnabout" (1932) into a screenplay for Howard Hawks at MGM in the early 1930s, the bankable studio star Joan Crawford became available, and Faulkner was forced to integrate a female protagonist into the all-male story at the behest of studio producer Irving Thalberg; Hawks recalled that Crawford was "the biggest star at that time," and MGM was not willing to "lose a million dollars" (Kawin, "Howard Hawks" 90–91) on the picture, which they would if they didn't include a female role, since women made up the majority of film audiences at that time. Although Faulkner may have treated this event as an imposition, famously stating that he didn't "seem to remember a girl in the story" (Blotner, *Biography* 307), such collaborative interventions could benefit the author's screenwriting, as well as his exploration of gender relations, which I explore in chapter 1. Due to the rewrite, a wartime buddy movie became a complex romantic film with a love triangle at its center, which addressed the theme of female sexual independence. In this case, a loss of authorial control enabled Faulkner to explore foreign positions in the exchange of sexual desire, charged as he was, as D. Matthew Ramsey describes, with "finding not just a way to include an important female character but to represent the point of a view of a woman sexually alluring, tragic, and noble all at once (in a very Joan Crawford way)" ("Stars" 100). An actress also came to unexpectedly dominate one of Faulkner's screenwriting projects for Warner Brothers in the 1940s. *To Have and Have Not* was the first film in which Bogart and Bacall starred as romantic leads, and they became actual lovers during filming. As Todd McCarthy describes, "the contagious thrill sparked by Bogart and Bacall's romance defined the prevailing mood of the shoot" (376), and Faulkner was tasked with writing increasing amounts of sexually charged dialogue between the pair, responding to the on-set improvisations, which marginalized a secondary love interest of Bogart's in the screenplay that Faulkner had written in a more misogynistic vein.[17] In both instances, Hollywood actresses could dominate Faulkner's screenwriting projects in ways that were potentially valuable to his craft.

This was not just the case for Faulkner's working relationship with his actors, but also with fellow screenwriters. While working at Fox, his co-screenwriter on "Splinter Fleet" (released as the film *Submarine Patrol* in 1938), Kathryn Scola, was assigned by studio producer Darryl F. Zanuck to "keep an eye on the storyline" to counterbalance the "poetic freewheeling" of Faulkner's work on previous projects for the studio (Blotner, "Hollywood" 278). As an example of stylistic regulation, it is also gendered, as this division of labor was designed to ensure that Faulkner adhered to a fast-paced structure that would match the more clipped register considered appropriate to the largely male cast of this World War I movie. Faulkner's writing was further policed by a female screenwriter in his work on the film noir picture *The Big Sleep*, for which he collaborated with Leigh Brackett. Brackett had already developed a successful hard-boiled writing style; Hawks brought her onto the project as he had been impressed by her recently published mystery novel, *No Good from a Corpse* (McCarthy 379). Hawks commented on their first meeting at his office on the Warner lot that "in walked a rather attractive girl who looked like she had just come in from a tennis match. She looked as if she wrote poetry. But she wrote like a man" (Francke 81). Additionally, when Bogart was asked to comment on the completed script for the film, he directed criticisms to Brackett about some of the lines he considered to be far too genteel. It transpired, however, that these were Faulkner's contributions. Consequently, Bogart nicknamed Brackett "Butch" and went to her with any dialogue that he felt needed roughing up (McCarthy 387). It is hard to imagine some of the dialogue Faulkner penned in their final screenplay being delivered by Bogart's laconic, wry detective persona. Bogart no doubt looked for Brackett's touch on typically Faulknerian lines such as "Pride is a great thing, isn't it? And courage—and honor—and love. All the things you read about in the copybooks—only in the copybooks nothing ever gets tangled. The road always lies so straight, and clear, and the signs say to love and honor and be brave" (Faulkner et al. 293). Brackett's work was more typically "masculine" in the hard-boiled vein, while Faulkner's garrulous, elaborate dialogue and set-piece speeches were deemed "feminine." Faulkner's collaborations with Scola and Brackett, then, created a series of gender crossings through the blurring of identity fundamental to the co-authorship of a single work, in which the female screenwriter is tasked with "butching up" her male collaborator's writing.

In contrast to these potentially tense encounters, Faulkner's closest collaboration in Hollywood was with Meta Carpenter. Carpenter would work for Hawks for over twenty-five years and by the late 1950s was one of the most senior women in the field of script editing (McCarthy 557). Faulkner and Carpenter's romantic affair lasted intermittently from the mid-1930s until the 1950s, and their collaborations on movies were tender and mutually educative. She was the first to explain to Faulkner the improvisational mode of developing dialogue that Hawks used on the set of his films, a technique with which the author became more familiar through working with the director on *To Have and Have Not* (*ALG* 38). The exchange of knowledge in the film community between Faulkner and Carpenter was reciprocal. When Carpenter questioned Faulkner on a line of dialogue in his screenplay for *The Road to Glory*, asking "you say—," he interrupted her: "I didn't say it.... The character said it" (*ALG* 84). This proved instructive for Carpenter, as she realized that Faulkner was telling her "that his characters [have] a life-force of their own" (*ALG* 85). Their cross-gender professional collaboration, complete with sexual charge, resulted in their productive pooling of knowledge on a series of film projects until the early 1950s.

Faulkner's Hollywood collaborations with women, whether active or involuntary, combative or tender, harmonious or dissonant, manifested themselves in his scripts and the films that would result from them, but Faulkner would also process these encounters through his fictions. In terms of theme, Faulkner said that he wrote *If I Forget Thee, Jerusalem* "to stave off... heart-break" (*SL* 338) after the cessation of his affair with Carpenter, and the novel addresses both the benefits and dangers of fusing artistic and sexual impulses through the actions of the idealistic lovers Charlotte and Harry, as I show in chapter 3. These collaborations also shaped the narrative structure of some of Faulkner's novels. Joseph R. Urgo has argued that Quentin and Shreve's shared construction, through collective narration, of the reader's image of the mythic hero in Faulkner's novel *Absalom, Absalom!* (1936)—Thomas Sutpen—was informed by Faulkner's experience in Hollywood of creative teams' production of coherent visual narratives.

As such, *Absalom* should be viewed as a "celebration of *collaboration* as a fruitful human exercise toward creating new works of art and reaching new levels of comprehension" (Urgo, "Absalom" 58). Faulkner would additionally meditate on the competitive nature of *cross-gender* collaboration through his fictions, responding to work alongside his female Hollywood co-creators in ways that brooded on the sexualized undercurrents of collective labor. In *Requiem for a Nun*—a text that emerged out of a hierarchical collaboration with a young female author and was penned with a specific Hollywood actress in mind for the lead role—Faulkner developed an improvisatory form of dialogue in which the female character, Temple Drake, participates in the collaborative construction of her personal narrative:

> GOVERNOR
> I know who Temple Drake was: the young woman student at the University eight years ago who left the school one morning on a special train of students to attend a baseball game at another college, and disappeared . . . until she reappeared six weeks later as a witness in a murder trial in Jefferson, produced by the lawyer of the man who, it was then learned, had abducted her and held her prisoner——
>
> TEMPLE
> —in the Memphis sporting house: don't forget that.
>
> GOVERNOR
> —in order to produce her to prove his alibi in the murder——
>
> TEMPLE
> —that Temple Drake knew had done the murder for the very good reason that——
>
> STEVENS
> Wait. Let me play too. (*N* 4: 557–58)

As a form of dramatic collective narration, Temple helps to compose her backstory along with the other characters, giving the reader what Gavin Stevens calls "a moving picture show for free" (*N* 4: 607), but it is also a competitive dynamic in which she is frequently drowned out and overruled by the Governor and Gavin. The dialogue here mimics the working processes that generated Faulkner's own screenwriting as, on projects such as *To Have and Have Not*, he was required to work with screenwriters, actors, and directors spontaneously and pragmatically to shape plot, dialogue, and character, sometimes parallel to the movie being filmed. Such explorations of the intersections between gender, power, and creativity permeate Faulkner's fiction and screenwriting from the 1930s to the 1950s. Collaboration in Faulkner's life and work should not, therefore, be understood as a creative practice that merely lies behind the composition of key works but as a process that repeatedly manifests itself in the textual fabric of his writing for literature and film.

Visual Media and Sexual Difference

As an extension of these intimate correspondences between literature and film, Faulkner shaped representations of women in his screenplays that helped to cement the status of woman as image in commercial cinema, but his Hollywood novels would go on to question such a framing. These connections between visual media and gender binaries were first powerfully examined in Laura Mulvey's essay "Visual Pleasure and Narrative Cinema" (1975), which fused feminist theory with psychoanalysis to expose the voyeurism and fetishism essential to film viewing within Hollywood cinematic narratives. For Mulvey, the Hollywood style successfully marshaled visual pleasure by coding "the erotic into the language of the dominant patriarchal order" ("Visual Pleasure" 835). Within this mode of viewing, cinematic spectatorship becomes structured around sexual difference. As Mulvey describes with respect to visual culture more broadly, "pleasure in looking has been split between active/male and passive/female. . . . In their traditional exhibitionist role women are simultaneously looked at and displayed, with their appearance coded for strong visual and erotic impact so that they can be said to connote *to-be-looked-at-ness*" ("Visual Pleasure" 837). Teresa de Lauretis also argues that this dynamic is essential to visual representations of women, proposing that the presentation of woman as spectacle "is so pervasive in our culture, well before and beyond the institution of cinema, that it necessarily constitutes a starting point for any understanding of sexual difference" (37–38). In other words, women are visually displayed as object, whereas men command the gaze and occupy the role of spectator within cultural representations of gender.

Within Hollywood film specifically, the status of woman as image is developed further, since mainstream cinema was able to fuse spectacle and narrative (Mulvey, "Visual Pleasure" 837), building "the way [the woman] is to be looked at into the spectacle itself" (843) through the fluid use of time (such as the editing of shots to form a narrative) and of space (such as variations in camera distance).[18] This occurs on two levels, both within the diegesis of the film itself and before the cinema audience, as the woman is presented as "erotic object for the characters in the screen story" as well as "for the spectator within the auditorium, with a shifting tension between the looks on either side of the screen" (Mulvey, "Visual Pleasure" 838). Faulkner's screenplays reproduced this structuring dynamic from the very beginning of his career, since as Kevin Alexander Boon points out, "it is the screenwriter who first shapes representation, who first frames the gaze" (121). For example, in Faulkner's early treatment for MGM, "The College Widow," which was based on the story he had written for Bankhead, Mary Lee Blair is stalked by a mysterious and sinister stranger with whom she had a short affair. In the text, Blair is positioned as the consumable object of the male spectator's gaze; the stranger sits outside her house, and "she knows that he has found her somehow and is waiting—lurking. She begins to feel that he is hidden, watching the house day and night . . . All day long she is in terror. She does not dare go out" (*MGM* 49–50). The stranger's gaze is so powerful that it paralyzes the female character in the position of a petrified spectacle, thereby controlling the film narrative. The stranger bears the look on behalf of the film viewer, gendered as male. Mulvey describes this type of dynamic when she observes that "the spectator identifies with the main male protagonist" and "projects his look on to that of his like, his screen surrogate, so that the power of the male protagonist as he controls events coincides with the active power of the erotic look, both giving a satisfying sense of omnipotence" ("Visual Pleasure" 838).

As in Faulkner's treatment, this relationship may frequently be expressed through violence within the diegesis of the film itself, since, as Mary Ann Doane elaborates, the "narrative's containment of the image of the woman is generally mediated by the male character who demystifies, possesses, or sadistically punishes the woman" (*Femmes Fatales* 101). According to the logic of Mulvey's psychoanalytic framework, this is because the female figure, through her lack of a penis, evokes castration anxiety in the male viewer ("Visual Pleasure" 840). The spectator has two options to manage these unpleasurable fears: either they can reenact the trauma through investigation, devaluation, or punishment of the woman or they can neutralize the threat the female figure presents through fetishization and overvaluation, such as through the activity of star worship (Mulvey, "Visual Pleasure" 840). In "The College Widow," Faulkner follows a punitive logic, situating the stranger as the spectator's "screen surrogate," as in the erotic contemplation of the female image the male viewer has complete mastery over the woman's role and trajectory in the narrative.

Faulkner also worked on one of the films Mulvey uses to illustrate the containment of the female image within classical Hollywood: *To Have and Have Not*. Mulvey describes how Bacall's character, Marie "Slim" Browning, is displayed as a sexualized object for the dual audience of the spectator in the cinema and the male protagonist within the film, but, by falling in love with Bogart's character, Harry Morgan, she "becomes his property" and "her eroticism is subjected to the male star alone" ("Visual Pleasure" 840). Faulkner's writing partly helped to reinforce this ultimate possession of the female character. In his story line for a new ending for "To Have and Have Not," dated 6 April 1944, Morgan is said to "compel" Browning to say she loves him, "believing that once she says it, she will commit herself and come to his whistle."[19] Faulkner's outline echoes the famous "whistle scene" that appeared in the final film, but instead of penning a line of dialogue that creates an impression of Browning's independence, here the whistle metaphor indicates her complete subservience to Morgan.

Although Faulkner may have followed a structure within his screenplays in which the gendered relationship between spectator and spectacle shapes the progression of the narrative, he would lament the status of woman as image in his Hollywood fictions. Criticism of this dynamic appeared in a work of fiction Faulkner published shortly before he began work for the studios in May 1932. In his story "Dry September," published in January 1931, a white spinster named Miss Minnie Cooper from a Southern town is rumored to have been attacked by a Black man, Will Mayes; these rumors lead to violence, which follows a racist logic of "defending" Minnie's virginity from perceived Black male hypersexuality, as a lynch mob forms to kill Will. Minnie, as a woman entering middle age, had ceased to attract the gazes of men in the town, "the sitting and lounging men . . . not even follow[ing] her with their eyes any more" (*CS* 175). However, speculation as to the nature of her relationship with Will leads to her becoming once more the focus of visual attention; she now approaches the town's square with "voices about her murmurous, also with that feverish, glittering quality of their eyes" (*CS* 180). As M. J. Burgess observes, this shift marks Minnie's acquisition of a "renewed status as a sexual commodity—in effect, her re-gendering" (99), a change that the character appears to savor "as children eat ice cream" (*CS* 180). Minnie's positioning as a spectacle of sexual interest comes to a head in a scene where she goes to the "miniature fairyland" (*CS* 181) of a picture show. The "silver dream" of the unfolding film gathers momentum and strength over Minnie, producing a violent laugh in her that grows in intensity even as she tries to suppress it, forcing her friends to escort her from the cinema, where "at the curb" her laughter continues "on a high, sustained note" (*CS* 181). Burgess argues that since Minnie is positioned as both spectacle for community gossip and spectator of the film in the cinema, she "cannot hold in their necessary equilibrium her simultaneous roles as watcher and watched, a disability that . . . breaks down into a laughter that is hysterical, even defiant" (100). Burgess concludes that the text, more broadly, "appropriates the narrative techniques of the cinema in order to explore the violence of its specular model of gender consumption" (100).[20]

Such an early challenge to the violence and voyeurism of filmic vision in Faulkner's work became explicitly tied to Hollywood, as both representational system and location, after he started in his role as a screenwriter. In Faulkner's short story "The Brooch" (1936), the focalizing character, Howard Boyd, appraises the beauty of his young, flapper-like wife, Amy. Her image somehow transcends her mediation, since she appears "not of the face whose impeccable replica looks out from the covers of a thousand magazines each month, nor of the figure, the shape of deliberately epicene provocation into which the miles of celluloid film have constricted the female body of an entire race" (*CS* 658–59). Howard appears to advocate for a form of primeval female beauty that predates modernity's channels of mediation, perceiving "a quality completely female in the old eternal fashion" (*CS* 659) in Amy. This instance of visual appreciation of the female image overruns and stalls the temporal progression of the narrative as a charged reverie, consistent with Mulvey's point that the woman's "visual presence" in cinema "tends to work against the development of a story line, to freeze the flow of action in moments of erotic contemplation" ("Visual Pleasure" 837).

Similar woes to those found in "The Brooch" are expressed in Faulkner's sole Californian story, "Golden Land." The male protagonist of the text, the middle-aged, wealthy real estate business owner Ira Ewing, bemoans that the female image has been collapsed into a reproduced, prosthetic sameness through its commercial mediation; when Ira watches his mistress making him a drink "in the bathing costume of the moment" he recalls that it is the exact replica "such as ten thousand wax female dummies wore in ten thousand shop windows that summer" and "such as a hundred thousand young girls wore on California beaches" (*CS* 718). Ira is disturbed by the reification of woman as consumable spectacle, and the attendant homogenization of a generation of women, leading him to make a sweeping, misogynistic statement that calls for the obliteration of *all* young female bodies: "would to God that all young girls, all young female flesh, were removed, blasted even, from the earth" (*CS* 718). In moments such as this, Faulkner could question the status of woman as image in acts of looking and simultaneously highlight the sadism of the male spectator.

These scenes are but two examples of male narrators or focalizing characters in Faulkner's fictions repeatedly using references, frameworks, and tropes from commercial film and mass culture to appraise the appearance of female characters. Women, in Faulkner's fictions, appear to be more readily associated with Hollywood products than men, as well as more susceptible to the movie industry's influences. In Faulkner's novel *If I Forget Thee, Jerusalem*, the following passage appears, as Harry looks past his lover Charlotte's features and out the bus window moving through the landscape; he observes "her head tilted back against the machine-made doily, her face in profile against the dark fleeing snow-free countryside and the little lost towns, the neon, the lunch rooms with broad strong Western girls got up out of Hollywood magazines (Hollywood which is no longer in Hollywood but is stippled by a billion feet of burning colored gas across the face of the American earth) to resemble Joan Crawford, asleep or not he could not tell" (*N* 3: 636). As Harry contemplates Charlotte's head rested against a cushion, his mind becomes distracted by the images of industrial reproduction that surround her: the "machine-made doily" and the glow of the "neon" signs, which are mirrored in the "burning colored gas" of Hollywood, littering the route of their journey. This framing stimulates a meditation on the artifice of "Western girls" aping the lives of Hollywood stars, turning themselves into images from mass-produced magazines. The association between mechanized production and commercial film echoes Walter Benjamin's fears that the "aura" of the work of art is diminished by its reproducibility, namely that "by replicating the work many times over, it substitutes a mass existence for a unique experience," of which the "most powerful agent," for Benjamin, was film (*Technological Reproducibility* 22). Here the "strong

Western girls" are denied a unique experience due to the reproducibility of their mediated, mass-market relationship to visual culture.

The scene restates the gendered spectator/spectacle opposition within filmic acts of viewing, as well as recirculating a modernist binary in which the writer maintains a masculinist distance from his female characters, embedding a hierarchy into the relationship between male creator and female creation. Huyssen uses the example of Gustave Flaubert to illustrate this point, describing how, in his most famous novel, "woman (Madame Bovary) is positioned as reader of inferior literature—subjective, emotional and passive—while man (Flaubert) emerges as writer of genuine, authentic literature—objective, ironic, and in control of his aesthetic means" (46). While Flaubert presented Bovary as a consumer of pulp fiction, Faulkner's female characters now passively consume Hollywood magazines. In moments such as this, which recur across Faulkner's Hollywood novels, there are two related cultural power dynamics at work that map onto sexual difference: woman as consumable object, man as voyeuristic spectator; woman as consumer of mass culture, man as synonymous with modernist, writerly detachment. However, Faulkner questions and undercuts these hierarchies and associations. He employs two principal strategies, drawing on his experiences in Hollywood, to destabilize these oppositions: disturbances of vision and the exposure of complicity.

Building on and qualifying Mulvey's arguments in "Visual Pleasure," theorists have shown how visual restrictions in relation to the female object within commercial cinematic narratives can unsettle the male spectator's default position of voyeuristic detachment. Doane insists that "feminist film theory must be especially sensitive to issues of iconography, of vision and its relation to forms of knowing, because femininity in modernity has become very much a question of hypervisibility. As soon as the relation between vision and knowledge becomes unstable or deceptive, the potential for a disruption of the given sexual logic appears" (*Femmes Fatales* 14). Although narrators and focalizing characters may ascribe Hollywood references to female characters as a tool of consumption in Faulkner's writing, such attributes can also, importantly, be presented as visual misapprehensions. In *Pylon*, for example, a male reporter working for a local newspaper describes the female protagonist and barnstorming flier, Laverne Shumann, in terms of her visual marketability, telling his editor that she had "Harlow-colored hair that they would pay her money for... in Hollywood" (*N* 2: 804). However, this description fails to align with Laverne's image at all, since her androgynous overalls are juxtaposed with her "Harlowcolored hair," an allusion to the hyperfeminine pre-Code actress Jean Harlow, creating a disconnect between the reporter's vision and his cultural knowledge. Through relations between characters such as Laverne and the reporter, Faulkner demonstrated that the male gaze could be challenged through strategies that disrupt vision, which, as I demonstrate in chapters 2 to 4 on Faulkner's Hollywood novels of the 1930s and 1940s, include transvestism, masquerade, inscrutability, and repulsion.[21] These techniques—derived from the Hollywood genres of melodrama, screwball comedy, film noir, and horror, among others—work to question the status of woman as consumable object in visual media.

Conscious of his own participation in the film industry, which helped to cement the status of woman as image in visual narrative, the objectification of women within Faulkner's Hollywood novels is also complicated by the collusion of his male characters in creating these spectacles.[22] While women may appear as both the consumers of filmic commodities and consumable images in Faulkner's Hollywood fictions, men are unable to disentangle themselves from them. In "Golden Land," when Ira comes down in the morning to collect the papers from the front door of his house in Los Angeles, an image of his daughter, Samantha, an aspiring Hollywood actress who has worked as a film extra for two years, stares up at him from the front cover. In the sensational language of the tabloid press he sees that "at his feet the black headline flared above the row of five or six tabloid photographs from which his daughter alternately stared back or flaunted long pale shins: APRIL LALEAR BARES ORGY SECRETS" (*CS* 705). These stories have appeared in the tabloids for a few days, as Samantha has been embroiled in a Hollywood casting-couch scandal, the details of which are being debated in court. In the newspapers, Samantha is abstracted both by the duplication of her image and by the use of her stage name: "Miss April Lalear of the cinema" (*CS* 708), as her brother playfully dubs her. Her physical abstraction is so complete that Ira is unable to read the material reproduction of Samantha's face, which "sprung out at him, hard, blonde and inscrutable" (*CS* 705).

However, Ira cannot disconnect from these objectified images of women, since he too participates in their generation by exploiting his daughter's newfound notoriety for his own ends. Ira has arranged for his secretary to break the story to a newspaper, and they have mocked up a page that advertises his company by virtue of being "APRIL LALEAR'S FATHER" (*CS*

715), which will be accompanied by a staged photo of Ira at the courthouse where his daughter is undergoing trial. Ira's commercial spirit is so self-serving that his secretary has to check him on it: "We can't expect them to put under your picture, 'Turn to page fourteen for halfpage ad'" (CS 715–16). Rather than establishing a dynamic of masculine detachment from mass culture, Faulkner's Hollywood fictions dramatize the complicity of men in the creation of woman as spectacle within commercial narratives, as I demonstrate in the subsequent chapters, whether it is the reporter composing titillating fare about the fliers' sex lives for his newspaper in *Pylon*, Harry penning confession stories about female sexual awakening for the popular magazines in *If I Forget Thee, Jerusalem*, or Ward Snopes drawing on his experiences of pimping and pornography for his new ambiguous role in Hollywood in *The Mansion*. These textual surrogates process Faulkner's own role in the construction of commercial images of women through his work in the studio system, but, crucially, his Hollywood fictions question the normative feminine and masculine positions in the relationship between spectacle and spectator.

Genre and Ideology

In a final dialogic pattern, Faulkner's Hollywood fictions engage with the conventional female roles of commercial movie genres, which he inhabited in his screenplays and appropriated for his prose. Faulkner's work for the studios, in part, served to uphold traditional presentations of female characters within generic templates. However, it is remarkable that the overall creative direction, across Faulkner's screenplays and Hollywood novels from the 1930s to the 1950s, moves towards a revision of depictions of women within commercial genres in ways that advanced popular characterizations of gender.

Hollywood genres work to present ideological perspectives, or systems of values, through patterns of convention. According to Thomas Schatz, we might consider genres primarily as "problem-solving operations" that "repeatedly confront the ideological conflicts (opposing value systems) within a certain cultural community, suggesting various solutions through the actions of the main characters" (*Hollywood Genres* 24). However, this does not mean that genres reach the same conclusions within these frameworks. As Schatz describes, the building blocks of film genres are both static and dynamic; on the one hand, they contain "a familiar formula of interrelated narrative and cinematic components that . . . continually reexamine some basic cultural conflict," but on the other hand, "changes in cultural attitudes, new influential genre films, the economics of the industry, and so forth, continually refine any film genre" (*Hollywood Genres* 16). This means that generic conventions can be deployed to different ends within Hollywood genre films, working "to both criticize and reinforce the values, beliefs, and ideals of our culture within the same narrative context" (Schatz, *Hollywood Genres* 35). Commercial films, then, may not necessarily be ideologically conformist, since they also work to criticize the value systems upon which the culture is built through staging conflicts between characters in discrete communities.

Consequently, character, as a conventional component of genre, has an ambiguous relation to the wider social and political climate, which is often expressed through the use of stereotype. Early feminist film theory by Marjorie Rosen in *Popcorn Venus* (1973) and Molly Haskell in *From Reverence to Rape: The Treatment of Women in the Movies* (1973) challenged the limiting stereotypical depictions of women in commercial film. Maggie Humm describes how their work created "a descriptive, emotional 'historiography' of Hollywood cinema showing how women's conventional roles, for example, as mothers or girls next door, had little representational bite on women's real identities and experiences" (13). However, directors and screenwriters within Hollywood have also been able to challenge such stereotypes. Claire Johnston has questioned the monolithic presentation of Hollywood as "repressive and manipulative" (31) in its stereotyping of women, since the iconography of commercial cinema, which includes character, can readily be reconfigured to question the myths with which it is generally associated and that it is marshaled to support.

Faulkner worked extensively on Hollywood genres that have been closely identified with specific female stereotypes and roles, such as vice and adventure films and film noir, but the author did not blindly support the status quo when mediating ideological conflicts pertaining to gender through genre conventions. Throughout his career, we see him continually questioning and revising genre-based representations of women as well as the system of values within which these portrayals are embedded. His work across film and literature demonstrates how conventions can be reconfigured from both inside *and* outside the studio system. In Faulkner's work on Hollywood genre pictures, we can observe him accepting and incorporating stereotypes into his writing, as manifestations of a broader sexist ideology. However, the general trend in his work across literature and film was to revise stereotypes actively through the reformulation of conventions across literature and film. As this activity attests, Faulkner viewed film and literature as distinctive but related mediums, and he took the opportunity to reimagine character types and plot devices within the new creative arena of cinema to engage new audiences. By moving between these two fields, Faulkner could both work within and transcend the popular cultural genres that Hollywood aimed to perfect.

In this way, Faulkner was not subverting Hollywood conventions as an outsider, but was instead a participant in the critical dialogic process through which commercial genres establish themselves and evolve. The Hawksian woman figure, a character type I describe in detail in chapter 2, was closely identified with Hawks's screwball comedies and adventure films from the late 1930s and 1940s. She has been seen as a "progressive" genre type, due to her masculine attributes and her ability to move into male zones of activity and maintain a degree of equality with men. But it is important to remember that such presentations developed in film history by combining stereotypical and novel features of characterization. In Faulkner's screenwriting, which advanced representations of the Hawksian woman, we can observe a perhaps surprising character hybridity. In his screenplay for the adventure film "Splinter Fleet" (1936), for example, Faulkner creates a double-sided portrayal of Susan as an incipient Hawksian woman. At times, she scorns sentimentality and the prospect of marriage and is introduced in the directions as "attractive, independent, self-contained" (*TCF* 393). Elsewhere, she pliantly acquiesces to the conventions of ritual courtship when she is pursued by a new suitor, breaking down in tears when she receives flowers from him, explaining that "I grew up on a ship, you see. Oh, I've known lots of men—good men like—but they never thought of giving me flowers" (*TCF* 468). Such inconsistencies result in a dissonant presentation that challenges the complacent investment of audiences in gender stereotypes.[23]

Faulkner similarly explored the ideological ambiguity of novel female characters within his writing for two 1940s genres at Warner Brothers: melodrama, or the woman's film, and film noir. In women's films of the late 1930s and 1940s, female characters struggle to reconcile their desires with marriage and motherhood (Haskell, *Reverence* 156), thereby expressing a challenge to conventional roles in the wartime and early postwar period. Types such as the suffering mother of the woman's film emerge during moments of social change or historical crisis, which are processed through a set of recurring conventions. The unhappy conclusions of these films, in which a woman may be exiled from her family or endure the death of a child, are intended to signal the dangers of female "errancy" in order to protect the nuclear family. However, there is still room for ideological resistance *within* this generic template. As Haskell points out, "the forced enthusiasm and the neat evasions of so many happy endings have only increased the suspicion that darkness and despair follow marriage, a suspicion the 'woman's film' confirmed by carefully pretending otherwise" (*Reverence* 124).

Faulkner had to be schooled in the resistant features of the woman's film when working at Warner Brothers, as he learned in Hollywood that certain genres could embrace a degree of formulaic subversion he may not initially have believed possible. Faulkner contended with the ideological inconsistencies of the woman's film genre in his review of a draft script titled "The Damned Don't Cry," based on Harry C. Hervey's 1939 novel of the same name, in November 1941 for Warner Brothers. His sensitivity to the conventions of the genre is such that he believes the narrative does not sufficiently resolve the ideological conflict the plot sets up, since he says the script "fails to state a definite problem, moral, personal, or sociological, and then proceed to solve it" (*SL* 145). In the script, a character called Zelda has an illegitimate child but "loves it too much to repudiate it completely" (*SL* 145) and so conceals this fact; however, Faulkner believes that Zelda is neither strong nor self-sacrificing enough to justify this course of action but merely keeps the child because she is ordered to do so. This means that the picture cannot generate audience pity, since once the child's existence is revealed, Zelda "simply shrieks and faints and after a while comes to, whereupon, thanks to the frantic efforts of everybody else in the picture except her, the situation is unchanged and therefore none of it need ever have taken place" (*SL* 145). For Faulkner, the script in its current form does not fully perform the ideological work of the woman's film in its use of the trope of sacrifice, in which a woman is often forced to give up someone close to her in order to preserve the family home. But in the script as it stands, Zelda is too passive to make a decision that addresses the problem the picture poses.

Faulkner asserts that the issue is compounded by the film's "happy ending," but he initially seems unreceptive here to a degree of ideological subversion that the genre was starting to accommodate. The experienced screenwriter is not satisfied by the resolution of the plot through Zelda's marriage to Dan, who Faulkner describes as "a poor sort" and not "the one she should have faded out with, unless something is done with DAN, either various stages of conflict shown between DAN and ZELDA, or an undeviating fidelity despite all odds" (*SL* 146). At the beginning of his work on the woman's film genre, Faulkner appears to overlook that the forced and unconvincing resolution of the plot through marriage or reunion is in fact consistent with the ideological ambivalence of many women's films, particularly as they developed in complexity into the 1940s. After Faulkner gained knowledge in Hollywood of the broader scope for these kind of ambiguities within the evolving genre, his final version of "The Damned Don't Cry," written at the end of 1941, would incorporate this trope; Zelda is suddenly reunited with Dan at the end of Faulkner's treatment, but the conclusion offers scant consolation for the exile from child and home that she now faces, with Dan offering Zelda a glib line about accompanying her away from her home town to "some end-line such as farther than that, until they die, etc." (*CL* 101). The ostensibly happy ending can barely mask the "darkness and despair" that lurk on the horizon. Faulkner's new version of a woman's film now embraces its increasing ideological complexity in ways that helped to revise the presentation of female attitudes toward marriage within melodrama. Indeed, as I will show in chapter 5, Faulkner's modifications of the conventions of the woman's film in *Requiem for a Nun* was such that his late-career Hollywood novel would become aligned with the more sophisticated, and ideologically resistant, family melodramas of the 1950s.

Around a similar time in cinema history, film noir mediated cultural conflicts related to gender through the antagonistic relationship between male and female characters. Noir explored troubled (or threatened) masculinity in the 1940s, a focus engendered by the conclusion of World War II and a shift in the position of women in American society as they moved to occupy more positions in the national labor force. Within these films, the figure of the femme fatale plays scapegoat for male self-doubt. Gender anxiety and antagonism are expressed in the conflict between the hero and the eroticized, deceitful femme fatale, who is diagnosed as the source of masculine insecurity and sacrificed to those fears. Across Faulkner's scripts that draw on noir characterization, the murderous femme fatale figure is repeatedly subjected to a violent death or imprisonment to neutralize the threat she presents: the spoiled daughter figure, Veda, is arrested at the conclusion of Faulkner's version of "Mildred Pierce" (1944); Marlowe arranges for the duplicitous Carmen Sternwood to be gunned down at the conclusion of Faulkner and Brackett's screenplay for "The Big Sleep" (1944); and Daisy Otis drives off the side of a mountain while being pursued by the police after attempting murder in Faulkner's screenplay "Stallion Road" (1945).[24] Such endings work to resolve the anxieties the female character produces in the male viewer, by containing the threat she presents through punishment.

However, we should not equate these films' conclusions *solely* with a reassertion of patriarchal dominance. Cowie believes that a focus on the masculinity of noir "obscures the extent to which these films afforded women roles which are active, adventurous and driven by sexual desire," arguing that "the fantasy of the woman's dangerous sexuality is a feminine as well as masculine fantasy, and its pleasures lie precisely in its forbiddenness" ("Film Noir and Women" 135–36). In other words, it is not just the patriarchy or standards of Hollywood censorship in the 1940s that require these expressions of female sexuality to be punished, since it is part of a broader transgressive model from which men *and* women can derive pleasure. We can see this in Faulkner's script for "Stallion Road," which was at one point intended to star Bogart and Bacall (Blotner, *Biography* 467) as another noir vehicle for the couple after the successes of *To Have and Have Not* and *The Big Sleep*. The plot clearly works to remove the threat Daisy poses to the men around her, however Faulkner nevertheless derives a transgressive pleasure from her depiction; one male character gives a warning to the hero about Daisy—"She's dangerous. She's poison. She's worse than that: she's dynamite" (*SR* 60)—which she herself later echoes when she goads the "virtuous" heroine, and her rival for the hero's affections, by asking, "Did it ever occur to you that a human being might be poison too? . . . That I am poison? Dangerous?" (*SR* 69). The pleasure Daisy derives from her fatal sexuality activates male anxieties in the screenplay. Nevertheless, such moments also offer exciting glimpses of unfettered female desire that threaten to overrun the ideological trajectory of the narrative towards containment of the fatale figure and thereby revise the conventions of the noir genre more broadly.

Faulkner's screenplays traffic in the tropes of commercial film in ways that gradually work to undermine the promulgation of conformist gender ideologies through genre conventions, and this process was also an ongoing transmedial dialogue with this prose. In his modernist novels, he recycled, reframed, and interrogated the genre conventions, and their associated gender portrayals, that he was tasked with transmitting in Hollywood. Chapter 1 begins this focus on the imbricated relationship between gender and genre through an analysis of Faulkner's first story outlines and treatments for MGM, which fuse the visual iconography of the flapper film, previously explored in his novel *Sanctuary*, with the genre conventions of the pre-Code vice film to warn against the "excesses" of new female roles. I pay particular attention to his portrayal of the figure of the "bad girl" from the vice genre, who transgressed sexual boundaries as a means of social advancement (Doherty, *Pre-Code Hollywood* 131), to suggest that Faulkner produced dissonant pre-Code works for MGM that both reveled in and condemned Hollywood vice. Faulkner wrote sexually vivid content appropriate for the pre-Code era, in which women get away with murder, but also invited the audience to find these women morally bankrupt. These early projects demonstrate Faulkner's understanding of how gender portrayals were embedded within commercial genre conventions, as the screenwriter incorporated new archetypes into his work to both engage and caution the popular appetite for filmic explorations of female sexual transgression.

Beginning in his work on "Turn About" for Hawks at MGM, and advanced in his screenwriting at Fox in the mid-1930s, Faulkner's Hollywood writing starts to integrate transgressive female characters without the need to "keep in check" their excesses. Chapter 2 pays attention to the collective working practices of Hollywood and studies Faulkner's creation of a number of Depression-era working women in his novels and screenplays, where sexuality was sublimated into cross-gender collaborative labor after the implementation of the Hays Code in 1934. Through the female roles he created in his screenplays for "The Road to Glory" and "Splinter Fleet" at Fox and "To Have and Have Not" at Warner Brothers, Faulkner both developed and built upon his portrayal of equivalent heroines in his fiction, such as Laverne Shumann from *Pylon*. He thereby actively participated in the construction of the masculinized, and socially progressive, heroines of Hawks's late 1930s and early 1940s screwball comedies and adventure films. The chapter approaches the distinctive "Hawksian woman" archetype as a figure that emerges collaboratively within studio networks and whose development highlights an aesthetic conversation between Faulkner and Hawks across literature and film through the 1930s and 1940s.

Faulkner continued to build on representations of the masculinized heroine in his 1939 novel *If I Forget Thee, Jerusalem* through the characterization of Charlotte Rittenmeyer, and chapter 3 is concerned not only with the novel's debt to the conventions of Hawks's films and Faulkner's screenplays but also the text's engagement with the gender oppositions of the high/low divide. In "The Wild Palms" sections of the text, Faulkner explores cultural divisions through commercial labor comparable to work in Hollywood, since its protagonists, Charlotte and her lover Harry, produce art shaped by the demands of the market to support themselves: sculpture and magazine writing respectively. However, Faulkner starkly contrasts Charlotte's and Harry's involvement with their work, since Charlotte's sculptures become increasingly experimental through her market commissions, a form of instrumentalized modernism, while Harry becomes fearful that his confession stories, written from female perspectives, will consume him. By ironically juxtaposing Charlotte's anxiety-free industry with Harry's paranoid labor, Faulkner undercuts the tired metaphorical approximation of women with "degraded" commercial art. This chapter also analyzes Faulkner's own teleplay adaptation of the "Old Man" sections of *If I Forget Thee, Jerusalem* in 1953. The work recasts a story of sexual horror as a commercial romance and therefore undermines many of the fearful ways in which men view women within popular cultural frames in both narrative threads of the original novel.

Chapter 4 moves the focus onto Faulkner's prose and Warner Brothers screenplays from the 1940s, specifically the genres of noir and the war film and their associated gendered ideologies. After working for Warner Brothers from 1942 to 1945, the first new prose work Faulkner produced was "Appendix Compson: 1699–1945," commonly known as the Compson "Appendix," for the collection *The Portable Faulkner* (1946), which provided a genealogy of the central family in *The Sound and the Fury*. This chapter demonstrates how Faulkner's new presentation of Caddy Compson traffics in the images of women contained in his noir and Gothic screenplays for Warner Brothers rather than his Yoknapatawpha fictions, particularly "The Big Sleep"; "Mildred Pierce"; "Dreadful Hollow," a little-discussed vampire horror screenplay from the mid-1940s; and "Stallion Road." Her revisualization also draws on images of World War II secret agents from Faulkner's movie scripts for "The De Gaulle Story" (1942), "Battle Cry" (1943), and "To Have and Have Not," all of which emphasized the indecipherability of the female figure. By depicting Caddy as femme fatale in his 1946 appendix, Faulkner incorporated a new gender archetype into his Yoknapatawpha prose and used the troubling opacity of her image to explore noir's close association of gender difference and the visual mechanism of film, in particular the notion that the fatale's presentation, as Doane describes, is "dependent upon perceptual ambiguity and ideas about the limits of vision in relation to knowledge" (*Femmes Fatales* 3). In rendering Caddy's image both commodified and inscrutable, Faulkner suggests that figures derived from noir resist deciphering and that established characters from his own fiction are open to visual reassessment.

Chapter 5 further considers the relationship between film genre and ideology. It approaches Faulkner's 1951 hybrid prose-drama narrative as an adaptation of two women's films that he worked on for Warner Brothers in the 1940s, "The Damned Don't Cry" and "Mildred Pierce." In *Requiem for a Nun* Faulkner returned to the theme of maternal sacrifice associated with the genre in his own Hollywood-inspired melodrama. Rather than creating an "homage," however, Faulkner drew on the drive for social conformity inherent in the genre but redeployed its tropes in a subversive fashion to launch a strong critique of the aggressive post–World War II domestic imperative. Faulkner challenged the ideological enforcement of limiting gender roles in Cold War Hollywood film by exaggerating and undercutting the sacrificial tropes of the woman's film and the sentimental features of race melodramas (such as 1939's *Gone with the Wind*) in *Requiem*. The self-conscious stylistic excess of the text unwittingly anticipated the direction some Hollywood family melodramas would take in the 1950s, particularly the films of Douglas Sirk, in which the director similarly employed self-ironizing techniques to undermine Cold War domestic norms. In Sirk's films, style is used as a method of undercutting dominant presentations of race, class, gender, and sexuality in American culture, while displaying them in recognizable fashion, through an exaggerated use of form.

Chapter 6 concludes by giving an overview of gender portrayals across Faulkner's Hollywood writing. It considers the character Linda Snopes Kohl from Faulkner's late-career work *The Mansion* as a generic hybrid of the cinematic archetypes he had developed in his fiction and screenwriting over the past few decades. The novel combines aspects of Faulkner's previous Hollywood screenplays and novels, since Linda embodies the sexual assertiveness of the bad girl, engages in the masculinized collaborative labor of the Hawksian heroine, possesses the dangerous inscrutability of the femme fatale, and sacrifices her lover for his own welfare within the template of the melodramatic woman's film. However, through Linda, Faulkner manages to revise the potential ideological limitations of some of these roles in a single text. By revealing such transmedial exchanges between literature and cinema, this book traces Faulkner's contribution to film history through both his screenplays and his displaced Hollywood novels across the breadth of his career.

1

Sanctuary, Flapperhood, and the Pre-Code Vice Film

FAULKNER'S FIRST IMPULSE TO journey to Hollywood was sparked on a trip to New York in November 1931, during which he met with a series of rival publishers. At this point in his career, he was beginning to garner a reputation as the author of *The Sound and the Fury* (1929), *As I Lay Dying* (1930), and, infamously, *Sanctuary* (1931), a novel set chiefly in the gangland underworlds of Mississippi and Memphis. During his stay in New York, Faulkner met the Southern actress of stage and screen, Tallulah Bankhead, who was an admirer of his work and who suggested he go to Hollywood to write a screenplay for her. Bankhead had been asked to approach Faulkner by her studio, Paramount Pictures. Faulkner was obliging, reputedly replying, "I'd like to help a Southern girl who's climbin' to the top. But you're too pretty an' nice a girl to play in anything I'd write" (Blotner, *Biography* 289). The author talked to a representative of Paramount in New York as a result. The idea of more lucrative writing projects appealed to Faulkner, and so he asked his agent to try and secure him a Hollywood contract, while he began work on a story for Bankhead. In a letter to his wife, Estelle, from New York on 13 November, Faulkner was enthusiastic about the well-paid contract that was being drawn up and excited at the prospect of the collaboration, explaining that he was "writing a movie for Tallulah Bankhead. How's that for high?" (*SL* 53).

In 1931, the year Bankhead met Faulkner, she had starred in a number of films shot at Paramount's Astoria Studios in Long Island that were typical of the pre-Code era of Hollywood cinema. In this period of cinema history, as described in the introduction, films that dealt head-on with themes of sex and violence did not face the stricter enforcement of the Motion Picture Production Code studio guidelines by the Production Code Administration, which would be set up in 1934 under the leadership of Joseph I. Breen. Bankhead had become synonymous with "fallen heroine" or "bad girl" roles through these movies, but she was tired of playing these parts, recalling that she "seemed sentenced for life to playing tarts, reformed tarts or novice tarts" (192). These films seemed to play on Bankhead's reputation from the 1920s as, in Molly Haskell's words, "the most thoroughgoing libertine and free-swinging flapper of the age" (*Reverence* 78). Bankhead was indeed famous for her hard-partying, chain-smoking, and drug-taking lifestyle. While she asserted that many of the stories about her were apocryphal, she nevertheless participated in the dissemination of "the carousing phase of [her] legend" by riffing off journalists' prurient interest in her lifestyle (Bankhead 92–3). While stories about Bankhead may be exaggerated, she nevertheless proclaimed in her autobiography to be "the foe of moderation, the champion of excess" (94).

Bankhead's meeting with Faulkner did indeed lead him to work for Hollywood, and his early work would play on the actress's reputation for "excess." Faulkner would, however, join the Metro-Goldwyn-Mayer (MGM) studio rather than Paramount. In April 1932, he signed a contract for $500 a week as a screenwriter with MGM and started work at the beginning of May (Blotner, *Biography* 302). Bankhead, too, would move from Long Island to Hollywood in 1932 to star in two more pictures for Paramount and one for MGM, meaning that both actor and author would come to work for the same studio on the West Coast after their first meeting in New York. One of Faulkner's first projects was to adapt a three-page synopsis he had typed out, called "Night Bird," into a treatment, or a story outline without dialogue, which he retitled "The College Widow." It is likely that "Night Bird" was the piece Faulkner had started work on for Bankhead in New York the previous November (Blotner, *Biography* 305). The project does nothing to distance the actress from the film roles for which she had been typecast; Bankhead summarizes that across her early 1930s Hollywood projects, which she called "fiascos," she invariably played "a wicked woman, inclined to be promiscuous, double-dealing and dark of design" (192). Reflecting these parts,

Faulkner's early treatments for MGM fuse the visual iconography of flapperhood, which he had previously explored in his novel *Sanctuary*, with the genre conventions of the pre-Code vice film, which often focused on women who used their promiscuous sexuality to climb the social ladder (Doherty, *Pre-Code Hollywood* 131). This chapter will demonstrate that the influence of Bankhead on Faulkner's early work for Hollywood was decisive, since the actress was both closely associated with the popular image of the partying flapper and had predominantly worked within the vice film tradition in her short-lived Hollywood movie career. Bankhead would also provide a bridge for Faulkner between the cultural networks of the South, the East Coast, and Hollywood, as well as an imaginative connection between his fiction and new screenwriting projects.[1]

In Hollywood, Faulkner would pen dissonant pre-Code film works for MGM that both reveled in and condemned vice through the figure of the bad girl, texts that policed the excesses they simultaneously sought luridly to depict. Faulkner's initial writing for MGM was actually in line with the code of standards that had been agreed upon by the studios in 1930 in dialogue with the Roman Catholic layman Martin Quigley and the Jesuit priest, Father Daniel Lord. These standards were a form of self-censorship and aimed to put limitations on the sex and crime pictures that were the main source of revenue for the studios. Robert Sklar describes how the agreement that was reached "allowed for a fairly wide leeway in depicting behavior considered immoral by traditional standards—adultery or murder, for example—so long as some element of 'good' in the story balanced what the code defined as evil. This was the formula of 'compensating moral value': if 'bad' acts are committed, they must be counteracted by punishment and retribution, or reform and regeneration, of the sinful one" (174). Although such a template was widely ignored in the early years of pre-Code cinema, Faulkner's early screenwriting registers the increasing pressure Hollywood would feel to bow to conventional morality and demonstrate its willingness to punish transgression.

Such portrayals of the bad girl were not entirely new, since Faulkner's depiction of the trope established a continuity with previous ambivalent representations of the hedonistic flapper in popular media, particularly those found in silent film of the 1920s and in his novel *Sanctuary*. These earlier works similarly displayed and warned against the norm-violating behavior of a different female figure: the flapper or New Woman. At MGM, Faulkner created hybrid characters in his screenwriting projects that brought together cultural attributes of the 1920s flapper and the early 1930s bad girl. This body of work therefore offers fascinating insights into Faulkner's sense of the role of female sexuality in attracting and cultivating popular audiences during this period of literary and cinematic production.

Faulkner would, however, not only create cautionary tales that kept in check the "transgressions" of certain female types and roles. In his later projects for MGM, the screenwriter would move beyond these depictions to write women for the screen who were neither punished nor denounced for their sexual independence. In "Turn About" (1932) and "Mythical Latin-American Kingdom Story" (1933), Faulkner would instead pen sympathetic female characters whose sexual pragmatism is presented as a justified response to broader social tensions, and it was precisely the productively competitive nature of the studio system that was the catalyst for this shift in character delineation and the screenwriter's increased readiness to flaunt moral standards in his work for film.

Sanctuary and the Popular Imagery of Flapperhood

Faulkner's engagement with cinematic iconography in his depiction of female characters predates his work at MGM. One of the major figures in *Sanctuary*, Temple Drake, is initially aligned with cultural presentations of the 1920s flapper. Peter Lurie has observed how Temple's identity appears to be "structured along cinematic lines" (42), which he attributes to the novel's persistent emphasis on her image as an object of voyeuristic consumption. More specifically, though, Temple's cinematic quality is derived from a series of archetypes and conventions from the silent flapper film.

Upon entering the novel, Temple is presented as a 1920s New Woman whose unorthodoxy is expressed through revelry and the courting of dangerous men. Temple indulges in the libertine lifestyle of the flapper by spending her time dating and dancing, but she also reflects the flapper's embodiment of increased social independence for women, since she is pursuing a college education. As Stephen Sharot highlights, "the term 'New Woman' began to be used in the 1890s to characterize middle to upper-middle class women who were engaged in educational, political, and occupational pursuits outside the home" (74) before it became more closely associated with sexual expressiveness and consumerism in the 1920s. Temple initially embodies these twin social and behavioral facets of the flapper.

Due to the challenge the flapper posed to social norms, she also provoked a backlash, and a wide range of social ills were attributed to the figure, including smoking, drinking to excess, wild nightlife, sexual immodesty, and generational dumbing down (Zeitz, introduction). Faulkner's novel also provides its own social criticism of the flapper figure through Temple. In adopting some of these traits of the fast-living New Woman, Temple will no longer receive the protection of the men around her, and she will go on to endure sexual abuse at the hands of a group of bootleggers and gangsters at the Old Frenchman place and in a Memphis brothel. According to the punitive logic of the novel, similar to what Faulkner's work at MGM would go on to do, the author depicts the "excesses" of certain female roles and archetypes while cautioning against them.

It is important to remember that the flapper was not just a social phenomenon but a cultural construction created by artists, writers, advertisers, and filmmakers, and Faulkner's representation of the figure was in dialogue with these different media sources. *Sanctuary* has frequently been appraised as a novel that incorporates contemporary pop cultural influences. Faulkner himself performatively described in his introduction to the 1932 edition of the novel that he had integrated all the elements of "what a person in Mississippi would believe to be current trends" (*ESPL* 177). These would include detective story conventions in its depiction of criminal underworlds (Fiedler 85) and tropes from the gangster fiction genre, particularly in its characterization of Temple's abuser Popeye (Lurie 33; Hanley 257). The novel consequently offers a medley of contemporary mass media genres. Additionally, in his depiction of Temple, Faulkner drew on images of the flapper that had been disseminated in the literature of F. Scott Fitzgerald and Hollywood silent cinema of the 1910s and 1920s. The flapper film displayed Jazz Age femininity on the screen, embodied by strong heroines played by Clara Bow, Louise Brooks, and Joan Crawford, who were associated with "modern styles of dress and decor, jazz parties and nightlife, dancing, drinking, smoking, and the erotic possibilities of everyday life" (Landay 224). In her appearance and proclivities, Temple initially resembles one of these flapper stars, what Leslie Fiedler calls "a typical longlegged teenaged flapper . . . a co-ed *demi-vierge* in scandalously short skirts" (89).

But it is not simply Temple's *image* that visually recalls these roles. The unfolding of the narrative after Temple's initial appearance as this type reflects the typical structural progression of the flapper film, which worked to dominate and control the figure by exposing her apparent artificiality. Since the flapper represented a challenge to established social and sexual mores of the age, flapper films had two primary approaches to undercutting the subversive modernity of the figure. As Sara Ross explains, movies in which the flapper appeared could, first, offer a "moral lesson" by showing the flapper to either succumb to a tragic fate or experience redemption after "wrong-headedly" embracing "the rhetoric of free love or feminism or the lure of the jazz age" (409). Alternatively, these films could choose to derive comedy from the transgressions of the flapper; the redemptive angle would be retained within the comedic genre "through the flapper's ultimate rejection of modern ways and recuperation into the family" (409), thereby neutralizing the apparent sexual "threat" the figure posed. These strategies lent the flapper film a highly paradoxical nature, since they invited moral condemnation of the transgressions they simultaneously celebrated. As Ross describes, in the flapper comedy genre, film producers targeted "a balance between 'spice' and acceptability" by introducing "narrative correctives to a character's 'bad' behavior," which, in this case, often showed the flapper "explicitly renouncing her experiments with the modern lifestyle and/or settling down in a relationship with a conventional man" (411).

The collegiate flapper story and Clara Bow vehicle *The Plastic Age* (1925), a film that resembles *Sanctuary* and was directed by Wesley Ruggles, fuses these two dominant strategies by undercutting the female star's "excesses" through comedy and by redeeming the figure in her partial relinquishment of the role. When the wealthy freshman and sports star Hugh Carver (Donald Keith) joins Prescott College, he quickly finds himself attracted to the energetic party girl Cynthia Day (Clara Bow). She takes him to dances and on moonlit walks when he should be training for football matches or studying. Sensuality is essential to Day's presentation as flapper in the film, but her desires are invariably tempered through comedy: Day exaggeratedly feigns modesty when she sees that Carver's knees are exposed beneath his nightclothes on their initial meeting (see fig. 1), and after their first kiss, she frenziedly runs away into the woods with her suitor pursuing her shouting, "Gee!!!" (*Plastic*). Carver's sports and academic careers both begin to suffer from all the partying, but the film demonstrates Day's honor in turning this around: she calls an end to their nights out, justifying that Carver is not part of the "fast crowd" and she doesn't want him to become like her. Here the flapper protects the sensitive, wholesome sports star from her own excesses. The sacrifice restores the hero to sporting success on the football field, and by the film's conclusion, Day has shed enough of the

FIGURE 1. Cynthia Day (Clara Bow) reacts to the exposure of Hugh Carver's knees in *The Plastic Age* (1925). (Preferred Pictures)

flapper's attributes—one of her former suitors says she's "changed a great deal—quieter—not the same girl"—to allow a reunion between hero and heroine. Even here, their kissing is rendered absurd by them falling backwards off a bench in a passionate embrace. While the attractiveness of the flapper remains undisputed, the film instructs that the iconic figure either has to sideline herself for the man to flourish or the flapper pose has to be shed and the woman's behavior reformed to allow romance to endure.

In *Sanctuary*, Temple's first appearance in the novel recalls *The Plastic Age* in its exploration of the attractiveness of the flapper figure within an educational environment as a figure of sexual interest and speculation. Temple is enrolled in college but is more devoted to dancing and dating than intellectual study. She steals out of the women's dormitory on weeknights to go joyriding with the local boys, an activity for which she has been put on probation. She fraternizes with uneducated, presumably working-class town boys, a group distinguished from the college boys, as they have a hard-boiled look, wearing "hats cupped rigidly upon pomaded heads, and coats a little too tight and trousers a little too full, with superiority and rage" (*N* 2: 198). There is a socially transgressive element to Temple's activities as the haute bourgeoise daughter of a wealthy family dating men from a lower-class position. Though Temple may still be a virgin, there are implications of her sexual knowingness and experience; her name is penciled onto the men's lavatory wall in Oxford's train station, and while ambiguous, this suggests a climate of seedy speculation around her activities.

In keeping with these early scenes' resemblance to a collegiate flapper film, Temple's entrance in the novel is cinematically framed. From the outset, Temple is associated with heightened, frenzied movement. We first see her with "a snatched coat under her arm and her long legs blonde with running, in speeding silhouette against the lighted windows" (*N* 2: 198); Temple's presentation here seems especially aligned with the flapper type as performed by Bow, whose style was typified by "energetic movements, and enjoyment of masquerade and posing" (Sara Ross 418). Indeed, Lori Landay asserts that "part of what made Bow the 'super-flapper of them all' was her embodiment of kinaesthetics" (240), reflective of a new age shaped by heightened mobility at "the confluence of moving pictures, moving women, and modernist acceleration" (231). However, it is not simply the speed of Temple's movements as a literal "fast girl" that mimics the flapper screen role but, additionally, the swift transitions she makes between different poses. As Ross describes, "one notable feature of Bow's style was the rapidity with which she changed her moods, expressions and movements, exaggerated even beyond the flapper's typical animation" (418). Temple's progression through different poses is similarly accelerated to the point of comedy; we watch her "vanishing into the shadow beside the library wall," with the narrator then speculating that there was "perhaps a final squatting swirl of knickers or whatnot as she sprang into the car waiting there with engine running" (*N* 2: 198). Typical of the flapper too, Temple's mobility is bound up with her love of music and dancing, as at the student balls she is "passed in swift rotation from one pair of black sleeves to the next, her waist shaped slender and urgent in the interval, her feet filling the rhythmic gap with music" (*N* 2: 198). These movements, though energetic and expressive, are shot through with a tone of foreboding, as we sense that Temple may lose control of her body as she is exchanged passively from partner to partner.

As a kinetic and cinematic embodiment of the flapper figure, Temple's movements attract male spectators, and it is here that Faulkner first interrogates the gendered voyeurism and fetishism that is fundamental to filmic spectatorship in *Sanctuary*, as has been elaborated in psychoanalytic feminist film theory, which I outline in this book's introduction. Temple attracts the gaze of the men, who consume her as erotic object; Lurie identifies her as "a popular cultural fetish or icon" (22) and "one of the novel's self-referential 'products' of commodified pleasure" (39), the subject of both the reader's and the male characters' voyeuristic gazes, reflecting commercial visual media. But Temple cannot control acts of looking herself. At the university dances, which she attends with fellow students, men from the town watch her from outside in the dark through the lighted windows of the gymnasium while drinking and smoking. The voyeurism of this activity is pointedly cinematic. It is reminiscent of Mulvey's description of the gender binary within visual media, in which man is positioned as spectator and woman as spectacle; for Mulvey, "the extreme contrast between the darkness in the auditorium . . . and the brilliance of the shifting patterns of light and shade on the screen . . . helps to promote the illusion of voyeuristic separation" ("Visual Pleasure" 836). Consistent with woman's position as object rather than bearer of the look, Temple is repeatedly associated with blindness in contrast to the men around her. As she emerges from the dance hall with her partner, where she has been a dynamic visual spectacle, the lounging men observe her: "Her eyes, all pupil now, rested upon them for a blank moment. Then she lifted her hand in a wan gesture, whether at them or not, none could have said" (N 2: 199). Temple is not able to return the gaze that consumes her but is accused of courting it through her movements. In Ruby Lamar's account to the lawyer Horace Benbow of the night of Temple's rape, she blames Temple for the apparent sexual provocation of her physical mobility at the Old Frenchman place, charging that events might have progressed differently "if she'd just stopped running around where they had to look at her. She wouldn't stay anywhere" (N 2: 291). In describing Temple's eyes as "like the holes in one of these masks" (N 2: 291), Ruby clearly, however, presents Temple as a blind spectacle, an object of voyeuristic fantasy.

The aftermath of the rape and abuse Temple suffers at the Old Frenchman place and at Miss Reba's Memphis brothel also reflects a core feature of the flapper film, in which the behavior of the flapper is presented as a superficial pose. The device ideologically suggests that the flapper's excesses only superficially mask her essentially virtuous nature. Consequently, the challenging modernity of the figure can be undone or stripped away, as occurs in *The Plastic Age*. Flapperhood in these films is undermined as a legitimate mode of being, presented instead as pure performance. As Ross describes, cinematic flapper roles "suggest that the transgressive behavior of the characters is removed from their 'true' nature. Narratively, the behavior is usually motivated as a whim produced by the influence of the media or a charismatic figure, or a pose assumed to shock or impress the other characters" (415). Indeed, the speed at which Temple moves between different types of behavior in *Sanctuary* implies that the flapper is just one role she assumes under external pressure.

In the second half of the novel, Temple's image is much more closely aligned with the role of the gangster's girlfriend, or the moll, than the flapper. After she is imprisoned by Popeye in the Memphis brothel, Temple rapidly transforms herself into a gun-toting, hard-living moll as a means of survival. Temple enters into a relationship of sorts with her captor and begins to adopt the language of her new gangland environment. In a scene at a Memphis club, Temple asks Popeye to dance, goading him with the line "call yourself a man, a bold, bad man, and let a girl dance you off your feet" (*N* 2: 342) as her hand works its way under his arm to touch the butt of his pistol. Of course, her shift in behavior does little to alter her situation; similar to the roles of women in the pre-Code films of the early 1930s that cemented the gangster genre, in which "the dames, molls, and dishes are pushed around and cast aside" (Doherty, *Pre-Code Hollywood* 150), Temple is subjected to continuing abuse within a masculine, hard-boiled environment. Deborah Clarke argues that Temple's behavior in this part of the novel reads as "a desperate attempt to articulate what she cannot speak verbally—a feminine discourse which will prove effective in the face of male aggression" (67). Scott Yarbrough, too, advances that Temple plays a role here in order to transcend her subjection and that her image in Memphis is allied to the roman noir tradition, the American crime genre that provided the source texts for many noir films that date from the early 1940s. He states that Temple "becomes a femme fatale because such a transformation and reconstruction of self are, to her, the only way to salvage her life and her soul" (Yarbrough 53). We view Temple's language and actions as an impotent response to the impossibility of her situation and the pervasiveness of male violence. But as an extension of this, we retrospectively read Temple's initial flapper stance as masquerade. Faulkner may, then, make us aware of the limited roles afforded to women within patriarchal structures, and the violent subjugation that underpins them, but he also neutralizes any threat the flapper figure may present to male dominance, by forcing us to consider the identity a mere pose.

Indeed, the rapidity with which Temple shifts between different roles and personas denies her character a stable identity. This is also the case in Bow's embodiment of the flapper role, in which "the distinction between the poses and her 'real' or innocent self is not marked" (Sara Ross 418). Such was the pace at which Bow shifted between these poses that she "blurred the line between pretending and 'being'" (420), allowing the film to display the unabashed sexual nature of the flapper while simultaneously presenting it is an act. When Temple gives a verbal account to Horace of the sexual abuse she suffered from Popeye, we see her inhabit a quick succession of different identities or positions. She imagines a number of hypothetical scenarios: that her legs were those of a boy (N 2: 328); that she was wearing a medieval chastity belt (N 2: 329); that she was lying dead in a coffin (N 2: 330); that she was a teacher in command at school (N 2: 331); and then, finally, that she was "an old man, with a long white beard," causing her to sprout a penis while Popeye is groping her (N 2: 331). As Clarke argues, Temple's attempts to fend off the men through language are ineffective, so she "is left with the alternative of becoming a man" (66), producing a series of "protective figurative fantasies" (68). In Temple's account too, as Caroline Garnier has argued, she "clearly establishes the adult male as dominant and confirms that she is devoid of power" (165) and that her "linguistic sexual aggressiveness can therefore be seen as resistance to subordination" (172).

It is also important to stress that Temple's discourse here is founded on hypothesis, and therefore her language is shown to be as provisional as the various poses she adopts. David Herman defines hypothetical focalization as "the use of hypotheses, framed by the narrator or a character, about what might be or have been seen or perceived—if only there were someone who could have adopted the requisite perspective on the situations and events at issue" (231). By speaking in hypothesis, Temple attempts to grant herself the agency and power in discourse that was denied to her at the Old Frenchman place. As a consequence of such language, we come to read all of Temple's many roles in the novel as tentative. Faulkner therefore extended the paradoxical image of the flapper, what Haskell calls the figure's "contradiction between the worldly woman and the breathless little girl" (*Reverence* 82), the flapper pose barely covering an essential vulnerability.[2] Faulkner, then, worked within the conventions of the silent flapper films of the 1920s to present Temple as a visual spectacle that threatened to collapse under its own contradictions, since her image is comprised of a series of artificial poses quickly assumed or revoked under external pressures.

Such contradictions were essential to the flapper's image in 1920s mass culture. Deborah Barker argues that at the beginning of *Sanctuary*, Temple never fully inhabits the "fun-loving flapper" role since she "draws the line at the sexual freedom" associated with the figure ("Moonshine and Magnolias" 150). But resistance to embracing a fully libertine identity was in fact a key feature of the American flapper's image in popular discourse. As Haskell describes, Bow was "the flaming incarnation of the flapper spirit" but didn't "stray any further from the straight and narrow than the distance of a long cigarette holder or a midnight joy ride" (*Reverence* 79). The flapper, consequently, only ever *superficially* challenged convention in her dominant filmic incarnations. Haskell uses the example of Zelda Fitzgerald, who became synonymous with the American flapper in the popular imagination, to describe this contradiction (and just like Temple, Fitzgerald hailed from the South and was the daughter of a judge): "Zelda's most uninhibited acts were grandstand public gestures: splashing around in the Plaza fountain in her clothes or staying up all night drinking champagne. She flew in the face of convention and her parents' morality to the point of notoriety, but without actually forsaking the safeguards and the protection of that morality" (*Reverence* 81). In Temple the contradictions of flapperhood are exemplified in her insistent refrain of "my father's a judge" (*N* 2: 199), with which she is associated from the very beginning of the novel during her courtship with the alcoholic Gowan Stevens, a means of summoning her privilege to assert her virtue. This is something Ruby challenges Temple on at the Old Frenchman place, stating that Temple will "slip out with the kids and burn their gasoline and eat their food, but just let a man so much as look at you and you faint away because your father the judge" (*N* 2: 218). These words prove prescient, as by the end of the novel, after everything she has endured, Temple is reassimilated into the patriarchal order, appearing beside her father in Paris's Luxembourg Gardens. In this final scene, Temple appears as an image of posed indifference, yawning and checking her makeup (*N* 2: 398). Faulkner said that the scene illustrated the wider message of the book that "women are impervious to evil" since "all of it [to Temple] was like water falling on a duck's back and sliding right off" (Blotner, *Biography* 294). The novel finally succeeds in containing the flapper figure by "recuperating" her into the restrictive social structures of her family and by implying that the identity was never anything more than an artificial pose. Faulkner cautions against the behaviors of the New Woman, in a seeming effort to neutralize her subversive potential by showing the apparent dangers that accompany the flapper's rebellious independence, which, in a final misogynistic turn in the novel, seem to render Temple shockingly numb to her own subjugation.

Pre-Code Vice and the Bad Girl

Faulkner would update the flapper figure he had initially explored in *Sanctuary* within his early screenwriting projects by engaging with the new conventions of pre-Code cinema at MGM. Faulkner's time at the studio coincided with the short period in which the content of Hollywood talkies was not regulated by the Production Code Administration. While the Motion Picture Producers and Distributors of America (MPPDA) had pledged to abide by the Production Code in March 1930, the Production Code Administration was only empowered to enforce it from July 1934 (Doherty, *Pre-Code Hollywood* 2). The Production Code was drafted by the Jesuit priest Father Lord and adopted in 1930, after silent film production had been largely discontinued,[3] to counter the moral profligacy of the 1920s through the advocacy of a coherent moral vision achieved through censorship. During this four-year period, the studios frequently disregarded these guidelines to produce eccentric, excessive, and provocative films; as Doherty summarizes, "pre-Code Hollywood did not adhere to the strict regulations on matters of sex, vice, violence, and moral meaning forced upon the balance of Hollywood cinema" (*Pre-Code Hollywood* 2) after July 1934.

This periodization should be qualified somewhat. Films of the early 1930s were themselves subject to forms of self-censorship, since an awareness of the Code was incorporated into the production process as part of an industry-wide policy (Maltby, "Fabrications"). While there are indeed clear differences between Hollywood films of the early and later 1930s, a clean break in modes of representation cannot be identified in all cases, as narrative conventions and systems of characterization evolved organically throughout the decade out of "experiment and expedient" (Maltby, "Fabrications"). It was also not the case that Hollywood films after this point gave up entirely on exploring "scandalous" topics, but rather the enforcement of the regulations ensured that the structures of "post-Code" Hollywood films had to work to support normative moral values (Jacobs 23). For example, David M. Lugowski has shown how representations of queer characters in fact "survived industry regulators" (9) during Depression-era Hollywood cinema, which he attributes to "the necessary role . . . [queerness] plays in public entertainment and other social performances," including as a moral warning, since alleged "weakness and perversion . . . must be shown in order to be ridiculed or rejected" (26).

In contrast, pre-Code cinema did not necessarily work according to a logic of moral retribution or the neutralization of perceived moral threats, what Maltby calls the "moral accountancy" that the Code sought to bring to bear on Hollywood plots, where "a calculus of retribution or coincidence invariably punished the guilty and declared sympathetic characters innocent" ("Fabrications"). Within this period of film production, a series of films emerged that explored sexual transgression within an upturned moral universe where vice went unpunished and virtue unrewarded (Doherty, *Pre-Code Hollywood* 103). These films frequently focused on female characters who challenged moral values and institutions (such as marriage) but neither repented nor experienced negative consequences. As Mick LaSalle describes, before 1934, "women on screen took lovers, had babies out of wedlock, got rid of cheating husbands, enjoyed their sexuality, held down professional positions without apologizing for their self-sufficiency" (introduction). *Variety* magazine summed up the trend for vice focused on women in its film review of the year for 1931: "Important ladies of the screen, those whose names mean drawing power, found smash films in the wages of cinematic sin. . . . Public taste had switched to glamourous, shameful ladies . . . Not too long ago, playing an unpunished fallen heroine would have jeopardized the career of a film actress. In 1931, it became her ticket to box office supremacy" (qtd. in LaSalle, ch. 4). At this point in cinema history, the fallen heroines of pre-Code Hollywood escaped retribution or moral judgment for their sexual activities.

The vice film genre loomed large over Faulkner's early screenwriting career. His arrival in Hollywood was followed shortly by MGM's release of *Red-Headed Woman* in June 1932, with a screenplay by Fitzgerald and Anita Loos, and the end of his work for MGM in May 1933 predated the Warner Brothers release of the film *Baby Face* (1933) by just a few months. Both Fitzgerald and Loos had popularized images of the flapper and Jazz Age femininity in their fiction, in works such as *Flappers and Philosophers* (1920) and *Gentlemen Prefer Blondes* (1925) respectively, and they were now working to disseminate images of the bad girl in their 1930s screenplays. Doherty describes *Baby Face* as documenting "a woman's vertical movement up the economic ladder via horizontal means" and, accordingly, as "the most notorious of the sex-in-the-workplace vice films of the Pre-Code era" (*Pre-Code Hollywood* 134). Faulkner's career at MGM was therefore framed by the release of two of the most influential vice films of the early 1930s.

We should, however, differentiate between the generic categories of bad girl and fallen heroine in terms of agency: according to Doherty, the fallen heroine "is a victim of economic or romantic circumstances, forced to make a desperate choice when buffeted by hard times and bad men," whereas the bad girl "is a calculating agent of her moral decline and financial ascent who treats sex like any other business transaction" (*Pre-Code Hollywood* 131) in pursuit of social advancement. Lea Jacobs similarly makes the case for distinct representations of womanhood in pre-Code cinema, identifying two types of "fallen woman" heroine: the first "commits a sexual transgression" and is punished with exile from her family and becomes an outcast, often working as a prostitute, ultimately dying by the end of the picture; the second incarnation of the type experiences expulsion from the domestic sphere too but, in contrast to the first type, climbs the ladder to improve her financial position by using men (x). The second delineation is closer to Doherty's "bad girl" type, and it was this kind of pre-Code heroine that particularly attracted the attention of the censors, since the heroine's fall appeared to be compensated by material advantage, in what Hollywood called the "Cinderella story" (Jacobs 11); as Jacobs elaborates, these films "undercut the narrative logic of sin, guilt, and redemption" (12) that had been upheld in the nineteenth-century melodramatic literary antecedents of the fallen heroine genre, in which the female character "experienced remorse, and suffered a pronounced degradation and decline" (11). After 1934, censors would actively alter the structure of this genre of films to redirect the narrative trajectory of the female role (Jacobs 23) in order to "bolster normative definitions of gender roles, marriage, and family life" (Jacobs x), which the bad girl and Cinderella films in their pre-Code iterations unscrupulously failed to do.

The story titled "Night Bird" that Faulkner had written for Bankhead in New York before coming to Hollywood was attuned to the conventions of such pictures. Indeed, it seems to have been written with an eye to the fallen heroine and bad-girl roles that Bankhead had repeatedly played in her early Paramount films. This demonstrates Faulkner's close awareness of the types of projects that could be used as a vehicle for a film star with a particular public image. *The Cheat* (1931), directed by George Abbott, for example, was a fallen heroine picture that resisted punishing the female protagonist. In the film, Bankhead plays Elsa Carlyle, the wife of a young broker named Jeffrey; she is an inveterate gambler whose sizeable debts threaten to destroy her life and marriage. A wealthy art collector called Hardy Livingstone overhears her troubles at a party he is hosting and offers her the money for her debts in return for sex. In a bizarre twist, Elsa's husband becomes a millionaire overnight, and she tries to pay back Hardy, but he insists that she has made a promise and he now considers her his possession. Hardy assaults Elsa, branding her with his personal crest, and she shoots him in return, which he survives. Utterly devoted to his wife, Elsa's husband takes the blame for the shooting and is imprisoned. It is here that the narrative trajectory clearly follows the script of the fallen woman film, as Elsa is victimized by her economic circumstances, although born out of vice, and expresses deep remorse for the choices she has made, telling Jeffrey in prison that she realizes "how wicked, selfish, and spoiled" she is and resolving that "from now on I'm going to be different. I'm going to be good" (*Cheat*). Living up to this commitment, Elsa confesses to the crime during Jeffrey's trial and redeems herself. Her expressions of sincere regret and her virtuous intervention save her; the indictment is dismissed, and she is reunited with her husband, their relationship now strengthened. The moral arc of the film allows the fallen heroine to enjoy material wealth by the conclusion of the film; while Elsa is victimized by economic hardship, she avoids final punishment for her "transgressions."

As is the case in *The Cheat*, Bankhead's film *My Sin* (1931), which was also directed by George Abbott, shows the female protagonist experiencing no great material or financial disadvantage as a result of her vices. In a significant contrast, however, the transgressions of Bankhead's character are more aggressively pursued, and the "bad girl" figure in this film undergoes neither moral epiphany nor ethical transformation in the process. Bankhead played, in her words, a "notorious hussy loose in the Canal Zone [Panama], up to some erotic nonsense in a cabaret" (191), taking on the role of a nightclub hostess called Carlotta, a hedonistic drinker, spendthrift, and gambler. She is attacked in her apartment by a man to whom she owes money and who wants to steal her savings. In a struggle, she shoots and kills the man but denies the accusation of murder. A dissolute, alcoholic lawyer named Dick Grady takes up her case and fabricates a story in the trial, which enables her to get off with a verdict of not guilty.

Dick advises Carlotta to reinvent herself in order to leave behind her reputation in Panama. Carlotta takes on a new name in New York—Ann Trevor—and becomes a successful interior designer dating a billionaire broker named Larry Gordon, who buys her a house in the country and knows nothing of her past. She is recognized by a Gordon family friend from her Panama days, Roger Metcalf, who threatens to out her. In a scene from the film, Larry and his mother debate whether a woman such as Carlotta should escape public judgment, while Roger tries to expose her. In this scene, Carlotta drops her glass when Roger begins to speak of Panama and reveals that he has invited Dick to dinner; the upper-class family performs the role of a censorious community, placing judgment on Carlotta, not knowing she is at the table with them. They challenge the decision the court reached, with Larry's mother stating that she doesn't think "public opinion is strong enough against women like that. It's all very well to be generous, but see what's happened. She's probably set free to go out and do a great deal of harm in the world" (*My Sin*). Larry also insists that, despite the alleged extenuating circumstances, "there must have been a rotten streak in her somewhere." The family subscribes to a clear binary in which, as Larry's mother declares, "Women are either good or bad." However, the film does not move towards punishment of the bad girl, instead choosing to reward her. Her relationship with Larry ends after she confesses her past to him, but she keeps her job and is reunited with Dick, who buys her the country house she had been promised and proposes to her. The film suggests that those who embrace moral relativism can find happiness. As these Bankhead vice films show, clear moral oppositions do not belong to the era of pre-Code cinema, in which women could be both "good and bad" without fear of repercussion or absolute judgment.

"Manservant," "The College Widow," and "Absolution"

Building on his knowledge of Bankhead's Hollywood movie career, Faulkner's early work at MGM would incorporate portrayals of bad girls and fallen heroines fundamental to the vice tradition of pre-Code cinema. Solomon has commented on the importance of contemporary gender roles to these early projects. He highlights how Faulkner joined a film community in which successful female screenwriters were working to bring images of the urban "New Woman" onto the screen, whether in the form of vamps, flappers, or working girls (*Screenwriting* 21), and he notes the significance of Faulkner's first impulse in Hollywood to build on his work in *Sanctuary*, which had interrogated the extent to which New Womanhood, which was typically associated with urban centers, could be extended to women from the rural South (*Screenwriting* 22). In my analysis of Faulkner's work for MGM, I specifically consider the screenwriter's dialogue with distinct filmic archetypes for women in these projects, namely the bad girl and fallen heroine, and therefore the wider cultural and generic significance of Faulkner's presentation of gender within pre-Code cinema history. Faulkner's early work for the studio inhabits the vice template but establishes an inconsistency in which vice may be celebrated or rewarded, but we are nevertheless invited to judge female characters for their sacrifice of virtue, thereby following a formula akin to that of "compensating moral value." At MGM, he wrote bad-girl roles for unmarried women who negotiate their position in society by expediently moving between sexual partners. Although these figures may experience loss, Faulkner generally invited audiences to condemn these women for their lack of remorse, denying them the freedom from moral judgment or punishment that the bad girl more typically enjoyed.

Faulkner's second project at MGM in May 1932 was to develop the synopsis for "Night Bird," which he most likely penned for Bankhead, into the treatment "The College Widow." The basic plot remained the same between synopsis and treatment: a young woman, the daughter of a university professor in a small Southern college town, flirts with college boys but soon becomes bored with them. The term "college widow" is itself slang for a noncollege woman who dates students (Kawin, "College Widow" 31). She encourages the advances of a sinister and mysterious stranger who has an hypnotic effect on her (*MGM* 44). They have an affair, but she begins to be frightened of him and breaks it off. She quickly marries her college sweetheart in a bid to escape the stranger, moving with her now husband to the city without telling him about her past, but the stranger becomes a stalker, following her to the city. Bruce F. Kawin parallels the plots of "Night Bird" and "The College Widow" with *Sanctuary*, highlighting their joint "emphasis on the way a teasing virgin becomes fascinated by a dangerous and possessive older man, courts damnation as well as a fall in social status, and becomes indirectly responsible for the deaths or ruin of the men around her" ("College Widow" 29). More significantly, Faulkner is exchanging broader cultural archetypes between fiction and film here, combining the cavorting flapper that he had explored in *Sanctuary* with the sexual assertiveness of the pre-Code bad girl, but once again meting out punishment to the figure. In the case of "Night Bird," the stranger finds her in her new home and attacks her, and her husband kills the man. After this episode, she suffers a miscarriage, her husband leaves her, and, in the more extreme punishment of the figure in "The College Widow," her mother dies of shock (*MGM* 51).

Faulkner previously used this trope, where the death of a child leads to the mother's increased promiscuity, in his first treatment for MGM, titled "Manservant," a colonial romance set in 1920s India. In this piece, Faulkner presents the female character Judy as a reformed fallen heroine; she had originally come to India on her honeymoon, and her husband was tragically killed by a tiger on a hunt. In grief, she fell into a period of "hysteria and fast living," during which she became pregnant by a man with a "very shady reputation," a figure Faulkner developed further through the stranger in "Night Bird" and "The College Widow." Judy's child dies after she gives birth (*MGM* 10). This second great loss leads her to move "into and out of affairs with civilian and military men" (*MGM* 10) in Calcutta. Her affair with the honorable Major Nigel Blynt returns her to a committed relationship, but her "reputation" (*MGM* 9) lingers over them, even though she is now "more impeccable than many actual wives" (*MGM* 11). After the death of his father, Nigel has to return to England, but Judy says she cannot accompany or marry him because of the harm her reputation would do to him. Here we see the female character protecting her lover from her past out of fear that knowledge of her previous "excesses" would destroy him. Indeed, the accumulation of Judy's losses, compounded after Nigel leaves India without her, causes her to chart the inverse path to the bad-girl archetype: she chooses to live "a life of almost nun-like seclusion, denying herself to all who knew her in the old days" (*MGM* 14).

In contrast to Judy's abstinence in "Manservant," after experiencing these losses, the protagonist of "The College Widow" treatment, Mary Lee Blair, more closely resembles the bad girl in her defiant and destructive behavior. Indeed, Faulkner's most significant development of the story between synopsis and treatment is that Mary Lee causes the destruction of the men around her through her "tarnished" attractiveness. A sincere suitor—who wants to "redeem" her after a series of scandalous affairs by marrying her—despairs at Mary Lee's disregard for her own honor. When she crashes a college dance with a tough-looking guy from town, she laughs in the suitor's face and "drinks from a flask in full sight" (*MGM* 52). He commits suicide that night. After the suicide, she is said to be "not remorseful . . . just quite weary" (*MGM* 52).

The device of an innocent man's suicide is used in Faulkner's third treatment for MGM, a wartime buddy film called "Absolution," dated 1 June

1932, in which two friends, John and Corwin, compete over a girl called Evelyn. Faulkner's portrayal of Evelyn extends his exploration of a bad-girl type who defiantly pursues her desires. Conflict between John and Corwin over Evelyn leads to Corwin's destruction on the war front in France: Corwin forces John into a game of aerial combat to resolve competition over Evelyn, even though this inevitably results in his death, since John is a far more experienced flier (*MGM* 67–68). Although Evelyn had been in a relationship with Corwin, she has not been waiting for her war hero's return: she has got engaged to another man while Corwin was away and feels relieved when she learns of his death (*MGM* 68). Shocked at her lack of honor, John goes to Corwin's grave and shoots himself. Evelyn is a bad girl who, similar to Mary Lee, indirectly destroys the men around her, but she experiences no negative repercussions by the treatment's end, only the audience's condemnation.

In "The College Widow," Mary Lee does show some capacity for self-sacrifice for the benefit of others. Her behavior results in her increasing social exclusion, and her father loses his job because of her reputation. She manages to have him reinstated by promising the university president that she will leave the town and never return. She finally becomes a prostitute in a neighboring city, living in an expensive hotel as "the companion of middle-aged men at night clubs" (*MGM* 53). This appears to follow the traditional template of the fallen heroine narrative, in which the transgressive female character experiences a series of losses before turning to sex work (Jacobs x), but within this model the film would generally conclude with the woman's tragic and untimely death. Instead, the conclusion of "The College Widow" cements the presentation of Mary Lee as a bad girl through an expression of her bitterly ironic relationship to her transgressions and losses. In the final scene, she sees her ex-husband and his wife at a nightclub:

> Mary Lee is in a gay party. . . . She lifts her glass and gives a toast:
>
> MARY LEE
> To the mother of my son! (*MGM* 53)

In this line of cynical defiance, and the only fragment of dialogue in the treatment, Faulkner ascribes Mary Lee the register of the pre-Code bad girl. As Solomon points out, the single line highlights the provisional nature of the treatment itself, since the "power of its climactic, ironic, and tragic final words" suggests the "promised value of dialogue" (*Screenwriting* 25) had the studio chosen Faulkner's script for production. It also elliptically signals the treatment's unrealized potential as a star vehicle for pre-Code actresses who cultivated images of sexual independence. Kawin suggests that this is the kind of dialogue that could have been delivered by "a daring actress" from the pre-Code era, a figure such as Greta Garbo or Mae West, who were known for playing "sexually active unmarried women" ("College Widow" 35). West perhaps most memorably embodies the frank sexuality of the pre-Code leading lady. In *She Done Him Wrong* (1933), directed by Lowell Sherman, she plays a saloon singer called Lady Lou in 1890s New York who moves between rich male partners as is financially expedient, wearing the diamonds she receives from them as trophies. The film was an adaptation of West's 1928 stage play *Diamond Lil*, which was considered so provocative that the Hays Office told Paramount to change the title and aspects of the plot and not to refer to the original play in any of the movie's publicity material (Watts 182). Despite a superficial change in title and character name, Lady Lou's lines were still shot through with suggestive humor, and she plays on her exploitation of the men around her for financial gain, wisecracking that she "wasn't always rich. . . . There was a time I didn't know where my next husband was coming from" (*Done Him Wrong*). This type of glamorous and hard-bitten self-knowledge, modulated through ironic humor, is echoed in the language of Faulkner's Mary Lee Blair. "The College Widow" would have provided an attractive and challenging role for one of MGM's roster of pre-Code actresses and vice film stars, such as Greta Garbo, who had appeared in 1931's vice picture *Susan Lennox (Her Fall and Rise)*, or Jean Harlow, who starred in the notorious bad-girl film *Red-Headed Woman*.

    A crucial difference between Faulkner's early treatments and a pre-Code vice film such as *She Done Him Wrong* is that West was one of the cinematic period's "sensualists without guilt" (Haskell, *Reverence* 91), meaning she escaped judgment and avoided being stigmatized as sexually destructive. West tries to seduce Captain Cummings (Cary Grant), the director of the city mission next door to the bar, whom she sees as different to the long list of criminal men from her past, but nevertheless believes he "can be had" (*Done Him Wrong*). At the end of the film, Cummings, who is revealed to be an undercover federal agent investigating the illegal activities of the bar, orchestrates a police raid. The bar owner is arrested along with other members of the criminal ring, and Cummings escorts Lou into a separate carriage. We expect Lou to face arrest too, after accidentally killing one crooked woman connected to the saloon and setting up the murder of a man who had aggressively pursued her. Rather than facing prison, however, Cummings jokes that he will be Lou's "jailor" as he slips an engagement ring on her finger and endearingly calls her a "bad girl." Although Sklar suggests that, in succumbing to marriage, Lou's "fate" is "perhaps a concession to the boundaries American moral precepts still imposed" (185), it is nevertheless a proposal based on an acceptance of the female character's transgressive nature rather than an attempt to reform her.

In "The College Widow," no such reconciliation occurs. Faulkner draws on the flapper figure he had explored in *Sanctuary*, but he adapts it to fit the cultural frame of pre-Code vice, since Mary Lee is an energetic hedonist with a streak of sexual aggressiveness. Mary Lee abandons the "the safeguards and the protection" (Haskell, *Reverence* 81) of established moral systems that had sheltered the flapper and exhibits glamorous defiance in the face of her loss of reputation, much more typical of a bad girl in the mold of West. Unlike Lady Lou, however, Faulkner invites us to judge Mary Lee for the trajectory of her fall; where the transgressions of Faulkner's bad-girl lead to the death of a virtuous man, the end of her marriage, and exile, West's Lady Lou receives a proposal of marriage from the upstanding Cummings without any suggestion that she is capable of being "rehabilitated," or indeed that this would be desirable.

Faulkner's ambivalence towards the vice film, and the role of female transgression within it, was also reflected in Paramount's own adaptation of *Sanctuary* as *The Story of Temple Drake*, "the most notorious vice film of 1933" (Doherty, *Pre-Code Hollywood* 108), directed by Stephen Roberts. On 16 June, shortly after Faulkner joined MGM, Paramount took a four-month option on *Sanctuary*, and the adaptation was released a little before Faulkner's studio contract ended. It was one of the films responsible for the Production Code crackdown in 1934, on account of its "excessive" sexual and violent content. The novel had previously been considered by Hollywood studios, in 1931, but was ultimately dismissed as unworkable. Paramount reconsidered the adaptation in 1932 after the publication of the Modern Library edition of *Sanctuary* in March and Faulkner's arrival at MGM in May, events that made the project seem commercially viable (Binggeli 90) and potentially presented a solution to Paramount's financial difficulties (Doherty, *Pre-Code Hollywood* 114). Doherty asserts that *The Story of Temple Drake* traces "the sexual contours of the extramarital vice film" (*Pre-Code Hollywood* 114), and Maltby suggests that Paramount's revisions of the screenplay moved the film away from the highly controversial gangster genre, which had faced prohibition from the Association of Motion Picture Producers (AMPP), towards a less contentious "fallen woman" film ("Production Code" 52).

The film also falls outside the bad-girl cycle of vice films, as it is a woman's subjugation rather than aggressive sexuality that invites moral debate. Temple Drake was played by Miriam Hopkins, an actress who didn't shrink from playing controversial roles. For example, in 1933 she also starred in the pre-Code comedy *Design for Living*, which depicted a ménage à trois between Hopkins and two male suitors, played by Fredric March and Gary Cooper. *The Story of Temple Drake* presents Temple's transgressions as a product of a split psyche or dual nature, as she claims at the beginning of the film that "it's like there were two mes."[4] Temple delivers this line as a justification for her refusal to marry her respectable lawyer boyfriend, Stephen Benbow, since the "bad" side of her character won't allow her to. Her face in close-up shows a mixture of fear and resignation in contemplation of her transgressive nature. Consistent with her presentation as a tease, the film shows graffiti on the wall that reads "Temple Drake is just a fake. She wants to eat and have her cake." The inscription could serve as a motto for the film itself, which hints at sexual transgressions that can neither be shown nor expressed; Stephen Benbow, for example, can only elliptically question Temple as to the nature of what she has endured at the hands of the gangsters: "Are you? Did he?" The film also works to "redeem" Temple; Stephen offers Temple the chance to take the stand to give her account of the deaths of Tommy and Trigger, an opportunity to triumph over her "evil streak," as Stephen tells her, going on to say, "You're a woman, but you're still a Drake. You want to act like one don't you?" (*Temple Drake*). Temple ensures that justice prevails by giving an honest testimony in the final courtroom scene, after which she faints. Stephen carries her out of the courtroom and says to her father: "Be proud of her judge—I am." The adaptation indulges in vice while shrinking from it, dissociating Temple from the vices to which she is attracted through tropes of doubling, and by finally delivering a clean break from her past. These features reflected the changing climate in Hollywood, since in 1933 the Catholic Legion of Decency was set up "to coordinate a campaign to boycott movies that the Catholic Church considered indecent" (Sklar 173), and the studios began to capitulate to such external threats to their profits.

Although this adaptation of *Sanctuary* would reach the screen, Faulkner's "The College Widow" was not approved for development, due to its high sexual content. The producers at MGM dismissed the treatment as too hot to handle. Anne Cunningham, a fellow screenwriter, wrote a synopsis and evaluation of the treatment in October 1934 that echoed Faulkner's own comments about Temple's character in *Sanctuary*, writing: "It is an evil, slimy thing, absolutely unfit for screen production, in the face of current censorship . . . or at any future time" (qtd. in Kawin, "College Widow" 36). Cunningham's response is particularly interesting in terms of the point in cinema history in which it is situated. Faulkner wrote the screen treatment in spring 1932 at the height of the pre-Code era. Thus Cunningham, in assessing Faulkner's work, applies post-Code standards—after Breen had been appointed head of the Production Code Administration—to a pre-Code work, retrospectively policing the products of a former cinematic age. Her comments came shortly before the release of MGM's *Forsaking All Others* in December 1934, which led to the first showdown between Breen and a studio in the newly tense, reactionary climate; Breen contributed dialogue to improve the moral fiber of the film, and his "successful intrusion into the process of motion picture editing marked a turning point in the balance of power" in Hollywood (Doherty, *Pre-Code Hollywood* 330). Faulkner's penning of a vice film in 1932 is entirely in keeping with an era of license and relaxed enforcement of moral guidelines for movies. Faulkner fused the energetic libertinism of the flapper with the assertive sexuality of the bad girl, but in both *Sanctuary* and his early MGM projects he discouraged audience identification with these figures by either punishing their behavior or emphasizing their cruelty to others. Faulkner's ambivalence towards female icons of popular cinema from the 1920s and early 1930s would, however, undergo significant changes in his subsequent projects for MGM.[5]

"Turn About" and "Mythical Latin-American Kingdom Story"

A remarkable shift takes place in Faulkner's representation of women in his film work on the project he began in July 1932. The director Howard Hawks had followed Faulkner's career since the publication of *Soldier's Pay* in 1926 and had even considered adapting *Sanctuary* for the screen, but he did not want to go through the process of trying to get such a project past the censors (Kawin, *Faulkner and Film* 76). Hawks had read the author's World War I story "Turnabout" (1932) in the *Saturday Evening Post* and bought the rights to the story through his brother, William Hawks, and now wanted Faulkner to adapt the story himself (Blotner, *Biography* 306). Faulkner had actually been taken off the MGM payroll by this point, but the assignment brought him back within the studio fold.

As mentioned in the introduction, when working on the screen adaptation of the story, which was released as the film *Today We Live* in 1933, Faulkner was asked to substantially rework the plot of his story to include a central female character in order for the studio to use the movie as a star vehicle for the actress and box-office draw Joan Crawford. It was common for studios to rework film projects based on the availability of the big stars, but it occurred just a week after the studio producer Irving Thalberg had told Hawks to shoot Faulkner's first script as it was (McCarthy 179). The power of an individual actor to shape narrative at MGM was particularly pronounced, since it was "the studio of stars" (Christensen 4), and actors such as Crawford would appear "in narratives in which the role of the individual star and the social, political, and economic value of the entertainment . . . she provided were consistently confirmed" (Christensen 4).

Faulkner's work for Crawford has particular significance at this point in MGM's history. After the beginning of the early sound era in the late 1920s, Crawford was one of the female stars who had made the transition to sound successfully. In contrast, the studio's elite group of male stars had not adapted well to the updated medium. The most dramatic fall of all was that of the silent star John Gilbert, who demonstrated "his inability to adjust an exaggerated pantomime style to the subtler technique of talking pictures" (Schatz, *Genius* 103). Gilbert left MGM in 1933 and was dead by 1936, and Buster Keaton's career was over by the early 1930s, demonstrating the vertiginous decline of iconic male stars of the silent era. MGM recruited a new group of male stars to replace them. New names such as Clark Gable and Robert Montgomery would appear in the studio's typical film products: high-gloss, stylish light comedies and romantic dramas (Schatz, *Genius* 103). Crawford's image had been synonymous with the "party girl" in the films of the 1920s and embodied a kind of sexual freedom without guilt that went beyond the American flapper's ultimate reticence (Haskell, *Reverence* 79). By the 1930s Crawford was securing roles in MGM's top-drawer star vehicles such as *Grand Hotel* (1932), the studio's biggest hit to date, featuring a long list of studio acting talent, including Garbo, John Barrymore, and Wallace Beery. Crawford's insertion into Faulkner's project then appears at a time when many actors from the silent age were facing obsolescence. Her strength was consequently bolstered by her ability to adapt and survive despite seismic changes to the film medium.[6]

Crawford was apologetic about her last-minute inclusion in "Turn About" and insisted that Faulkner "write for her the same clipped British dialogue he had written for Claude and Ronnie so that the picture would be less sentimental than MGM had apparently intended it to be" (Kawin, "Turn About / Today We Live" 104). This led to some of the gender-crossing elements of Crawford's delineation in the film; Hawks apparently said that "Joan wanted to talk like the boys . . . I couldn't blame her" (Hogue 54). But the results on screen were mixed, with the elliptical dialogue being labeled "Hemingwayesque" by some viewers (McCarthy 185). MGM attempted to counterbalance Crawford's masculinized dialogue by assigning the costume designer Adrian—who worked on a large number of MGM films between 1928 and 1941, including *The Wizard of Oz* (1939)—to produce a series of ornate gowns and suits for her, an embellishment of the role that highlights the dissonant quality of the newly inserted female lead. By the end of August, Faulkner had completed "Turn About" and added a role for Crawford to an all-male war story by giving Ronnie, one of the two male protagonists of the story, a sister, Ann. In turn, he made the other male character, Claude, a ward of the family. In the screenplay, the three of them grow up together and a love triangle develops, in which Claude satisfies the incestuous desire of Ronnie for his sister by acting as surrogate; as Dallas Hulsey advances, "through active mediation Ronnie redirects his desire for Ann through Claude" (74). Since Claude is not a blood relative, he dispels the threat of incest, but as a member of the family he is sufficiently closely related to Ronnie and Ann to perform a sanctioned version of Ronnie's perverse fantasies.

"Turn About" is the Faulkner-authored screenplay that has attracted by far the most critical attention, perhaps because this was the only adaptation of his own work that reached the screen in which the author exerted a large influence over the film's content, and it is the only screenwriting project that went into production during his time at MGM. Both John T. Matthews and D. Matthew Ramsey suggest that Faulkner's work on the film forced him to consider the relationship of his characters to cinema audiences in gendered terms. For Matthews, through the character of Ann, Faulkner demonstrates that he "understood that the female romantic lead exists to be desired as object by the male audience, and to be identified with as the desiring subject by female spectators" ("Culture Industry" 66). Matthews therefore sees Crawford's image operating as both object and subject of the gaze (its recipient and bearer) to cater to both genders that comprise mass cinema audiences. Ramsey emphasizes the significance of Crawford to the project, suggesting

Faulkner was necessarily made to feel subordinate to the tastes of women in the film industry, as "MGM largely catered to the female audience (seven out of ten film-goers in the 1930s were women)" ("Stars" 86).

Collaboration with an actor was therefore instructive in reshaping Faulkner's screenwriting at this point. Ramsey perceives the potential benefits of collective working processes in Faulkner's "relative loss of control" ("Stars" 89), as he was "forced to imagine a different space for women than he might have been used to.... Suddenly the author was presented with the task of imagining female desire" ("Stars" 100). Ramsey helps us see work on this collaborative product as a power struggle between competitive agents in the Hollywood studio, a struggle in which he sees Crawford emerging as the dominant player, since her star status overrode the film. Indeed, Crawford would become a major player in the studio system by the 1940s, one among a handful of stars "powerful, eccentric, or intimidating enough to choose their projects and determine their own images, for at least some of their careers" (Haskell, *Reverence* 9).[7]

The role of the other Hollywood screenwriters assigned to the project was equally significant in generating this feeling of a "loss of control" in Faulkner's work for a new medium. After Faulkner's third draft of the screenplay, the head of the Story Department from 1930–37, Sam Marx, drafted in Anne Cunningham—who later reviewed and expressed her deep distaste for "The College Widow"—to write a long treatment of the story from the woman's point of view to develop and flesh out Ann's character, but these contributions were dismissed as being too "sentimental" (McCarthy 184). After that, the script was passed on to Edith Fitzgerald, a veteran screenwriter who had mainly worked on early 1930s "women's pictures," including the *Laughing Sinners* (1931), in which Crawford had starred. Fitzgerald wrote Ann a number of strong scenes focusing on her activities as a nurse and her friendships with other women (Kawin, "Turn About / Today We Live" 108). Fitzgerald ultimately received screen credit along with the young screenwriter Dwight Taylor for the screenplay, while Faulkner was credited with "Story and Dialogue." Faulkner lost mastery over his material to women during the writing process, as his creative work was significantly reinvented after he exited from project. This loss of ownership was a phenomenon typical of Hollywood in the classical era, where it was rare for a writer to be involved with a screenwriting project for the duration. Already a radical departure from his original story, the female character the studio demanded had to be further reworked to exploit the "women's angle" by appealing to female mass audiences. The fact that a number of these collaborators were women, tasked with bringing psychological credibility to Faulkner's characters, would have been a new experience and would have challenged his sense of authority over his work. At MGM in the early 1930s, many of the top staff writers were women, including Frances Marion and Loos, who had both successfully made the transition from writing for the silents to the talkies. This could lead to gendered power struggles within the studios' writing networks. On the film *Red-Headed Woman*, for example, F. Scott Fitzgerald was taken off the project and replaced with Loos, as Thalberg thought Fitzgerald was doing a bad job and wanted an injection of Loos's unique brand of "sexual banter and playful eroticism" (Schatz, *Genius* 118). Fitzgerald resented being replaced on the film and Loos receiving solo screenwriting credit, as Hollywood enabled the more prominent and acclaimed novelist to be usurped by a writer who was not so highly regarded outside of the film community at the time.

In various ways, then, the project was a disruptive one for Faulkner. Interestingly, the disruptiveness of Crawford's role comes across in the presentation of Ann in both Faulkner's screenplay and the final film; we can perceive this in Ann's language (that clipped masculine dialogue of hers), costume (her elaborate gowns by Adrian, which jar with the austere wartime setting), and the plot (since, significantly, she refuses marriage to her presumed suitor, choosing an American pilot named Bogard over Claude). These aspects bear out Matthews's observation that, tasked with accommodating Crawford within the adaptation, Faulkner reflexively engages with the inclusion, by making the screenplay consider the problem of the woman's place in the movie ("Culture Industry" 66).

The characterization of Ann additionally reflects the circumstances of the screenplay's production through the use of historical setting. Just as Faulkner was forced to imagine a different kind of female character through a loss of control over his material, Ann's "transgressive" behavior in Faulkner's screenplay appears to emerge as a product of temporary conditions outside the individual characters' control, specifically the effect of World War I in England on sexual norms. During World War I, there were widespread debates concerning the potential upending of sexual and gender roles as a result of the conflict. Many feared that the absence of men due to mass mobilization was, as Susan R. Grayzel describes, "overthrowing conventional morals and encouraging women to become sexually promiscuous"

(65) and that the conditions of wartime threatened to "upset traditional gender arrangements" (77). Faulkner's screenplay for "Turn About" explores such wartime reconfigurations, but without judgment being placed on female transgression. In one scene, Ann comforts Claude, who is afraid of battle and turning increasingly to drink, by having sex with him out of wedlock, but she insists: "It's not love, though, Claude," to which he replies, "Gad, no. Love dead now. Maybe come back to life someday," the refrain even coming from behind Claude's closed door as he takes Ann to his bed out of the scene dissolve, "but not love, Claude! Not love!" (*MGM* 190). Here a woman authoritatively uses her sexuality to calm Claude's fears of war, and, as Rollyson observes, "only in the pre-Code era could Faulkner have Ann actually go to bed with Claude before they are married" (*Past* 361). It is Claude rather than Ann who attempts to rehabilitate their actions by insisting "we'll be married as soon as it's over. If it ever is," to which Ann replies, "yes. If that matters. But weddings are as dead as peace" (*MGM* 193). Claude invests in Ann's understanding of wartime sexual politics when he tells her brother Ronnie, after being persuaded by Ann, that they "didn't wait," justifying the decision by explaining that "we talked about how it would be in the chapel, with Mr. Thorndyke and veils and wreathes and the voice that breathed O'er Eden? . . . that chapel and Mr. Thorndyke seem a million miles away, and there's not any Eden anymore, and the wear is khaki and not veils" (*MGM* 194). Claude's speech to Ronnie asserts that war, with the looming possibility of death, allows for unorthodox sexual arrangements. Ronnie has already tacitly communicated his acceptance of Ann and Claude having slept together, by kissing his sister, in a moment that is framed highly romantically in the film as Ronnie tenderly lifts up Ann's face towards him (*MGM* 191; fig. 2). The kiss partly expresses Ronnie's relief that the taboo of incestuous attraction has been diffused by the suitor he has appointed for Ann, but it also shows his recognition that war allows for unorthodox sexual arrangements.

A similar scene also occurs in the last full-length screenplay Faulkner produced for MGM in March and April 1933, an adventure film that was given the working title of "Mythical Latin-American Kingdom Story." The project continued Faulkner's new focus on "fallen" women whose sexual transgressions escape judgment within the context of international conflict. The property drew on the historical background of political unrest in Cuba between 1929 and 1933 (Blotner, *Biography* 314) and focuses on

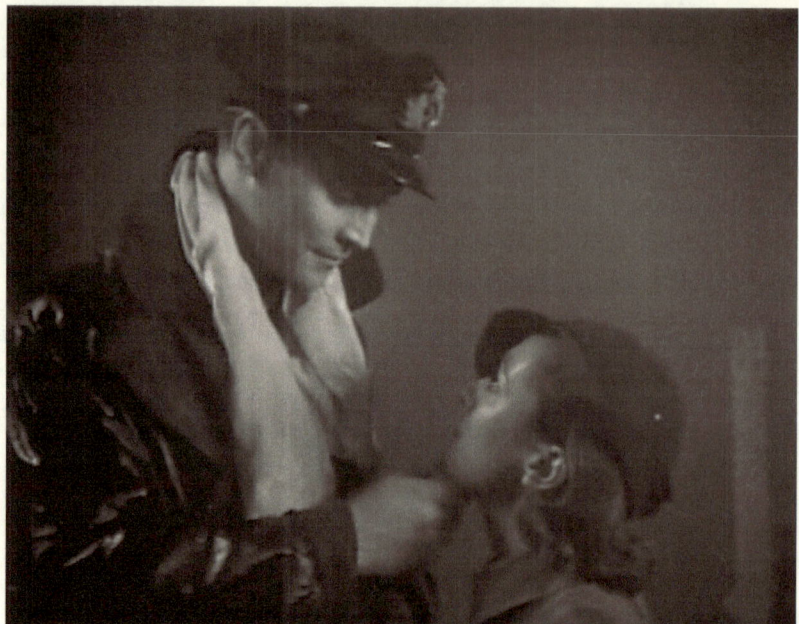

FIGURE 2. In *Today We Live* (1933), Ronnie Bogard (Franchot Tone) moves to kiss his sister Ann Boyce-Smith (Joan Crawford) by lifting up her chin. (MGM)

the actions of a group of exiled revolutionaries of an unnamed nation, whose activities lead to the involvement of American characters.[8] In a revolutionary plot, Maria Rojas appeals to the femininity of a young woman named Marion. Maria believes that Marion will be able to seduce an American pilot called Bowden, allowing them to hijack for their cause a plane full of gold that he is responsible for getting out of the country, arguing that "tears are a woman's heavy artillery, as a glance of the eye is her single neat thrust of the dagger" (*MGM* 464). Marion is taken to Bowden's room and dressed in a loose-fitting negligee to perform this deed, but rather than judging Marion for her transgressive actions, Bowden senses that they are a product of her vulnerability and her co-option into the revolutionary cause out of desperation. When Marion asks Bowden how it feels to be in love, he replies, "You mean, you haven't got . . . anybody but these—(jerks his hand savagely as shadow of sentry passes again) You poor kid. You poor, damned—" (*MGM* 522). Condemnation of female sexual transgression is again suspended, since it is recognized as instrumentalized and as a response to wider political upheavals and personal losses outside the individual woman's control.

More active than Marion in defending her actions, in "Turn About" Ann also resists judgment of her relationship with Claude by her love interest, Bogard:

BOGARD
    ... God, you are a filthy lot, aren't you?

ANN
    Filthy?

    (She looks at him. They look at one another. Then she goes to the door and holds it open)

BOGARD
    Forgive me.—for saying that. I'm not cringing, understand. I just ask pardon for saying what I should not have said even to a streetwalker. (*MGM* 221)

Ann upbraids Bogard for his lack of understanding of the effect that the exceptional circumstances of war can have on sexual practice, challenging him with a simple question and gesturing to the exit in the final directions for the scene.

Perhaps disappointingly, Faulkner's screenplay concludes with a restoration of order. Claude and Ronnie die in a joint mission in October 1918. After the war, Bogard and Ann marry in the chapel in England where she grew up with Claude and Ronnie. However, this formulaic resolution of the Hollywood romance occurs parallel to the end of World War I once the aberrant social conditions it imposed have been removed. The suspension of sociosexual conventions during the war in this screenplay reflects a shift in Faulkner's depiction of women in his screenwriting, as the penitent fallen heroines and damned bad girls of his cautionary early pre-Code treatments for MGM are replaced with a female character who is presented as neither remorseful nor irredeemably sexually assertive.

Reflecting the wider conditions of Faulkner's work in Hollywood, "Mythical Latin-American Kingdom Story" also meditates on the challenging of men by women in positions of authority. Among the screenplay's revolutionaries, Maria is presented as a woman of aggressive dominance and unwavering devotion to the cause, as her husband says of her proudly, "It might be better said of her that she is a giver of grief rather than a victim of it" (*MGM* 458). Maria appears to violate the gendered binary among the revolutionary group, in which men are associated with deeds and women with language, as the Chief asserts in the planning of their revenge against the new leaders of their home nation: "This is an affair for men and courage, not women and words" (*MGM* 459). Maria repeatedly challenges this absolute division, insisting, "I do not think; I do" (*MGM* 461) and "I do not threaten; I do" (*MGM* 512). These gender-crossing elements of Maria's presentation appear to speak to Faulkner's own anxieties about his position within the collaborative communities of Hollywood. When Maria attempts to persuade Marion to join the revolutionary cause and avenge the death of her mother, Marion expresses her wish to be "a man! Just for one month. A month? A day, and [sic] hour!" (*MGM* 466), so she could violently right the wrongs done to her mother, but she looks at her hands and believes a woman's hands are not equipped to perform such a task. Maria also looks at them and observes that "one would scarce call them . . . the hands of a woman even now" and goes on to say that "they look quite capable of performing the act of any man" (*MGM* 466). With this, she places on Marion's hand the bloodied glove that saved the Chief's life from the assassin's bullet. Faulkner offers a statement on the politics of gendered labor in which women take on men's roles and even take control over the tools through which men perform their authority. This appears to muse on the contrasting ways in which the products of Faulkner's labors for MGM in Hollywood had been reshaped by women, particularly through the work of his female co-screenwriters. In exerting control over his work, the Hollywood women Faulkner encountered proved themselves fully capable of performing the acts of a man.

The ways in which Faulkner's early MGM treatments portray women situate them within the vice tradition due to their focus on unmarried women who actively pursue their desires, use their sexuality to maintain material comfort, and experience no shame nor regret in the process. Vice goes unpunished (or at least the women remain unrepentant), while virtue goes unrewarded. However, these works do not allow us to revel in the liberated universe of moral relativism that pre-Code cinema more widely celebrated. Although Faulkner could write the bad-girl role, he could not promote identification with the figure, as we are invited to judge the actions of women that lead to the needless sacrifice of young virtuous men. In this way Faulkner built on his portrayal of the energetic libertine flapper in his novel

Sanctuary to explore the sexual aggressiveness of the bad girl in works that all ultimately cautioned against the behavioral excesses of these figures. As Elizabeth Binggeli has commented in her analysis of Faulkner's statements about *Sanctuary*, "Faulkner attempted to cast himself as both the naughty peddler of obscenity and the high-minded literary artist" (95), and for Florence Dore the novel itself shrinks from its own excesses by operating "according to a proleptic logic that prohibits disclosure," avoiding direct references to sex as part of a narrative strategy marked by "a tendency not to say" (79–80). Faulkner also pursued this strategy of public self-correction or narrative reticence while at MGM, where he wanted to both have his cake and eat it: to write sexually vivid content appropriate for the pre-Code era, in which women get away with murder, but also to invite us to find his characters morally bankrupt. In doing so, Faulkner simultaneously performs the roles of libertine and censor in relation to his textual creations. It was only when the author was forced to include a role for a woman in his adaptation of "Turnabout" that a new vein of female characterization emerged in his Hollywood work: Faulkner would now write women for the screen who escape judgment for being sexually pragmatic, at least in exceptional circumstances, or who challenge male authority without experiencing punishment. In this way, Faulkner took the inverse journey to the studios during the pre-Code era; whereas his early treatments follow the formula of moral compensation that the studios had largely ignored since 1930, his later works evidence the blurring of moral lines from which Hollywood films started to shrink due to external pressures from around 1933.

Faulkner's work at MGM reveals a number of interesting things about his relationship with Hollywood. Even at this early stage in his screenwriting career, he had a clear idea of the kind of picture that could be used as a vehicle for a star with a distinctive public persona, such as Bankhead. Additionally, it demonstrates his willingness to recycle and rework material between his modernist novels and Hollywood screenplays, since he drew on *Sanctuary* for "The College Widow" to reinvent the flapper as a bad girl, and he even considered adapting "Mythical Latin-American Kingdom Story" into fiction. It also shows his understanding of how gender portrayals were embedded within commercial genre conventions; women, as Doherty describes, were the subject and main audience for Hollywood vice (*Pre-Code Hollywood* 125), and MGM was largely targeting the female demographic in drawing on its roster of popular stars, such as Crawford. As a pre-Code Hollywood screenwriter, Faulkner demonstrated that he could incorporate new archetypes into his work to engage the popular appetite for filmic explorations of female sexual transgression. In his subsequent projects at Twentieth Century–Fox and Warner Brothers, in collaboration with Howard Hawks, Faulkner would actively advance female characterization in late 1930s and 1940s Hollywood cinema in projects that sublimated female sexuality into collective labor, as he participated in the construction of the socially progressive Hawksian woman archetype.

2

Collaborative Labor and the Dialogic Construction of the Hawksian Woman

PYLON (1935) WAS THE first novel Faulkner completed after a working spell at MGM, which came to an end when he was fired from the studio in May 1933 (Blotner, *Biography* 217). *Pylon* in fact arose from conversation with Howard Hawks. After leaving MGM, Faulkner had turned to work on *Absalom, Absalom!* (1936) but needed relief from the intensive and consuming labor on this highly experimental novel. Faulkner asked Hawks's advice for a new project, and the director suggested that he write about something other than "those damned hillbillies" (Kawin, *Faulkner and Film* 88) of the rural South. A story about a couple of fliers and a woman they both sleep with appealed to Faulkner, so Hawks told him to write it as a novel (Kawin, *Faulkner and Film* 88). The novel is not set in Faulkner's fictional Mississippian county as his previous five novels had been; *Pylon* instead focuses on a triad of barnstorming fliers in and around New Valois, a fictionalized version of New Orleans.

Its deviation from his previous work is, however, not only geographic but also cinematic. Tom Dardis contends that when Faulkner wrote *Pylon* in 1934, he additionally hoped to sell it to Hollywood, but no one was interested in such an adaptation, not even Hawks (101). *Pylon* was, then, conceived out of creative dialogue and commercial intentions in Hollywood, yet the novel's filmic properties have been little discussed, specifically its debt to a range of filmic genres for which Faulkner had written in his early work for Hollywood. These include his many MGM movie projects concerned with flight and aerial stunts within the context of war; for example, his script for the World War I–era romance "Turn About" / *Today We Live* and his treatment for the airmail service picture "Flying the Mail," both completed in 1932. As Michael Zeitlin reminds us, many of Faulkner's collaborators in Hollywood believed the author's self-invented myth that he had been a flyer in World War I, and Faulkner was, therefore, in part employed at the studio "because he was expected to know something valuable about the conduct of the war in the air" (*Faulkner, Aviation, and Modern War* 172).[1]

Pylon also draws on Faulkner's work on melodramatic and adventure films (genres that Faulkner fused in "Mythical Latin-American Kingdom Story" [1933], his fantastical script about a band of revolutionaries, shot through with heightened dialogue and strained action). Faulkner's description early in *Pylon* of the action that centers around the New Valois airport reflects the novel's Hollywood-inspired genre hybridity, describing how "the rotundra [sic], filled with dusk, was lighted now, with a soft sourceless wash of no earthly color or substance and which cast no shadow: ... [it] presented the furious, still, and legendary tale of what man has come to call his conquering of the infinite and impervious air" (*N* 2: 799–800). The otherworldliness of the scene evidences melodrama's anti-realist hyperbole, while the planes' "conquering" of the air suggests how much technological advances have historically functioned to open up new spheres and means of conflict.[2]

As well as being initially inspired by Hawks, Faulkner also absorbed a subgroup of Hawks's films into the novel. Dardis sees *Pylon* as Faulkner's "homage" to Hawks and the cinema of the early 1930s, as it resembles pre-Code films like Hawks's *The Crowd Roars* (1932) and *Tiger Shark* (1932), "rough and tough, fast-talking films about people in 'dangerous' occupations" (100). In *Tiger Shark*, a group of sailors engage in risky fishing missions from San Diego's port into shark-infested Mexican waters where shipwrecks are a frequent phenomenon. Romance and hazardous action are shown to intersect and further one another. The violent death of the old fisherman Manuel Silva, who is pulled into the water by a shark, leads to Captain Mike Mascarenhas's seduction of the deceased man's grieving daughter. The captain describes the role of the sharks in their community, while gesturing at his prosthetic hook: "They took my hand and give me this. They took your father and give me you. They settle everything" (*Tiger Shark*). In *Pylon*, too, the risks of barnstorming shape the relationships between the characters, establishing and severing connections and heightening erotic tension. More than his previous novels, then, which seem indirectly shaped by cinema as a feature of modernity, *Pylon* bears the direct imprint of the genres Faulkner had been exposed to and written for himself in early 1930s Hollywood.

This chapter considers *Pylon* as marking the beginning of a dialogue between Faulkner and Hawks that would extend throughout the 1930s and 1940s and reflects fundamental shifts in the representation of women in Hollywood cinema. At MGM during the pre-Code era, as discussed in the previous chapter, Faulkner worked within the genre of the vice film in his early treatments, focusing on sexually transgressive female characters who aggressively disrupt moral values and institutions without remorse. However, by the time Faulkner came to work on *Pylon* in the fall of 1934, the Production Code Administration had been given the remit to implement the Motion Picture Production Code (or Hays Code), rendering such directly sexual portrayals of women onscreen impossible. The strict application of the Code after July of that year resulted in the "working woman" pictures more typical of the later 1930s as the female star was forced out of the bedroom and into the workplace due to censorship. As Molly Haskell argues, the Hays Office was inadvertently responsible for creating "the driving, hyperactive," down-to-earth working woman associated with late 1930s and early 1940s pictures, who was "more at ease pursuing a career, whether for its own sake or as a pretext for finding a husband, than languishing in a love nest" (*Reverence* 92).

The working-woman archetype was embodied in figures and performances such as Ginger Rogers as Polly Parrish in *Bachelor Mother* (1939) and Rosalind Russell as Hildy Johnson in the Hawks-directed *His Girl Friday* (1940). *Bachelor Mother* is an anarchic romantic comedy that begins with the heroine losing her job as a seasonal worker in a department store over Christmas. Shortly after, Parrish is mistakenly identified as the mother of an abandoned baby that she finds outside a foundling home and is given back her job on the condition that she accept responsibility for it. Defying traditional plot expectations, Parrish needs to *have* a baby in order to keep her job, and the child (who is rarely referred to by name) functions as a symbolic device to generate a series of frenetic, madcap scenarios typical of screwball comedies. These create romance between Parrish and the owner of the department store, Mr. Merlin, who are both repeatedly mistakenly identified as the parents of the child; Parrish and Merlin eventually accept the roles society has ascribed to them as the baby's mother and father, and the film concludes with Merlin proposing marriage. Within this vein of films, and the new vision of filmic womanhood they present, work is the context in which romance is furthered, motherhood is presented as a sudden imposition, and sexual impropriety is entirely absent.

Faulkner registers this move from bad-girl to working-women pictures from the mid-1930s in *Pylon* by fusing aspects of pre- and post-Code characterization in his portrayal of the female protagonist: a barnstorming mechanic, wing-walker,[3] and parachute jumper named Laverne Shumann. Laverne's sexuality is still vividly presented, but it is primarily sublimated into cross-gender collaborative labor in her work on aerial stunts. Laverne represents the first of a number of androgynous Depression-era working women that would appear across Faulkner's novels and screenplays in the 1930s and 1940s. Additionally, Faulkner's distinct portrayal of Laverne as an active woman who works alongside men appears to have had a strong impact on Hawks, as she resembles the masculinized heroines of the director's late 1930s and early 1940s screwball comedies and adventure films, the widely recognized "Hawksian woman" archetype. In *Pylon* we encounter the figure in incipient form, and it was also a portrayal Faulkner revised and extended through the female roles he collaboratively created in two of his mid-1930s screenplays for Twentieth Century–Fox, written under the directors Hawks and John Ford, and his work on 1944's *To Have and Have Not*, which was also directed by Hawks, at Warner Brothers. Laverne's characterization is a significant departure from cultural representations of women within both Hollywood film and the literary sources that inspired the genres of commercial cinema. Significantly, the novelty of her representation also disrupts modes of viewing in the novel, as Laverne's image is shown to challenge the male gaze by questioning the status of woman as consumable object in visual media, principally through the character's acts of transvestism and masquerade (Doane, *Femmes Fatales* 25).

In establishing the exchange of certain archetypes between the works of Hawks and Faulkner, archetypes rooted in the diverse genres of war and adventure films and the screwball comedy, it is possible to reveal an enduring aesthetic conversation between director and author during Hollywood's Golden Age and the high point of North American modernism. This exchange reframes iconic figures from film not as the product of the singular imagination of an "auteur" but instead as derived from collaborative networks that extend across literary and filmic communities. Faulkner's principal and most enduring creative relationship in Hollywood was with Hawks, which may have resulted in the minimization of Faulkner's contribution to the Hawksian oeuvre, since the director would become a favorite of auteur theory, a school of analysis that works to extract "the distinguishable personality of the director as a criterion of value" (Sarris 452). Distanced from an auteurist approach that reads films as indicative of the director's authorial "signature" (Sarris 452), the exchanges I trace between Hawks and Faulkner help us to see studio filmmaking instead as a process "of negotiation and struggle" (Schatz, *Genius* 12) between diverse actors.

The Origins of the Hawksian Woman

The Hawksian woman figure is most closely associated with the director's films from 1939 to 1948—from *Only Angels Have Wings* to *Red River*—that are believed to offer a distinctive vision of gender relations. In this series of films, Hawks presented balanced relationships between men and women in which differences are first acknowledged and questioned. This leads, however, to a deeper recognition of commonalities between hero and heroine, and the achievement of mutual respect allows for a meaningful union. This is reflected in these films' quick-fire, wisecracking dialogue, an expression of sexual tension that is also a form of pleasurable sparring between equals. Todd McCarthy goes so far as to claim that "the feeling of mutual respect and equality-as-ideal that is generated between the best of Hawks's couples" (12) is the most emotionally compelling aspect of the director's work.

These core aspects are well illustrated in the director's 1940 screwball comedy *His Girl Friday*, in which Hawks explored the mutual adaptation of hero and heroine. The action centers around the office of a newspaper and explores conflicts between work and family in relation to female identity. The two main characters of the film are the editor of the paper, Walter Burns, played by Cary Grant, and his ex-wife and former star reporter for the paper, Hildegard "Hildy" Johnson, played by Rosalind Russell. Hildy is poised to marry a dull insurance man named Bruce Baldwin and settle down to become a mother. Walter dreams up a series of elaborate tactics to prevent the marriage and win Hildy back and in the process gets her hooked writing up a new "scoop" for the paper. The film concludes with a traditional Hawksian ending of reconciliation between hero and heroine in which both parties have accommodated each other's differences. In Hildy's delineation, we see a character who acquiesces to Walter and reenters the combative world of creative work, leaving marriage and motherhood behind, yet, in the pleasure she derives from the scoop and the value Walter places on her distinct feminine perspective as a journalist, she is able to resist her complete co-optation into the system.

Many of these elements and qualities of female characterization in the Hawksian screwball comedies of the late 1930s and 1940s find their origins in literature and film from the early to mid-1930s, for which many writers, screenwriters, and directors can take credit. Biographers and critics of the director have, however, described the Hawksian woman as a figure that appears fully formed in cinema from the late 1930s without any clear antecedents. Arguably Hawks didn't need to look further than his own home for inspiration when he worked these gender portrayals into his films, as he was married to Nancy "Slim" Keith during the period he directed the films that solidified the popular image of the Hawksian woman in the wartime and immediate postwar period, even naming Marie "Slim" Browning from *To Have and Have Not* after his wife. Hawks's image of this heroine can be seen, in part, as a tribute to Slim Keith. She writes in her 1990 biography that "for [Hawks], I was a fabulous armpiece, the ultimate decoration, the embodiment of the Hawks woman," as the director "liked a no-nonsense femininity" (Keith 200). The cross-dressing heroines of her husband's films are mirrored in Slim's preference for wearing "well-cut, man-tailored suits" (Keith 200). Keith, then, embodied the gender hybridity that often typified the Hawksian heroine as a seductive transvestite.[4] Transvestism was also crucial to the genesis of *His Girl Friday*. The film is based on a play, *The Front Page* by former Chicago reporters Ben Hecht and Charles MacArthur, which, Hawks said, "had the finest modern dialogue that had been written, and I asked a girl to read Hildy's part and I read the editor and I stopped and I said, 'Hell, it's better between a girl and a man than between two men'" (Bogdanovich 57). The director proceeded to change the gender of one of the actors in the film adaptation of the two-hander.

It is sometimes overlooked that the gender-crossing element of characterization in Hawks's films may apply as much to male as female characters. As Peter Wollen points out, Hawks's comedies of "sex reversal and role reversal" focus on "domineering women and timid, pliable men" (*Signs* 74) caught up in shifts across a gendered power divide. Elizabeth Cowie does not draw such a sharp distinction between Hawks's dramas and comedies in this respect, arguing instead that gender-crossing permeates both genres, since across these films "not only do women act like men, but men act like women," and it is "the lack of fixity of the conventional characteristics of masculine and feminine" that make his films distinctive (*Representing* 30). Cowie uses the example of *His Girl Friday* to show how Hildy's masculinity—since her role in the film was a male part in the original play—is counterposed with Walter's function as "the 'female' who is messing her life up" (*Representing* 31). It is the world of work in the film that sets up "a play of reversals and inversions in relation to sexual difference" (Cowie, *Representing* 31). Hildy's professional return to journalism is presented as an invitation to remasculinize herself, since her desire to leave the newspaper business had been in order to "go some place where [she could] be a woman" (*His Girl Friday*): the domestic sphere. Hildy ultimately realizes that she's "no suburban bridge player" and rejects her effete fiancé, Bruce; on the contrary, she realizes she's "a newspaperman," thus spelling her complete remasculinization through work and rejection of suburban domestic femininity.

Consistent with Slim Keith's claim, several decades after these films were actually made, to have inspired the figure, definitions of "the Hawks woman" are almost exclusively retrospective and did not emerge until the 1970s. Haskell was among the first to make an argument for the progressive qualities of Hawks's heroines from the 1930s and 1940s. She observed that Hawks "never excludes [women] from the action, never even implicitly suggests that a woman occupies a fixed space—the home, society—or that she is man's subordinate" ("Favorite Sport" 109). This early study from 1971 highlights the transgressive quality of this modern heroine, as she moves into traditionally masculine spheres of action. The domestic sphere is entirely absent from these films, only ever vaguely alluded to. As Leigh Brackett also observed in 1971, "Hawks's people are not domestic types; nobody ever talks about getting that little spread and settling down to raise a family" (120). Although a film like *His Girl Friday* presents Hildy's sense of conflict between work and family, the action never moves into the home, remaining focused on the newspaper offices; their relationship is ultimately an expression of the value of collaboration in professional settings (fig. 3).

This separation of spheres was also a key aspect of the exotic adventure films that helped cement the popular image of the Hawksian woman, such as *Only Angels Have Wings* from 1939, which presents a female interloper into the "masculine" territory of dangerous work. The film is set in a South American trading port and centers around a group of mail-running pilots. Into this insular community arrives an independent heroine, Bonnie Lee

FIGURE 3. Hildy Johnson (Rosalind Russell) and Walter Burns (Cary Grant) work alongside each other in the newspaper office in *His Girl Friday* (1940). (Columbia)

from Brooklyn, who is a carefree, thrill-seeking professional (as a musician, specifically a pianist and nightclub singer) and financially independent. Crucially, Bonnie's movement is not presented as a violation of masculine territory but rather produces the very energy that invests these Hawksian relationships with their attractive vitality. On the one hand, Bonnie surprises the hero, Geoff Carter, played by Cary Grant, by resolving to remold herself to this new environment, reassuring him that "I'm not trying to tie you down. I don't want to plan. I don't want to look ahead" (*Only Angels*). She therefore learns to embrace the unpredictable and high-risk world of the hero. On the other hand, Bonnie finally gets Geoff to express his emotion-led *desire* for her presence, when he offers to toss a coin to help her make her decision about whether or not she should leave the community; disappointed at first, Bonnie discovers that the coin is double-sided, and so his answer would always be that, yes, she should stay. Brackett summarized this development as follows: "When the hero can accept [the Hawksian woman] as he would another man, with the masculine virtues he values, then he can start thinking about her as a woman" (121). Typical of Hawksian mutual adaptation between the two protagonists, Bonnie is willing to remain, but it has to be the hero's will for her to stay.

Contemporary to Haskell's work in the early 1970s, Naomi Wise's essay on the figure of the Hawksian woman retrospectively described how Hawks's films broke with the previous presentation of women in Hollywood cinema by moving away from a binary of stock heroines as either fair-haired virgins or tainted sex objects; Hawks instead presents a fusion of the good-girl and bad-girl categorical poles "into a single, heroic heroine, who is both sexual and valuable" (Wise 112). The Hawksian woman's distinctive characteristics were generally identified by critics such as Wise as her experiential wisdom, often achieved through suffering, streetwise maturity, independence, competence, and strength of will, all qualities that are embodied in both the director's screwball and adventure films by characters such as Hildy Johnson and Bonnie Lee.

The Hawksian woman should also be understood as very much a post-Code film heroine whose sexuality was sublimated into work and collaborative labor in order to conform to the new moral climate in Hollywood. Women in this period of Hawks's films often work in the entertainment industry, most frequently as club singers or musicians, as is the case in *Only Angels Have Wings, Ball of Fire* (1941), and *To Have and Have Not* (1944). While these careers turn the heroines into something of a spectacle, their competence and hard-bitten business sense is often conveyed through their work as entertainers. It also seems to prepare them to cross over into male-dominated environments and labor alongside men, particularly in *Only Angels Have Wings*, where the piano-playing entertainer Bonnie adapts successfully to the world of the group of fliers. Bonnie's own father was a trapeze artist who died in a fatal accident while performing, and her background in this risky entertainment industry is her way into understanding the dangers of flying. Wise adds that "while the men in Hawks's adventure films are professionally skilled (as fliers, gunmen, racing drivers, etc.), Hawksian women are professional human beings" (114). It is the professional adaptability of these heroines that is striking here as they move into hypermasculine zones of activity. This shift away from the fallen women or bad girls of early 1930s films is not solely due to the Production Code, though; it also reflects historical developments. Women were relatively protected from the job losses of the Depression, as "certain essential jobs (such as clerical work, and domestic and personal service) were so clearly marked as women's work that the economy could not survive without women's contributions in these areas" (Ware 37), while during World War II more women were required to work in industrial roles vacated by men engaged in military service overseas. This historical context contributed to widespread cultural representations of the working woman.

After these initial definitions, the Hawksian woman figure did come under greater scrutiny from feminist critics who were less inclined to see progressive aspects in the character's delineation and observed that she is subjected to the same processes of male voyeurism and fetishism through which the female image in cinema has traditionally been viewed. Laura Mulvey argued that Lauren Bacall in *To Have and Have Not* is displayed as an object of the "combined gaze of spectator and all the male protagonists of the film" and is presented as "isolated, glamorous, on display, sexualised" ("Visual Pleasure" 840), but as the film progresses, she becomes the hero's property after she falls in love with him. Mulvey claims that Bacall's "eroticism is subjected to the male star alone. By means of identification with him, through participation in his power, the spectator can indirectly possess her too" ("Visual Pleasure" 840). One of the most prominent Hawks scholars, Robin Wood, responded to Mulvey's challenge that the male gaze fetishizes and possesses the Hawksian woman in his 1981 addition to his landmark 1968 work on the director, a short appendixed essay titled "Retrospect." Here he concedes that women in Hawks's films "are clearly conceived from the male viewpoint: one would not wish to claim that women find a 'voice' in the films that is not male-determined" (Wood 171). Wood acknowledges the limitations of his earlier reading by highlighting the lack of female communities in Hawks's films, arguing that women exist relationally to the hero as his rivals. He offers the challenge that their presence is surprising nevertheless, since they do not operate within traditional patriarchal structures to perpetuate inheritance: they are boldly anti-maternal. For Wood, this is crucial, as Hawks's women "are anomalous and threatening, but *there* . . . they remain obstinately men/women, demanding a recognition somewhat different from that exchanged between the males; they are a permanent problem" (176), with "problem" conceived in a constructive sense from a gender-theory perspective. Wollen also identifies the "threat" that women pose to the Hawksian hero (*Signs* 71). He states that Hawks's heroes are "habituated to danger and living apart from society" (Wollen, *Signs* 66) and describes the admission of the Hawks woman into the idealized, exclusive, all-male community as a protracted process in which the female character comes to understand the rituals of the exclusive group (Wollen, *Signs* 71). As Cowie highlights, this process is essentially one of masculinization, since "once she has become 'one of the boys' she is no longer a threat" (*Representing the Woman* 29). Even though the "threat" of the female figure may eventually be neutralized, Wood praises Hawks for incorporating such a disruptive force into his films—a challenge to tradition—that he could just as easily have suppressed. Women in these films are ultimately able to achieve a measure of equality with men by playfully assuming masculine attributes and contributing to the labor of predominantly male communities.

While I would not contest the claims made by film scholars such as Haskell, Wise, and Wood that the Hawksian woman reaches her apotheosis in the films of the late 1930s and early 1940s, stressing the newness of this figure within popular culture has resulted in her antecedents in literature and film frequently being overlooked. Haskell, for example, argues that the androgynous heroine "does not really blossom until the late Thirties" ("Masculine Feminine" 35). However, proto-Hawksian women recur repeatedly across Faulkner's fiction and screenplays from the mid-1930s, and they embody many of the qualities I have outlined, suggestive of the diverse influences that helped to create the modern heroine. The screenwriter Jules Furthman, for example, worked on both *Only Angels Have Wings* and *To Have and Have Not*, where he drew on the roles he had written for Marlene Dietrich on pre-Code films such as *Morocco* (1930) and *Shanghai Express* (1932). Actresses such as Jean Arthur, Barbara Stanwyck, and Rosalind Russell also invested the developing image of the Hawksian woman with their own distinctive screen personas. Faulkner was, however, the most high-profile novelist to be directly involved in the construction of this type through his screenwriting, and he didn't simply write these portrayals under commission but rather drew on his own fiction from the same period. In fact, the female protagonist of *Pylon* is perhaps the earliest example of an already highly developed image of the Hawksian woman in American letters, since Laverne embodies a number of the distinctive qualities of the figure, specifically androgyny, transgression into masculine spheres of action, eroticized collaborative labor alongside men, and an anti-maternal streak, fusing many of the Hawksian woman's key components in embryonic form. In the exchange below, for example, Laverne engages with Jiggs, the other airplane mechanic,[5] and a single unit of dialogue distils many of these features:

> She was dressed, the trenchcoat belted; she gave the room a single pale comprehensive glance, then she looked at him, brief, instantaneous, blank. "Drinking a little breakfast," he said.
>
> "You mean supper," she said. "You'll be asleep in two hours." (*N* 2: 853)

The rapidly delivered quip, taken in conjunction with her masculine dress and the impassive gaze, reflect her steely composure and playful manner of negotiating her position within a masculine community. In her strength, candor, playfulness, and androgyny, I believe that Laverne ought to be considered alongside the evolving heroines of Hawks's films. As I will go on to show, drawing on feminist theories of filmic spectatorship, Faulkner partially works to challenge the status of the female figure as a fetishized object of desire within mediated acts of looking through the disruptive novelty of Laverne's presentation. *Pylon* was published four years in advance of the supposed emergence of the fully formed Hawksian woman in *Only Angels Have Wings*, presenting the possibility that Hawks's portrayals of women in his films may have been influenced by the novel he initially encouraged Faulkner to write. Indeed, it was a portrayal Faulkner would develop in his subsequent screenplays penned for Fox, inspired, in part, by his own intimate encounters with potential models for the Hawksian woman during his time at the studio.

The Masculinized Heroine and Labor

Pylon principally establishes Laverne as a masculinized heroine through her labor as an aviator and entertainer alongside men. Through the figure, Faulkner revised and updated his portrayal of women within male-dominated flying communities that he had previously documented in his fiction. Across the wide-ranging body of work this chapter covers—Faulkner's short stories, fiction, and screenwriting, as well as the work of his Hollywood collaborators—we can trace an evolution in cultural understandings of gendered attributes during the 1930s and 1940s, and the ways in which gender is communicated and mediated to both coterie and mass audiences. Faulkner's frequent updates to his portrayal of the androgynous working heroine across literature and film demonstrate that the meanings creators and audiences attach to gender are not fixed. In this regard, Faulkner's work appears to be particularly in sync with the Hawksian oeuvre, since, as Cowie observes, "Hawks's films demonstrate the ways in which the meanings, the definitions, of masculinity and femininity are determined through the textual system" (*Representing* 34). In other words, a Hawks film does not rely on a stable, preexisting gender binary to convey interactions between men and women; instead, each individual film by the director produces its own definitions of masculinity and femininity through establishing specific "distinctions around sexual difference," which it proceeds to play with and interrogate (*Representing* 31). Similarly, across Faulkner's fiction and screenwriting, we see images and attributes of masculinity and femininity subject to continual flux across textual systems of representation in exchanges between the author's heroes and heroines.

Faulkner first explored a love triangle between barnstorming fliers in his 1930 story "Honor." The story describes the experiences of Buck Monaghan as a wing-walker after World War I; he has an affair with a woman named Mildred, the wife of Rogers, a pilot in the flying circus. It appears Rogers is aware of the affair from the beginning, and he agrees to give her up to Buck, as Mildred pragmatically explains: "We've talked it over and have both agreed that we couldn't love one another any more after this and that this is the only sensible thing to do. Then he can find a woman he can love, a woman that's not bad like I am" (*CS* 557). Competition over Mildred is expressed through the final wing-walking show over an amusement park, in which Rogers and Buck try to outdo each other in a daredevil loop, but Rogers ultimately has to save Buck from a failed wing-walk. After this episode, Mildred returns to Rogers and they have a child together, Mildred later telling Buck in a letter that he is to be the godfather. The story contains the themes of sexual unorthodoxy, barnstorming entertainment, and contested paternity that would later animate *Pylon*, but Mildred does not fully align with the features of masculinized heroines in Faulkner's work of the mid-1930s, since she first appears as a vision of feminine domesticity in "an apron on over one of these little pale squashy dresses, with flour or something on her arms" (*CS* 553), and neither does she engage in the flying shows alongside the men.

Pylon may also have been influenced by Harry Behn's adaptation of Faulkner's "Honor" for MGM, and in this project definitions of "masculinity" become markedly associated with images of collaborative labor in dangerous situations. Behn produced a synopsis of the story dated 13 January 1933, and when Faulkner left Hollywood after working on *Today We Live* for Hawks, he was supposed to build on Behn's synopsis. Faulkner was assigned to the "Honor" project from November 1932 to February 1933, but it appears he never carried out any revisions (*MGM* 421). Behn produced a first full-length script for "Honor," dated 24 January 1933, and Bruce F. Kawin argues that much of this script more closely resembles *Pylon* than the original story, which raises the possibility that Faulkner may have drawn on the adaptation when composing the novel, as he had read Behn's synopsis for the same project at an earlier date (*MGM* 425).[6] *Pylon* can therefore be seen to follow the inverse trajectory to the one we would typically associate with adaptation; rather than a work of fiction being used as the property for a film, *Pylon* could be considered a "novelization," an instance in which Hollywood screenwriting provoked the creation of an additional prose work.[7] In Behn's version, Mildred actively participates in the air shows as an accomplished parachutist (*MGM* 425), and her performance demands considerable personal danger since she injures her ankle in one stunt (*MGM* 423). The screenwriter Jules Furthman was also involved in this project, adding notes to Behn's first script while he worked on his revisions (*MGM* 423); as previously mentioned, Furthman later wrote the screenplay for *Only Angels Have Wings* and shared credit with Faulkner, among others, on *To Have and Have Not*. As such, Faulkner's 1930 story "Honor," Behn's 1933 screenplay adaptation, *Pylon,* and the Hawksian films of the late 1930s and 1940s all stand in complex genetic relationship to one another in their evolving portrayals of women in dangerous communities and occupations.

In building on and moving beyond these literary and filmic sources to imagine an active, female wing-walker in *Pylon,* Faulkner also drew on a real-life counterpart, who was similarly viewed as being masculinized by her labor. In February 1933 Faulkner began taking flying lessons from Vernon Omlie, a former Army aviator and seasoned barnstormer, to regain his nerve for flying and acquaint himself with up-to-date flying technology. Omlie was married to a woman called Phoebe who would take part in air shows with her husband as a wing-walker "swinging from one plane to another, then jumping, cutting away her parachute and falling free until she popped open a second one" (Blotner, *Biography* 315). They went on tour as part of a flying circus, then, after hitting rock bottom financially, they set up a successful flying school, took up a variety of charter jobs, and in the process became celebrities (Blotner, *Biography* 315).

Phoebe Omlie impressed Faulkner as a "masculinized" woman performing a dangerous job in a male-dominated world and pursuing an unorthodox lifestyle. Among the trophies in Vernon and Phoebe's Memphis apartment was the iron mouthpiece that Phoebe swung from during barnstorming performances with "her hair cropped and her face scarred" (Blotner, *Biography* 315). Indeed, Phoebe not only crosses gender through her association with such images of masculinity but triumphs over the men around her. In a *New York Times* article from September 1931, the headline reads that "MRS. OMLIE BEATS 36 MEN IN DERBY; Declared Grand Prize Winner of 52 in Flight From Coast" (Lyman 8). To Faulkner, Omlie would have represented not only gender transgression but successful performance and even dominance within a masculine environment through feats of physical skill.

As an amalgam of these diverse sources in literature, screenwriting, and sport culture, Laverne is presented as an active, androgynous figure who engages in labor within a community of men, and it is partly her transvestism that frustrates the male gaze within the novel. While *Pylon* only briefly alludes to Hollywood and California, Faulkner is particularly concerned with exploring the ways in which Laverne's activities within the air shows are both mediated through commercial narratives and visually consumed. Faulkner uses daredevil flying as a constructed visual mode, what Peter Lurie calls the novel's exploration of "communal perceptual experience and ... individual characters' acts of seeing" (15), through which the author can explore his evolving perspective on mass entertainment and commercial film.

As part of the novel's reflection on processes of mediation, a nameless reporter working for a local paper in New Valois is attempting to sell a germ of a story about the barnstorming fliers to his editor, Hagood. The reporter is primarily interested in the unorthodox relationships between the barnstormers; Laverne is married to Roger Shumann, a racing pilot, but is also lover to the parachute jumper Jack Holmes, and it is unclear which of the two men is her son Jack's father. This is part of the challenge the novel poses to patriarchal systems. John N. Duvall views the sexual configuration of the three fliers as a critique of bourgeois marriage, an institution which furthers the patriarchy (82), and, in Roger, Duvall sees a man, in his acceptance of his partner Laverne's child despite its unknown paternity, who "subverts patriarchal values by accepting a woman whose sexuality breaches cultural limits" (83). The reporter believes that the unorthodoxy of this three-way relationship, within the context of the dangerous activity of barnstorming, is viable fodder for the paper, as he defends to Hagood, "I thought that women's bedhabits were always news" (*N* 2: 808). Hagood is less interested in the "bedhabits" of the fliers than in the commercial spectacle itself. He asks the reporter for a visual document of the air races, namely "an accurate account of everything that occurs out there tomorrow that creates any reaction excitement or irritation on any human retina" (*N* 2: 808), frustrating the latter's sexual fascination for the fliers. As Taylor Hagood comments, the editor here acts as a censor of the reporter's copy, "enforcing [the newspaper's] role as promoter of 'accuracy,' of a report that is more than simply information and less than the subtle and questioning medium of fiction" ("Media" 114). It is in this sense, as John T. Matthews points out, that we can view the reporter as a surrogate for Faulkner, "as another kind of writer who reckons awkwardly but hopefully with modern ways" (*Seeing* 63). Karl F. Zender also suggests that the reporter's disenchantment with the newspaper business and his "sense of the compromises inherent in the medium" (*Crossing* 51) echo Faulkner's anxieties about money and his need to labor in Hollywood. It is through the reporter that Faulkner appears to express his ambivalence towards the screenwriting profession; as a character who deploys and struggles against features of commercial writing, the reporter resembles a stock figure of a Hollywood novel, a screenwriter-adjacent type who expresses both his "contempt for the convention-driven films that are generally produced and [his] investment in these same formulas" (Rhodes 6).

Due to such creative conflicts with figures who adhere to economic imperatives, *Pylon* has been frequently read as a critique of the struggling role of the artist (whether barnstorming flier or writer) as a paid worker within capitalist economic structures and technological modernity.[8] The novel's bleak vision of the contemporary position of the artist has been interpreted, by extension, as an indictment of Hollywood; from this perspective, the novel's focus on the deleterious impact of money on artistic practice reflects Faulkner's own experiences in Hollywood. The novel is undoubtedly concerned with the function of art in cultural modernity, and Hollywood was crucial to Faulkner's thinking here, since, as Matthews argues, in *Pylon* Faulkner "draws on a sense of the seismic shifts in social and sexual mores, cultural forms, mass behavior, and economic relations that his life in the Hollywood film colony cued him to" (*Seeing* 60). Among these shifts, Faulkner worked a novel portrayal of the androgynous working woman, born out of his collaborations in the Hollywood community, into his fiction. While *Pylon* may partly reflect Faulkner's sense of his commodity value after his work in Hollywood, it has thus far not fully been considered that the novel in fact derives much of its communicative power from mass art due to its debt to Hollywood conventions and Faulkner's screenwriting.

These influences make it difficult to read the novel as an unambiguous condemnation of the economic instrumentalization of artistic practice.

This is not to say that the presentation of Laverne shouldn't be understood as an act of mediation driven by financial need, since the reporter has tasked himself with producing a titillating narrative about visual entertainment and sexual unorthodoxy for consumers of the newspaper. However, Laverne's masculine qualities repeatedly refuse a neat co-option into the reporter's framework, contesting the very construction of woman as image within visual media. As previously discussed, the woman in cinematic narrative is generally positioned as the passive bearer of the look and "can be said to connote *to-be-looked-at-ness*" (Mulvey, "Visual Pleasure" 837). The female image, as Mary Ann Doane describes, "is theorized in terms of a certain *closeness*, the lack of a distance or gap between sign and referent" (*Femmes Fatales* 18). The association between femininity and the closeness of the image problematizes the voyeuristic separation essential to cinematic spectatorship, since "for the female spectator there is a certain overpresence of the image—she *is* the image" (Doane, *Femmes Fatales* 22). For Doane, the female spectator can therefore be understood as a form of "transvestite" who shifts between active and passive, masculine and feminine positions, both masochistically identifying with the image of the female character while also identifying with the agency of the hero who controls the gaze in the film narrative (*Femmes Fatales* 24). By extension, female transvestism, as both practice and cinematic device, can be seen as an effort to establish distance between woman and image, since the woman as transvestite "adopts the sexuality of the other" (Doane, *Femmes Fatales* 25) through clothing in order to attain "a mastery over the image and the very possibility of attaching the gaze to desire" (Doane, *Femmes Fatales* 24).

In *Pylon*, Laverne's transvestism similarly functions to violate the positioning of the female as a consumable image of desire, and she can be seen to assume a degree of "mastery" over her presentation by distancing herself from the familiar visual signifiers of her gender. The novel initially emphasizes Laverne's masculinity in dress, hairstyle, and physique, a description that seems to recall Omlie: "looking almost like a man in the greasy coverall, with the pale strong rough ragged hair actually darker where it was sunburned, a tanned heavyjawed face in which the eyes looked like pieces of china" (*N* 2: 790). As Dardis suggests, "like all Hawks's 'tough women,' Laverne has a certain strain of pseudo-masculinity about her" (100). Both an ambivalently gendered figure and the mother of a child of unknown paternity, Laverne presents a threat to masculine domination, and the cultivation of her image visually expresses her desire for autonomy, as it "converts practical necessity into social sign" (Matthews, "Autograph of Violence" 261). But her image should also be considered *culturally* subversive in its status as visual spectacle.

The reporter's first description of Laverne to Hagood, in a scene I briefly analyze in the introduction, highlights her transvestism and masculine attributes, but her image exceeds and frustrates his reference points within contemporary commercial art, as he relays seeing her "out there in the hangar this morning in dungarees like the rest of them, with her hands full of wrenches and machinery and a gob of cotter keys in her mouth like they tell how women used to do with the pins and needles before General Motors begun to make their clothes for them, with this Harlowcolored hair that they would pay her money for it in Hollywood and a smear of grease where she had swiped it back with her wrist" (*N* 2: 804). The reporter draws on commodified images of female beauty derived from Hollywood and appraises Laverne's visual marketability. This initially seems to chime with Doane's point—in an analysis of George Cukor's 1949 workplace screwball comedy *Adam's Rib*—that "male transvestism is an occasion for laughter; female transvestism only another occasion for desire" (*Femmes Fatales* 25). However, what is remarkable about the reporter's encapsulation of Laverne's image is the incongruity of her apparent filmic beauty and commodity value: her "Harlowcolored hair" that she could profit from in the commercial film center. Such incongruities are revealing, since Laverne, as Marta Paul Johnson rightly emphasizes, "exists multifariously in the imagination of others," meaning that her character "suffers a range of distortions" (289). Her androgynous dress, working in the overalls of a mechanic, contrasts starkly with the femininity of her hair, likened to that of the quintessential blonde bombshell of 1930s cinema, Jean Harlow. Indeed, the "smear of grease" on her face manifests her challenging androgyny in a single image, as the feminine eroticism of the smudged lipstick has been transformed into the grease of the engineer's trade, a stereotypically masculine pursuit. It is a striking early presentation of the feminine-masculine Hawksian type that highlights how the reporter, as Johnson asserts, "is not a reliable reflector of Laverne" (293) as well as deviating significantly from cinematic presentations of women synonymous with Harlow and the pre-Code films in which she starred. Harlow portrayed sexually active, independent women, and she was particularly associated with the figure of the bad girl through her work on *Red-Headed Woman* (1932), the kind of role in which the female protagonist is portrayed as improving her financial situation through a transactional use of sex. Bad girls like Harlow seduced their way up the social ladder, but they did so by appearing as unambiguously feminine images of desire. Although the reporter attempts to place Laverne in one visual frame derived from Hollywood, her image, in its striking and dissonant androgyny, frustrates such a direct approximation. Disrupting the putative "closeness" of woman as image, Laverne's self-presentation becomes distanced from the reporter's attempt to position her as a fetishized object of desire.

The Erotics of Collaboration

Within the novel, Laverne's labor within the community of aviators masculinizes her, but it also imbues cross-gender collaboration with an erotic charge. This invites comparison with Faulkner's own participation in the collaborative communities of Hollywood, where he worked alongside women in artistic exchanges that, as Robert Jackson suggests, were often characterized by a sexual energy arising from the pooling of creativity (33). Jackson argues that Hollywood production was in part animated by the fraught nature of creative competition, the "difficult, painful process in which the personal and the aesthetic are confused, often erotically, in shifting relations of sex and power" (36). In portraying Laverne's collaborative creativity and bringing forth its sexualized undercurrents, Faulkner provides a fictional equivalent of the dynamics of Hollywood working practices behind the scenes that are energized by struggles over creative control and competitive desires.

In addition to reflecting the behind-the-scenes activity of the studio system, *Pylon* is also in dialogue with tropes of contemporary cinema. As previously outlined, Laverne's presentation in the novel reflects that of the post-Code Hollywood heroines, whose sexuality was sublimated into work due to industry censorship. However, Faulkner's portrayal of the group of barnstormers does not simply submit to the new moral climate that shaped his Hollywood work after 1934. Instead, he lays bare the ways in which the Code remade commercial art, by rendering the sexual sublimation fundamental to post-Code cinema explicit through a heightened portrayal of female desire. Matthews has commented on this exaggerated portrayal of Laverne's sexuality as representing "the furthermost evolution of the sexually defiant young woman in Faulkner's fiction. In fact, she's way over the top" (*Seeing* 62). However, I believe such excess has a specific critical intent within the novel, as it constitutes another method through which Faulkner establishes distance between Laverne and the consumable "closeness" of her image, namely that of masquerade. Doane describes the "masquerade of femininity" in cinema as "a kind of reaction-formation against the woman's trans-sex identification, her transvestism" in which a woman may "flaunt her femininity, produce herself as an excess of femininity" (*Femmes Fatales* 25). By highlighting the artificiality of self-presentation, masquerade keeps femininity at a distance; its challenge to patriarchy can therefore be located "in its denial of femininity as closeness, as presence-to-itself, as, precisely, imagistic" (Doane, *Femmes Fatales* 25).

We can observe the subversive potential of female masquerade most vividly in Faulkner's description of Laverne's first wing-walking stunt with Roger. In the buildup to this scene, Laverne suggests joining Roger in the aerial show, and he accordingly drills her in "the simple mechanics" (*N* 2: 908) of wing-walking and operating the parachute. Faulkner's focus here on shared labor in the production of elaborate spectacle reflects the studio system in which cross-gender teams, of which he was a part, worked to produce visually arresting entertainment. The prose also registers surprise at the type of gender crossings that attend such creative networks, as women are apparently masculinized by their participation within them; the narrator is shocked to find that at one point it is Laverne rather than the mechanic who takes it upon herself to repair the flier's airplane, observing that "they had almost reached the airplane before they discovered that it was the woman and not Jiggs at work on it and that she had put the supercharger back on with the engine head still off and the valves still out. She rose and brushed her hair back with the flat of her wrist, though they had asked no question" (*N* 2: 880). The lack of a question—or indeed, a challenge—from her male collaborators indicates their deference towards Laverne's skilled labor.

Before the jump that follows her first wing-walk, the show deviates from its course when Laverne initiates sex with Roger. After climbing into the cockpit of the plane, straddling Roger while facing him, the pilot's reaction is described as follows:

> In the same instant of realising (as with one hand she ripped her skirthem free of the safetywire with which they had fastened it bloomerfashion

between her legs) that she was clawing blindly and furiously not at the belt across his thighs but at the fly of his trousers he realised that she had on no undergarment, pants. She told him later that the reason was that she was afraid that from fear she might soil one of the few undergarments which she now possessed ... soon he had two opponents; he was outnumbered, he now bore in his own lap, between himself and her wild and frenzied body, the perennially undefeated, the victorious; ... the bereaved, the upthrust, the stalk. (N 2: 908–9)

Duvall asserts that the episode showcases the reversal of "the binary of male as acting subject and female as passive object," viewing Laverne's sexual assertiveness here as "a furious affirmation of self" (87). Technology appears to be central to this process, and Vivian Wagner has observed a wider pattern in *Pylon* in which machines can function "as the signs and symbols of a liberation from normative gender relations, with airplanes providing a utopian space for articulating this liberation" (81). By disrupting gender norms through the collective labor afforded by new forms of technology, Faulkner was in step with the gender presentations of Hawks's films in which heroines were masculinized by becoming active and conventional definitions of sexual difference were challenged. As Cowie summarizes, "the simplistic representation of the sexual relation as one of domination/submission is one which Hawks's films tend to oppose, instead they assert the figure of a woman who is equal to the man" (*Representing* 32). In a vivid demonstration of this relation in the cockpit, Laverne is presented as both the initiator and dominant party, while Roger struggles feebly with his "two opponents," becoming dissociated from his own sex.

Although Laverne's sexual assertiveness is of course highly significant here, the performative nature of the episode as an act of masquerade is also of central concern. Laverne's act takes place within the frame of a show with "the money collected and the crowd waiting" (N 2: 908) and as such comments on the intersections of mass entertainment, consumerism, and sexuality.[9] In order to turn herself into a spectacle for consumption, Laverne has to mask her gender ambiguity and display her femininity: "She wore skirts; they had decided that her exposed legs would not only be a drawing card but that in the skirt no one would doubt that she was a woman" (N 2: 908). As opposed to the transvestism of her labors on the ground, in this aerial scene Laverne establishes distance between herself and her image in a different way, in the sense that, for Doane, "masquerade doubles representation; it is constituted by a hyperbolization of the accoutrements of femininity" (*Femmes Fatales* 26). Laverne's presentation of her femininity through masquerade manifests in both the exaggeration of her gendered appearance in the construction of the spectacle and the sudden flaunting of her sexual desires in midair. By doing so, Laverne momentarily achieves a degree of control over her image, as her excessive self-presentation demonstrates "the effectivity of masquerade . . . in its potential to manufacture a distance from the image, to generate a problematic within which the image is manipulable, producible, and readable by the woman" (Doane, *Femmes Fatales* 32). When Laverne descends from the skies in a "ruined dress" and "parachute harness," she becomes an exaggerated icon "in the very traditional symbology . . . of female bondage" (*N* 2: 909). In such moments, images of femininity can become defamiliarized through acts of excess.

It is also a revealing scene in terms of its position in cultural history. Rather than submitting to post-Code modesty, the scene makes work unabashedly sexually provocative and highlights tensions in the relationship between entertainer and audience in the creation of spectacle, as Laverne's performance provokes diverse reactions from the assembled crowd. Specifically, it exposes the hypocrisies of an audience who simultaneously wish to censor and are titillated by mass entertainment. While Roger lands the airplane, Laverne endures the following: "she had come down with the dress, pulled or blown free of the parachute harness, up about her armpits and had been dragged along the ground until overtaken by a yelling mob of men and youths, in the center of which she now lay dressed from the waist down in dirt and parachute straps and stockings" (*N* 2: 909). Jumping from the plane, Laverne descends into the center of her audience, the "yelling mob." As a result of what happens here, Diane Roberts labels Laverne's first jump a pornographic scene, "a male fantasy of the receptive female that comes out of nowhere, legs spread" (*Southern Womanhood* 206). The pornographic aspect is of course derived from the show's relation to the crowd. While Laverne has initiated the sex act in the sky, which appears improvised and spontaneous rather than calculated for its economic return, she loses control of how she is observed in her descent. Wagner comments that once Laverne "leaves [the] utopian space of the airplane, all these blurred boundaries and gender distinctions are history" (93). This threatens to negate her active stance in the cockpit, as Duvall argues, "despite Laverne's action, which presents her as a desiring subject, once she makes her jump she becomes the universal object of male voyeuristic fantasy" (87).

I believe that Faulkner wishes us to pay particular attention to the ways in which masculine voyeurism and fetishism go hand in hand with censorship in relation to the object of desire. Among the mob that gathers around the compromised body of Laverne is a young village officer with a "sadistic" (*N* 2: 909) face who bars Roger from getting to her. The officer relishes the policing of sexuality within his small geographical territory, which has now grandly extended to the skies themselves. He is something of a diminutive Joseph Breen, the censor who led the Production Code Administration from 1934 and was responsible for pulling pre-Code films from circulation and refusing to release them "unless rendered moral" (Doherty, *Pre-Code Hollywood* 19); the character is described in the novel as "a man besotted and satiated by his triumphs over abased human flesh which his corrupt and picayune office supplied him" (*N* 2: 909). The young officer feels he has experienced the "ultimate shape of his jaded desires fall[ing] upon him out of the sky" (*N* 2: 909), reflecting the way in which film reflects our fantasies back to us in visual form, tracing the shape of our desires.

Within the structure of any form of entertainment, the crowd seeks repetition, as "the mob's immediate object happened to be the same—to see, touch her, again" (*N* 2: 910). The irony here is that the censor only intensifies his desire for the object that he removes from visual consumption, a truth unconvincingly masked by offended moral sensibilities. We witness this kind of unsettling illogic in a later scene when the police officers deliver Roger and Laverne from the small town in a car, and one of them rubs his flank up against Laverne's body (*N* 2: 911), creepily undermining the performance of his duties to enforce moral codes.

As punishment for such "transgression," Laverne is arrested and taken to jail by the officers. When Roger finally gets to see her, she is dressed in a raincoat to cover her modesty. Laverne and Roger are expelled from the village community, as her parachute jump has awoken the violent collective desires of the repressed moralizers. The officers drive them to the airport where their plane was left. Roger is told to perform their exit flight despite the danger—there are no lights to guide him—as the police are worried that they cannot hold back the crowd. Laverne's return to the plane after a night in jail is spectacularly depicted: "holding the raincoat about her" she must "run down the long tunnel of the cars' lights and climb into the airplane and vanish" (*N* 2: 911).[10] The young officer has been driven "mad" and "insane" (*N* 2: 911) and exhibits a desperate desire to turn the image he has witnessed descend from the skies into a sexual reality; he screams after them, "I'll pay her! I'll pay either of you! Name it! Let me fuck her once and you can cut me if you want!" (*N* 2: 912). The crazed man's moral hypocrisy is indicated by his desperate pursuit of the plane, screaming "whore and bitch and pervert" (*N* 2: 912) as Roger takes off. The scene renders transparent the sexual redirection of visual mass entertainment undertaken by the Production Code Administration, by creating an exaggerated spectacle of erotic labor. It serves to highlight the fundamental hypocrisy of the new moral climate of Hollywood at the time Faulkner composed *Pylon,* in which the censor represses and removes from the screen the very things he desires.

Challenging the Maternal Role

In addition to engaging in masculinized labor suffused with an erotic charge, Laverne is shown repeatedly to refuse, or to be unable to perform, a prescribed role of devoted wife and mother, another feature consistent with the Hawksian woman archetype. After Roger dies flying the pylons in a faulty aircraft the reporter had arranged for him to use, Laverne and her son are perceived according to generalized, commercial stock archetypes as "the dead pilot's wife and child" (*N* 2: 938) by the newspaper photographer documenting the search for the plane and Roger's body in the lake. However, Laverne exhibits her resistance to being consumed as a reified "type" in a visual commercial narrative. She reacts to the sight of the plane crash that kills Roger as follows: "she did not scream nor faint (she was standing quite near the microphone, near enough for it to have caught the scream) but instead she just stood there and watched the fuselage break in two and said, 'Oh damn you, Roger!'" (*N* 2: 936). Laverne prevents her scream from being caught on the microphone and confounds the expectations of the crowd by cursing Roger as the aircraft breaks in two.

Laverne's final appearance in the novel further distances her from the "proper" role of grieving widow and suffering single mother. Laverne travels with Jack Holmes and her son by cab in the snow to the home of Roger's parents, where she will make the decision to give up her child into their care. She believes she cannot support her son Jack anymore, as she is pregnant with her second child, and this time Jack Holmes is definitely the father (*N* 2: 987). She observes the house from the waiting car, gazing on a scene that appears staged in its artificial reproducibility:

it seemed to the woman that almost at once the car had stopped and looking out through the snow she saw a kind of cenotaph, penurious and without majesty or dignity, of forlorn and victorious desolation—a bungalow, a tight flimsy mass of stoops and porte-cochères and flat gables and bays not five years old and built in that colored mud-and-chickenwire tradition which California moving picture films have scattered across North America as if the celluloid carried germs, not five years old yet wearing already an air of dilapidation and rot; a quality furious and recent as if immediate disintegration had been included in the architect's blueprints. (*N* 2: 984)

The image of the "celluloid . . . germs" distributed across the North American continent recalls the colonization of culture Clement Greenberg sees as being effected by kitsch as a "mass product of Western industrialism, [which] has gone on a triumphal tour of the world, crowding out and defacing native cultures in one colonial country after another" (103). The proliferated cinematic images of Hollywood are presented as a disease that has got into the body of the nation. From the perspective of the individual spectator, it is as if Laverne is scarcely able to perceive the individuality of the building due to its mass reproduction on the cinema screen, what Taylor Hagood describes as an example of "film's propensity to naturalize simulation" ("Media" 109), and indeed this whole scene has a self-conscious reflexive quality. It appears that the mise-en-scène, within which the Shumann family's flimsy bungalow is centered, is purpose-built for the action. The building is practically new, but wears its decay as image, a ready-made illusory ruin built to project an idea of the occupants' taste and social milieu to the camera using visual shorthand.

As Laverne steps out of the cab to walk to the house, she is again evaluated according to her failure to live up to a predefined social role. The driver places judgments on Laverne's character from the car, piecing together what he has heard of her story in his internal monologue: "So that's her. . . . Only she dont look a whole lot like a widow. But then I hear tell she never acted a whole lot like a wife" (*N* 2: 985). So too, when Laverne debates the future of her son with her father-in-law, Doctor Shumann, he seems bent on framing Laverne according to the bad-girl archetype, unearthing Laverne's previous assertion that she was "born bad and could not help it" (*N* 2: 986). Building on this, when they find the money the reporter has hidden in the child's toy airplane, the Doctor and his wife first presume Laverne has put it there, then imply that she has gained the money through prostitution, his wife questioning, "where would she get a hundred and seventy-five dollars that she would have to hide from both of them in a child's toy?" (*N* 2: 990). In keeping with the bad-girl image, Roger's parents presume that any financial advancement on Laverne's part can only have been achieved through sexual transactions.

In the verbal exchange where Laverne expresses her intention to leave her son with his putative grandparents, her delivery is again not consistent with the language of a suffering widow, indeed it is marked by emotional control, even coldness. When she laughs, in response to the doctor's suggestion that her child will soon forget her, it is "short, mirthless, not moving" (*N* 2: 986). When the Doctor gives her more time to make up her decision, she insists, "I have decided now" (*N* 2: 986), and she actually reverses the offer, saying that she would be happy to give *him* more time to decide whether he feels able to take the child. When he gives her the grand ultimatum that she is "to make no attempt to see [her son] or communicate with him as long as [he and his wife] live," she simply replies, "Yes . . . I have to do it" (*N* 2: 986–87). Laverne's decision is a pragmatic response to economic necessity; she cannot afford to feed and clothe her son, as she is expecting another child, which is definitely not Roger's. Self-conscious and in control, she delivers her final line "as though for a record" (*N* 2: 988).

Duvall asserts that in Laverne's actions here she fails to escape the patriarchal system, since she is forced to relinquish her child to an alternative father figure who can provide for him economically (93). Roberts also reads the scene as demonstrating Laverne's transformation "from gender-breaching archadultress to reformed Magdalen . . . speaking the words of the self-sacrificing mother [she is] the 'loose woman' facing up to both the economic and moral responsibilities of maternity, her sexual and social independence abrogated once and for all" (*Southern Womanhood* 207). While Laverne's agency is indeed limited by patriarchal structures, her image does not derive from established archetypes in cultural discourses pertaining to womanhood and motherhood. Laverne's presentation has little in common with the self-sacrificing mother's travails in the restrictive family home, as presented in women's films of the late 1930s and 1940s—the conventions of which Faulkner would later explore in his screenwriting for Warner Brothers and his 1951 novel *Requiem for a Nun*—since *Pylon* insists on Laverne's distance from the domestic sphere. In fact, the text repeatedly highlights her deviation from such gendered cultural frames as the blonde bombshell, the suffering mother, or the bad girl. Instead, her image disrupts the expectations of the characters around her; she is presented as anti-maternal and undomestic, pragmatic rather than self-sacrificing, cold and controlled rather than emotionally expressive, and performative and self-conscious rather than more directly sincere, all features consistent with the presentation of the Hawksian woman in Hollywood films from the late 1930s.

Faulkner would further advance his portrayal of this type of heroine within his fiction in "The Wild Palms" sections of his 1939 novel *If I Forget Thee, Jerusalem*. "The Wild Palms" describes an unorthodox romance between Harry Wilbourne, a trainee doctor at the city hospital, and Charlotte "Charley" Rittenmeyer, an artist. It begins at a bohemian party in New Orleans hosted at a painter's studio on the evening of Harry's twenty-seventh birthday. Harry doesn't have any appropriate dress clothes, so his roommate in the interns' quarters lends him a tuxedo to wear. Inspecting the paintings hung around the walls at the party, Charlotte approaches him and asks, "What do you think about it, mister?" (*N* 3: 520). Harry struggles to articulate an opinion, and so Charlotte ventures, "'Marshmallows with horseradish,' she said, too promptly. 'I paint too,' she added. 'I can afford to say. I can afford to say I can beat that, too. What's your name? and what have you got all this on for, just to come slumming? So we can all know you are slumming?'" (*N* 3: 520). Charlotte's character delineation is distilled quite clearly here; she has a creative yet playful eye, asserts the value of her own work above that on display, and quips about Harry's inappropriate dress as a form of flirtation. Upon her entrance into the novel, Charlotte is immediately presented as a tough, assertive, desirable, sexually unorthodox, androgynously attractive, anti-maternal, creative, and witty heroine. As a sculptor working on commission, Charlotte continues Faulkner's focus on post-Code, Depression-era "working woman" heroines within his 1930s fiction and screenwriting. In the more developed exploration of her playfulness as an expression of creativity, Charlotte is of a piece with the androgynous sparring playmates of the Hawksian screwball comedies that were to come. The term "screwball" was in fact first used to describe the comedy genre's heroines, indicating their "crazy energy and a certain nonconformity" (Mortimer 11), qualities that Laverne and Charlotte, in parts of Faulkner's 1930s novels, embody.

Although the genre is not one we readily associate with Faulkner, he would become well versed in screwball films and would even begin a couple of film projects in this vein in the 1940s. In a letter from Faulkner to Hawks in June 1948, in reference to a project called "Morningstar," Faulkner demonstrates his knowledge of the director's screwball comedies and expresses his wish to create a movie similar to Hawks's *Ball of Fire*, "where a sexy young woman got involved in a household of old mossback professors and turned everything upside down." What follows is a two-page outline for a film titled "Morningstar," in which a beautiful woman from Venus journeys across the universe to recruit men for her "manless" land; in the proposed picture, the old scientists—among whom Faulkner envisaged a role for Cary Grant—compete for the opportunity. Faulkner imagined comic scenes in which "we could show them boasting or trying to prove their virility with false teeth clashing and secret bottles of glad-restorer pills falling out of their coat-tail pockets."[11] In an earlier screwball project, the treatment "Continuous Performance" from February 1946, Faulkner also suggested Grant as the male protagonist, and the relationship between the leads in the treatment (Henry and Nancy Smith) recalls the rapport of Grant and Katherine Hepburn in *Bringing Up Baby* (1938). In one scene, Henry "enters the diningroom [sic]. It looks like a stadium almost. A table a furlong in length is set for dinner for about 20 people, with flowers and silver, his and Nancy's places at either end dim by distance from one another, so that they would need a courier or at least radio to communicate."[12] The treatment highlights the comical absurdity of established social conventions, which screwball comedies work to challenge and even overturn.

In their association with more masculinized actions and modes of behavior, and the kind of gender reversals and inversions we associate with screwball comedy, Laverne and Charlotte prefigure the "superwoman" of the 1940s Hollywood cinema, who, as Haskell defines, "has a high degree of intelligence or imagination, but instead of exploiting her femininity . . . adopts male characteristics in order to enjoy male prerogatives, or merely to survive" (*Reverence* 214). While Faulkner contributed towards the emerging image of the Hawksian woman in his novels from the 1930s, he was also developing his vision of this archetype in his screenplays for Twentieth Century–Fox.

"The Road to Glory" and "Splinter Fleet": Laboring on the Warfront

Encouraged by Hawks, Faulkner signed a contract with the studio Twentieth Century–Fox in December 1935 that would last until the middle of 1937 (Gleeson-White, "Introduction" 2). Faulkner produced five screenplays for the studio during this period, working sometimes independently and sometimes in a collaborative team of writers. It is particularly in the genre of the war film that Faulkner developed the novel presentation of gender relations he had begun in *Pylon*. Contrary to his claim that "warfare [is] . . . the only condition under which a man who is not a scoundrel can escape for a while from his female kin" (*SL* 153), his Fox screenplays feature female interlopers into scenes of international conflict. Consistent with Cowie's point that the films of Hawks and his collaborators toy with and expose the constructedness of definitions of gender (*Representing the Woman* 31, 34), Faulkner's screenwriting for Fox serves to demasculinize popular images of warfare through a series of role reversals and gender crossings on the front.

Faulkner's screenplay for *The Road to Glory* (1936), directed by Hawks, was his first assignment at the studio and the only one of these projects for which he received screenplay credit.[13] *The Road to Glory* is set in the French trenches of World War I and explores the productive labor of women within male-dominated zones, the Hawksian woman's key mode of action. Fox had acquired the rights to adapt an existing French movie, *Les Croix de Bois* (1932), based on the 1919 novel of the same name by Roland Dorgelès, into a Hollywood film, a project initially titled "Wooden Crosses." The studio decided to remake the film and to include some of the battle footage from the original in the new version (Gleeson-White, "Road to Glory" 44). The 1932 film, directed by Raymond Bernard, was dominated by interactions between the soldiers, who were played by French veterans, so we should consider the masculinized heroine of the Hollywood adaptation to be an invention of the collaborators on the later project. Faulkner was brought on board in December 1935 to produce the first screenplay along with fellow screenwriter Joel Sayre. Their work was set against the backdrop of European turmoil and the threat of war, since by the mid-1930s Hitler was already in power and increasing his nation's military capacities.

One has to bear in mind that the first screenplay of "The Road to Glory" is a collaborative work. As such, assigning sole authorship of a given scene to Faulkner is difficult. One could, therefore, argue that decisions regarding matters of characterization were not entirely Faulkner's own. However, as argued in the introduction, I believe we should challenge critical attachment to the myth of individual authorship, by considering how both Faulkner's screenwriting *and* fiction arose from collaborative processes of creation. Additionally, although Faulkner may have penned certain characters according to the requirements of the Hollywood projects in which he was involved, the presence of equivalent types in his fiction suggests that we should consider them to be part of his wider oeuvre. The writing on "The Road to Glory," while produced by two screenwriters, can nevertheless be placed in close dialogue with Faulkner's fiction from the same period, particularly *Pylon*.

As Sarah Gleeson-White describes, Faulkner and Sayre co-authored three virtually indistinguishable drafts of the screenplay dated between 31 December 1935 and 27 January 1936 ("Road to Glory" 46). I cite from both the 31 December first temporary version, published by Southern Illinois University Press in 1981, and the second 24 January "final" version, which contains a number of revisions and retakes made up until April 1936 and which Gleeson-White attributes to Faulkner ("Road to Glory" 46), published by Oxford University Press in 2017. These versions merit contrasting, among other aspects, for their divergent treatment of the project's central love triangle; Darryl F. Zanuck, producer at Fox, was unhappy with the depiction of this element in Faulkner and Sayre's 31 December screenplay, complaining that "we simply have two lovers . . . that happen casually to fall in love with the same girl" (Gleeson-White, "Road to Glory" 48). In reaction to such criticism, the later screenplay further develops this dynamic.

In the 31 December screenplay, Monique is presented as torn between suitors: the older, honorable, yet staid Captain Paul Marache, to whom she has promised herself, and the passionate and impulsive Lieutenant Delaage, to whom she feels a more intense physical attraction. The tension is resolved by Paul's blindness as a result of war. Paul sacrifices himself on the battlefield to avoid confronting the loss of his love. The screenplay repeatedly emphasizes female labor in a male-dominated environment, since Monique has an active role on the war front as a nurse. The screenplay is at pains to show us her physical work:

> 228. CLOSE SHOT MONIQUE
>
> *on her knees. She is dressed in the fatigue uniform of a probationary nurse. She dips a scrubbing brush into a pail of water and scours the floor. She wields her brush energetically for a few moments, then*

> stops to brush the hair out of her eyes with her wrist. She sits back and listens to the strains of "Ave Maria" which are heard on the sound track. She looks about her carefully, then rises to her feet, wiping her hands on her apron. (Sayre and Faulkner 138)

The description recalls Laverne's intense labor on the fliers' airplane as the only woman on the repair lot, with Monique instead getting her hands dirty working as a nurse on the war front. Monique also dons men's clothes to infiltrate deeper into the conflict when she cross-dresses as an orderly in order to learn more of the fate of the men with whom she is romantically involved at the front (Sayre and Faulkner 141). The ability of Monique to cross gender through masculinized dress and engage in intensive physical labor alongside the "hero" is a central early hallmark of the Hawksian woman.

The 24 January final screenplay further develops the love triangle feature by showing how Monique manages her position in relation to the two men by insisting on her professional independence and playfully calling attention to the artificiality of Delaage's romantic advances. When Delaage protects Monique from a nearby explosion, he speaks of the dangers he can shelter her from as a "veteran" (*TCF* 66) who has spent two years at the front. Monique challenges his hyperbolic assertion that the sky is "full of death" by pointing out that "when the rain comes, the planes go away" (*TCF* 66). After Delaage admits the failure of his strategy to seduce Monique on the basis of experiences of war, she evaluates that "perhaps it's because—I'm a veteran too!" (*TCF* 66). Delaage later challenges that Monique is "much too young and sweet to be such a veteran," to which she offers the retort that she's "very busy . . . for the duration of the war" (*TCF* 107). In such instances, Monique forces Delaage to abandon a cliched romantic script that emphasizes female vulnerability by insisting on the value and extent of her *own* labor at the front. Indeed, Monique repeatedly calls attention to the staging of Delaage's attempted seductions. Delaage suggests that the constant threat of death should invite them to seize the moment—"A bomb or a shell may get me tomorrow. And you, too"—but Monique checks such contrived excesses, countering, "*(politely, after a pause)* That was very dramatic" (*TCF* 67). This response typifies Monique's playful sparring with Delaage.

Monique is not framed solely within this competitive dynamic. Faulkner and Sayre also recognize that through identification with the perspective of the noncombatant, she is essential to the audience's emotional engagement with the dangers of war. In a technically interesting scene from Faulkner and Sayre's first screenplay, the writers recognize how the visual enlargement of the female image can be used to generate mass affect:

> 262. ATMOSPHERIC SHOT
>
> *Monique's face, agonized by her experience in the hospital, fills the screen. Superimposed are the faces of the wounded and dying, the endless lines of stretchers, the faces of officers bawling orders, the priest uttering prayers of absolution, a surgeon's gloved hand holding a scalpel, etc. On the sound track are heard the booming of the guns, the clang of ambulance bells, the groans of the wounded, and the cries of "Nurse . . . nurse . . . nurse!"* (148)

The disturbing layering of images and sounds before the fade-out recalls some of the innovative techniques of visual and aural double exposure Faulkner used in his treatment for "Sutter's Gold," written in July 1934, in which he experimented with "the nonsynchronous relation of sound and image" (Gleeson-White, "Auditory Exposures" 97), having been influenced by the work of the Soviet filmmaker Sergei Eisenstein. Faulkner wrote this treatment for Hawks at Universal based on Blaise Cendrars's 1926 novel of the same name, having carefully read a previous scenario penned by Eisenstein at Paramount in 1930 (Gleeson-White, "Auditory Exposures" 88).[14] Faulkner incorporated harsh cuts into his treatment that recall the jarring effects of Eisensteinian montage. Returning to this technique in "The Road to Glory," in the Faulkner and Sayre screenplay the female face occupies the whole screen, and the images that are "superimposed" across Monique's face convey her psychology and the overwhelming competition of demands she withstands. The arresting visual potency of this close-up derives from the anti-realist suspended psychological time it inhabits. The screen-wide presentation of Monique's face demands the audience's empathetic engagement with the horrors of war as they imprint themselves on the individual psyche.

It is interesting for a modernist writer such as Faulkner, whose fiction was so concerned with using innovative techniques to represent consciousness, to have found a way of rendering psychic turmoil visually in the screenplay form, perhaps building on what he had learned from Eisenstein's scenario for "Sutter's Gold." Béla Balázs argues that silent cinema's images of the human body gave rise to a reassertion of embodied interiority in popular cultural experience. He asserts that "the whole of mankind is now busy relearning the long-forgotten language of gestures and facial expressions... the visual corollary of human souls immediately made flesh" ("Visible Man" 96). The language of cinema makes the abstract mind visible. The face of the actor, most powerfully in the close-up, communicates character and narrative development through a visual language that is rich, polyphonic, individualized, and unregulated; indeed, during the close-up, the face *becomes* the drama. Balázs goes as far to say that the lyricism of the actor's facial expressions is "incomparably richer and fuller of nuance than literary works of whatever kind" ("Visible Man" 99), due to the fact that these expressions are much more numerous than words. In this scene from "The Road to Glory," Faulkner too explores the rich language of visible interiority, which also signals a loss of authorial control, as the close-up's language is expressed through the unique facial communication of the actor. In terms of the wider evolution of cinematic gender archetypes, "The Road to Glory" precedes the Hawksian woman's cinematic apotheosis around World War II, but it offers an important stage in the figure's development in the mid-1930s, born out of dialogue between Hawks, Faulkner, and Sayre.

Faulkner further developed the figure of the wartime masculinized heroine at the center of a love triangle in his screenplay for "Splinter Fleet," written with Kathryn Scola in late 1936 and directed by John Ford. Scola was a prolific screenwriter during the 1930s who, in a parallel with Faulkner, also had previous experience working on pre-Code vice material that pedaled in violence and sex, as she co-wrote screenplays with Gene Markey featuring controversial female leads for the films *Baby Face* and *Female* (both 1933) at Warner Brothers and *Midnight Mary* (1933) at MGM. She was also a favorite of Zanuck and worked with him extensively at Warners; Zanuck respected her work, and when he left Warner Brothers to found Fox, Scola followed him and remained at the new studio for most of her career (Nelmes and Selbo 837).

The film on which Faulkner and Scola were to collaborate was an adaptation of Ray Millholland's World War I memoir, *The Splinter Fleet of the Otranto Barrage* (1936), which gives, as described by Gleeson-White, "an account of his experiences as an engineer officer on a submarine chaser in World War One" ("Splinter Fleet" 379). The figure of a masculinized heroine at the center of a romance is entirely absent from Millholland's memoir, which is, as Gleeson-White summarizes, "more or less limited to battle and technical detail . . . ; there is little characterization and next to no narrative arc" ("Splinter Fleet" 379). The memoir focuses on the activities of the Splinter fleet, which formed part of an Allied barrier across the Adriatic to defend the shipping routes of the Mediterranean against Austrian and German submarines (Millholland 109–10). As Millholland elaborates, the fleet of "United States Submarine Chasers were the first vessels on the Otranto Barrage which were specifically designed and equipped for just such work. . . . The chasers were large enough to perform their work against submarines only, our three-inch popgun being no match for the heavier guns of the enemy destroyers" (110–11). Using this historical backdrop, Faulkner produced two versions of the screenplay with Scola: a first draft dated 7 December 1936 and a first draft continuity-dated 22 December 1936. Zanuck divided up the work on the property systematically, making Scola responsible for the story line and Faulkner for the dialogue (Gleeson-White, "Splinter Fleet" 376), building on a story outline produced by Karl Tunberg on 4 September 1936, which was structured around the love triangle and the efforts of the splinter-boat sailors (Gleeson-White, "Splinter Fleet" 377–79). It was, therefore, on Tunberg's depiction of the love triangle that Faulkner and Scola built their screenplay rather than Millholland's memoir.

The character Susan, the love interest of two chief petty officer sailors, Fender and Perry, exhibits many of the key hallmarks of the Hawksian woman but was written for a John Ford film, challenging the idea that the archetype only appears within the films of a single director. To introduce her in the screenplay, Faulkner and Scola describe Susan as "attractive, independent, self-contained. (Suggestion—Jean Arthur) She knows the answers for all such as Fender. He is a wise, tough chief gunner. (Suggestion—Spencer Tracy)" (*TCF* 393). Susan demonstrates the self-sufficiency and verbal sparring of the Hawksian woman, and the casting suggestion of Jean Arthur further contributes to the distinctiveness of the archetype, since Arthur would star in the first of Hawks's films credited with a more complex exploration of gender relations, *Only Angels Have Wings*.

Susan's language expresses her strength and independence through her wit and playfulness, and indeed it was Faulkner who was primarily responsible for ensuring the success of the dialogue. Similar to Monique, she does not expect the hero to conform to a romantic script; when Fender jokes that he would "even marry" her, she ironically responds, "Guns Fender condescending to *marry*? I can't believe it" (*TCF* 395). The retort highlights the consistent function of the wisecrack when deployed by women in Faulkner's Hollywood fictions of the 1930s: it subtly undermines masculine authority, ironizes any notion of female passivity, and challenges traditional romantic roles. For example, when Susan sees the "small and unimpressive" (*TCF* 397) submarine chaser Fender will be sailing in, she exclaims in amusement, "Chief Petty Officer Fender—the great Guns Fender—to the Splinter Fleet" (*TCF* 398), gently emasculating him. So too when her rival suitor Perry drives past in a taxi and splashes her with mud, she takes control of the situation by calling attention to his position through humor, expressing "caustically," "I suppose if you'd been an admiral you'd have run *over* me!" (*TCF* 399). Perry makes a chivalrous gesture of trying to wipe away the stain on her skirt, but she rapidly responds, "No, thanks. Not with that four dollar handkerchief!" (*TCF* 400). In keeping with the mutual gender crossings of Hawks's films, these exchanges highlight Perry's femininity as much as they emphasize Susan's masculinity.

In moments such as these, Susan's language is the primary tool through which Faulkner and Scola call attention to gendered hierarchies and explore the possibility of their disruption within the screenplay. Additionally, her rapid-fire wisecracks expose and challenge the class dynamics within the love triangle. Both Susan and Fender are from precarious, working-class backgrounds, while Perry comes from wealth, Fender labeling him a "cream-puff" (*TCF* 428). Susan refers to Perry's trips to the dock to see her as examples of "slumming" (*TCF* 422),[35] and she ironically contrasts Fender's rough manners with Perry's chivalry (*TCF* 425). While conscious of her different class background, she emphasizes Perry's privileged class position in order to assert the value and necessity of her labor. Susan lives on a docked tramp steamer called "The Nancy Jones" with her father, Captain Leeds, where she has lived since her mother died when she was three years old. Susan informs Perry that they are sailing into the war zone in Italy with cargo the next day; they are selling guns and munitions to the army and have already made several trips. Recalling the attitude of the reporter towards Laverne in *Pylon*, Perry registers the audience's shock, viewing Susan as an interloper into a dangerous masculine territory of action: "So you actually serve under fire!" (*TCF* 433). However, Susan is at pains to highlight that this is not a gender transgression but a natural manifestation of her work ethic: "I belong to the—common people. I don't know what Park Avenue thinks about slacking" (*TCF* 433). Such verbal countering occurs again when Perry and Susan later meet in the war zone of Corfu; Perry tries to comment on the incongruity of a woman working in such a dangerous environment, arguing that the military "don't need you to fetch and carry for them," to which she responds in simple economic terms: "That's our business. Corfu's the base for the Allies" (*TCF* 466).

Such features—the socially critical wisecrack and the apparent gender transgressions of productive collaborative labor—clearly point to an incipient portrayal of the Hawksian woman. Nevertheless, some aspects of the screenplay suggest that we should still see Susan as a stage in the process of the archetype's development rather than its complete crystallization. For example, Perry tries to engage in traditional courtship of Susan, to which she responds with tears: "I know I must look silly—but nobody ever gave me flowers before" (*TCF* 468). Susan has previously resigned herself to men like Fender who could not engage with her in such a conventional manner, more interested in play than chivalry, but her reaction suggests she has merely repressed her desires for scripted romantic gestures rather than ridding herself of them. Additionally, when Susan smuggles herself onto the ship heading for the Second Battle of Durazzo to ensure the welfare of Perry and Fender, she does not actively participate in "manning" the engine room, although presumably she has the skills from her work with her father, as the directions indicate that "Susan is sitting on a stool, crouched against the wall, watching Perry. He pays no attention to her—works grimly at the engines" (*TCF* 495). The film does, however, conclude with the suggestion of a balanced Hawksian relationship between Susan and Perry in its resolution of the romance plot through compromise and sacrifice; Perry forgoes a more senior role in the military to stay with Susan and remain a seaman at the warrant officer grade. The development of a relationship between equals through the pooling of knowledge and the achievement of mutual understanding in fact reflects Faulkner's own romantic experiences in Hollywood.

Faulkner and Meta Carpenter, "Sweetheart and Pal All in One"

A key figure who may have influenced Faulkner's portrayal of nascent Hawksian women during his time at Fox was Hawks's script supervisor, Meta Carpenter Wilde. Faulkner worked with Carpenter (her surname during their courtship) on *The Road to Glory*, as well as *Banjo on My Knee* (1936) and *The Last Slaver* (1937) for Fox, and *The Left Hand of God* (1955) for Winchester Pictures and RKO (Gleeson-White, "Road to Glory" 45), and it was during their time at Fox that they began a long affair. In 1930s Hollywood, Carpenter would have been dubbed a "script girl" (indeed she herself uses this label in her memoir), a term that evolved into the gender neutral "script supervisor" by the 1950s due to more men taking up the position and out of recognition of the heavy demands and complex function of the role, an acknowledgment not contained in the original diminutive title. As a script supervisor, Carpenter ensured the film's continuity and would document the production unit's progress in filming the screenplay.

In her memoir, which describes her relationship with Faulkner, Carpenter made the following comment on the potential inspiration for the "archetypal Hawks heroine":

> Jean Arthur [the star of Hawks's film *Only Angels Have Wings* and Faulkner's casting suggestion for Susan in "Splinter Fleet"] in all her variations, incapable of guile or artifice where her man was concerned, straight-shooting, accommodating, undemanding, sweetheart and pal all in one. Clearly, Howard Hawks knew far more about his blonde secretary and her relationship with William Faulkner than I had deduced from his uninquisitive manner and masklike face. I make no pretense to having served as the model for the classic Hawks heroine, comfort and joy of the noble, stalwart Hawks hero. The coincidence of timing and likeness, however, cannot be entirely ignored. (*ALG* 108)

What should we make of this coincidence? It seems unlikely that Carpenter would have been Hawks's first encounter with a "straight-shooting, accommodating, undemanding" woman in Hollywood. Certainly, the director would have been familiar with the practical reality of screenwriters hundreds of miles from home and family, as was the case for Faulkner, taking a lover in Hollywood. However, Faulkner's affair with Carpenter may have had a different effect on him. As an intermittent laborer in Hollywood, rather than a successful insider as Hawks was, Carpenter as script supervisor may have represented to Faulkner a more modern, professionalized idea of womanhood that he was able to carry over into his screenplays.

Faulkner had of course already begun to accommodate this new feminine ideal within his writing through his depiction of Laverne in *Pylon*, yet his contact with Carpenter may have informed, or been the catalyst for, his further development of the figure in "The Road to Glory" and "Splinter Fleet" during a period in which they were collaborating. As Matthews argues, Carpenter may have embodied Faulkner's image of the film community: "Meta *was* Faulkner's Hollywood—young, seductive, modern, emancipated, and even Southern" (*Seeing* 75). Despite this "metaphor," as Matthews describes, Carpenter was not such an easy fit for New Womanhood from the beginning of her affair with Faulkner; in accordance with her background, she subscribed to the notion of the sanctity of Southern womanhood—despite being a young divorcée—and resisted the sexual excesses of Tinseltown: "William Faulkner, away from his wife, out of sight of the all-knowing burghers of Oxford, intended to have a holiday, not enforced monogamy. . . . But I was not yet ready to become involved with another woman's husband. What I had seen of married men on the prowl collided with a Southern puritanism that I wore like a fender" (*ALG* 22). Carpenter's account of their affair in the memoir, which was kept up periodically until well into the 1940s, charts her process of shedding the Victorian morality of traditional Southern womanhood and adopting a more modern attitude towards sex. In her narrative, she casts Faulkner as a Hawksian hero, noble and stalwart, in her definition "restrained" and "remote" (*ALG* 62). But this role also conflicts with his posturing as a Southern gentleman, at least in her depiction; Faulkner idealizes Carpenter, writing her overwrought poetry and covering their bed in blossoms. Carpenter feels caught between two modes of seduction, associated with the romance and decadence of literature and Hawksian films respectively. She elaborates that "if Script Girl found it extravagant, straight out of the Swinburnes and Lord Byrons to whom he had introduced her, an excess of sentiment that would have made Howard Hawks groan, Finishing-School Graduate, who had not yet relinquished her hold on me, saw it as a declaration of elegiac love" (*ALG* 79).

What potentially modifies Faulkner's sentimental romantic ideal of Carpenter—as presented in her memoir—is their professional collaboration. In this role, she acted as an intermediary between the screenwriter and the director to ensure smooth progression in the ongoing cutting and editing process. This was a full-time job, rather than the more project-by-project role of the studio screenwriter, which was labor-intensive and required considerable flexibility and diplomacy. Working for Warner Brothers in the early 1940s, Carpenter found that after John Huston commended her as a script supervisor on *The Maltese Falcon*, her reputation became such that directors began to specifically ask for her to work on their films. She recalls that at Warner Brothers "a picture would 'wrap' on Friday and on Saturday [she] would be given the screenplay of a new film beginning the following Monday" (*ALG* 264). This workload took its toll, as Carpenter wrote in a letter to Faulkner in Mississippi around this time that she'd "become a workhorse" and needed him "to rub the harness sores away" (*ALG* 264).

Though she also worked as Hawks's secretary, typing out the writers' screenplays as they were dictated to her, she first acted as script supervisor on Hawks's film *Barbary Coast* (1935), in addition to her secretarial duties. As part of these responsibilities on *The Road to Glory*, Carpenter had to manage Faulkner's writing progress, monitoring inconsistencies in his screenplays. She also had access to knowledge that remained opaque to Faulkner. In two important examples, Carpenter had more in-depth awareness of the technology of film production and the star system, as her work required more close contact with on-set film production. Thus, in editing Faulkner's scripts, Carpenter had a much more practical visual sense of what could be achieved technologically on-set and how his writing would have to fit with the manufactured personas of the studio's roster of stars. Carpenter was essentially educating Faulkner in the nature of collaboration within a corporate structure. As Jerome Christensen argues, neither an auteurist model, which valorizes an individual's contribution, such as a director or screenwriter, nor a materialist or collectivist model, which views a "set of industrial conditions or group as the functional equivalent of the individual author" (13), provide an adequate account of the authorship of studio films. Instead, it is more helpful to think of the corporate studio itself as an author that works to achieve its objectives through the operation of different forms of power (Christensen 18–19). Carpenter understood that Faulkner's work had to align with the aims of the Fox studio as a corporate "intending author" (Christensen 13).

Such close collaboration with men turned Carpenter into something of a masculinized heroine akin to the figures in Hawks's films. Carpenter describes the gender-crossing behavior she had to assume in order to survive in Hollywood, asserting that "a woman who works behind the camera, even today, must have a strong personal life to counteract the mutative process that occurs when she is thrown with a company of men. . . . It is not that these lonely women take on the masculine grain but that their womanliness is chipped away in the daily give-and-take with male co-workers whose hostility pours from them like sweat. Her voice unconsciously deepens. Her stride bespeaks efficiency and resolution. Outwardly, she becomes androgynous" (*ALG* 313). Faulkner's sense of being feminized by his work in Hollywood—he called his fellow screenwriters "whores" (*ALG* 185)—is reflected in his script supervisor lover's need to masculinize herself as defense against a hostile work environment. While there is an absence of the "noble and stalwart" Hawksian hero in the ranks of male employees of the studio system as Carpenter sees it, a screenwriter and director such as Faulkner and Hawks may have drawn on the image of these tough, decisive, androgynous female collaborators in shaping the heroines of the films on which they worked.

From Faulkner's perspective, it is arguable that this was his closest and most sustained encounter with a financially independent and professionally ambitious woman within a workplace. Some of Carpenter's influence bled into Faulkner's depiction of Monique in the film on which they worked alongside each other at Fox. We see Monique as a nurse at the front among men in the thick of the action, much as Carpenter was in the context of the collaborative labor of the studio writers' offices (or "The Ward" to insiders). Carpenter's love of music as an amateur pianist is also reflected in Monique's passion for the instrument. Monique listens "with a rapt expression and softened eyes" (*TCF* 108) to the music the talented Delaage is able to play, a tool of his seduction. An interest in music is one Faulkner professed not to share with Carpenter, but he recognized, and perhaps envied, the hypnotic power it had over his lover; he told her at one point as she listened to a record, "You are a sight to behold, my beauty. Those hands flailing in the air, that maniacal look on your face" (*ALG* 138).

While I think that the behavioral aspects of the Hawksian heroine do not fully chime with Carpenter's character, at least as she portrays herself in the memoir, the emphasis on successful collaboration between men and women—in industries where the most senior roles were and continue to be dominated by men—and the unorthodox sexual arrangements prevalent in the Hollywood community do anticipate aspects of the figure. Building on *Pylon* and his encounter with Carpenter at Fox, Faulkner borrowed details from literature and life in his depiction of Monique for "The Road to Glory" and Susan for "Splinter Fleet." The productive and intimate collaboration Faulkner engaged in with Carpenter may well have shaped his presentation of modes of artistic exchange and shared labor in both his screenwriting and modernist fiction of the 1930s.

Sexual Competition in "To Have and Have Not"

Faulkner's screenwriting for *To Have and Have Not* under the direction of Hawks at Warner Brothers in 1944 develops his distinctive 1930s heroines still further and contributes to the creation of perhaps the most enduring screen image of the Hawksian woman: Lauren Bacall's portrayal of Marie "Slim" Browning.[16] Jackson's notion of the "sexuality" (33) of Faulkner's collaborative communities, in which men and women compete for artistic influence and mingle identities within a collective project, has particular relevance for *To Have and Have Not*. Across the projects Faulkner worked on in Hollywood, this film possesses a particular sexual charge derived from collaboration, as it was the first film in which Humphrey Bogart and Bacall starred as screen lovers—they famously fell in love during the making of the picture. Kawin asserts that *To Have and Have Not* is the produced film from Faulkner's Warner Brothers period that has "scene for scene and structure for structure, the most of Faulkner's actual writing in it" ("Film Career" 180). Consequently, in writing Bacall's role as Slim, Faulkner was instrumental in the construction of a filmic feminine archetype that he had been developing for over a decade across his fiction and screenplays and which had now reached its apotheosis.

In responding to the themes and ideas generated by a collaborative community, yet still mediating them through his own imagination, Faulkner was able to create a young, eroticized female figure who nevertheless displays "masculine" strength and resourcefulness and is more closely associated with action than passivity, which contrasts starkly with a secondary female character Faulkner wrote for the film. Marie is in fact more progressive than the equivalent presentations of Laverne in *Pylon* and Charlotte in "The Wild Palms," taking into consideration the ways in which these works conclude, as we will see.

Wood highlights how the differences between the more solitary labor of writing fiction and the more overtly collaborative processes central to filmmaking had an important bearing on the 1944 film adaptation of Hemingway's 1937 novel *To Have and Have Not*. In Hawks's adaptation of Hemingway's book, Wood sees the director as escaping the limiting "ideological determination" of a so-called "outspokenly anti-Establishment 'protest' work" (173). Such transcendence of the original material through collaboration has implications for gender representations in the film, which differ from the sexism inherent in Hemingway's novel. Wood argues that

Hemingway's "book's morbid preoccupation with impotence on the one hand and the fantasies of super-sexuality embodied in Harry Morgan on the other goes with our sense of Hemingway's isolation and clearly determines the presentation of Marie. . . . It is the Hawksian context, similarly, that makes possible the Marie of the film. . . . Hemingway's Marie has no meaning after Harry's death; Hawks's is a woman who will always be able to take care of herself, whatever happens to her man" (174). In the Hemingway novel, Harry is married to Marie, a middle-aged woman with whom he has two daughters. Marie is a thinly sketched character in Hemingway's text, who lacks the tough resourcefulness of the Hawksian woman. On a failed swindling mission, Harry speculates misogynistically on what will happen to Marie after his death: "She's too old to peddle her hips now" (Hemingway 121). Marie is rendered hollow by Harry's death and is unable to attend his funeral. Her ability to start a new life after him appears to be hampered by the limited view Harry had of her, since she believes that her age—"I'm big now and ugly and old and he ain't here to tell that I ain't" (Hemingway 179)—and her dependency—"he always made money some way and I never had to worry about money, only about him, and now that's all gone" (Hemingway 179)—render the future hopeless. Through adaptation, the collaborative network involved in film production can therefore transcend the ideological limitations of a literary work that promotes the idea of masculine isolation and female dependency. Again, as was also the case for "The Road to Glory" and "Splinter Fleet," the Hawksian woman can be most closely identified with the films of Hawks and the work of his diverse screenwriting collaborators, since she is absent from the source works for all these cinematic adaptations.

Faulkner's role on the film began when the author returned to California in February 1944 to write a version of "To Have and Have Not" for Hawks, where he worked until mid-May. He collaborated on the project with Jules Furthman, who had been producing screenplays since 1915 and was therefore an adaptable and valued screenwriter. Furthman had previously worked on *Come and Get It* (1936) and *Only Angels Have Wings* for Hawks. Apparently the project began when Hawks tried to persuade Hemingway to adapt one of his novels for the screen and challenged the author that he could make a film out of even his worst book, which Hawks judged to be *To Have and Have Not*. Hemingway thought the task impossible, even for himself; Hawks responded "OK, I'll get Faulkner to do it. He can write better than you can anyway" (Kawin, *Faulkner and Film* 109). Faulkner was brought in after Furthman had finished work in February 1944 on the first "final" draft of the screenplay. As Faulkner writes in a letter to his wife in March 1944, he did not think much of this version, stating that he was "working with Hawks, on a book of Hemingway's 'To Have and Have Not.' It was a poor book. A write [sic] named Furthman, $3000.00 per week, worked since last October on a script. It was no good. Hawks asked the studio for me as soon as I got here. We are now writing a new script from day to day as he shoots the picture. That's how I happened to be working directly with the actors."[17] As this letter intimates, Faulkner's work for Warner Brothers required significant improvisatory skills as he had to respond to highly changeable conditions: fluctuating budgets; creative clashes between writers, directors, actors, and studio bosses; and the restrictions of studio resources.

Kawin's comparison of Furthman's, Faulkner's, and Hawks's versions of the screenplay in his introduction to the published version leaves out a key period of development in the genetic evolution of the film's content. Kawin compares Furthman's final screenplay (completed February 1944) with the second revised final (last script changes completed 22 April 1944), of which Kawin believes Faulkner to be the sole author ("No Man Alone" 27, 32–33). The four revised screenplays and collections of revised and additional scenes I have studied in the Brodsky Collection at Southeast Missouri State University help to fill the developmental gap between these two screenplays and Hawks's final shooting script, as well as expanding our understanding of Faulkner's contribution to that development.[18] Faulkner's changes emerged largely in tandem with the nine-week-long shooting of the film from 6 March 1944 to 10 May 1944, which was a highly spontaneous and collaborative method of working. Bogart commented in an interview during his work on the film that Faulkner, Hawks, and himself were devising new scenes, dialogue, and gags as they went along on the set (Kawin, "No Man Alone" 33). Meta Carpenter also recalled that

> every morning Bill arrived at the studio and pounded out pages that would be filmed the following day for Bogey, Bacall, Hoagy Carmichael, Walter Brennan . . . and assorted villains. *To Have and Have Not* was almost pure Faulkner, superimposed on what was left of the Furthman script. There was simply no time for Hawks to ask his cast how they would say the lines or to call in a third writer. Bill worked slavishly, employing a remarkable discipline in order to stay ahead of Hawks and his cast. He liked hearing his words spoken as written. . . . *To Have and Have Not* succeeded mainly because of

Faulkner, the screenwriter who was thought by other inhabitants of The Ward to know little or nothing about the screenplay form. (*ALG* 299)

Carpenter's comments confirm that by this point in his film career, Faulkner was a screenwriter of considerable skill.

The film of *To Have and Have Not* is set in Vichy-controlled Martinique in the summer of 1940; the action centers on Harry Morgan, a jaded, cynical fishing-boat captain played by Humphrey Bogart, who is gradually persuaded to involve himself in a mission to smuggle French Resistance fighters onto the island. The striking element in the development of Faulkner's revisions for the film is the split portrayal of Marie and Helene that emerges, which dramatizes a tension between Faulkner's representational modes for women; his portrayal of Helene is indicative of the lure of a more stereotyped characterization—a "hysterical," fickle, and emotionally impressionable figure—whereas Marie, as the quintessential Hawksian woman who had been emerging in his writing throughout the 1930s, stands for the imaginative potential of the new feminine-masculine type. While both these women are inherited characters, the way Faulkner nurtures and develops them demonstrates the plasticity of his imagination.

Kawin argues that one could "organize the versions of the ['To Have and Have Not'] script in terms of the gradually larger and more daring roles they offer Marie" ("No Man Alone" 19). Faulkner's contribution was to fuse the Dietrich-like portrayal of Marie inherited from Furthman, who had worked on several films for Josef von Sternberg starring the German actress, with Hawks's and Bacall's on-set improvisations (Kawin, *Faulkner and Film* 111); as Hawks himself asserted, "Bacall is a warmer version of Dietrich" (Bogdanovich 60). In contrast to the expansion of Marie's role, by the time the character Helene reaches the screen via Hawks's version of the shooting script, "nearly all of Helene's serious lines and erratic behavior are cut out" (Kawin, "No Man Alone" 36). The shooting script lacks the love triangle element present in the series of revised scenes in which both Marie and Helene vie for Morgan's affection, as Faulkner ultimately decided to leave Marie as Morgan's only viable love interest. It is, however, in this competitive romantic structure, which Faulkner gradually dismisses across his work on the revised screenplays and additional scenes, that the oppositional clash of these two female archetypes is most apparent, providing us with an insight into Faulkner's divided representational craft.

Among the scenes Faulkner crafted alongside the on-set improvisations, Marie impresses as a figure who is able to assert her strength within a male-dominated world. Morgan and Marie cooperate to achieve certain functional ends, such as in an illuminating scene where they collaborate in an operation on a wounded Resistance fighter, as Marie administers ether and hot water to the patient.[19] This practical streak is in keeping with Hawksian heroines' close association with productive action as essential to their well-being. As Haskell observes, Hawksian heroines are "at ease with their bodies when their bodies are in motion, doing things" (*Reverence* 138). In this way, actions rather than words are the expressive mode in Hawks's films; in terms of romance, deeds supplant words as the vehicle of emotional exchange and, ultimately, seduction.[20] Consequently, Marie is able to come closer to Morgan through sharing physical work with him. As Wood argues in his assessment of the director's legacy, "Hawks is above all a *physical* director" and "the cinema is the perfect medium for expressing emotion or moral values through actions" (24).

Faulkner's writing for the film demonstrates how Marie is not rendered passive by her emotions but is rather able to channel them into deeds. In Faulkner's work on one scene, Morgan buys Marie a ticket to San Juan to escape the trouble that might befall them both after the rescue operation. She sustains her signature ironical repartee; mirrors the physical gestures of the hero, who takes the initial physical romantic initiative, drawing his head down to kiss him as he has stooped to kiss her; and only permits herself to reveal more intense emotions after he has left her. After Morgan walks away, Faulkner gives the direction: "He rumples her hair and starts out toward front. Marie looks after him, her eyes slowly filling with tears."[21] Faulkner depicts Marie here as consciously sidelining emotion from her interactions with Morgan. In Faulkner's work on "To Have and Have Not," Marie transmits the intensity of her feelings through both a controlled register and structured gestural engagement with the hero, rather than the content of her words. Verbal emotional outpourings are thus repressed and highly stylized exchanges favored. This suppression of emotion is a gender-crossing element of Marie's delineation. Marie resists being categorized as an impractical, overly sensitive figure by demonstrating putative "masculine" qualities in her actions—her cool-headedness, her keenness to "muck in," her pragmatism, and her resourcefulness, demonstrated in her assistance of Morgan in the operation scene. In behaving this way, Marie comes closer to Morgan, action bringing them gradually into a partnership structured around mutual respect.

Faulkner's work displays Marie's self-control and her free expression of identity within the masculine territory of action through her use of irony and sense of playfulness. A good example of this is when Morgan spontaneously attempts to seduce Helene after she has fainted observing the operation on her husband, Paul. Holding her passionately as she begins to stir, Morgan is interrupted by Marie in Faulkner's section of the treatment with the witty line: "What are you trying to do—guess her weight?"[22] One might expect Marie to react to Morgan's intimacy with a sexual rival as betrayal—instead she avoids the loss of power such a reaction would precipitate and deflects the potentially painful awareness of Morgan's desire for another woman through piercing irony. In this register, she is able to police Morgan's sexual instincts without him feeling constrained or emasculated, playfully reminding him of his duties to Helene's husband, lying unconscious next door. Morgan meets Marie on this verbal plane, as they engage in rapid-fire repartee expressive of sexual equality.

In another of Faulkner's scenes, Morgan threatens to turn Helene and Paul in to the authorities for a ransom. In the action that precedes the following excerpt, Helene tries to raise the money to save them, negotiating with the "hard, ruthless" Morgan by offering herself sexually to him, an idea which Morgan, only half-seriously, indulges.[23] Morgan insensitively asks Marie to select some clothes for Helene to groom her for the enactment of their agreement.

MORGAN'S ROOM
>... a knock comes ... It is Helene, dressed carefully in one of the new dresses.... He asks her what she wants.

HELENE
>Isn't that obvious? I had to come. You knew that. Don't pretend you didn't expect me. It won't be the first time I've bought Paul's freedom from the Gestapo.

She watches him a second, then walks toward him.

HELENE
>So you won't take my simple word. You must have a surety before Renard comes. Very well.

> *She lifts her arms to embrace him. He catches her wrists, stops her.*

MORGAN

Wait till I send in the bill, will you? What are you trying to do? Push me into turning you in just to get rid of you, before I have even made up my mind?

HELENE

Why should I trust your word that you won't turn us in, when I don't expect you to trust mine that I'll pay the bill?

MORGAN

I get it now. You are the one that wants the surety.

> *They stop, turn their heads toward the door, as feet SOUND beyond it. . . .*
> *Morgan turns quickly, drags her roughly to the bedroom, thrusts her in. When he releases her to take hold of the door, she stops and faces him, provocative and inviting.*

MORGAN

Oh, So [sic] you like to balance each page before you turn it, too—huh?[24]

In stark contrast to the verbal jousting with which Marie engages with Morgan, Faulkner writes Helene as consistently shrinking from shifting her register into Morgan's playful mode. Morgan speaks figuratively of a sexual metaphor of debt, while Helene engages literally in what they are about to do as a direct sexual transaction, surrendering herself dramatically to him, with recourse to her account of submitting herself to the Gestapo to save her husband. Although Helene expresses a form of love for Morgan, she will never be successful in persuading him to take her on as an equal in a positive union. Helene later asserts that she "can be hard, but only as women can be hard."[25] In moments like this, she marks herself as female, foregrounding her relative "weakness," and as such is unable to engage in the gender-crossing elements of the more progressive heroine's actions. In fact, in exploring this "type," Faulkner's characterization of Helene causes him to indulge some of his misogynistic tendencies. In a draft of the scene where Morgan collects Helene and Paul in his boat, Faulkner writes that "Morgan turns away. He pauses, sniffs, as if he had suddenly smelled something, turns his head from side to side, sniffing, raises the hand with which he had helped Helene into the boat, sniffs at it, smells the faint scent which she had left, ~~turns his head and spits over side~~. *dips hand in water to wash it off.*"[26] Both the strike-through and the addition, which I have italicized, are Furthman's changes to Faulkner's writing, suggesting that his cowriter was on hand to soften Morgan's misogynistic reactions to Helene's more traditionally feminine characterization.

As Faulkner's work across the screenplay revisions progresses, Helene is increasingly marginalized as a love interest for Morgan. Faulkner positions Marie, the Hawksian woman, as Morgan's predominant and most fitting romantic sparring partner. As such, Marie more confidently identifies herself as the masculinized heroine and mocks Helene's outmoded femininity: "What'll we do with her? I know. Maybe she can cook. Because I can't."[27] Faulkner also suggests that Morgan's ultimate disinterest in Helene may be linked to her conformity to stereotypically female modes of behavior, in contrast to his attitude to Marie. When Helene, in an agitated state, asks for emotional reassurance from Morgan that she can trust him, Faulkner indicates Morgan's actions and thoughts in the set directions: "He tries to calm her. He is annoyed. This is a fine time for her to pick, here at the last minute when he and everybody else is busy as hell, to go female on him."[28] In contrast to Helene's apparent weakness, Marie becomes yet more self-ironizing, triumphant in the face of obstacles to romance with Morgan, singing her signature song "How Little We Know" defiantly at Morgan when he seems to distance himself from her,[29] and her honor is emphasized, rather than her cynical exploitation of circumstances.

In one of Faulkner's new scenes for his work on the penultimate set of revised scenes, Marie refuses to escape from Martinique with Morgan using the money he has exploited from the Gaullists. Morgan's knowledge of Marie's resistance to corruption redeems him in turn: "you've gone pretty far for honor, and I just found out about somebody else I know that went pretty far for it. So maybe there's something in it, after all."[30] Finally comprehending Marie's honorable nature, Morgan returns to the island to be with her. Faulkner's writing then concludes on a note of mutual respect in a balanced heterosexual union that proves educative to both parties.

The project as a whole shows Faulkner's ability to inhabit the Hawksian style, adapting it to his own through his deployment of appropriate action and language, and to submit to the tempering influence of other writers. Kawin, however, supports auteurist readings of the film by arguing that *To Have and Have Not* "reveals the guiding influence and personal vision of a single artist, Howard Hawks" ("No Man Alone" 9). Yet, as I have argued, a female protagonist such as Marie is not entirely unique in the Faulknerian canon. Laverne from *Pylon,* Monique from "The Road to Glory," Susan from "Splinter Fleet," and Charlotte Rittenmeyer from *If I Forget Thee, Jerusalem* can be read as 1930s prototypes of the Hawksian heroine as she later appears in World War II–era cinema. All these figures from Faulkner's novels possess similar gender-crossing qualities to Marie while maintaining their professional independence and sublimating their sexuality into action and work. Most of these figures, that is, bear many if not all of the key androgynous marks of the Hawksian heroine, as they appear masculinized, creative, resourceful, independent, brave, and anti-maternal. Laverne and Charlotte crucially divert from the archetype in that their character delineation seems to shape their fate. Laverne's partner dies in a plane crash, and she is forced to give up her son into her husband's parents' care, while Charlotte dies after a botched abortion at the hands of her lover: Laverne loses her child and Charlotte her life. In building on these female figures with Hawks, Furthman, and the cast of the film, Faulkner is able to visualize a more positive outcome for such a character within his screenwriting, thus demonstrating how the networks of Hollywood had an ameliorative effect on Faulkner's vision of the tragic fate of certain gender portrayals.

In shaping Marie, Faulkner was able to revisit those women who prefigure the Hawksian woman in his own fiction from the 1930s. The adjustment of her narrative fate in his work on "To Have and Have Not" suggests that by 1944, through a process of revisualization and collective labor, he was able to provide a more positive representation for film of the sociosexual mores of his age. In such a model, we find Faulkner *benefiting* from Hollywood work, despite its more explicit market conditions, and from the need to inhabit different registers of expression within that community. In looking back at those previous figures in Faulkner's fiction and screenwriting that anticipate the portrayal of Marie in *To Have and Have Not*, it becomes apparent that the Hawksian woman was not spontaneously invented by the director but rather emerged out of an intimate dialogue between novelists, screenwriters, actors, and script supervisors that developed over more than a decade, a dialogue that Faulkner was instrumental in furthering.

3

If I Forget Thee, Jerusalem, Corporate Artists, and Hack Writers

RETURNING TO MISSISSIPPI AFTER working intermittently for Twentieth Century–Fox from December 1935 to August 1937, Faulkner would begin writing a new novel, which would eventually be published as *The Wild Palms [If I Forget Thee, Jerusalem]* in 1939.[1] The text is composed of two narratives, "The Wild Palms" and "Old Man," which alternate in counterpoint, creating a form of textual montage in which the themes of the dual sections contrast and complement one another. "The Wild Palms" sections focus on a doomed romance between Harry Wilbourne and Charlotte Rittenmeyer. The couple try to escape bourgeois constraints—Harry's professional medical career, Charlotte's husband and children—to enjoy a fugitive romance that is, in Charlotte's words, "all honeymoon" (*N* 3: 551). The couple move from New Orleans to Chicago, to a cabin in the Wisconsin woods, to a mining camp in Utah, on to Texas, back to New Orleans, and finally to the Gulf Coast. Faulkner professed that he composed these sections of the novel to process his affair with Meta Carpenter in Hollywood. Around the time he began work on "The Wild Palms," he was forced to confront the end of his relationship with Carpenter when he met her and her new husband, the pianist Wolfgang Rebner, in New York. Before meeting them, he had engaged in a destructive bout of drinking, struggling with the thought of seeing her "belonging to someone else" (Blotner, *Biography* 387). After this encounter, he would go on to rework "The Wild Palms" as a tragic love story, and he would quote the final lines of the narrative—"*Between grief and nothing I will take grief*" (*N* 3: 715)—repeatedly to Carpenter (Blotner, *Biography* 388, 509).

The novel was, then, partly inspired by one of Faulkner's most important personal and professional relationships in Hollywood. Building on this history, *Jerusalem* offers a commentary on the relationship between popular culture and high art, as well as the status of artistic practice under the pressures of the market. The two protagonists of "The Wild Palms" produce commercial art shaped by market demands to support themselves during their roving affair. Through the creative labors of Charlotte (a sculptor) and Harry (a pulp magazine writer), Faulkner presents a series of analogies to the screenwriting craft that acknowledge both the compromises and potential of the medium, as well as his ambivalence towards the instrumentalized working conditions of the Hollywood studio.

As described in the introduction, the novel's profound engagement with the circulation of popular culture has led a number of critics to label *Jerusalem*, usually with a focus on "The Wild Palms" portions, Faulkner's "Hollywood novel" of sorts, due to its meditation on the relationship between art, commerce, and wage labor (Grimwood 115; Godden and Knights 203; Zender, *Crossing* 43). The commodified art Charlotte and Harry produce is conceived of as proof of their "selling-out" within this dynamic, and the artistic and commercial realms in the novel are set up in conflict. However, the novel starkly contrasts the artistic engagements of Charlotte and Harry with the market. Indeed, claims that the market is synonymous with damaging processes of commodification and compromise in the novel have to be founded overwhelmingly on Harry's relationship to popular culture, since wage labor plays different roles in the lives of the novel's two principal characters. Charlotte's artistic engagements with the market are pragmatic and receptive, marked by a lack of anxiety and the preservation of an autonomous creative signature. As an independent but practically minded artist, Charlotte both submits to and subverts commercial expectations; she is neither totally absorbed by the market nor strictly oppositionally resistant to it. My close analyses of Charlotte's work therefore afford new insights into Faulkner's sense of the relationship between artistic practice and the mass market at this stage in his career, after having labored in Hollywood since 1932 for a series of studios. While "The Wild Palms" undoubtedly explores the difficult cohabitation of commerce and art, the novel also recognizes the affordances of popular media through a series of creative acts that appear analogous to aspects of screenwriting and Hollywood work.

In addition to the novel's exploration of commercial labor akin to Faulkner's work in Hollywood, *Jerusalem* also draws on conventions from his screenwriting. As discussed in the previous chapter, similar to Laverne Shumann in *Pylon*, Faulkner portrays Charlotte in the same vein as the masculinized heroines of his Fox screenplays, which he would further develop in his productive collaborations with Hawks into the 1940s. When we first encounter Charlotte in the novel, she is immediately associated with an assertive masculinity when she takes Harry by the wrist with "a grasp simple, ruthless and firm" (*N* 3: 520). Faulkner borrowed from his scripts in his penning of Charlotte's dialogue too; her "short brutal sentences like out of a primer" (*N* 3: 634) recall the clipped dialogue Faulkner had to write for Joan Crawford on *Today We Live* (Kawin, "Turn About" 104). Duvall labels the relationship between Harry and Charlotte one of a number of "counterhegemonic alliances" in Faulkner's 1930s fictions that serve to "invert the hierarchy of male dominance (the males are passive; the females, active)" (xiv) and argues that Faulkner's androgynous women, such as Charlotte, "desire roles not traditionally allowed them by their cultures" (Duvall xiv). Charlotte's challenging androgyny additionally provides another striking example of dialogue between Faulkner's screenplays and fiction, and it forms part of a pattern of repeated gender-crossing in the novel.

This blurring of binaries ties into the novel's wider interrogation of the relationship between modernism and popular culture—and by extension between experimental fiction and the Hollywood screenplay—as a gendered opposition. Andreas Huyssen shows how fears of the masses during the period of modernization and social upheaval from the late nineteenth to early twentieth centuries has also been expressed as male fear of women (52), and he asserts that masculine modernism insistently gendered mass culture as female in order to Other the threat it posed to their practice (47, 53). Huyssen summarizes that "the fear of the masses in this age of declining liberalism is always also a fear of woman, a fear of nature out of control, a fear of the unconscious, of sexuality, of the loss of identity and stable ego boundaries in the mass" (52). Implicit in Huyssen's description of this fear is the belief that it produces an exaggeration of the scale of the threat from women. This fear is sublimated into men's production of cultural images that fuse women and mass culture symbolically. Men express their dominance over these symbols to compensate for their sense of anxiety. It is a creative but "paranoid view of mass culture," within which "the modernist aesthetic itself... begins to look more like a reaction formation, rather than like the heroic feat steeled in the fires of the modern experience" (Huyssen 53). Faulkner interrogates the great divide of high and mass culture in *Jerusalem* by ironizing the cultural fears that sustain such an opposition through Harry's disproportionate anxiety in producing material for the mass market. As I will show, in "The Wild Palms" Faulkner uses the tensions and conflicts of Harry and Charlotte's affair to meditate on the interactions between modernism and mass culture through vexed gender relations. In a series of allusions to the screenwriting profession, Faulkner ironically juxtaposes Charlotte's anxiety-free industry on experimental sculptures for the market, an activity that is coded as masculine, with Harry's fearful labor on magazine confession stories, which the character associates with his own feminization. Faulkner thereby works to undercut the tired metaphorical approximation of women with "degraded" commercial art through a series of cultural and gender slippages.

In asserting the gendered significance of Charlotte's and Harry's diverging experiences in relation to artistic practice and the market, I build on Anne Goodwyn Jones's critique of the novel, in which she observes that in Charlotte, Faulkner explores a third position in terms of gender. Jones sees the author as negotiating the ambivalent ways in which women are simultaneously exalted and degraded in American culture, "to explore and contest the ontological certainty of the gender dichotomy itself" (143). She argues that Faulkner achieves this in *Jerusalem* by seeking "the sources of that dichotomy in the stories men tell out of their deepest fears" (143); in other words, paradoxical cultural representations of women are exposed as the product of male paranoia. She argues that, as a modernist, Faulkner subscribes to a dichotomy between high art and mass culture as good versus bad, which he then presents symbolically in his fiction as a clash between men and women. Jones sees Faulkner literalizing this divide most explicitly by coding popular culture as a "bad—that is, sexually promiscuous—woman" in his modernist fiction (144). For Jones, "Faulkner comes closest to exposing the dichotomy between the genders as an artifact of patriarchal culture," and the novel "locates the interests served by these dichotomies of gender and culture, and finds those interests to be a patriarchal oxymoron: masculine fears" (145–46).

Charlotte's divergence from established gender conventions in Faulkner's fictions and Harry's anxieties in relation to popular culture, however, need to be understood within a Hollywood matrix and placed in dialogue with Faulkner's screenwriting and modes of work within the studio system. Jones sees Charlotte as a unique figure in Faulkner's work who breaks down the cultural dichotomy as an "adult woman who is both actively and happily sexual and also appears to have intelligence, imagination, and a certain independence of spirit" and whom Faulkner treats "with a respect . . . that is absent from his treatments of other sexually active and assertive and intelligent women"; as such, he seems to have "broken through the conventions marking good from bad women on the basis of their sexual autonomy" (145). While Charlotte of course disrupts gender categories in Faulkner's work, in situating her artistic practices in relation to different aspects of screenwriting, as well as set design, I position her within a lineage of agents Faulkner encountered in Hollywood and wrote into his 1930s fiction and screenplays.

Specifically, we see Charlotte moving between creative commissions and across artistic registers in a role akin to a mobile studio laborer, designing a "stage" in the window of a department store to attract the eyes of consumers, and finally engaging in a politicized act of storyboarding.[2] Equally, I analyze Harry's panicked interactions with the mass market in relation to the particular anxieties of the male screenwriter in 1930s Hollywood, namely fears that "hack" writing destroys talent and emasculates male authors and that female actors and writers had come to dominate popular visual modes of communication in the studio's Golden Age. While Faulkner may have shared some of these professional fears, he nevertheless interrogates them in the novel through exaggeration.

These features of "The Wild Palms" stand in dialogic relation to the "Old Man" narrative. In both sections of the novel, Faulkner shows how the relationship of men to women within a popular cultural framework is undermined through failures of vision that are equated to the attachments, limits, and potential discomfort of filmic spectatorship, which Faulkner explores using conventions from the popular genres of melodrama, horror, and erotic cinema. In my analysis of Faulkner's own teleplay adaptation of "Old Man" from the early 1950s, I show how the author recast the 1939 story of sexual horror as a commercial romance. Those fear-inspiring images of women from the novel are shown to be subjectively produced, since, within the exteriorized visual medium of television, such presentations disappear from Faulkner's writing.

Charlotte's Corporate Art

In "The Wild Palms" sections of the novel, Faulkner places Charlotte and Harry's attitudes to art and the market in stark counterpoint. Charlotte's artistic practice most closely reflects that of the salaried screenwriter through her flexible ability to move between diverse projects and contracts according to market demands. From 1932 to 1936 alone, Faulkner worked for MGM, Universal, Fox, and RKO on a diversity of genre pictures. Charlotte's artistic style, similar to that of creative figures in the studio system, is both distinctive and inflected by the market. As Schatz describes, in the classical period of Hollywood there was "a melding of institutional forces" in which "the 'style' of a writer, director, star—or even a cinematographer, art director, or costume designer—fused with the studio's production operations and management structure, its resources and talent pool, its narrative traditions and market strategy" (*Genius* 6). At its most extreme, Hollywood films can be viewed as a form of "corporate art" that may obscure the contribution of individual artists; Christensen elaborates that "whether corporate art is represented by General Motors' commissioning of massive murals painted by Diego Rivera in the courtyard of the Detroit Institute of Arts in 1932 or Warners' hiring of Howard Hawks to direct *Scarface* the same year, the key to understanding that art is to plumb the strategic intention of General Motors and Warners, not Rivera or Hawks" (2). However, rather than Charlotte's sculptures undergoing thoroughgoing corporate standardization, her works become increasingly experimental through her market commissions. As we will see, it is a striking representation of instrumentalized modernist practice in Faulkner's work, in which art and the market are shown to productively interact in the hands of a female artist.

Although Charlotte's work is produced with commercial intentions, it is important to observe the way in which it develops and retains its particularity under market pressures. Charlotte's first collection of small sculptures is produced to dress the window of "a leading department store" (*N* 3: 554) in Chicago. Here she takes on a role equivalent to that of 1930s Hollywood set designers—who designed movie sets in order "to set trends, arbitrate public taste" (Esperdy 198)—arranging her figures within a restricted space to entice the eyes of consumers. She produces a series of realistic representations of natural figures, "deer and wolfhounds and horses and men and women, lean epicene sophisticated and bizarre, with a quality fantastic and perverse" (*N* 3: 554). Her later work maintains this signature style, for her future commercial projects exhibit the same "bizarre, fantastic and perverse" (*N* 3: 555) quality previously described in the prose.

Most strikingly, Charlotte's second group of figures for the department store, a batch of "historical figures about Chicago, this part of the West" (*N* 3: 554), have evolved from a realist mode of representation to modes of increasing abstraction, and it is the market that has provoked this artistic transition, not the autonomous will of the artist. Rather than this signaling her co-optation, she adapts the commissions she receives to reflect her own creative whims, maintaining an independence of vision that is distinctly modernist. Her experimentalism here also reflects the work of early Hollywood set designers. Gabrielle Esperdy explains that although each studio had a signature look—MGM was known for art deco and Warner Brothers for its urban realism (200)—set designers were instrumental in establishing these visual styles and were therefore "able to transcend at least some of the broader regulatory pressures of the studio system" (200). This meant that they had "a large measure of design freedom" (Esperdy 200) within which to experiment. Two principal factors lay behind these design innovations. First, motion picture set design was only emerging as distinct from stage set design in the 1930s, allowing the production of "unprecedented designs" making use of "new materials and technologies" (Esperdy 200). Second, the interwar period was a transitional phase in American architecture and design, "with tradition and modernity in conflict as never before" (Esperdy 200), meaning that Hollywood art directors "unfettered by high art agendas and canons of taste . . . created a free-wheeling eclecticism that borrowed liberally, and often simultaneously, from traditional and contemporary sources of architecture and design" (Esperdy 200). Charlotte's work exhibits an equivalent artistic freedom to experiment across cultural categories of taste within the bounds of corporate art. Her commissioned work—"an order for a hundred dollars" (*N* 3: 554) from the department store—stimulates her to consider a number of high/low figurative fusions that might satisfy her client's need for figures with a local character from "this part of the West" (*N* 3: 554) while remaining diffuse in their allusiveness. As such she dreams up "Mrs O'Leary with Nero's face and the cow with a ukulele, Kit Carson with legs like Nijinksy and no face, just two eyes and a shelf of forehead to shade them with" (*N* 3: 554). Her work here blends popular cultural, high art, and classical references in ways that are formally innovative and complex.

Charlotte's evolving aesthetics demonstrate her increasing embrace of design innovation. On Harry and Charlotte's arrival at a cabin by a lake in Wisconsin after leaving Chicago, Charlotte jumps out of the car and runs to the edge of the water, having seen a stag on the beach in the dawn light. The approach of the car scares the deer away, "its white scut arcing in long bounds," and Charlotte cries out, "That's what I was trying to make! . . . Not the animals, the dogs and deer and horses: the motion, the speed" (*N* 3: 562).³ The presence of the stag in the natural landscape causes her to recall her early realistic figures but to describe them as undeveloped, an incipient attempt to capture the abstract qualities of bodies in motion. Her comment also reflects Faulkner's own statement of the artist's purpose "to arrest motion, which is life, by artificial means and hold it fixed so that 100 years later when a stranger looks at it, it moves again since it is life" (*LG* 253). Both Charlotte and Faulkner seek to arrest the motion of life through artificially imposing formal stasis upon it so that the viewer or reader may reanimate the life of the work in the imagination. As Cynthia Dobbs comments, Faulkner considers this artistic goal to be "a particularly masculine aim. For Charlotte's longing to 'still life,' to arrest the flow of time, is enacted through her very rebellions against conventional notions of femininity" (827). Indicative of an artist growing in "vision," the figures that she makes display an artistic unity, being "component parts like the parts of a tableau or a puzzle, none more important than another" (*N* 3: 557). As part of a tableau, they are all mutually dependent, an organic whole; if they were merely commodities, to remove one as a consumable unit would not endanger the whole.

Faulkner additionally presents Charlotte's commercial creative practice at key points in the novel as a surrogate for his own. The state in which Charlotte continues to work is one of indefatigable industry, her "deft untiring hands" shaping her "effigies" (*N* 3: 555). Charlotte's tactile, energetic craftsmanship in making these figurines is close to what Faulkner views as the process involved in the creation of works of genuine aesthetic value, in which there is a direct relation between labor and aesthetic achievement. In an introduction to *The Sound and the Fury* (1929), Faulkner illustrates this correlation when he commented on the process of writing that early novel: "I can make myself a vase like that which the old Roman kept at his bedside and wore the rim slowly with kissing it. So I, who had never had a sister and was fated to lose my daughter in infancy, set out to make myself a beautiful and tragic little girl [Caddy of *The Sound and the Fury*]" (*ESPL* 299–300).

In Charlotte's own composition of "actual figures almost as large as small children" (*N* 3: 556), there is the sense that she is fashioning her own offspring to fill a parental lack: the children she has left behind to pursue her affair. Similar to Faulkner's desire to hoard his vase at his bedside, Charlotte too believes that her work should be protected from external influences in order to preserve its value, seeing the effigies "like something created to live only in the pitch airless dark, like in a bank vault or maybe a poison swamp, not in the rich normal nourishing air breathed off of guts full of vegetable" (*N* 3: 555–56). However, this never prompts Charlotte to divorce her work from the market.

After the orders from the department store end, McCord, a newspaper man and friend of Charlotte and Harry, enters into a new collaboration with her, in which "she was to make puppets, marionettes, and he to photograph them for magazine covers and advertisements" (*N* 3: 556). In a single period of intense creative activity, which is described as "dense and concentrated fury" (*N* 3: 556), the new marionettes reference Miguel de Cervantes (Don Quixote), William Shakespeare (Falstaff), and Edmond Rostand (Roxane and Cyrano de Bergerac). Her state of mind and the conditions under which she produces her work in fact mirror Faulkner's own composition of an early modernist novel. Where Faulkner allegedly "wrote *As I Lay Dying* in six weeks, without changing a word" (*ESPL* 177–78), Charlotte produces her figures "in one sustained rush of furious industry . . . a single interval interrupted only by eating and sleeping" (*N* 3: 557). What might the intention of Charlotte's exhaustive allusions be here? The common theme between all the figures is that they variously point to modes of emasculation: masculine delusion and impracticality (Quixote), masculine incompetence and cowardice (Falstaff), and the physical inadequacy of men to attain worthy women (Cyrano). Charlotte's playful work chooses to focus on compromised mock-heroic figures. For a female artist, who maintains her artistic integrity within the market, to produce such objects clearly sets up a gendered oppositional structure within cultural practice. While male agents may direct capital within the market, female creativity can subvert such a power dynamic by producing work that is critical of the structural hierarchy itself.

The requirements and expectations of the magazines and advertisers for which Charlotte produces this new work do not completely reshape her artistic output. Rather than the market dictating the content of her work, she gathers her environment into her practice. For example, her Falstaff is presented as disfigured by sexual activity, with "the worn face of a syphilitic barber" (*N* 3: 556), an allusion to Harry's first job in Chicago as a laboratory assistant in a charity hospital "making routine tests for syphilis" (*N* 3: 552). Indeed, James D. Bloom suggests that these figures reference different aspects of Harry and Charlotte's relationship through the carnal motivations of Falstaff, sexual competition over Roxanne, and the "'damned and doomed' idealism of Quixote" (86). Though it could be asserted that her miniaturization of protagonists of great literary works is a bastardization, a trivialization of the Western canon for sale, I see them differently. In a deft blending of "high" and "low" imagery, Charlotte moves across cultural categories in a wild combination of visual allusions in a practice similar to that employed by T. S. Eliot in *The Waste Land* (1922). Charlotte references great works of Spanish, English, and French literature in her work and produces a Falstaff that brings to mind the popular entertainment form of the bear fight, with "the man struggling with the mountain of entrails as the keeper might wrestle with the bear" (*N* 3: 556); a Roxane who looks "like the sheet music demonstrator in a ten cent store" (*N* 3: 557); and a vaudevillian Cyrano. Bloom comments that these figures "at once deform, deride, *and* reassuringly replicate and recall the mass-entertainment formulas that constituted Hollywood's precursors (sheet music, vaudeville)" (86). They succeed, therefore, in being simultaneously "popular and subversive, heterogeneous and canonic" (Bloom 86) in their relationship to mass culture. Consequently, Charlotte's high/low fusions do not indicate her selling-out but rather her skillful grasp of a wide range of seemingly incompatible influences.

Charlotte's art neither entirely undercuts nor completely succumbs to corporate values; while she follows economic imperatives and adapts to the demands of the market, she uses the opportunities she is given to produce work that surprises by insistently collapsing and realigning cultural distinctions. Furthermore, her parade of disempowered men expresses her transcendence over a number of modernist clichés associated with womanhood and the market. Goodwyn Jones, building on Huyssen's work in her analysis of *Jerusalem*, describes how "like 'man,' for instance, modernist 'art' is thought to be autonomous, while mass culture, like 'woman,' is contingent upon larger forces (such as market research and ultimately profit). Like 'man,' art transcends everydayness; like 'woman,' mass culture is embedded in it" (144). Feminine dependency is equivalent to mass culture's dependency on other imperatives, economic for example, which are at odds with the idealized autonomy of modernism. Charlotte's work, however, challenges notions of "feminine" market dependency and submission by creatively disempowering men within her distinct yet saleable modernist aesthetic.

Charlotte is confronted with commercial failure when the initial commission from the department store abruptly ends, but her reaction to this development again communicates her resistance against total market dependency, which masculinizes her in the eyes of the men around her. When her art objects exceed demand, she continues to work despite the loss of consumer interest; after the orders stop, she works "at night altogether now, since she was out with her samples, her completed figures all day" (*N* 3: 555). Rejection by the market is perhaps predetermined by Charlotte's motivations in creating in the first place, justifying that she expected the consumption of her work to reach "saturation point" since she made the figurines principally for "fun" (*N* 3: 555). The financial setback, when her figures for store windows no longer sell, grants Charlotte strength and stature, as "failure, reacting upon her like on a man" invests her "with a sort of dignified humility" (*N* 3: 558). This is similar to Bourdieu's notion of the "game of 'loser wins'" (Bourdieu 39) in which creative agents garner cultural capital through "a systematic inversion of the fundamental principles of all ordinary economies" (39); Charlotte's work is no longer aimed at consumers and seeks neither profit, power, nor institutionalized cultural authority (39). Charlotte is, at this point, ascribed the transcendence of autonomous modernism, even though her experimental aesthetic has ironically been cultivated within the market economy. Her work as a whole presents a new perspective on art in Faulkner's fiction; while the artist cannot fully resist the market's demands, they can nevertheless realize a form of aesthetic individualism within the bounds of the commission. Just as Charlotte moves from one commercial project to another while maintaining a distinctive artistic voice, so too Faulkner's screenplays could coexist in complex dialogue with his modernist fiction, despite the former's more overtly instrumentalized conditions.

Harry as Hack Writer

Charlotte's activity as a sculptor contrasts with Harry's forays into creative work. He pens confession stories for popular magazines, written from female perspectives, that he fears will reshape his life with Charlotte. Faulkner presents Harry as a similar figure to the Hollywood hack, the artistic sellouts that the author had called "whores" (*ALG* 185), perceiving them to have been feminized by their commercial labors for the studios. Harry considers himself in such negative terms as a hack writer who pens pop material that he consistently denigrates and tries to divorce himself from.[4] However, Faulkner exaggerates Harry's fears. If we consider the hyperbolic tone of Harry's sneering attitude to his work, it seems Faulkner seeks to create a self-critical distance between himself and Harry's obsessive fixation on the dangers of commercial work.

In readings of this character's distinctive register, the conventions of the novel, as filtered through Harry's perspective, have been studied according to the features of commercial genres such as melodrama and romance. Peter Lurie advances that the novel functions as a critique of the conventions and sentimentalizing narratives of cinematic and theatrical domestic melodrama by parodying the "classically melodramatic plot of misguided love" (131, 146), as part of which Harry casts Charlotte as a "wanton woman" in his imagination (147). Jones argues that Faulkner critiques the romance plot of the popular novel, in which she sees "The Wild Palms" as a "bad romance," a "bad" inflection of the genre, as it has a man as its main protagonist and filtering consciousness rather than a woman, and it features "physical torture, a weak hero, and a sad ending" (154). Jones genders the genre in the case of "The Wild Palms" as a "masculine popular romance plot, a plot written by men for men, a plot that derives specifically from male fears and that attempts to warn men away from the dangers it articulates" (156). Rather than pursuing an overarching genre-based reading of "The Wild Palms," I pay careful attention to those aspects of Harry's creativity that approximate the screenwriting profession, and I consider Harry himself to be a producer of diverse mass cultural genres, as Faulkner had been, rather than conforming to a specific generic type.

Where Charlotte's harmony with her artistic products is foregrounded, Harry is always in conflict with his work. Harry's creativity is disembodied and numb, what Faulkner names "the anesthesia of his monotonous inventing" (*N* 3: 578). Harry describes his writing process using an American football metaphor, another form of mass entertainment. He sees himself as a school halfback who "grasps the ball"; yet crucially it is not the "opposing team" or the arbitrary rules of the game that antagonize him, but the object of play itself, the ball, "his Albatross, his Old Man of the Sea . . . his sworn and mortal enemy" (*N* 3: 577). Harry's tools, which fashion his "moron's pap" (*N* 3: 578), seem to threaten him more than other agents in the cultural marketplace. Harry fetishizes the pen as the location of compromise, typical of the tone of an embittered 1930s Hollywood "hack" such as F. Scott Fitzgerald, who in "The Crack Up" lamented that he "had been only a mediocre caretaker of most of the things left in [his] hands, even of [his] talent" (71). Harry's metaphor foregrounds the impotence of the male writer as he misapprehends the strength of his artistic tools to rise up against him. Faulkner seems to mock Harry here, as the character's paranoia has led him to view his own writing in overblown terms as his "sworn and mortal enemy."

Harry is feminized by his mass cultural work, as his writing for popular magazines adopts female subject positions, crafting "stories beginning 'I had the body and desires of a woman yet in knowledge and experience of the world I was but a child' or 'If I had only a mother's love to guard me on that fatal day'" (*N* 3: 577). The close link between commodification and feminization is also explored in a work of fiction by Faulkner's fellow Hollywood modernist, Nathanael West. West's *Miss Lonelyhearts* (1933) is a tragicomic novella in which a vice columnist answers anguished letters, principally about sexual issues. This role inspires increasingly grandiloquent language and messianic ideas in the writer. The opening line reads: "The Miss Lonelyhearts of The New York *Post-Dispatch* (Are-you-in-trouble?—Do-you-need-advice?—Write-to-Miss-Lonelyhearts-and-she-will-help-you) sat at his desk and stared at a piece of white cardboard" (5). Though more darkly comic in tone than *Jerusalem*, the striking gender slippages in this passage communicate the gendered anxieties that accompany men composing populist fare to alleviate feminine troubles. In their focus on naive virgins and fallen women, Harry's own tales recall the female archetypes of Faulkner's early 1930s Hollywood writing: Temple Drake of *Sanctuary* and the protagonists of his early treatments for MGM within the vice tradition. We find Harry in a similar position to Faulkner in Hollywood, trading on the allure of transgressive female sexuality for a popular audience, as Harry produces "his latest primer-bald moronic fable, his sexual gumdrop" (*N* 3: 578). However, Faulkner does not invite us to share Harry's sexual shame in writing these texts but to view the writer's fears as disproportionate, particularly in contrast with Charlotte's creative labors in the market.

A scene in the department store offers an interesting contrast between gendered modes of participation in the cultural marketplace. Harry's nightmarish vision of the consumer industry and Charlotte's workplace transforms it into a "synthetic marble cavern" populated by "satin-clad robot-like saleswomen" and "jointless figures with suave organless bodies" (*N* 3: 576–77). This is not, however, a view shared by his lover, since Harry's fear of the store is juxtaposed with Charlotte's uncomplicated immersion in its processes of exchange as she is seen to "vanish" (*N* 3: 577) into its crowds. Harry observes Charlotte and qualifies that she does "not disappear: he would see her from time to time, consulting in pantomime with someone over some object which one of them held, or entering or leaving a window" (*N* 3: 577). In contrast to Harry's fearful state of removal, Charlotte moves fluidly around the store engaging in the exchange of commodities and interacting physically with the space for her new creative commission. As Dobbs observes, "Charlotte is less troubled and more fluid in her movement between a romantic ideal of living beyond and above social and economic concerns and an engagement with that very social world" (828).

In these differing poses or stances, Harry and Charlotte seem to offer a dual commentary on the flâneur figure, as explored in Walter Benjamin's *The Arcades Project*. This mammoth book, through a collage of primary sources and authorial commentary, documents how the bourgeoisie of nineteenth-century Paris would promenade through the crowds that congregated in the city's arcades, its covered avenues that were also commercial spaces. Benjamin explores the dangers the flâneur experiences in this activity as "within the labyrinth of the city, the masses are the newest and most inscrutable labyrinth. Through them, previously unknown chthonic traits are imprinted on the image of the city" (*Arcades* 446). This certainly chimes with Harry's underworld image of the "charwomen" in the department store, who to him seem to have "crawled molelike from some tunnel or orifice leading from the foundations of the earth itself" (*N* 3: 577). Harry's detachment from the activity of the department store, sitting for two to three hours reading an evening paper (*N* 3: 577), is a form of flâneur-like resistance, since, for Benjamin, "the idleness of the flâneur is a demonstration against the division of labor" (*Arcades* 427), labor in which Charlotte is engaged within the "arcades" of the department store. Charlotte seems to subscribe to a different vision of the broadening effects of the metropolis, shopping, and the crowd as she immerses herself in its shapes and activities. For Benjamin, "empathy with the commodity is fundamentally empathy with exchange value itself. The flâneur is the virtuoso of this empathy. He takes the concept of marketability itself for a stroll. Just as his final ambit is the department store, his last incarnation is the sandwich-man" (*Arcades* 448). Charlotte's easy movements through the crowds of the department store demonstrate her empathetic engagement with the marketplace within the commercial metropolis, while she also resists her total commodification, embodied, for Benjamin, in the figure of the "sandwich-man." Dobbs argues that through such feminine mobility in the novel, "Faulkner explores his culture's fears of radical fluidity in ways that connect women's bodies (as powerful sites of origin, seduction, and contamination) to both a radically feminized landscape and a dangerously volatile free-market economy" (811–12). However, Harry's panicked equation of Charlotte with capitalism is relativized through her anxiety-free dealings and movements within its structures. While Harry appears representative of the flâneur's withdrawal from the dangers of the city, Charlotte suggests that same activity's potential for a new, exhilarating expansion of the self.

Significantly, Harry's fear of being devoured by the crowd at the department store is explicitly expressed as a fear of women, when he observes the charwomen appearing from an "orifice" of unquantifiable depth. In his paranoiac imaginative fusion of the crowd with womankind, woman becomes not just his Other, but even "another species" (*N* 3: 577). Huyssen's diagnosis of the bourgeois artist's anxious gendering of the crowd could apply to Harry, as he too projects "male fears of an engulfing femininity . . . onto the metropolitan masses" (53). Harry's nightmarish vision of the store is equivalent to what Huyssen identifies as the process by which "the haunting specter of a loss of power combines with the fear of losing one's fortified and stable ego boundaries, which represent the *sine qua non* of the male psychology in that bourgeois order" (53). The specter that haunts Harry is the modernist artist's same "nightmare of being devoured by mass culture through co-option, commodification, and the 'wrong' kind of success" (Huyssen 53). Faulkner complicates this masculine vision of commodity culture and the masses through Charlotte's easy participation in this world. She is the artist working within a modernist aesthetic who enjoys a relaxed immersion in the crowd of consumers, and her actions serve to ironize Harry's terrified remove from the masses.

Harry has a disproportionate conception of the threat his pop-cultural writing poses to him and Charlotte. Religion and myth also become structured by the degrading power of mass mediation in Harry's mind; "God's voice" is supplanted by the "radio" and Venus transmutes into "a soiled man in a subway lavatory with a palm full of French postcards" (*N* 3: 587, 588). Harry's fears are echoed in Eliot's denouncement of mass culture in *Notes towards the Definition of Culture* (1948), where the modernist insisted upon the elitist preservation of high culture as a "minority culture" and advanced the generalizing claim that "a 'mass-culture' will always be a substitute-culture; and sooner or later the deception will become apparent to the more intelligent of those upon whom this culture has been palmed off" (107). Harry appears equally sensitive to a perceived ersatz quality of mass cultural transformations. Karl F. Zender claims that *Jerusalem* champions a form of materialism beyond money, since Faulkner "needed to find a way to rescue materialism from itself, in the sense of finding a way to reject excessive dependence on money without at the same time rejecting the life of the flesh" (*Crossing* 53). But Harry's fears appear to be specifically bound up with the relation between commercial activity and gender fluidity. Dobbs highlights this link in *Jerusalem*, which for her explores "the ways in which fears of a seemingly natural feminine fluidity bleed into cultural anxieties about the unforgiving vicissitudes of a constitutively fluid free-market capitalism" (812). In this case, the market causes the returned figure of Venus to turn into a man and grasp after pornography, indirectly expressing Harry's own anxieties about the gender slippages of his feminizing pulp. He believes that "there seems to be no limit to what [he] can invent on the theme of female sex troubles" (*N* 3: 587), fearing that his fictional fantasies may transform him utterly and may in fact be uncontainable.

The generalizations of Harry's popular cultural paranoia, when counterpointed with Charlotte's pragmatic and calm engagement with the market, ask us to view them critically as exaggerated misapprehensions. Harry's production of "sexual gumdrop" for the magazines would, at first glance, seem to uphold a strict cultural binary, since, as Max Horkheimer and Theodor W. Adorno assert, "the culture industry does not sublimate; it represses," elaborating that "works of art are ascetic and unashamed; the culture industry is pornographic and prudish" and "the mass production of the sexual automatically achieves its repression" (140). However, Charlotte's artistic labors produce works for the masses that are infused with her sexual energies; the erotic, for Faulkner, is, then, not necessarily repressed by its circulation in the marketplace. Harry recognizes that Charlotte appears impervious to the same repressive, bourgeois seduction he fears, quipping "she's a better man than I am" (*N* 3: 586) when McCord highlights her ignorance of the constraints of respectability. In his own eyes, Harry's participation in the market unmans him, and he is doubly emasculated by Charlotte's invulnerability to his materialist fears and the effeminacy of his writing. This causes him to police the fluid gender roles that he is anxious may have become visible to observers. He worries, for example, that the manager of the apartment in Chicago that he and Charlotte have been renting might presume that he, Charlotte, and McCord are in a three-way relationship, in which gendered roles are subjected to flux: Harry lightheartedly defends that it is "just two of us . . . None of us are androgynous" (*N* 3: 583). There is a need here to reassert the fixity of gender signifiers, and the way they interact with cultural distinctions, as Harry is all too aware that he plays the role of feminized hack writer to Charlotte's masculinized experimental artist on commission.

Hollywood Stars and Pop Seductions

While Charlotte and Harry's love affair is detailed in the "Wild Palms" narrative thread of *Jerusalem,* it is interspersed with the "Old Man" narrative, which focuses on an escaped convict who is caught in a Mississippian flood and rescues a pregnant woman. The tall convict, similar to Harry, feels threatened by the allure of pop culture, including Hollywood's images of women and the emotions they inspire in viewers. The following lines appear as the woman lowers herself into the convict's boat: "even in durance he had continued (and even with the old avidity, even though they had caused his downfall) to consume the impossible pulp-printed fables carefully censored and as carefully smuggled into the penitentiary; and who to say what Helen, what living Garbo, he had not dreamed of rescuing from what craggy pinnacle or dragoned keep when he and his companion embarked in the skiff" (*N* 3: 596). Lurie is correct in his assessment of the passage that "the convict is shocked at how much his real charge is at odds with a popular-cultural or Hollywood version of the female in distress" (137), as "the deformed swell of belly bulging the calico, suspended by its arms" (*N* 3: 596) fails to live up to the convict's idealized vision of femininity gleaned from pulp novels and movies. Lurie analyses the convict's investment in the image of Greta Garbo as being indicative of his "mental operation of projecting himself into an imaginary or fantasized role" (137), as film viewers do. John T. Matthews perceives a class element in this activity, in that "pop industrial culture puts false dreams of agency and success before the minds of the working class. . . . Stuffed with such fantasies, the Tall Convict can't be expected to think through the conditions that trap him" (*Seeing* 71). Clearly, the convict's ability to liberate himself is hampered both by the presence of the pregnant woman in his getaway craft and his investment in a commercial and visual fantasy of romance. He fantasizes the woman into the role of the enigmatic film star or the damsel in distress in an adventure movie and consequently casts himself within the role of desiring subject. In fact, the sexual economy of both narrative threads of *Jerusalem* has been infiltrated by commercial cinema. Men, intoxicated by the beauty of Hollywood actresses, wish to translate the cinematic objects of their desire into the realm of the real. When Harry visits a brothel to attempt to procure Charlotte an abortion, the madam describes the cultural demographic of her employees: "I got American girls here or Spanish (strangers like Spanish girls, once, anyway. It's the influence of the moving pictures, I always say)" (*N* 3: 638). The sex industry has responded to the demands of male consumers to be seduced by Hollywood women. Her throwaway remark that men only enjoy the girls "once" shows how shallow and exoticizing this kind of pleasure is. In such cases, as King suggests, Faulkner "overtly explores the dangers of 'pulp fiction' and the culpability of those who create them" (522–23).

Nevertheless, I would argue that the novel appears less critical of commercial narratives and images themselves than of readers' and spectators' uncritical engagement with them. The reference to Garbo from "Old Man" has particular resonances in terms of masculine spectatorship within the 1930s Hollywood imaginary. Roland Barthes says of the actor in his essay "The Face of Garbo" that she "still belongs to that moment in cinema when capturing the human face still plunged audiences into the deepest ecstasy . . . when the face represented a kind of absolute state of the flesh, which could be neither reached nor renounced . . . Garbo still partakes of the . . . rule of Courtly Love, where the flesh gives rise to mystical feelings of perdition" (471). Garbo's image arrests and arouses the viewer by virtue of its materiality. Barthes highlights the chivalric element of beholding Garbo, as the passage from the novel does, but he also chooses to foreground the female flesh as origin of a form of power that inspires idealization but also endangers the subject. Haskell recognizes the position of Garbo within cultural and social networks as one of striking independence; for her, she is "the anima of no single *auteur* or even society, but is a natural force, a principle of beauty that, once set in motion, becomes autonomous" (*Reverence* 107). The scene in the skiff illustrates the potency of Garbo's image. The convict is disempowered through his projection of Garbo's Hollywood roles onto the woman, since his chivalric actions will ultimately result in his return to a state of incarceration as he succumbs to "mystical feelings of perdition." This stands in stark counterpoint to Charlotte's engagement with popular romance narratives. She instead displays a practical ability to differentiate between fiction and reality when she says to Harry, "the second time I ever saw you I learned what I had read in books but I never had actually believed: that love and suffering are the same thing and that the value of love is the sum of what you have to pay for it and anytime you get it cheap you have cheated yourself" (*N* 3: 526). Distinct from the convict's activities, lived experience causes Charlotte to retrospectively reread and reassess the "truths" of artistic knowledge as they touch upon romance.

The convict's loss of agency in this scene, through his conflation of fantasy and reality, also subverts the typical gendered binary of spectator and spectacle within the cinema. Doane argues that Hollywood cinema traditionally positions the female spectator in a naive relationship to the images of film as she struggles to differentiate between the image and the real, therefore misattributing desire (*Desire to Desire* 1). Doane describes "the image of the longing, overinvolved female spectator" that circulates in culture as emphasizing "proximity rather than distance, passivity, overinvolvement and overidentification" (*Desire to Desire* 2). Faulkner seems to suggest that this is a form of spectatorial closeness in relation to the images of commercial cinema to which men may be susceptible. By invoking a Hollywood female archetype, the filmic imagination of Faulkner's tall convict sets an autonomous image in motion, which overruns the narrative by placing him in a predetermined role.

Garbo would also have strong resonances for a male screenwriter of the 1930s such as Faulkner, particularly in terms of the autonomy of her beauty. Whereas during the 1920s there was a significant amount of professional and social networking among women in Hollywood, from the 1930s the more common all-female team in the film community would be between writers and actresses at the studio (Francke 32). Lizzie Francke describes in particular the long creative association between the screenwriter Salka Viertel and Garbo at MGM, where Faulkner worked in the early 1930s (35). This monopoly of the image management of a particular actress presents the relationship between female writer and film star as a closed circuit that excludes the male writer. For Faulkner, Garbo may have been an impermeable symbol produced by women that his imagination was unable to inhabit creatively. The autonomy of Garbo's image within *Jerusalem* taps into its exclusivity and its marginalization of men on the level of production. Garbo as spectacle may appear especially threatening to the author because she cannot be constructed through the male imaginary but only beheld. In the allusion, Faulkner seems to acknowledge the Hollywood woman's potential to give rise to moments of rapturous power that can lead to men's ruin through their overinvestment in and lack of critical distance from the image.

Desire on the Small Screen: Faulkner's Television Adaptation of "Old Man"

Faulkner adapted "Old Man" for television in 1953; although the teleplay was never produced, it does reveal how the images of women within *Jerusalem* are conditional on the perspective of the male subject. In this teleplay, Faulkner elided the cinematic fantasies that imperil the convict in *Jerusalem*. The transmedial adaptation in fact resulted in a remarkable generic shift between fiction and television, as Faulkner moved "Old Man"—in its treatment of the relationship between the convict and the pregnant woman—from the conventions of horror to those of the vice film and commercial romance.

In the "Old Man" narrative from the novel, the convict considers the woman to be a burden that inspires fear and potential violence within him. She takes on epic proportions in his imagination, as the spectacle of the pregnant woman becomes "a separate demanding threatening inert yet living mass of which both he and she were equally victims" (*N* 3: 599). The convict even meditates on the possibility of drowning the woman to overcome the trial that he sees as afflicting them both. In entertaining such a violent discarding of his "burden," he has to dehumanize her, comparing her to "the living timber in a barn which had to be burned to rid itself of vermin" (*N* 3: 599).

The convict's conception of the woman turns her into a monster: "the woman had ceased to be a human being and . . . had become instead one single inert monstrous sentient womb from which, he now believed, if he could only turn his gaze away and keep it away, would disappear" (*N* 3: 605). His belief that he can dispel this monstrous image by ceasing to behold it positions him in a role akin to the spectator of a horror film. In Barbara Creed's essay on horror and the "monstrous-feminine," she utilizes Kristeva's theory of the maternal figure's abjection to show how films within this genre often portray "the archaic mother, the reproductive/generative mother" as "a *negative* figure . . . seen only as the abyss, the monstrous vagina, the origin of all life threatening to reabsorb what it once birthed" (47, 54). For Creed, this creates a distinct relationship between the spectacle of the monstrous feminine in film and the spectator in the cinema, as "the suturing processes are momentarily undone" (57)—the viewer cannot bear the sight of the horrific image any longer and looks away. The convict wishes to erase the image of the woman in the same fashion. Creed argues that this repulsion of the gaze shows the spectator is momentarily able "to withdraw identification from the image on the screen in order to reconstruct the boundary between self and screen and reconstitute the self that is threatened with disintegration" (58). The image the convict invokes of the archaic mother endangers his sense of self, as he is fearful of maternal engulfment, but it is, ironically, a horror film of his own projection that he wishes to stop viewing. For the convict, the penitentiary, in contrast, becomes an imaginative space of security and sanctioned pleasure; he reflects nostalgically on "the Sunday ball games and the picture shows—things which, with the exception of the ball games, he had never known before" (*N* 3: 607). The convict responds to the memory of curated and structured leisure; the picture shows in prison, scheduled and managed, contrast starkly with the horrific image of the procreative that repels him.

Faulkner's 1953 adaptation of the "Old Man" story as a teleplay for the William Morris Agency rejects conventions from horror in favor of those from the vice film and romance. This shift seems to indicate Faulkner's acknowledgment that the discrepancy between fantasy and reality in fiction cannot be fully rendered in television without significant experimental innovation within the form in what was a relatively young mass medium. There can be no doubt that Faulkner's motivations in writing the piece were principally financial, but he defends the work in a letter to Saxe Commins from 24 December 1952 as a cultural product that he stands by, despite his editor's fears that its circulation may damage his reputation. Faulkner stated that the work "is (mildly) amusing, honest as regards the people. That is, as you know, if I had felt otherwise, that it was false, I would not have put my name on it . . . I doubt if what a tv screen shows is going to hurt what Random House prints in books, any more that [sic] what movie screens have shown that I did" (*FBC* 2: 103–104).[5]

In a crucial difference in characterization in this transmedial adaptation, the teleplay gives the pregnant woman a backstory: "She is an orphan, daughter of Delta tenant farmers. When her parents died, she was about

13–14. She went to live with a sister ten years older, married to another tenant farmer. Her position in the house was almost that of a servant. . . . She has a little more education than the Convict."[6] She escapes to Memphis after being raped by her brother-in-law, where she discovers she is pregnant by him. She tragically turns moral judgment for these events upon herself. As in the novel, the woman is rescued by the convict in the skiff during the flood. In the teleplay, however, the convict has been imprisoned for killing a rival who slept with his girlfriend.

Faulkner's script goes on to show life in the penitentiary and expands our insight into the sexual activities of the convicts. He initially frames the piece as a sex and crime picture in the vein of his early 1930s writing for MGM in pre-Code Hollywood, entirely unsuitable for television in 1950s America. As Thomas Doherty describes in relation to Cold War US television, the networks and independent stations "kept well clear of political and cultural controversy" as they were profit-driven and under government oversight and, due to the revenues they derived from advertising, "television was exquisitely sensitive to viewer protests and product boycotts" and therefore attempted to avoid offending any consumer demographic (*Cold War* 61). Despite such restrictions, in Faulkner's scene, which takes place on the fifth-Sunday visiting day to the prison, "a special train, known to the convicts as the Midnight Special, stops at the prison. It is filled with women, black and white, the wives and sweethearts of the prisoners, and a few extra prostitutes. There is nowhere for the couples to go except a field full of tall weeds. At midnight the women are all allowed to enter the compound where the convicts are waiting for them, and the pairs scatter into the weeds to make love, nobody paying any attention to anyone else."[7] The scene is as regulated as the penitentiary's ball games and picture shows in which the tall convict of the novel finds comfort, and it involves a dissolution of sexual boundaries. Faulkner indicates that "there's something orgiastic about it: the convicts, black and white, crowding against the fence, waiting for the stroke of midnight and the gates to be thrown open, chanting, singing, 'Let that Midnight Special shine its light on me tonight,' the women on the other side of the fence, waiting. Then the gates are open, the guards leap for their lives almost as the two groups, men and women, pour together and in pairs hurry off into the weeds."[8] The convict is positioned in the same relation to the scene as Faulkner intended the viewer to be: arrested by the visual action but detached from it, "an outsider, watching, drawn to the scene, he probably does not know why, left at last alone of all of them, solitary, lonely, but still convinced that he wants none of it after what happened to him through a false woman twenty years ago."[9] It takes the flood to divide the orgy, as "the levee breaks. Guards arrive with lorries, the convicts are herded out of the weeds and the arms of their screaming women, loaded into the lorries and rushed to the levee for rescue work."[10]

After this point, Faulkner moves the script towards a commercial romance. The next morning, the convict is in the skiff in which he rescues the girl from the top of a house where she has taken refuge. Faulkner cross-references with the novel and outlines that "we follow the story line in the book, except that it is a love story now."[11] The convict's initial reaction to the woman is to treat her as a burden from whom he wishes to free himself in order to return to the penitentiary. The convict's protective regard for the girl deepens when at the last minute he refuses to turn her over to the men in a shanty-boat that offer to take her aboard, as he fears she will be raped by them.[12] When he finally gets the skiff ashore, he begins as if to throw her onto the bank, then they hold each other's gaze, and instead of the convict being repelled by the image of the woman, they share a kiss in a sentimental exchange:

> CONVICT (holding her)
>> Why in hell didn't you climb down that bank back there and get the hell out of this like I told you?
>
> GIRL
>> Why didn't you leave me on that shanty boat and get the hell out of this when *you* had the chance?
>
> CONVICT (holding her)
>> Well, I didn't. So what?
>
> GIRL (desperately)
>> Nothing! Just get me up the bank where I can lie down.[13]

Writing for the medium of television, Faulkner has the convict perceive romance rather than horror in the "burden" of her pregnancy, and their dialogue resembles that of a screwball comedy such as *Bringing Up Baby* (1938), with its mixture of flirtation and antagonism in the midst of an anarchic predicament.

Where the "Old Man" narrative from *Jerusalem* communicates the convict's rejection of the familial, the teleplay shows him gradually embracing domesticity within the conventional genre of romance. Once the convict and the woman reach the relative stability of the alligator-hunting camp in the novel version, they achieve "that rapport of the wedded" born out of joint suffering (*N* 3: 667); the convict thinks of himself and the woman as a couple whose relationship has depersonalized and desexualized them: "the old married . . . the electroplate reproductions, the thousand identical coupled faces with only a collarless stud or a fichu out of Louisa Alcott to denote the sex" (*N* 3: 667). The convict's contempt for the domestic takes on the familiar overtones of the modernist neurotic, as when he sees "tomorrow propped by a thousand morning sugar bowls or coffee urns" (*N* 3: 667), the presence of Eliot's J. Alfred Prufrock is apparent, who himself admits to having "known the evenings, mornings, afternoons, / . . . measured out my life with coffee spoons" (*Complete Poems*). The convict's surrendering of himself to the penitentiary, after having relieved himself of the "millstone" of the woman, allows his monastic refusal of sexual communion with women to prevail. When the plump convict commiserates that the extension of the tall convict's sentence due to his escape in the skiff will result in "ten more years to do without a woman," the tall convict answers with a highly misogynistic and elliptical equation that concludes the novel: "Women, shit" (*N* 3: 726).

In a marked contrast, the teleplay foregrounds a union between the convict and the woman. After the birth, with the convict serving as midwife, Faulkner outlines that

> each scene between them from now will have that quality, that overtone of tenderness, love, between them—a love which they don't have time to acknowledge yet for the reason that they are too busy staying alive; this is probably when he tells her how he got into the penitentiary; she may tell him where the baby came from. Her attitude toward him is already that of a secure and comfortable wife of about a year, say, the marriage just old enough for the first child to have come; without being conscious of it, they have settled down into a sort of domesticity.[14]

This shift towards a domesticated relationship springs out of endurance, the shared histories of trauma, and the convict's paternal attitude towards the baby: it leads the convict to contemplate eloping to Mexico with the woman to start a new life. The girl contends that for true freedom, the convict must return to the penitentiary for the remaining three years of his sentence, so that the child will not be brought up as a fugitive. The action then returns to the penitentiary on a fifth Sunday for its final scene, another Midnight Special event:

> *The convict is among them, shaved and clean. The train arrives, the gates are opened, the first scene is repeated as the men and women rush together, then break into couples, hurrying into the bushes. The girl has come, with the baby. She and the convict stand holding hands, watching the frantic couples rushing away into the bushes, until they are alone. The same thought seems to occur to both of them, but the girl says,*
>
> GIRL
> No. Not yet. We're going to do it right. We've waited this long; we can last out the rest of it.[15]

As viewers, not participants, of the orgiastic scene, the couple refuse to yield to their instincts. For the convict of Faulkner's television adaptation, his refusal of sex has become a strategy of delay to facilitate romance.

Though it would be difficult to uphold the value of the teleplay as an example of creative adaptation or innovative use of the televisual format, it indicates Faulkner's pragmatic will to create something "honest" that is palatable for a mass audience. He reformulates the novel's story to demonstrate how fear of the feminine and commercial visual culture, explicit within the novel, is redundant within a form destined for visual transmission that typically resisted experimentation or provocation. Faulkner recasts the novel's sexual horror story, in which the convict shrinks from mediated images of women, as a popular romance for television. While this no doubt indicates his impulse to mine his work for financial opportunities within a burgeoning medium in the 1950s, it also shows how the image of the horrific maternal only functions within the text when channeled through an individual consciousness that conditions the spectacle. When Faulkner comes to expand the story for a mass audience, the warped image of the pregnant woman that repels the convict becomes untenable. In the original novel, we view the woman within a fearful Hollywood imaginary. In the teleplay, as Faulkner exteriorizes the story for a diffuse audience of spectators, the anxious cinematic images of the convict's projection evaporate.

Visual Misapprehensions and the Tyranny of the Woman Writer

In connection with Harry's narratives for the confession magazines, "The Wild Palms," which is mediated primarily through his consciousness, attempts to cast Charlotte within frames of reference from Hollywood and commercial visual culture. As Harry strives to compare Charlotte to Hollywood types, it becomes apparent that she is a poor fit for such images, failed comparisons that seem to comment on the limitations of masculine creativity within 1930s cinematic production. Indeed, Charlotte's characterization challenges the restrictions of the commercial cinematic lens that Harry imposes upon her. On one occasion, Harry watches Charlotte wander naked around the cabin at their Wisconsin woods retreat, preparing for a morning swim, and Faulkner makes the following reference to the Californian industry: "[Charlotte] slid out from beneath the blanket. He watched her, the grave simple body a little broader, a little solider than the Hollywood-magazine cod liver oil advertisements, the bare feet padding across the rough boards" (*N* 3: 569). The comparative admission that she is "a little" different from the models in Hollywood magazines attempts to demonstrate Harry's mastery of her image by positioning her within popular culture, but it in fact only confirms his failure to contain her. It is what is elsewhere referred to as the "hard impact of [Charlotte's] presence" (*N* 3: 570) that resists commodification here.

This moment is one in a series of Harry's unsuccessful attempts to apply a commercial viewpoint to Charlotte, a failure that stems from his inability to read her body. Charlotte enjoys a sexuality that is unabashed, dominant, and authoritative. When Harry observes her in the novel, the incapacity of the male gaze to successfully apprehend her physicality is emphasized. At the beginning of their passionate flight to Chicago, the following lines appear when Charlotte initiates sex with Harry in a train drawing room: "When he turned she had removed her dress; it lay in a wadded circle about her feet and she stood in the scant feminine underwear of 1937, her hands over her face. Then she removed her hands and he knew it was neither shame nor modesty, he had not expected that, and he saw it was not tears. Then she stepped out of the dress and came and began to unknot his tie, pushing aside his own suddenly clumsy fingers" (*N* 3: 535). Charlotte surprises Harry with a sexual authority that he struggles to translate and does not meet his expectations of feminine timidity or frailty. He fails to even settle on ascribing an emotion to her before physical contact disarms him. In this scene, Harry tries to frame Charlotte's desire through her modish underwear. Her physical gestures, however, cannot be confined within this visual framing. Similar to his earlier recourse to the Hollywood magazines to describe Charlotte, Harry's attempt to consume her image within the terms of catalogue fashion falls equally flat. Charlotte resolutely refuses to be read as commodified object by dint of the strong sexual desire that challenges Harry's faltering gaze. Part of Harry's unease here seems to derive from Charlotte's sexualizing gaze being turned upon him, in which *he* is positioned as an erotic spectacle. Pardis Dabashi observes a similar moment in *The Sound and the Fury*, in which Miss Quentin stares down her uncle Jason, which "reverses the typical gender dynamic of cinematic looking"; Dabashi suggests that "Jason's fear of being the object of spectacle betrays a fear of feminization" (545). At the end of the scene from *Jerusalem*, which concludes the second part of "The Wild Palms" thread of the novel, Faulkner freezes the action at a moment of misapprehension to illustrate the gap between commercially generated fantasies and sexual reality, at a moment when the binary of female spectacle and male spectator is unsettled.

This disparity appears to indicate Faulkner's awareness of the difficulty of communicating female desire within visual narratives. In a broad sense within commercial visual culture, female sexuality may always remain a mystery to the male spectator. Linda Williams has identified the contradictions and conflicts of filmic pornography, a genre that encounters difficulty "in figuring the visual 'knowledge' of women's pleasure" (*Hard Core* xvi). Female sexuality remains opaque within hard-core porn despite its apparent hypervisualization of the woman's body and desires. As Williams describes, "the woman's ability to fake the orgasm that the man can never fake (at least according to certain standards of evidence) seems to be at the root of all the genre's attempts to solicit what it can never be sure of: the out-of-control confession of pleasure, a hard-core 'frenzy of the visible'" (*Hard Core* 50). For Williams, this desire for proof of female pleasure is the animating drive behind the production of hard-core cinema, which seeks to visualize what "can never be objectively measured" (*Hard Core* 50), since the woman's orgasm can neither be visualized nor proven. Harry is placed in a similar position, attempting to visually savor Charlotte as commodified object but finding her desires inscrutable.

In addition, Faulkner was directly confronted with the essential unreadability of female desire—or its refusal to be visually rendered in commercial genres—through his work in 1930s Hollywood. In the studios at that time, screenwriting was considered a viable profession for many women, in which they could achieve a measure of equality with their male colleagues. Sonya Levien—one of the most prolific screenwriters in Hollywood history and who worked without a collaborator—wrote in Catherine Filene's 1934 edition of *Careers for Women* that "a woman has as good a chance as a man to become a successful screenwriter. Her sex creates no awkwardness or difficulty. She has always been a familiar figure in the screen ranks" (qtd. in Francke 33–34). Filene's book also elaborates that women in the studio system of the 1930s could in fact find themselves being actively sought out for writing roles. In 1934, B. P. Schulberg, head of Paramount, had recently announced to the Association of Motion Picture Producers a new initiative to promote women in key production and creative positions, of which "the purpose will be to accentuate the woman's angle and make certain that films appeal both to women and men" (qtd. in Francke 34). Francke asserts that "Schulberg's proposal makes clear that producers believed that women writers were better able to cater for the tastes of a female audience, which were often construed as rather mysterious and something that men could not necessarily recognize" (34). Demystifying the female audience was a crucial task for the writing team of a film, since women made up the majority of cinemagoers at that time. This would have affected Faulkner, particularly at MGM, as "during the 1930s the link between the 'woman's film' and the woman screenwriter was most obvious" at the studio where "the roster of women writers was extensive and illustrious" (Francke 34), with literary figures Anita Loos and Dorothy Parker among them.

This large female presence was at times perceived as a threat to men in the same profession, as the screenwriter Frances Marion, who had a fifty-year career in Hollywood, recalled: "When we carried the scripts on which we were doing re-writes, we made sure that they were in unmarked, plain covers. But we knew male writers were complaining about the 'tyranny of the woman writer' supposedly prevalent at all studios then, and particularly at MGM" (qtd. in Francke 35). In this anecdote, the fear of emasculating male writers is compensated by masking the potential threat: women writers redraft their male counterparts' work but defend masculine pride through concealment. Francke believes that this notion of the alleged "tyranny of the woman writer" at 1930s MGM was attributable to the head of studio production, Irving Thalberg, who had encouraged women writers to work for the studio, as he believed that "women were better suited to writing material for female stars and that a 'woman's touch' would bring to the script a certain authenticity of feeling" (35).

A screenwriter's commercial value, then, was in part attached to their ability to inhabit female psychology and desire, particularly within the lavish melodramas that were MGM's signature product under Thalberg. Faulkner would no doubt have reflected on his own imaginative capital within such an environment. This was a creative community in which the communication of the female perspective by and for women was prized. Harry's misrecognition of Charlotte's desires in the novel's mobile sex scene on the train echoes the difficulty male writers experienced in 1930s Hollywood in translating female psychology to the screen to sate the demands of the market. Harry struggles to narrate his lover's interior life, preferring to attribute commercial signifiers to her sexuality and body. Through the gap between Charlotte's impulses and Harry's comprehension, Faulkner appears to concede at this point in his career that there is only so far a man can go in imagining female desire as it will always be observed rather than inhabited.

Visual Communication and Unionized Labor

Charlotte's creativity will once again mimic the activities of the Hollywood screenwriter in the novel in ways that highlight her productivity and solidarity with her fellow workers. Her work continues to contrast with the anxiety and alienation of Harry's engagement with commercial visual culture. When Charlotte has to demonstrate the dire employment situation to the workers in a mining camp in Utah,[16] where the lovers conduct part of their affair, she uses an illustrative technique that resembles that of the storyboard:

> and now they all watched her, the five women pushing forward also to see, as she fastened with four tacks produced from somewhere a sheet of wrapping paper to the end of a section of shelves where the light from the single window fell on it and began to draw swiftly with one of the scraps of charcoal she had brought from Chicago—the elevation of a wall in cross section with a grilled window in it unmistakably a pay window and as unmistakably shut, on the one side of the window a number of people unmistakably miners (she had even included the woman with the baby); on the other side of the window

an enormous man (she had never seen Callaghan, he had merely described him to her, yet the man was Callaghan) sitting behind a table heaped with glittering coins which the man was shovelling into a sack. (*N* 3: 630–31)

Charlotte finds a practical and potentially liberating way of communicating through visual language that approximates the filmic technique of montage, through which overall meaning is conveyed through a succession of snapshots. Charlotte can use a range of modes of artistic production at her disposal to achieve a desired result. Her storyboard has a visual directness in which intention and performance directly correlate. Despite having never met Callaghan, the corrupt owner of the mine, Charlotte gleans from the source material she has at her disposal (in this case oral accounts) to create an artistic correspondence with reality.

Lurie describes Charlotte's cinematic communication to her audience, in what he identifies as a nod to silent cinema, as a form of exploitation through melodramatic representation that seeks "to quell or re-contain an outburst of proletarian energy" (151) in that her drawings dispel the miners' potential resistance despite their miserable circumstances. It is still additionally true that Charlotte is sympathetic to the laborers' cause, having been a contracted laborer herself, and wishes to offer support through clarification. As Bloom comments, "Charlotte's cartoon proves consciousness-raising for its audience, for at least *some* workers of the world" (87). The fact that Charlotte is the generator of these images also has a gendered significance, as we find a woman wielding the tools of visual communication to generate identification from her audience. Charlotte's success as a storyboarder may sublimate Faulkner's awareness that there were more female screenwriters in Hollywood in the 1930s than at any other period in film history, at least up until the 1970s (Haskell, *Reverence* 151). Read in this light, "the five women pushing forward also to see" (*N* 3: 630) Charlotte's drawing may represent a collaborative community of women collectively appraising a film project.

This community also suggests the potential for unionization around a common labor-based cause. Writing about *Absalom, Absalom!*, Charles Hannon considers how volatile working relations during the Hollywood of the 1930s filtered into Faulkner's 1936 novel. Hannon describes how the studio system that Faulkner participated in "was fraught with disorder as a consequence of battles over the unionization of Hollywood workers," screenwriters and technical workers alike, who "fought for, and were fought over by, the various guilds and unions that sought to represent them in contract negotiations with the studios" (82–83). In particular, Hannon references the 1932 strike threatened by the International Alliance of Theatrical Stage Employees (IA), the year Faulkner moved to Hollywood. He believes that anxiety over the nature of the dissemination of the story of Thomas Sutpen, as intellectual property among the many narrators in *Absalom, Absalom!*, echoes this strike. He highlights "the atmosphere of distrust and suspicion in 1930s Hollywood labor relations that resulted from disputes over the distribution side of the industry," since "studio leaders in the 1930s and 1940s claimed that they were at the mercy of the IA, which could use the threat of a strike among union projectionists in any contract negotiations" (83). Hannon sees this as being translated into the fraught "labor of textual production" (82) within Faulkner's novel.

Hollywood labor was galvanizing, then, at the time Faulkner was living and working there in the years before he wrote *Jerusalem*. Charlotte's drawing may not be just a warning gesture of solidarity but an actual call to arms to unionize around a common purpose: the pooling of influence between contracted laborers. Carpenter comments in her biography on the excessive number of court actions in Hollywood in 1936, which pitted "actors against producers, producers against directors, actors against agents" (*ALG* 153). Out of this turmoil a group of directors formed the Screen Directors Guild to combat the studio producers, and Carpenter herself joined the Script Clerks Guild in 1936. The Screen Writers Guild (SWG), an organization of Hollywood screenplay authors, formed as a union in 1933; Francke asserts that this was the "one place where women could rise to positions of power" within the studio system (41). The veteran screenwriter Frances Marion was voted vice president of the SWG in its first year, and another woman screenwriter, Mary McCall Jr., was voted the first female president of the SWG in 1942 (Francke 41–2).

This resonates with the creative community who gather around Charlotte's images, which communicate employment rights to the workers, as Faulkner seems to have written the convulsive studio politics of the 1930s into the novel. Charlotte's drawing attempts to construct a creative network for women by expressing solidarity with her audience—who are also her co-workers—against oppression. Yet, within such an analogy, Charlotte goes much further than her counterparts in Hollywood, as Francke argues that despite the fact that successful women screenwriters' "lives were testimony to the possibilities for women," they nevertheless "could not or did not want to inscribe it on to their work to bring about larger changes" (43). In this sense, Charlotte unifies her creative activities with a desire to alter working conditions for the community. She serves as Faulkner's radical vision of the shaping potential of women within commercial visual culture, and by extension Hollywood institutions and networks such as the SWG.

Charlotte's Death and Masculine Creative Failure

Any analysis of *Jerusalem* that finds in Charlotte a progressive portrayal of womanhood within the Faulknerian canon must reconcile itself with the violence of her death after Harry performs an illegal abortion on her. While this conclusion subjugates women—and the erotic and artistic values Charlotte represents—Faulkner invites us to consider the act a further creative failure on Harry's part, since his hand is steered by fears that do not correspond to the body of the woman he is operating on. On one level, Harry's surgical failure derives from his exaggeration of the difficulty of the operation, since he has previously performed the operation successfully on the Utah mine manager's wife. Harry internally justifies this failure by considering that he couldn't perform the abortion, as he loved Charlotte too much (*N* 3: 696). He uses a revealing metaphor to qualify the disarming influence of that love: "A miser would probably bungle the blowing of his own safe too. Should have called in a professional, a cracksman who didn't care, didn't love the very iron flanks that held the money" (*N* 3: 696). Harry uses the language of possession to refer to Charlotte's body. In defending his failure, he exposes how much his relationship to her is still connected to his own economic status and the dynamics of ownership. Zender challenges that Harry's distracted contemplation of the class system, his wrangling with the concept of respectability, may have played a role here, that "he may have internalized middle-class values so completely as to be physically incapable of performing the operation" (*Crossing* 57).

Certainly, Harry's miser metaphor bears this reading out, but there is evidence to suggest that his failure is also linked to his inability to fully comprehend Charlotte's body. While Faulkner removes a description of the abortion from the narrative, in the operation's aftermath Harry ascribes cultural metaphors to the dying Charlotte that jar with his professed love for her. In his attempts to keep Charlotte alive, a reference to an Owen Wister pulp Western novel intrudes abruptly into his thoughts: "He was trying to remember something out of a book, years ago . . . the whore in the pink ball dress who drank the laudanum and the cowboys taking turns walking her up and down the floor, keeping her on her feet, keeping her alive" (*N* 3: 689). Consistent with their relationship thus far, Harry is unable to manage the cultural imaginary in relation to Charlotte's body, viewing her through a mixture of fearful and degrading perspectives. Despite Harry's impressions of her, Charlotte's art and life stand as testament to her pragmatic and eroticized creativity; she even restates her personal manifesto on her deathbed to Harry, asking him, "Jesus, we had fun, didn't we? bitching, and making things. In the cold, the snow" (*N* 3: 689). Tragically, Harry's cultural and sexual fears, which are revisited throughout the novel, appear to have sealed Charlotte's fate.

The conclusion of the novel extends this focus on failures of male creativity. Harry is imprisoned for the crime he has committed on the Gulf Coast. He masturbates over his remembered images of Charlotte, now seemingly incarnating the Venus figure with the French postcards he had feared his mass-market writing would transform him into. Harry's relation to Charlotte here appears as a shallow attempt to revivify intimacy with a body whose sexual desires he had failed to interpret. Harry attempts to erect a monument to his lover based around her deathbed philosophy, "remembering, the body, the broad thighs and the hands that liked bitching and making things" (*N* 3: 715). Harry does appear to have learned from Charlotte the value of rooting experience in corporeal reality, acknowledging that "memory, forever and inescapable" is dependent on "flesh to titillate" and that "memory could live in the old wheezing entrails" (*N* 3: 714, 715). It is highly unfortunate that his embodied epiphany relies on Charlotte's death for its catalyst, revealing Harry's lack of creative engagement with his lover while she was alive. Minrose C. Gwin views Charlotte's death before Harry (or the reader) can fully comprehend her artistic manifesto as one of a series of examples in which "women's voices" in Faulkner "are silenced before we really know what they are saying" ("Feminism and Faulkner" 62). Harry's act is a shallow restatement of masculine control of the hand after the violence of Charlotte's exit from the novel, as the tactile female artist figure no longer threatens the masturbating male protagonist.

In keeping with these themes, Faulkner's assigned title for the novel from Psalm 137 appropriately meditates on the struggles of the artist with a focus on an artist's hands: "How shall we sing the LORD's song in a strange land [Babylon]? / If I forget thee, O Jerusalem, let my right hand forget her cunning" (*King James Version*). Critics of the novel have highlighted how the titular citation from the Bible can be seen to represent Faulkner's trials as a Mississippian novelist having to perform the job of Californian screenwriter. The author wishes to "sing" of the South by composing serious, refined modernist novels in his home territory (Mississippi is viewed as the psalm's Jerusalem), but is however constrained into producing compromised art in a "strange land" (in which Hollywood becomes Babylon).[17]

Beyond such a simplifying dualism, the second half of the verse that follows Faulkner's chosen title is highly suggestive: "let my right hand forget her cunning." The pronoun "her" points to a feminine presence that works on the male authority of the psalm's artist figure. Feminine cunning within the psalm is an alien, external influence that apparently guides the male artist's hand against its will. That this cunning has Babylonian origins is left in no doubt, given the reference to the female "daughter of Babylon, who art to be destroyed" in the penultimate verse of the psalm. It is not a coincidence that the disempowered hand of the psalm resembles the failure of the abortionist's hand in the novel. Thus, feminine cunning in Babylon (and Hollywood, by implication) is set up as a seduction of the male artist or masculine creativity.

Crucially, though, in the novel itself, Faulkner presents fears of such a degrading seduction as a misapprehension. Harry's hands consistently appear dispossessed of their agency by a nebulous feminine threat whether he is acting as an artist, a lover, or a physician. The hands of men are disempowered by the artist's disproportionate fear of reprimand for his collusion with Babylon's daughters, which in Harry's case is most vividly represented by his "descent" into penning female confession stories. Indeed, hands in the novel continually disrupt assumptions of masculine ownership, and if a resistant capacity can be ascribed to any artist's hand within the novel, it is to Charlotte's and the experimental craft she engages in. In contrast, it is a mix of cultural paranoia and sexual fear that guides Harry's hands when they produce art for the market. The novel thereby serves to dismantle and disrupt the male/female cultural dichotomy of pure praise and compromised performance sustained within the psalm's verses. It does so by juxtaposing an androgynous experimental corporate artist with a fearful male hack writer of feminizing pulp. The novel, as a whole, shows us how wantonly the threat of mass culture is exaggerated and misread by men. If there is a unifying critique in *Jerusalem*, then, it is not aimed at mass cultural production itself but at a grosser "sin": the tired metaphorical approximation of women with commercial art and visual culture.

4

Inscrutable Images and Cultural Migrations

Wartime Noir and the Compson "Appendix"

IN JULY 1942, FAULKNER signed a seven-year contract with Warner Brothers. The studio was particularly drawn to the production of noir films at the time, keen to capitalize on the successes of their noir pictures from the early 1940s: the 1941 detective film *The Maltese Falcon* and the 1942 wartime espionage thriller *Casablanca*, both starring Humphrey Bogart. Between 1942 and 1945, Faulkner was at the center of the second wave of the studio's noir output, working on all three projects that defined the studio's film noir aesthetic in the mid-1940s: *To Have and Have Not* (1944), *Mildred Pierce* (1945), and *The Big Sleep* (1946). These three films represent the noir movement's exotic intrigue, melodramatic woman's film, and crime incarnations respectively. During this time, Faulkner would become highly versatile in his writing for the dark cinema of wartime Hollywood. This also coincided with the period when he produced his most adept and mature work for the screen, as he had already gathered extensive experience in the screenwriting craft during his stints at MGM and Twentieth Century–Fox in the 1930s.

After walking out on his contract at Warner Brothers in September 1945, the first new prose work Faulkner produced was "Appendix Compson: 1699–1945" (originally titled "1699–1945 The Compsons"), which he completed in mid-October. The text was published in 1946 as a gloss to an extract from *The Sound and the Fury* (1929), which appeared in an anthology of the author's work titled *The Portable Faulkner*. The "Appendix" provides a genealogy of the central family of *The Sound and the Fury* over almost two centuries. Of all the members of the dynasty described, the section devoted to Caddy is both the longest, running to six pages, and the most dramatic in content. Faulkner describes Caddy's life after her last appearance in *The Sound and the Fury*, where we see her upon her return to Jefferson on the day of her father's funeral in 1912. Faulkner's "Appendix" tells us that in 1920 Caddy marries "a minor movingpicture magnate" (*N* 1: 1133) in Hollywood, whom she divorces in Mexico in 1925. She then reappears in 1940 in occupied Paris, only to vanish mysteriously. We learn more about Caddy's experiences in wartime Europe when, in 1943, the Jefferson county librarian, Melissa Meek, finds a picture of Caddy in "a slick magazine" (*N* 1: 1134). The photograph shows Caddy in a sports car in Marseilles beside a German staff general. The way in which these new images depict Caddy differs considerably to her presentation in *The Sound and the Fury*. Indeed, perhaps the most remarkable aspect of the whole "Appendix" is Faulkner's reimagining of Caddy in this later depiction as a transnational femme fatale, or potentially even a World War II secret agent.

In this chapter, I will show how this new presentation of Caddy traffics in the imagery of Faulkner's noir and war screenplays rather than his Yoknapatawpha fiction. Faulkner draws particularly on the female image from his noir scripts for "The Big Sleep" (1944) and "Stallion Road" (1945), his portrayals of Gothic women in his screenplays for "Mildred Pierce" (1944) and an unproduced and critically neglected vampire horror film titled "Dreadful Hollow" (c. 1944), and his depiction of World War II secret agents in his war scripts for "The De Gaulle Story" (1942), "Battle Cry" (1943), and "To Have and Have Not" (1944). In these scripts, Faulkner was able to build on his depiction of the European femme fatale from a non-Yoknapatawpha short story titled "Snow," which was written in 1942 but remained unpublished during the author's lifetime. By depicting Caddy as a femme fatale in his "Appendix" from 1946, Faulkner brought a distinct new gender archetype into his Yoknapatawpha prose. To comprehend the significance of this inclusion, one has to consider how Faulkner developed the gender portrayals of "Snow" within his Hollywood work. I will suggest that his use of a popular noir figure has a number of implications for our understanding of Faulkner's writing for page and screen in the 1940s. First, the troubling opacity of Caddy's image reflects noir's close association of gender difference and the visual mechanism of film, in particular the notion that the femme fatale's presentation is "dependent upon perceptual ambiguity and ideas about the limits of vision in relation to knowledge" (Doane, *Femmes Fatales* 3). This recurring feature in Faulkner's 1940s writing, namely the inscrutability or opacity of his women characters, drew on commercial visual culture and was dependent on the circulation of conventions between his modernist fictions and noir screenplays. Second, Caddy's movements as femme fatale from Hollywood to Mexico, then on to occupied France with a German companion, illustrate the transnational migrations and exchanges between the United States and Europe that would stimulate both the genesis of noir film production in the early 1940s and its critical reception as a cultural movement in the postwar years. As we will see, the close relationship established between modernist literature and noir cinema across Faulkner's 1940s works reveals their many cultural intersections during a period when international audiences came to reassess both these genres.

The Genesis of the Compson "Appendix"

The Portable Faulkner was a chronological anthology of Faulkner's work, a compilation of extracts from his Yoknapatawpha fiction and some of his short stories. It was edited and compiled by the writer, critic, and journalist Malcolm Cowley. Cowley's aim was to establish Faulkner as a canonical writer within contemporary American letters, since Faulkner's books had largely fallen out of print in the United States by the mid-1940s. As Cowley recounts in *The Faulkner-Cowley File* (1966), he was attempting to reconcile Faulkner's poor reputation among publishers with the admiration he attracted from literary critics. However, the volume is more than an attempt to grant Faulkner's oeuvre more widespread attention—it is also an ideological project. In this sense, the collection is as noteworthy for what it includes as for what it suppresses. Cowley's aim was to unify the collection under the banner of a "Mississippi series" from Faulkner's fiction, with the intention of giving the reader "a picture of [Yoknapatawpha] county ... from Indian times down to World War II" (22). Cowley, therefore, wished to present Faulkner's work as an organic unity, circumscribed by the borders of Yoknapatawpha. This was a program Faulkner bought into at least notionally, agreeing to collaboratively construct something approximating "a Golden Book of [his] apocryphal county" (Cowley 25), a project he had imagined saving for old age. This project, which Faulkner elsewhere described as his final "Doomsday Book . . . of Yoknapatawpha County" (*LG* 255), was intended to provide "a genealogical survey of his fictional county" (Meriwether 94). It was never fully realized, but Faulkner described the Compson "Appendix" to Cowley as a "genealogy" (Cowley 44), and, as James B. Meriwether points out, the work "appears to fulfil exactly, though on a reduced scale" (95) the idea behind the "Golden Book." Faulkner's additional suggestion for Cowley's proposed project was the inclusion of new material in the form of an "Appendix," "a page or two of synopsis to preface [the final 'Dilsey' section from *The Sound and the Fury*], a condensation of the first 3 sections" (Cowley 31). What Faulkner wrote was not a brief synopsis but, as Cowley summarizes, "a manuscript of twenty or thirty pages, a genealogy, rich in newly imagined episodes" (36).

The "Appendix" that emerged is an extension of the Mississippi series that Cowley had lifted from Faulkner's work, but also a disruption of it, since it intervenes in the Mississippi writing Cowley had considered an impermeable organic whole. Faulkner himself immediately flagged up the disruptive potential of his "Appendix." He composed it without actually owning a copy of the novel it was intended to gloss, resulting in discrepancies of chronology and textual detail. Faulkner's sense that the new work could "stand as it is, as a piece without implications" (Cowley 37), hermetically sealed and innocuous, belies its actual function. The "Appendix" in fact features inconsistencies that overtly contradict its predecessor with which it is codependent. Faulkner would defend these inconsistencies to Cowley, stating that they "prove to me the book is still alive after 15 years, and being alive is still growing, changing; the appendix was done at the same heat as the book, even though 15 years later, and so it is the book itself which is inconsistent: not the appendix" (Cowley 90). Faulkner's estimation of the work's importance, that it brings *The Sound and the Fury* "into pattern like a jigsaw puzzle when the magician's wand touched it" (Cowley 36), suggests that Faulkner did in fact see the "Appendix" as radically realigning and retrospectively clarifying his novel from 1929. Its "implications" are evidently more wide-ranging than he elsewhere states. Among the disruptions the "Appendix" causes, Faulkner's genealogy of the Compsons stretches from 1699 to 1945, whereas the original novel's narratives stretch from 1910 to 1928. This time span disturbed the strict temporal structure of the anthology, which Cowley chose to organize chronologically according to the fictional time the selected works occupy; indeed, as Cheryl Lester argues, "with its two connected dates, which indicate a continuum or span of time rather than a point within one, the title of the appendix precludes and disrupts Cowley's system" (379).

Even more radically, the explicit reference to Hollywood in Caddy's section of the genealogy alludes to a level of subversion that Faulkner himself would not perhaps have conceded. Faulkner wrote in a letter to Cowley that he believed he had the "movie work locked off into another room" (Cowley 16), away from his prose. Indeed, Faulkner felt that he had to consciously expel the influence of Hollywood in order to create the "Appendix," and assesses its value in terms of its distance from his screenwriting: "I think this is all right, it took me about a week to get Hollywood out of my lungs, but I am still writing all right, I believe" (Cowley 37). Faulkner's defense of inconsistencies in his writing, too, can be read as an anti-collaborative impulse, perhaps wishing to distance himself from the overtly networked labors of Hollywood; as Erin Penner highlights, "by attesting to the need for characters to 'grow,' [Faulkner] erected significant defenses against editorial and readerly intrusions" (113). Caddy's marriage to a Hollywood magnate surfaces as if to undermine Faulkner's professed distance from or imperviousness to commercial filmmaking when writing experimental prose. The text itself conversely highlights the text's closeness to Hollywood, as Faulkner places a Yoknapatawpha heroine in the very center of the studio system through her five-year marriage to a movie magnate. Contrary to what Faulkner expresses to Cowley, the explicit reference to Hollywood in the "Appendix" invites us to view Caddy's new presentation in dialogic relation to Faulkner's contemporaneous screenplay work.

Caddy Compson in the "Appendix"

Faulkner devotes a whole section of the "Appendix" to Caddy, and his new descriptions of the character move beyond her depiction in *The Sound and the Fury*. From the very beginning of this section of the genealogy, Caddy is associated with doom, first through her own self-knowledge ("Doomed and knew it, accepted the doom without either seeking or fleeing it" [*N* 1: 1132]), and second, through her brother Quentin's fetishistic sense that his sister's loss of virginity will bring about the Compson family's downfall; Faulkner calls Quentin "that bitter prophet and inflexible corruptless judge of what he considered the family's honor and its doom" (*N* 1: 1132). Through the knowledge of her and Quentin's shared doom, Faulkner even ascribes Caddy a murderous quality. He asserts that since Caddy was aware of Quentin's death drive, she "would (and perhaps in the calculation and deliberation of her marriage did) have handed him the hypothetical hemlock" (*N* 1: 1132). It is this combined focus on Caddy's destructive and deadly instincts that first brings her image in line with the fatale from noir.

Faulkner's first depiction of Caddy in the "Appendix" after the events of *The Sound and the Fury* positions her in cultural and national environments alternative to those presented in the 1929 novel. Faulkner recounts that she

> was two months pregnant with another man's child which regardless of what its sex would be she had already named Quentin . . . when she married (1910) an extremely eligible young Indianian she and her mother had met while vacationing at French Lick the summer before. Divorced by him 1911. Married 1920 to a minor movingpicture magnate, Hollywood California. Divorced by mutual agreement, Mexico 1925. Vanished in Paris with the German occupation, 1940, still beautiful and probably still wealthy too since she did not look within fifteen years of her actual fortyeight, and was not heard of again. (*N* 1: 1132–33)

In this passage, Caddy enters a Hollywood marriage that culminates in divorce in Mexico. Her doom—a word repeated four times at the beginning of her section—seems to be linked to her commodity value, as she moves between marriages for financial gain. Her image is essentially inscrutable here, as the description makes a series of abrupt temporal leaps from 1910 to 1940, concluding with her sudden and mysterious disappearance in occupied France. In this new depiction, Faulkner exposes Caddy to the intimate influences of both mass culture (Hollywood) and transnational flows and exchanges (Mexico and Western Europe). Perhaps reflecting Faulkner's cultural biases, Caddy's contact with Hollywood is framed as a further stage in her degradation, for she is seduced by the economic allure of commercial film. Despite the seismic changes in her life, Caddy maintains her ageless beauty and wealth, with Faulkner suggesting that the former enables her to procure the latter.

Caddy's image is mediated further through her second "appearance" in the "Appendix" in a magazine photograph discovered by Meek. The prose describes "a picture, a photograph in color clipped obviously from a slick magazine—a picture filled with luxury and money and sunlight—a Cannebière [sic] backdrop of mountains and palms and cypresses and the sea, an open powerful expensive chromiumtrimmed sports car, the woman's face hatless between a rich scarf and a seal coat, ageless and beautiful, cold serene and damned; beside her a handsome lean man of middleage in the ribbons and tabs of a German staffgeneral" (*N* 1: 1134). Building on the first description, Caddy's proximity to a Nazi officer, as well as her apparent enjoyment of luxury, seems to indicate her increasingly mercenary nature. It is also in this "picture," however, that Faulkner cements his presentation of Caddy using the visual vocabularies of the dark sexualities of wartime noir and the Gothic film. Caddy is aligned with the iconography of the femme fatale through her association with European excess, dangerously attractive men with tarnished reputations, and the speed of technological modernity, while her timeless and dangerous beauty, more iconic than palpably human, is markedly Gothic in its delineation.

To put these descriptions in the context of the whole work, Caddy's section of the "Appendix" is interposed between those devoted to her brothers Quentin III and Jason IV. The "Appendix" first describes the patriarchal ancestor of Yoknapatawpha, Ikkemotubbe, "a dispossessed American king" (*N* 1: 1127), and then moves on to the Compson line from the eighteenth century, a succession of men who enjoyed less than illustrious military careers and also experienced their share of flight and dispossession, until it reaches Caddy's father, Jason III, who sells off the last of the Compson land. At this point, the progress of the Compson line encounters a dead end, as the three last male bearers of the family name are dead (Quentin), castrated (Benjy), and a childless bachelor (Jason). The line is only able to continue through the Compson women and Caddy's daughter, Quentin. Faulkner in fact ascribes a similar destructive fate to Caddy's daughter, who he claims was "already doomed to be unwed from the instant the dividing egg determined its sex" (*N* 1: 1139). Quentin also vanishes, when she runs away with her pitchman lover. Yet, lest the reader be tempted to draw too many comparisons between mother and daughter, Faulkner details that "whatever occupation overtook her would have arrived in no chromium Mercedes; whatever snapshot would have contained no general of staff" (*N* 1: 1141). The "Appendix" concludes with the terse and dismissive description of the Black characters who served the last of the Compsons: TP, Frony, Luster, and Dilsey. Though neglected, Faulkner grants them the quality of stoicism in a tokenistic gesture with the final line "They endured" (*N* 1: 1141).

Minrose C. Gwin argues that in the "Appendix," Caddy "is the voice of alterity to the long list of failed men of Faulkner's Appendix" (*Feminine and*

Faulkner 61). And in the catalog of dispossessed patriarchs, Caddy's section is something of an anomaly, the sections given to the female Quentin and the Black non-Compsons notwithstanding. Additional elements, though, contribute to the "alterity" of her section. As mentioned, Caddy is the only remaining member of the Compson family to produce a child, and therefore the only one who contributes to the continuation of this strange, arrested genealogy. Her otherness is also emphasized by the singularity of her fate, which contrasts starkly with what Faulkner predicts will befall her daughter. Finally, from a formal perspective, as Joseph R. Urgo points out, it is the only section of the appendix to employ present-tense action and dialogue (*Apocrypha* 41), granting it a heightened dramatic quality. But it is through references to cinema that Caddy's otherness is most explicitly presented. Thadious M. Davis argues that the debt of the "Appendix" to film is manifested through its "visualization of *The Sound and the Fury*," by recasting and reforming the plot in an omniscient narrative that can be scrutinized from the outside in rather than the inside out, and in its role as "a self-enclosed, self-referential inscription of the author as inventor, filmmaker, screenwriter, and cinematographer" (243). In addition to this sense of the "Appendix" formally mimicking the cinema, I would like to consider how the text alludes to the films Faulkner worked on in the 1940s before its composition.

The femme fatale image also appeared in Faulkner's non-Yoknapatawpha prose contemporary to the writing of his noir and Gothic screenplays. Faulkner submitted the story "Snow" to his agent Harold Ober in February 1942 (*SL* 149), and he revised it again in July of that year. In a letter to Ober received on 22 July, Faulkner stated in reference to the story, "you had this before. It is rewritten, simplified, still an implied story as before, but I have tried to fill the gaps, etc. and make it explicit as well" (*SL* 161). Faulkner would begin work at Warner Brothers on 26 July, so "Snow" was the last piece of fiction the author worked on before traveling to California, and its conventions would remain prominent in his mind at the studio. By 1949, Ober had still failed to place the story with a publisher (Cantrell 325), and it remained unpublished during Faulkner's lifetime, although aspects of the work would have an afterlife in his screenwriting and published fiction. In "Snow," a short news story appears in an American paper around the time of Pearl Harbor with the caption "Nazi Governor of Czodnia Slain by Companion" (*US* 665). The piece elaborates that a German governor of Serbia, General von Ploeckner, has been stabbed to death by his companion of several years, a Frenchwoman. The newspaper story is accompanied by two images, one which depicts "the cold, satiated, handsome Prussian face," the other "the woman's face . . . a little older than . . . fifteen years ago and no longer a peasant's face now" (*US* 665). The text then flashes back to prewar (and pre–Nazi era) Europe and a Swiss alpine region through which two Americans are traveling in a story that offers, as Solomon suggests, a "retroactive premonition of Nazism" (*Screenwriting* 122). The Americans come across the woman who will later go on to murder the German governor. She has come back to her home village in "a [Paris] hat and a fur coat that were not bought in any Swiss city" (*US* 669) for her husband's funeral, a mountaineering guide who died in a climbing accident. One of the Americans, named Don, suspects that the woman may have conspired to murder her husband with a rich German, "The Big Shot" (*US* 673). The woman and the German also took part in the fatal climb but survived. Don's suspicions are further aroused when he hears that the day after the guide fell from the mountain and was lost, his wife and the German took the train to Milan together. She later returns to the funeral in opulent clothes. The story implies that she has been involved in the murder of two of her partners, one a Swiss mountain guide, the other a Nazi governor.

The woman's transition from a rural background to close association with corrupt wealth and power through expedient relationships mirrors Caddy's own movement from the rural South to the wealthy circles of Hollywood and the French southern coast.[1] The woman in "Snow" also possesses the murderous instincts that Faulkner only subtly ascribes to Caddy in the "Appendix." In "Snow," the woman's inscrutability is also illustrated; though the newspaper identifies her as French, it transpires that the woman is in fact Swiss, despite her predilection for expensive Parisian fashion. The wartime neutrality of Switzerland adds further ambiguity to her allegiances; her motivations remain similarly opaque, as we are unsure whether she has killed the Nazi for personal or political reasons. Most important for my analysis, this image is saturated with the imagery of the femme fatale. This is a gender archetype Faulkner would develop further in Hollywood and later embed in the "Appendix," by which point he had decided that one of his most famous fictional creations should inhabit the persona in a major retrospective of his work.

Such an exchange suggests that Faulkner was at least keyed to the iconography of the cinematic femme fatale shortly before his trip to Warner Brothers, as evidenced by his delineation of the murderous wartime woman in "Snow," and was able to further his portrayal of the figure in his Hollywood work. It also indicates the circulatory nature of Faulkner's exchanges with cinema; Faulkner drew on the images of "Snow" for his work on his film scripts such as "The Big Sleep" and "Stallion Road," which he could in turn draw on for his Yoknapatawpha fiction after leaving Hollywood. In the "Appendix," he would explore the strength of the femme fatale's image by dramatizing a meditation on indecipherability, a central component to female characterization and narrative plotting in noir. Although Frank Cantrell reads the complexities of the murders in "Snow" as "extreme" to the point of making the tale "virtually incomprehensible or incredible" (330), such indecipherability is in fact typical of noir. What "Snow," Faulkner's Gothic and noir screenplays, and the "Appendix" all have in common is a central focus on the destabilization of the image through filmic or photographic mediation. These circulatory exchanges with commercial visual culture culminate in the mass cultural inscrutability of Caddy's presentation in the "Appendix," which, as I will demonstrate, is distinct from the modernist inscrutability that defines her presentation in *The Sound and the Fury*.

The Dark Sexualities of Wartime Noir and the Gothic Woman

Caddy's section of the "Appendix" is framed by Quentin's anxieties about the detrimental effect his sister's unbridled sexuality will have on "the family's honor" (*N* 1: 1132), or the patriarchal Compson line that the "Appendix" otherwise describes. Such a fraught relationship structured around fear, fetishism, and overinvestment reflects the wartime gender conflicts that inform female characterization in noir. To summarize the social importance of this widely discussed filmic archetype, the fatale is a figure of female independence and unsettling sexuality who endangers the men around her through her essentially destructive nature. As described in the introduction, film noir explored threatened masculinity after the conclusion of World War II, as during the war many women had "usurped" men on the domestic front in positions of work. The response to this development after the end of war was a strident reassertion of domestic life in national narratives and ideology, and the widespread expulsion of women from their newfound roles. Faulkner himself expressed fear about the development of women's social roles during World War II. He visited an aircraft factory in 1942 as research for a Warner Brothers war movie titled "The Life and Death of a Bomber / Liberator Story." He notes under a section elliptically titled "Women": "Do all types of work, drop hammer, spot welding, painting and doping, sewing linen. Man & wife not permitted to work at same job . . . Will they want to quit after the war?"[2] Although the tone of Faulkner's note is neutral and descriptive here, his final question nevertheless addresses a broader contemporary American sociosexual anxiety that the men fighting in war may have been permanently usurped by the housewives they left behind.

In film noir, it is the figure of the sensual and duplicitous femme fatale who plays scapegoat for such male insecurity and the challenge posed to male dominance. As E. Ann Kaplan outlines, "noir *expresses* alienation, locates its cause squarely in the excesses of female sexuality . . . and punishes that excess in order to re-place it within the patriarchal order" ("Introduction" 17). What the audience is granted is a masculine view of female sexuality, where an overinvestment in the femme fatale's allure imperils male subjectivity; that threat is mastered through the sadistic apparatus of the noir movie, which frequently concludes with either the violent death or imprisonment of the fatale figure. This movement is essentially allegorical, reflecting male anxieties in postwar America, and the associated impulse to control the woman and her unbridled sexuality so as not to be overthrown by it.

Most applicable to my understanding of Caddy's image in the "Appendix," however, are the indecipherable, inscrutable, and unknowable qualities of the femme fatale in noir. Mary Ann Doane argues that the fatale "harbors a threat which is not entirely legible, predictable, or manageable. In thus transforming the threat of the woman into a secret, something which must be aggressively revealed, unmasked, discovered, the figure is fully compatible with the epistemological drive of narrative, the hermeneutic structuration of the classical text" (*Femmes Fatales* 1). In other words, it is the fatale's duplicitous or deceitful nature that is exposed by the narrative movement of noir films. Perhaps unsurprising in this medium, the illegible threat the fatale poses is linked to limitations of vision. As Doane elaborates, film noir "establishes a disturbance of vision as a premise of the film's signifying system. The lighting style implies a distortion of an originally clear and readable image and the consequent crisis of vision. Since the epistemological cornerstone of the classical text is the dictum, 'the image does not lie,' film noir tends to flirt with the limits of this system, the guarantee of its readability oscillating between an image which often conceals a great deal and a voice-over which is not always entirely credible" (*Femmes Fatales* 103).³ This aesthetic presentation of epistemological crisis is linked to the inscrutability of the female, since, for Doane, "the woman confounds the relation between the visible and the knowable at the same time that she is made into an object for the gaze" (*Femmes Fatales* 103). As such, the femme fatale is a threat both to systems of knowledge and to cinematic narrative itself. We find Caddy in a similar position in her section of the "Appendix," as her mediated image frustrates visual knowledge, denying the text closure, while at the same time propelling the visual speculation that generates the narrative.

In his screenplay work for Warner Brothers in the mid-1940s, Faulkner would develop his portrayal of the femme fatale's hard-boiled sexuality, which he would later draw on for the Compson "Appendix." He was instrumental in the construction of damned, destructive, sexually charismatic women in his co-authored screenplay for "The Big Sleep," as well as his unproduced screenplay "Stallion Road." His writing for these pictures explores a wartime sense of erotic threat that either needs to be purged or has the potential to redeem the hero.

Faulkner explored the redemptive quality of the hero's relation to the dark noir heroine in his screenplay for "The Big Sleep," produced with his fellow screenwriter Leigh Brackett. Brackett would develop a strong working relationship with Hawks that would last for over twenty years after they collaborated on this noir film. As Kristina Hackel summarizes about Brackett's career, the screenwriter "thrived writing for male characters" in noir and Western films (741), and Brackett herself stated that "Hawks and I kind of tuned in on the same channel with regard to the characters" (qtd. in McGilligan, *Backstory 2* 18). In relation to female characterization, Brackett stated that "conventional heroines bore [Hawks]; he can't 'have fun' with them" (120); Brackett believed her own science fiction presented unconventional female characters "with independent lives and thoughts of their own, capable of being comrades and mates but always of their own free choice and always as equals. . . . So the Hawksian woman fitted my typewriter well" (121). Faulkner and Brackett divided the work up evenly between them to produce their final screenplay, dated 26 September 1944, the version from which I cite. Brackett stopped work on the project after this, and Faulkner's last contributions to the screenplay appear to be some story changes he made in December 1944 (Solomon, *Screenwriting* 180, 184). The major change the writers made in adapting Raymond Chandler's novel from 1939 was to make the private detective hero, Philip Marlowe (played by Bogart), fall in love with the daughter of the general who has hired him, Vivian Sternwood (played by Lauren Bacall). This adaptation resulted in the tough, evil Vivian of the novel being transformed into a "good-bad girl"; Doane argues that in relation to this specific variant of the femme fatale, the narrative of the noir film serves to reveal that "feminine evil is not a fundamental condition but an accessory, an accident" (*Femmes Fatales* 108). Faulkner and Brackett's changes lent a haziness to Vivian's motivations that was essential to Marlowe's quest; in the screenwriters' handling, the narrative serves to decode Vivian, to expose how "good" she really is beneath her tough exterior.[4] Vivian's indistinctness in their screenplay is essential to the classical delineation of the femme fatale, whose very seductive potency "exemplifies the disparity between seeming and being, the deception, instability, and unpredictability associated with the woman" (Doane, *Femmes Fatales* 46). In their list of characters, Faulkner and Brackett outline Vivian's character as "spoiled, exacting, smart, ruthless, with a habit for getting married" (Faulkner et al. 140), the last quality particularly reminiscent of Caddy in the "Appendix." In addition, in quintessential femme fatale delineation, she is described as "beautiful, giving the impression of strong will and strong emotions—the dangerous unpredictable type" (Faulkner et al. 140). It is the elements of danger and unpredictability that contribute most strongly to Vivian's inscrutability. These facets of Vivian's character are developed throughout the screenplay in both dialogue and set instructions; at one point, Marlowe compares Vivian to "a stick of dynamite. Smooth on the outside—but it makes a mess when it goes off" (Faulkner et al. 313). The "dynamite" image illustrates Vivian's inscrutability well. Elsewhere, Faulkner and Brackett indicate that Vivian looks "exhausted, stony, but giving an impression of submerged but volcanic emotion" (Faulkner et al. 301); the implication is that her genuine emotions or psychological state are buried deep beneath her "stony" hard-boiled presentation.

Also central to Vivian's presentation as a fatale are her destructive impulses. In the screenplay, Vivian wears her "vices" of drinking and gambling addiction lightly, and there is a continual emphasis on her fatal attitude, her belief in her damnation, and her sense of the impossibility of her redemption in lines such as "I've learned not to believe in anything. I don't need you, Marlowe. I don't know how you got here, but I don't want you" (Faulkner et al. 211). In one fight scene with Marlowe, Vivian bites his wrist, as well as shooting a hijacker when she leaves the casino with her winnings, aggressive details omitted in Hawks's filmed version (Faulkner et al. 217, 255–56). She is also fixated on the "corrupt blood" of the Sternwood daughters, exclaiming to Marlowe at one point that "we're [General Sternwood's] blood. That's where the hurt is. That Father might die despising his own blood. It was always wild, but it wasn't always rotten" (Faulkner et al. 260). Vivian's sense of belonging to a corrupted patriarchal line is mirrored by Caddy's own self-knowledge that she is part of a doomed genealogy.

Despite the danger Vivian poses to Marlowe through her unpredictability and apparent appetite for self-destruction, Faulkner and Brackett develop romance between the pair. Part of Marlowe's attraction to Vivian as presented by the screenwriters is his respect for her hard-boiled nature; he believes that had she committed the murder of Regan, she would have shot him from the front rather than the back. Echoing this, Marlowe's determination to find Regan whatever the cost and the dangers involved stimulates Vivian to feel genuine affection for him. This eventually leads to the revealing of Vivian's good nature beneath her ambiguous good-bad girl image, a process of unmasking that redeems the lovers. Both Faulkner and Brackett's screenplay and Hawks's film emphasize Vivian's honor in being willing to take the rap for her sister, who, it transpires, is the murderer. Vivian hired a gangster to cover up Carmen's guilt. The screenplay elaborates Vivian's honor within criminal circumstances: "I had prayers said for him in the Cathedral. And I brought the Father out here, too. I couldn't lie to him. He stood beside the sump and blessed Shawn [Regan]. I prayed too—for me, at least" (Faulkner et al. 326). This knowledge is the reward for Marlowe's quest to reveal Vivian's true self, as he discovers her capacity to maintain a moral code whilst engaging in ethically questionable action, a system by which he also lives. The film concludes with lines that imply that Marlowe and Vivian's union is structured around his ability to redeem her past actions; when Marlowe asks Vivian what's wrong with her, she replies, "Nothing you can't fix," as the police sirens come over the soundtrack (*Big Sleep*). In Faulkner and Brackett's conclusion, however, which takes place in the Sternwood mansion, Marlowe tells the police, "you won't have to hold me here. I've decided already myself to stay" (Faulkner et al. 329). The line implies that rather than Vivian needing Marlowe to repair her, he has actively chosen to step into her world after having decoded her character, able to perceive the mode of being that underpins her behavior and reflects his own. The goodness that is finally revealed beneath her hard-boiled exterior conquers both of their cynicism.

The last screenplay Faulkner completed for Warner Brothers, in September 1945 before walking out on his contract and returning to Mississippi, was his adaptation of the Stephen Longstreet novel of the same name, *Stallion Road*, published in 1945. In his screenplay, Faulkner presents the femme fatale, Daisy Otis, as both excessive and dangerous. But in contrast to his work on "The Big Sleep," "Stallion Road" presents the fatale as a figure that has to be destroyed to ensure the hero's survival and happiness. The final "reveal" here is different; while "The Big Sleep" serves to expose Vivian's essential good nature, "Stallion Road" uncovers Daisy's evil character. In the screenplay, two women, Daisy and Fleece Teller, compete over the love of the young veterinarian, Larry Hanrahan. Faulkner's portrayal of the dangerously attractive Daisy is in keeping both with his consistent flouting of the strict rules of the Production Code in relation to sexual content, and the hard-boiled presentation of female sexuality he had developed in "The Big Sleep." Daisy is described in Faulkner's cast of characters as being "attractive as hell—and she knows it . . . she has a roving eye and body" (*SR* 2). She is an effective seducer, a mercenary lover (she married a man for his money while her former lover Larry was at war), and a cynic deploying a quick-fire succession of disarmingly arch one-liners: as another male character describes her, "she's dangerous. She's poison. She's worse than that: she's dynamite" (*SR* 60), recalling the metaphoric description of Vivian in Faulkner and Brackett's screenplay.[5]

As part of her hard-boiled demeanor, Daisy comfortably asserts her sexual appetite, deviancy, and self-interest and derives pleasure from violence. During a fight with Fleece, Daisy claws at her rival's face, then sinks her teeth into her wrist, as Vivian does to Marlowe in Faulkner's writing for "The Big Sleep." In her most excessive act, Daisy, fearing rejection, attempts to murder Larry by injecting him with pure anthrax; when she steps back to observe the big hypodermic needle dangling from his arm "she watches, her teeth bared, her eyes glittering" (*SR* 87), almost in a state of arousal. Her capacity for violence is the aspect of her character that seems to most violate the expectations male characters place upon her; as one character concludes, "don't talk to me about frail females, Señor. But then, she was born and raised in these mountains" (*SR* 92). In contrast to the good-bad girl, Daisy as evil fatale has to be destroyed. Fleeing the destruction she has left in her wake, and in pursuit by the police, "going fast, grim and now frightened," Daisy loses control of the coupe she is driving, skids off the road, and tumbles down the side of a mountain (*SR* 96). Daisy's attempted murder of Larry and self-destruction are Faulkner's additions to Longstreet's story, and her death serves a purgative function as the dark woman dies to allow for a reunion between the two characters most suited to each other, Larry and the animal-loving Fleece. Daisy's murderous nature, potent sexuality, and association with self-destructive excess and speed all seem to anticipate the image of Caddy in the "Appendix." The process of unveiling the femme fatale in Faulkner's noir screenplays leads to the divergent conclusions of "The Big Sleep" and "Stallion Road," where the heroine either redeems the hero through her essential, but hidden, goodness or the murderous woman is destroyed in order to save the hero. Such an unmasking, however, is never completed in relation to Caddy in the "Appendix," a lack of closure that contributes to the enduring instability of her image.

Allied to Faulkner's visual presentation of the femme fatale is his depiction of the Gothic woman in his redrafting of the screenplay for "Mildred Pierce," which he completed in December 1944. Similar to the femme fatale's inscrutability, the Gothic female in this script is presented as visually deceptive.[6] Albert J. LaValley describes Faulkner's additions to the script as emphasizing "the lurid, the extravagant, and the outrageous" (31), and it was particularly the changes he made to the depiction of Mildred's spoiled, capricious, and manipulative daughter Veda that pushed the script for a melodramatic women's picture in the direction of Gothic excess.[7] In one such scene, after Mildred's younger, innocent child, Ray,[8] dies, Faulkner illustrates Veda's grief.[9] Veda enters Mildred's bedroom in her nightdress, moving "like a sleep-walker, stiffly."[10] Faulkner indicates that "in the dim light [Veda's] face is a ravaged mask of grief, her eyes deeply circled with shadow, staring as she enters slowly, one hand extended, looking at no one, apparently seeing nothing."[11] Mildred frantically tries to comfort her daughter, but when touched, Veda "gives a shuddering sigh and collapses, apparently unconscious."[12] Mildred carries Veda back to her room, struggles to lower her daughter onto her bed, but then notices something on the front of her own negligee, "a long black stain ... where Veda's head rested."[13] There is then a close-up of Veda's face; she has her eyes closed, but "what looked like heavy circles of grief under Veda's eyes is now revealed as carefully put on mascara where Veda has made herself up to simulate sorrow."[14] In this troubling scene, Veda uses her sister's death as an opportunity to manipulate her mother. Veda's cruelty is closely linked to her inscrutability, as her face falsely manifests a mask of grief.

To overcome Veda's unreadability, Faulkner uses narrative development to expose Veda's true nature to the other characters. At the wedding party for Mildred's second marriage, to Monte Beragon, an aristocratic rake, Faulkner writes that Veda "is dressed for the celebration, but she is not in it. She is looking at the group from partial concealment. Her face is no longer just inscrutable. It is cold, speculative, vicious; her true self shows and her face is not one to pass lightly."[15] Through jealousy of her mother, Veda's enigmatic quality begins to evaporate. At the close of Faulkner's screenplay, when it is finally revealed that Veda is guilty of Monte's murder, a crime for which Mildred attempts to take responsibility, Mildred tries to embrace her daughter, but Veda exclaims, "pah! Save it for yourself. You'll need it, even if they don't give me a chance to come back and haunt you."[16] Faulkner insistently calls attention to Veda's uncanny quality and her deathliness, in scenes that seem to advance a vision of Veda as a repressed, threatening, and potentially fatal side to Mildred's own character. This sense of Veda as an obverse or hidden version of Mildred adds to Faulkner's presentation of the inscrutability of the Gothic woman.

The Gothic strain to Faulkner's female characterization in his 1940s screenwriting comes to the fore most prominently in his unproduced horror screenplay "Dreadful Hollow." Howard Hawks bought the film rights for the vampire novel *Dreadful Hollow* in November 1944 for $2,500, which was written by Helen Mary Elizabeth Clamp under the pseudonym Irina Karlova and published in 1942 (McCarthy 403). Hawks specifically wanted Faulkner to adapt the novel, and Faulkner probably produced his screenplay around December 1944 (Solomon, *Screenwriting* 15). Despite Hawks's enthusiasm for the script, both Warner Brothers and Fox were not interested, even after the director's repeated attempts to get the picture made (McCarthy 403). Set in a house in England called the Grange, Faulkner's script introduces the Countess Czerner, a female Dracula, who is initially described thus:

> The countess sits in a high-backed chair almost like a throne, close to the hearth on which a fire burns even though it is June. There is something strange about her. At first glance, she appears to be an old woman. But something is wrong. She was beautiful once. She looks frail and wrinkled, her face is lined and the hand which she holds out to the fire looks like a claw. Yet her hair is raven black, her eyes and teeth are those of a young woman. Even her voice is young in pitch, with only a slight crack in it.[17]

The countess is an unnerving collection of discordant images and sounds, which variously signify youth, old age, and a bestial quality. The character possesses a compelling attractiveness that serves to make potent female sexuality monstrous; as Jack Halberstam points out within his analysis of Bram Stoker's *Dracula* (1897) and the Gothic tradition, "vampiric sexuality blends power and femininity within the same body and then marks that body as distinctly alien" (100). Michelle E. Moore also highlights that the countess's confusing appearance is synonymous with "a form of feminine masquerade that endangers men and young girls" ("Vampires"). The countess's otherworldly femininity is most directly presented as a threat to the heroine of the screenplay, the young Jillian Dare, who has been employed as a paid companion for the mistress of the Grange. Dare finds a photograph of her employer from the past: "It is a heavy tarnished silver frame; Jillian recognizes it to be the countess, but younger, in an older day. She is beautiful, proud, with a wild strange look, slender, in the riding habit of a bygone day, posed, slim-waisted, in a full skirt and a hat with sweeping plumes."[18] The image recalls Caddy's presentation in the magazine clipping as "ageless and beautiful, cold serene and damned" (*N* 1: 1134), as well as the perplexing enduring youth Faulkner attributes to Caddy: "she did not look within fifteen years of her actual fortyeight" (*N* 1: 1133). Both "Dreadful Hollow" and the "Appendix" place an emphasis on the viewer's struggle to interpret the inconsistencies of the female image.

Beyond this sense of the Gothic inflection of Caddy's image in the 1940s, though, the countess's depiction suggests that the image has an affinity to a corpse until it is revivified by new viewers. When Jillian looks up at the countess's window from the garden, she sees that in her bedroom

> facing the window is a big, regal-looking canopied bed. The countess lies in the bed, propped on pillows. She looks like a corpse, motionless, her eyes closed, her clawlike hands on the covers above her. Suddenly her eyes open. They are looking straight at Jillian. For a moment more she does not move. Then the frail wasted [woman] is galvanised into motion. The countess flings the covers aside, gets up and runs toward the window with amazing agility and speed. Her face is wild-looking, urgent and importunate. She stops, pressed to the glass, making a beseeching gesture of supplication with her hands, her lips moving, her voice coming thin and faint through the glass.[19]

Similar to the image of Caddy in the "Appendix," we sense that the corpselike image comes to life again once it is reinvested with the imagination of the spectator. Maurice Blanchot argues that "the cadaver is its own image. It no longer entertains any relation with this world, where it still appears, except that of an image, an obscure possibility, a shadow ever present behind the living" (258). As the presentation of the countess from "Dreadful Hollow" illustrates, both the corpse and image are held in a state of fixity that haunts the viewer. But the way in which the countess springs to life, "galvanized into motion," is pointedly filmic, recalling André Bazin's notion that in the cinema, "the image of things is likewise the image of their duration, change mummified" (15). Cinema's preservation of change, sparing it death, cannot be reanimated, of course, until it is viewed. This is a parasitic exchange where the dead image depends on new viewers to restore it to life; indeed, the countess says to Jillian that her very presence as a viewer restores her, and "that's why it is good to have you here—young, warm, pretty, with the hot sweet blood of youth in your veins to share with me—make me young again."[20] Faulkner's work on cinematic archetypes for women in his 1940s screenplays, then, consistently emphasized the female image as destabilized, unpredictable, and potentially deceptive, features that should be considered in relation to Faulkner's depiction of Caddy in the "Appendix."

Female Sacrifice in the World War II Film

The indecipherability of Caddy's image also relates to its historical framing during World War II, when she disappears in Paris during the German occupation, as Faulkner drew on his Warner Brothers war scripts for her new presentation in the "Appendix." Faulkner began work at the studio just seven months after America's entry into World War II, at a time when the studio was rapidly increased its war movie output. He worked on a number of war films there, including two scenes for 1943's *Air Force*, which was crucial in representing national attitudes towards the early US war effort, as "millions of Americans relived the startling news of Pearl Harbor and the first, disastrous months of war in the Pacific with the crew of the 'Mary Jane' in *Air Force*" (Baker 45). Warner's big hit of 1942 was *Casablanca*, a spy thriller movie set in French Morocco that explored fascist control. Indeed, as Solomon has commented, Warner Brothers grappled with the threat of Nazism in their war pictures at an earlier stage than other studios, through films such as 1939's *Confessions of a Nazi Spy*, which explored the infiltration of Nazis into the United States (*Screenwriting* 123). Films such as *Casablanca* reflected the realities of war and its effects on human relations, as they dealt with "displaced people—characters who were fugitives from the Nazis, or anti-fascists who had become aliens within their own societies" (Baker 46). In terms of female characters, women in these films "were rejected by the men they loved; they were compelled to give up their dreams of pleasant, secure homes; and they had to cope with a continual life of flight, or the terrors of forced prostitution, or the reality of Nazi sterilization laboratories" (Baker 46). Given Faulkner's exposure to wartime studio work and participation in national propagandist war movies, it is possible to reframe his wartime Caddy as a figure not unlike Ingrid Bergman's Ilsa Lund from *Casablanca*. Caddy, like Ilsa, is a displaced figure in flight in wartime Europe, her disappearance shrouded in mystery. Also, in the way Baker sees war shaping the lives of women, when we view Caddy in the magazine clipping with the German staff general, perhaps our judgment of her is mitigated by an awareness of the tropes of the movies in which the wartime woman appears—she is a figure in exile, rejected by previous lovers, and perhaps even forced into prostitution. Caddy can be seen to flee from one oppressive system only to get caught up in another, as she escapes the moral judgments of the American South only to be trapped within a fascist system that used the sexual exploitation of women as a tool of war.

But what if Caddy's intentions were more subversive than they might superficially appear? The heroism of female secret agents airlifted into occupied France in World War II was documented heavily by male writers and filmmakers during the war years. We can productively compare Caddy's presentation with the politically subversive heroines of Faulkner's wartime screenplays: Emilie in "The De Gaulle Story"; Clemente in "Battle Cry"; and Helene in "To Have and Have Not." Cross-referencing with these works implies that Caddy's situation could be anything between a captive and a resistance worker. Faulkner used a similar body of material for his screenplays on occupied France across these works, all of which are indebted to *Casablanca*.

The same month that Faulkner completed his revisions to "Snow," he started work on his first war picture for Warner Brothers, "The De Gaulle Story." He returned to the French episode he wrote for this film in his writing for "Battle Cry," "which was conceived as an epic film with separate chapters depicting American, British, French, Russian, and Chinese resistance to the Axis powers on various fronts" (*FBC* 4: xix). In "Battle Cry," Clemente

Desmoulins, a young Frenchwoman who was formerly a prostitute, becomes lovers with a British corporal, Albert Loughton. Like Caddy, the sexual judgment of the community condemns Clemente; she attempts to escape her "tainted" past but is continually confronted by the judgments of Parisian society. She explains the "shame" of her previous circumstances to Albert after his marriage proposal: "It was cold, too. Winter, and coming from the Midi, where it is never cold except when the mistral . . . There was just one, an old man he seemed to me then. As old as my father might have been. Then the police . . . I don't know how it happened, but one day there they were. They registered me, gave me the card. And so ever since—every six months . . . If I didn't, they would arrest me, you see" (FBC 4: 372–73). When the Germans invade France, Albert escapes at Dunkirk, but Clemente is trapped in Paris, where she is raped, forced to become the mistress of a German officer, and has to return to prostitution to support herself. She is subjected to the degradation and sinister ideology of a sexual parade for a Gestapo officer:

OFFICER
>   . . . what better way to put an end forever to this useless strife between us, than to mix our blood. What better destiny for the young women of France, than to bear children to the young soldiers of victorious Germany (FBC 4: 377–78)

The women are dressed up by the German policewomen in "negligee, boudoir" (FBC 4: 379), allotted numbers on placards, and made to parade before a peep show, behind which the German officers choose the girls they are interested in. Even after her rape and return to prostitution, Clemente's resistant quality persists: "the character and courage which enabled her to resist the Germans in Paris to the last is still there" (FBC 4: 381). Clemente looks for help from Henri Ballin, who has become an Underground agent for General de Gaulle. Clemente forgoes her chance to escape France for England with the Underground agents and instead involves herself in the Underground cell's strategy to sabotage a planned German invasion of England. She seduces a German officer to prevent his giving the order that might halt the debarkation of the doomed German troops (FBC 4: 395), as Faulkner sets up a clear link between female sexuality, sacrifice, and freedom that recurred across his war scripts of the early 1940s.

The character Helene in Faulkner's screenplay revisions for "To Have and Have Not" is also revealed to have prostituted herself in order to secure her and her French resistance fighter husband's escape from the Nazis in France: "It won't be the first time I've bought Paul's freedom from the Gestapo."[21] Women of occupied France in Faulkner's Hollywood writing sacrifice their bodies to sustain faith in abstract and imperiled ideas of nation and sovereignty, as neither borders nor bodies can be protected in an exceptional state of war. Faulkner's character Emilie in his screenplay "The De Gaulle Story," however, expresses her ultimate faith in the Underground movement in France: "It exists. Stronger than you think. It will be stronger still, as we learn better how to be Underground. We were free too long. But soon all Frenchmen will belong to it" (*FBC* 3: 167). As Emilie elucidates, strength in wartime France is subterranean rather than visible. Caddy of the "Appendix" is one such mysterious wartime subject with inscrutable motivations and allegiances. This suggests that the opacity of Caddy's image may be politically essential. Urgo sees the "Appendix" as Faulkner's lament for suppressed resistance during a wartime context, arguing that when Faulkner "places Caddy in the back seat of that German Mercedes, he imagines precisely the implications of the trammeled, cornered spirit and vividly portrays the perversion of life where rebellion is suppressed" (*Apocrypha* 42). Yet given Caddy's striking affinities with Faulkner's war movie heroines, perhaps the potential for resistance is still alive in her.

Cultural Migrations and Exchanges between Wartime Hollywood and Europe

In addition to the significance of the female image's unreadability in the "Appendix," Faulkner's positioning of Caddy in both Los Angeles and Paris in his 1946 text, an oscillation of a modernist figure between two cultural metropolises, alludes to cultural migrations and exchanges between Hollywood and Europe in the 1930s and 1940s. Caddy's migration from Hollywood in the 1920s to the heart of fascist Europe in the 1940s mirrors the inverse migration of commercial filmmakers from Germany to the US in the 1930s. German émigrés fled to the US before the outbreak of war and formed a cultural elite in Hollywood. A large amount of those émigrés who were influential in the emergence of Hollywood noir were Jewish exiles (Brook 9). Austrian-Jewish artists such as Billy Wilder and Fritz Lang arrived in Hollywood in the 1930s and would go on to direct classic noir films such as *Double Indemnity* (1944) and *Scarlet Street* (1945), the noir aesthetic enabling them to express a gloomy existential outlook colored by the horrors of Nazism and the war. Many of these directors employed German Expressionist stylistics in their work on American noir movies. Paul Schrader highlights how the German expatriate group deftly fused Expressionism with postwar realism in noir films, and that in these pictures they were able to fully draw on Expressionist techniques, such as chiaroscuro lighting and camera angles that favored oblique and vertical lines over horizontal ones (10–11). Lang, especially, was credited with smuggling the Expressionist stylistic features of Weimar cinema into his Hollywood films, building on his 1931 German thriller *M*, which was an important precursor to American noir. Many of the Jewish exiles in fact journeyed from Germany to Hollywood via Paris. As Brook highlights, "several of the Jewish refugees who would help jumpstart film noir were not only aware of French films of the 1930s, but in fact had made many of them. Before moving on to Hollywood, figures such as Lang, [Robert] Siodmak, Wilder, [Curtis] Bernhardt, and [Max] Ophuls, spent time . . . working in the French studios" (3). As a form of cultural exchange between Hollywood, Paris, and fascist Europe, Caddy's movements recall those of the German exiles to Los Angeles in the 1930s.

In addition to stimulating production, cultural exchanges between the US and Europe were crucial to the popular reception of both American novels and films from the interwar and wartime period. In many ways the imagery of the dark sexualities of wartime cinema aligns comfortably with Caddy's new depiction in the "Appendix," as American modernism and film noir were to become natural bedfellows. Indeed, Caddy's image parallels Cowley's postwar rehabilitation of Faulkner's prewar writing. Both Faulkner and noir movies received delayed critical appreciation. In the mid-1940s, *The Portable Faulkner* revalued Faulkner's modernist work, the vast majority of which was produced before the war,[22] just as French critics in the postwar period began to appraise wartime noir movies as a distinctive film cycle. We might consider the Faulknerian modernist canon and noir cinema alike as genres that were revisited after the high point of production had elapsed, and Faulkner's "Appendix" provides a striking example of cultural circulation between these two bodies of work in the immediate postwar period.

The new way of understanding 1940s hard-boiled cinema began when the postwar market in France was saturated with American cultural products; after this influx, French cinema critics were the first to champion film noir movies and identify them as a genre for scholarly analysis. The first writings on Hollywood noir appeared in French film journals in 1946, the same year

The Portable Faulkner was published, and began to consider this group of films as a distinct and sophisticated cinematic movement. The term "film noir" was penned by Parisian critics in post–World War II France when the nation was attempting to regain, or at least revisit, the influential cultural role it had enjoyed in the 1920s and 1930s. France's desire for cultural resurgence was expressed partly through critical evaluation of Hollywood movies, as James Naremore describes, "Paris was once again a staging ground for revolutionary artistic movements, a capital of jazz, and a cheap haven for foreign writers. The initial discourse on Hollywood's dark cinema therefore coincides with one of the last important moments in the history of international modernism" (41). Through a late modernist Parisian critical lens, American noir was appraised by critics such as Raymond Borde and Étienne Chaumeton in *Panorama du film noir américain, 1941–1953* as rendering "gangsters more psychologically complex and sympathetic, horror more quotidian, and detective fiction less rational," which, Naremore argues, if you look beyond the popular formula references had been "more or less the values of modernist literature since the beginning of the century" (40).

In terms of American modernist fiction, Faulkner's reputation before the publication of *The Portable Faulkner* was much stronger in France than in America, where translated copies of his books remained largely in print; Jean-Paul Sartre famously called Faulkner "un dieu," a statement that Cowley relished relaying to Faulkner during their correspondence (Cowley 24). Indeed, with landmark French translations of Faulkner, John Dos Passos, Ernest Hemingway, Erskine Caldwell, and John Steinbeck appearing between 1929 and 1939, the 1930s became known in France as the "age of the American novel" (Menand 208). Maurice Coindreau, who undertook a number of these major French translations of Faulkner's work, comments that "the young Frenchmen who had lived through the dark years of the Occupation and who had, or thought they had, something important to say, found a stimulating encouragement in these [interwar] American writers; in their haste to express themselves, they accepted them unreservedly" (86). Thus the American modernist writers whom the French read and translated before the war now had a strong influence upon a new generation after the Liberation, at the same time the French intelligentsia were consuming and praising American film noir. Indeed, the French can actually be credited with having "discovered" a number of American modernist and hard-boiled novelists as well as, later, the Hollywood auteurs of the 1940s (Naremore 23). Furthermore, Naremore sees Paris and Los Angeles as twin centers of high modernism: Paris as a cultural hub pre- and postwar, and Los Angeles, namely Hollywood, as a wartime home for European émigrés and major American writers like Faulkner (41).

The postwar French cultural community, then, simultaneously found value in Faulkner's modernist novels and the films from the time he worked at Warner Brothers (*Mildred Pierce* and *The Big Sleep* among them). As such, Faulkner's positioning of Caddy in France—when she disappears in Paris in 1940 and drives beside her lover against "a Cannebière backdrop of mountains" (*N* 1: 1134)—is an acknowledgement from Faulkner that in Cowley's project of national reputation construction, it is fitting that a key character from his modernist fiction should be transplanted to Europe, where his work was much more successful, in order to cultivate a new domestic American audience. Caddy, presented as a more typically 1940s filmic heroine in Europe, also anticipates the reappraisal of the tropes and figures of noir that would flow back from the film critics of France, which in turn stimulated American film scholars to reflect on the sophisticated films produced in their own backyard. Faulkner's depiction of Caddy on the Riviera shows that in the postwar period, American modernism, Faulkner, and film noir alike had to be regarded through a French lens in order to reassess their value within the American market. It was through including the archetype of the European femme fatale in his 1946 "Appendix" that Faulkner explored the historical closeness of modernism and Hollywood noir.

The Indecipherability of Noir

In addition to migration, cultural circulation is another form of movement that animates Caddy's section of the "Appendix." We see this enacted when Meek takes Caddy's image from the glossy magazine on a tour of Jefferson and Memphis. The librarian presents the photograph to Caddy's friends and relatives in order to decide what to do about her reappearance in Nazi-occupied Europe, and by doing so, as Penner suggests, she "does more than any other character in the 'Appendix' to expand Faulkner's fictional world" (117). The image invites the characters from *The Sound and the Fury* to speculate on her state as an individual and, on an allegorical level, as a visual commodity. The responses Caddy's image elicits are diverse: Meek wishes to liberate her ("We must save her!" [*N* 1: 1135]); Caddy's brother Jason reacts first with laughter, then shifts to denial ("That Candace? . . . Dont make me laugh. This bitch aint thirty yet. The other one's fifty now" [*N* 1: 1135]); Caddy's nurse Dilsey professes her inability to see the image at all ("My eyes aint any good anymore . . . I cant see it" [*N* 1: 1136]), though this may be feigned, as Dilsey interrupts Meek's attempt to call the woman's daughter Frony to corroborate whether it is indeed an image of Caddy. Faced with these responses, the librarian at first feels distressed, "crying quietly" (*N* 1: 1137) on the bus back to Jefferson from Memphis, but then ultimately decides to conceal the image, justifying to herself that "you could close the covers on it . . . and turn the key upon it" (*N* 1: 1137). By the time the photograph has completed its tour of Mississippi and Tennessee to be finally hidden in the library, the reader is left unsure whether the clipping does actually even contain a picture of Caddy. The plural and contradictory responses Caddy's image elicits suggest how unreadable her image has become.[23]

It is in this part of the "Appendix" that Faulkner explores a central feature of noir plots and characters: indecipherability. This aspect of the noir genre was illustrated to Faulkner during his work on *The Big Sleep*. During filming, out of confusion Bogart asked Hawks who had actually committed the central murder in the plot. Hawks admitted that he didn't have any idea, and when Faulkner and Brackett confessed that they couldn't figure it out either, the director wired Chandler, who tersely responded that he himself didn't know. Faulkner and Brackett would respond to this problem by expanding a scene of Chandler's in which the detective discusses the case to date with the district attorney. However, Hawks cut this scene from the picture upon its general release, thus reinstating the mystery around the murder (McCarthy 382). In Bosley Crowther's review of the film from 1946, he comments negatively of this aspect of *The Big Sleep*:

> If somebody had only told us—the script-writers, preferably—just what it is that happens in the [film], we might be able to give you a more explicit and favorable report on this over-age melodrama . . . But with only the foggiest notion of who does what to whom—and we watched it with closest attention—we must be frankly disappointing about it.
>
> For "The Big Sleep" is one of those pictures in which so many cryptic things occur amid so much involved and devious plotting that the mind becomes utterly confused. (6)

Crowther's frustration and bewilderment is a natural response to many of the new noir films of the time, in which, as William Luhr highlights, "a tension is apparent between the clear plotting associated with earlier detective films and the growing importance of evocative subtextual substructures that by their very nature defy clarity" (107). The preponderance of incoherent plots and enigmatic characterization in noir spills across Faulkner's prose and screenplay work, as we consider the indecipherable plot of *The Big Sleep* alongside the indecipherable characterization of Caddy as noir heroine in the "Appendix." Caddy's image is taken around a community of readers by Meek in Jefferson, just as Chandler's text is exchanged among directors, actors, and screenwriters in Hollywood. In both instances of circulation, the readers attempt to decipher the cultural object and speculate on its meaning. However, such efforts only serve to confirm the fundamental unreadability of the noir image or text.

Modernist and Mass Cultural Inscrutability

As an unreadable femme fatale, the portrayal of Caddy in the "Appendix" differs considerably from that in *The Sound and the Fury*, a distinction which leads to a divergent understanding of the female image's inscrutability in both texts. Though she is sexually rebellious in that earlier work, we sense that Caddy's isolation from the Southern community as a "fallen woman" defines her; she returns to her hometown in 1912 as a pathetic figure grieving for her father and her brother Quentin "in a black cloak, looking at the flowers" (*N* 1: 1032), her hands full of money with which she tries to buy her daughter back, gained, Jason believes, through prostitution. Caddy has rebelled against the Southern patriarchal codes for female sexuality—chastity and modesty—by getting pregnant out of wedlock and marrying Herbert Head so that her child might have a father. In light of this, the reader can only conceive Caddy in *The Sound and the Fury* according to her distance from the Southern context and the family from which she has been expelled. We never in fact see an image of Caddy after 1912 in the novel, even though three of its four narrative sections take place in 1928, and Caddy does not appear at all in the final section of the novel, which focuses on Dilsey. In the "Appendix," Faulkner gives us snapshots of Caddy from the 1920s to the 1940s, which do not solely focus on her as a figure whose sexual errancy is defined in opposition to the South; no longer the expelled fallen woman, the sister who grieves remotely, or the absent mother, she is a character defined in new contexts that do not frame her in relation to what she was forced to or chose to leave behind in Mississippi. In doing so, her image becomes informed by the iconographical systems outside of the Southern imagination that Faulkner had direct access to in the 1940s through his work in Hollywood. Where *The Sound and the Fury* positions Caddy within the Southern logic of what Diane Roberts calls "the chaste woman / fallen woman binary" (*Southern Womanhood* 122), the "Appendix" opens her image up to transnational flows and exchanges.

Of course, in a sense, *both* texts present Caddy as essentially inscrutable. As Eric J. Sundquist argues about Caddy in *The Sound and the Fury,* "there is probably no major character in literature about whom we know so little in proportion to the amount of attention she receives" (37). This earlier Caddy has repeatedly been viewed as a fixed or frozen image by critics. André Bleikasten claimed that as the "empty center" (51) of the novel, she is "first and foremost an image; she exists only in the minds and memories of her brothers . . . She is in fact what woman has always been in man's imagination: the figure par excellence of the Other, a blank screen onto which he projects both his desires and his fears, his love and his hate" (65). This notion of Caddy as a "blank screen" derives from her status as an object of fascination for her three brothers' unique subjective first-person narrative consciousnesses, which alternatively fetishize (Benjy), idealize (Quentin), and demonize her (Jason). Caddy in the novel is, then, also presented as an image that does not relinquish meaning, but I believe that this inscrutability, though also linked to fetishism and investment, should be understood from a modernist perspective rather than a mass cultural one.

This production of mass cultural inscrutability is furthered by cinematic elements of the Compson "Appendix," particularly its focus on mediation and externalized forms of vision. Most explicitly, as Davis also argues, Faulkner moves from the first-person narratives of *The Sound and the Fury* to the third-person narrative of the "Appendix," as the eye of the subject is replaced by the all-seeing eye of the genealogist. Although the last section of the novel is narrated in the third person, the other three sections, the vast majority of the text, are written in the first person. In a sense, the "Dilsey" section represents the narratorial bridge between *The Sound and the Fury* and the "Appendix." However, since this section does not feature Caddy, the inscrutability we associate with her character is only furthered in *The Sound and the Fury* by the three first-person narratives of her brothers. As such, the wholly omniscient vision of the "Appendix" represents a move toward the objective and the visual rather than the layered rendering of subjectivity that dominates the original novel. In addition, Gwin highlights the mediating quality of the "Appendix," as for her the genealogy functions in the "space *between* text and reader" (*Feminine and Faulkner* 61). In particular, we see Faulkner interposing the "Appendix" between *The Sound and the Fury* and the reader, thereby filtering our vision of the novel, a function that in part explains Faulkner's explicit references to Hollywood and photography in Caddy's section.

These different forms of inscrutability are, however, made most apparent through the processes of reading that structure both texts. *The Sound and the Fury* presents a series of tessellating first-person perspectives on the Compson daughter, which in turn create an almost Cubist presentation of Caddy for the reader, as we try to picture her image as a whole by reading through the interlocking planes of vision that the three narrative subjects of Benjy, Quentin, and Jason offer. In *The Sound and the Fury*, Caddy's image is fixed via the constraining subjective narratives of her brothers, discourses that objectify her and deny her a voice or narratorial perspective.[24] In the "Appendix," however, Caddy's image is fixed through its mass cultural mediation, turned into an object within "a slick magazine" (*N* 1: 1134). It is this objectified vision of Caddy that is circulated among the community of readers in Jefferson and Memphis. Where *The Sound and the Fury*, in typical modernist fashion, presents individual perspective as acting to limit our understanding and mental image of others, the "Appendix" presents the multiple perspectives of Yoknapatawpha's readers as speculative, limited by the inscrutability of the objectified image itself. This also contrasts with the early commodified presentation of Temple Drake in the modernist novel *Sanctuary*, where Drake's image is readily and voyeuristically consumed by the gazes of the men around her without visual obstruction or obscuration. *The Sound and the Fury* demonstrates how the mediating viewer may turn another subject into an object. In contrast, the "Appendix" considers how an objectified subject may be viewed through mass spectatorship and popular circulation. In a sense, Faulkner considers how Caddy as modernist figure is now circulated as a commodity, as he perhaps saw himself and his own work at the time he was submitting himself to the marketing project of *The Portable Faulkner*.

In the Compson "Appendix," Faulkner presented the femme fatale as a figure that resists deciphering. Caddy is unreadable as an image fixed in a genealogy and a magazine, precisely because she draws on the symbolic properties of the wartime heroines of Hollywood, whose subterranean intentions were investigated by narrative movement. This stands in contrast to Caddy's inscrutability as a modernist subject in *The Sound and the Fury*, where her image is rendered opaque by the operation of subjective discourse. In his prefatory note to the "Appendix," written around May 1946, Faulkner argues that *The Sound and the Fury* was only completed through the "Appendix," as the original novel was "the homemade, the experimental, the first moving picture projector—warped lens, poor light, undependable mechanism and even a bad screen—which had to wait until 1946 for the lens to clear, the light to steady, the gears to run smooth" (*ESPL* 301). The irony of this statement is that although Faulkner describes the "Appendix" as the visually clear cinematic counterpart to the visually obscure *The Sound and the Fury*, by drawing on noir in his text from 1946, the author in fact borrowed elements from a filmic movement that consistently emphasized the obscurity of the image, through its use of "poor light" among other techniques. This progression from modernist to mass cultural inscrutability between the publication of *The Sound and the Fury* and *The Portable Faulkner* suggests that Faulkner's vision of his writing had been mediated by his work for Hollywood, most explicitly through the traffic of images of the wartime woman between "Snow," his Warner Brothers screenplays, and the Compson "Appendix." Such a circulatory exchange indicates the porous relationship between his modernist fiction and screenplays; indeed, the exchanges the "Appendix" charts are not only aesthetic but also transnational, as Caddy's movements mimic the transatlantic migrations that shaped the production and reception of noir and modernism from the 1930s.

Where does Faulkner leave Caddy at the end of the "Appendix"? Melissa Meek, in her role as a censor and cultural archivist, places Caddy's image out of sight just as she conceals other "obscene" texts in Jefferson's library, such as James Branch Cabell's *Jurgen* (1919) and Henry Fielding's *Tom Jones* (1749). Caddy's image is locked up and hidden away due to the evidence it contains of her intimate connection to the darkest figures in wartime history. Meek's final gesture does, in fact, reflect the ultimate impulse of the noir film itself, in its "redoubling of efforts toward containment" of the femme female (Doane, *Femmes Fatales* 116). Yet, conversely, the very plurality of responses that Caddy's photograph provokes among its community of readers suggests that she is too open to continual reassessment to be reduced to an immutable aesthetic object and that her inscrutability is precisely the quality that leads to the enduring fascination her image attracts.

5

Requiem for a Nun and Cold War Hollywood Melodrama

FAULKNER CONCEIVED OF THE dramatic sections of his 1951 work *Requiem for a Nun* as a "good vehicle" (*SL* 318) for the Southern actress of stage and screen Ruth Ford, and he would continue to insist that the role of Temple Drake in *Requiem* was Ford's alone, even after other actors were suggested as alternatives (Rollyson, *Alarming Paradox* 497). Faulkner's Hollywood work with fellow screenwriters and actors may have primed him for his close collaboration with Ford in adapting the work as a play for the stage. In fact, he seemed to be comfortable with such collaborative work for the theater, writing in a letter from December 1951 that "producing a play is not a one- or two-man job, nor even just a ten man job" (*SL* 323), and Ford would alter dialogue and movement for the stage adaptation (*SL* 417).[1] Faulkner and Ford's relationship as creative colleagues predated their work on *Requiem*, however. Faulkner first promised to write a play for Ford when they were both working at Warner Brothers in 1943 (Rollyson, *Alarming Paradox* 357), and Ford had acted in the kind of 1940s Hollywood genre pictures that Faulkner himself had penned for Warner Brothers, as discussed in the previous chapter: noir (*Circumstantial Evidence*, 1945), horror (*The Woman Who Came Back*, 1945), and World War II espionage movies (*The Gorilla Man*, 1943). Ford even had an uncredited role as a nurse in *Air Force* (1943), to which Faulkner had contributed a number of scenes. In addition to these genres, Faulkner came to write for Warner Brothers in the vein of the maternal melodrama, a subgenre of the woman's film, through his story treatment of "The Damned Don't Cry" (completed in 1941, released in 1950) and his revision of the screenplay for "Mildred Pierce" (completed in 1944, released in 1945). In his work on these movies in the 1940s, Faulkner explored themes of maternal suffering and sacrifice and reproduced a formula wherein female transgression beyond the strict boundaries of the home and the nuclear family unit is met with severe punishment. The films' tragic conclusions—where distance between the mother and her children is enforced through death, imprisonment, or exile—warn of the perils that await women who fail to commit themselves fully to domestic cohesion.

From the late 1940s, after his work on these projects, Faulkner witnessed the repurposing of tropes from the woman's film in Cold War Hollywood melodramas, where the American family was upheld as an inviolable component of national strength and integrity. As John Sbardellati highlights, these films "played up the threat of Communism to American institutions" and "presented the church, school, and family as the most powerful bastions against red encroachment" (175). Melodrama was not only the favored genre for presenting Cold War anxiety in cultural products, but it was also a prevalent genre in contemporary American politics. Elisabeth R. Anker highlights how "melodramatic political discourse" disseminates the notion, in moments of historical crisis, that the innocent, virtuous nation-state has been injured, legitimating "heroic retribution" against the "villains" responsible, leading necessarily to the violent expansion of state power through acts of war and global control, actions that the discourse imbues with moral authority (2–3). She describes how the discourse grew in importance after World War II, during which time its conventions helped justify the growth of the national-security state and contributed towards the legitimation of anti-Communist international relations (Anker 3).

The Cold War Hollywood melodrama's focus on threats to the domestic sphere was symptomatic of a fundamental aspect of this melodramatic political discourse.[2] Elaine Tyler May uses the term "domestic containment" to describe the postwar phenomenon in which adherence to the home was linked to the national anti-Communist drive, arguing that "within [the home's] walls, potentially dangerous social forces of the new age might be tamed, so they could contribute to the secure and fulfilling life to which postwar women and men aspired" (16). In other words, the need to ensure national security by containing the global threat of Communism was reflected in the containment of middle-class nuclear American families within the home. In this model sexuality was not repressed but was confined within marriages in which normative gender roles were upheld, and a "reproductive consensus" endorsed motherhood as married women's primary duty (May 152). The political and cultural discourses of Cold War containment functioned melodramatically, as the moral polarities they propounded drew on oppositions between the West and the East, democracy and totalitarianism, pitting the "virtuous" American nuclear family against the "villainous" collectivism of the Soviet Union.

Away from Hollywood Faulkner himself returned to the tropes and themes of the woman's film in his fiction, producing his own Cold War Hollywood-inspired melodrama that explored domestic containment ideology. In 1951 he published *Requiem for a Nun,* which explicitly borrows from the woman's film's conventions and adapts a central focus of these films, the vexed status of the mother in American society, to meditate on Cold War anxieties. However, his updated version deviates significantly from the compliance to nuclear family values exhibited in the majority of contemporary Hollywood melodramas. Writing at a remove from commercial cinema, Faulkner drew on the drive for social conformity inherent in the woman's film but redeployed the genre's tropes, devices, and figures in a subversive fashion to launch a strong critique of the aggressive Cold War domestic imperative. In *Requiem* Faulkner created a warped Hollywood-inflected melodrama in which "family values" are presented as illusory, arbitrary, violently enforced, socially exploitative, and therefore poorly placed to defend against Red infiltration. By doing so Faulkner unwittingly anticipated the autocritical direction of some 1950s Hollywood melodramas, which similarly employed self-ironizing techniques to undermine Cold War domestic norms.

Defending Domestic Cohesion in the Woman's Film

Through his screenwriting work in 1940s Hollywood, Faulkner was educated in melodramatic tropes that enforced compliance to normative family values and gender roles. Molly Haskell identifies the middle-class domestic prison as the key generator of conflict in the late 1930s and 1940s woman's film genre, in which female protagonists wrangle with their desires for a world of risk and passion outside marriage (*Reverence* 156, 159). In essence, the woman's film explores a woman's pursuit of or simply desire for a mode of being that challenges social norms for women in the wartime and immediate postwar periods. As Pam Cook argues, in the woman's film "the heroine's transgression resides in her desire to act against socially accepted definitions of femininity, bringing her face to face with society" (254). In its exploration of such confrontation, the woman's film, more than any Hollywood genre that preceded it, intended to generate lachrymose identification from female spectators by using women as the dominant narrative viewpoint and foregrounding their suffering and the dilemmas they encounter. Rather than using such trauma to *critique* the constraints of the domestic sphere, however, these films' predominantly tragic endings warn against female transgression and thereby seek to uphold order within the family unit.

Haskell divides women's films into four principal thematic categories: sacrifice, affliction, choice, and competition (*Reverence* 163). For his subsequent work in *Requiem*, Faulkner drew on the sacrificial strain of the genre that he had explored in his wartime screenplays. In this subgenre female protagonists struggle to weigh conflicting commitments to their children, marriages, love interests, and careers. As such, the heroine is forced to make a sacrifice, the negative, often tragic consequences of which reinforce the idea that there is only one legitimate path for women: absolute devotion to the preservation of domestic cohesion. In Faulkner's screenplays it is specifically the heroine's relationship to her children that catalyzes the difficult sacrifices she must make. As a result, the woman's victimization through maternal suffering is the central point of identification for the putative female viewer.

Faulkner's story treatment of *The Damned Don't Cry* contains several key tropes of the woman's film. The treatment from November or December 1941 is one of five that Faulkner completed between late 1941 and early 1942 on a freelance basis with the intention of luring Warner Brothers into offering him a contract, which he ultimately secured in July 1942. It is a reworking of a previously rejected screenplay based on Harry C. Hervey's novel of the same name published in 1939 (Hamblin and Brodsky, preface 9). After reading the screenplay in November 1941, Faulkner suggested heavy revisions to the central role of Zelda, who has an illegitimate child and, as Faulkner summarized, loves it too much to disown it (*SL* 145). However, Faulkner found that the screenplay did not give enough credible motivation to Zelda's actions as either "a woman of unusual character" or an individual "doing it for the child's good and at sacrifice for herself" (*SL* 145). He sensed that the film could be successful if Zelda's role were strengthened and the plot pushed in the direction of the sacrificial maternal melodrama, in which she "would have had to choose between the child and herself and gained admiration and pity both" (*SL* 145).

Acting on these criticisms, Faulkner completed his treatment in late 1941.[3] In his version Zelda gets pregnant out of wedlock by a man who deserts her after a brief affair. Zelda puts her child, Glynn, into an orphanage and learns of his progress from a distance. She supports Glynn's education at "a good eastern prep school" through the underworld business ventures she inherits from her murdered gangster husband, including a "high-class exclusive and very profitable brothel" (*CL* 93), while also trying to protect him from the potential scandal of his family's activities and her sexually transgressive past. Zelda's observance of her child's progress from afar to avoid the taint of their mutual association strongly recalls a classic of the woman's film genre, *Stella Dallas* (1937), which concludes with a mother giving up her child into the care of her husband and his new partner, who are deemed to be a more "stable" family unit. Glynn ultimately learns of the brothel's existence and, in a fight at the treatment's conclusion, he inadvertently kills someone. Zelda frames herself for the manslaughter, and although she is freed after the trial, she is banished from the city and never sees her son again. Faulkner's version of "The Damned Don't Cry" requires Zelda to sacrifice both her own freedom for her child's and contact with her child for his welfare. Although the treatment concludes with a reunion between Zelda and a former suitor, this offers scant consolation for exile from child and home. According to the traditional script of the sacrificial woman's film, Zelda, although she now attracts admiration and pity, must leave her illegitimate son and seedy business behind to preserve normative family values.

In November and December 1944, Faulkner revised the script for the woman's film *Mildred Pierce*, an adaptation of the 1941 hard-boiled novel by James M. Cain and the screenwriter's second project in the genre. Faulkner changed it enough to constitute his own version, particularly through his addition of a number of "Gothic and outlandish" features (LaValley 34), including the characterization of Veda, which I analyzed in chapter 4. In this sacrificial woman's film, conflict between marriage, children, and work creates a series of painful dilemmas for the heroine. The film documents the progression of Mildred Pierce's destructive fixation on her materialist daughter Veda, which leads to separation from her husband and what is deemed her "transgressive" entrance into the world of work to fund Veda's excesses. At the end of the film, out of jealousy, Veda murders her stepfather, Mildred's second husband, the dissolute aristocrat Monte Beragon. Similar to Zelda in Faulkner's treatment of "The Damned Don't Cry," Mildred attempts to take the blame for the murder. When the film concludes, one of Mildred's children is dead and the other imprisoned, and the protagonist is reunited with her first husband, the morally upright counterpart to Monte. The implicit logic is that Mildred's failure to defend domestic coherence by alienating her husband and doggedly pursuing her career ambitions results in tragedy. Faulkner's work for "The Damned Don't Cry" and "Mildred Pierce" illustrates what Linda Williams identifies as the woman's film's "device of devaluing and debasing the actual figure of the mother while sanctifying the institution of motherhood" ("Maternal Melodrama" 3). While bourgeois domestic stability might be complicated in women's films, it is finally reinforced in their conclusions, which "re-inscribe the feminine in its location as defined by the patriarchy" (Kaplan, "Theories of Melodrama" 45) through either a reassertion of family order or the destruction of the "dysfunctional" family unit.

For his 1940s Hollywood women's films, Faulkner worked in the traditional melodramatic mode, where the moral complexities of historical crises are presented through simplified symbolic oppositions between vice and virtue (Brooks 14).[4] Peter Brooks sees melodramatic authors—including Faulkner—as tapping into a submerged reservoir of meaning, the "moral occult," which is "the domain of operative spiritual values . . . both indicated within and masked by the surface of reality" (5). Melodrama, in Brooks's assessment, "becomes the principal mode for uncovering, demonstrating, and making operative the essential moral universe in a post-sacred era" (15). This has a strong impact on characterization, as the words and gestures of the melodramatic player become hyperbolic with the intention of referencing an obscured moral order. Moral oppositions in melodrama become personalized through characters who embody good and evil. Due to this, characterization in the genre, while vividly drawn, contains little psychological depth (Brooks 16).

In keeping with this tradition, Faulkner uses the players in *Requiem* to perform excessive symbolic functions. The two protagonists of the dramatic sections, the married couple Temple Drake and Gowan Stevens, perform excessive gestures to indicate a submerged spiritual plane. Early in act 1, Gowan "stands, his back to the audience, and draws another long shuddering breath and then draws both hands hard down his face" (*N* 4: 523). Later in the same act, Temple "makes a gesture something like Gowan's in scene 2, except that she merely presses her palms for a moment hard against her face, her face calm, expressionless, cold" (*N* 4: 537). The mirrored gestures indicate a communion between the players in the midst of a moral crisis; crucially, although Temple and Gowan's spiritual affinity is made legible to the audience, it remains opaque to the individual characters since neither observes the other's gesture. The symbolic function of gesture is most strongly illustrated through the affinities of the players' movements with the architectural framework in which they are presented. Décor serves to create character rather than acting as a backdrop to the characters' development. Gowan, for example, is described as "almost a type" (*N* 4: 508) allied to a particular form of architecture in the 1920s and 1930s; Faulkner elaborates that "there were many of him in America, the South, between the two great wars: only children of financially secure parents living in city apartment hotels" (*N* 4: 508). Within such a framework, where architecture determines character, Faulkner is keen to foreground the limitation of space in his mise-en-scène. The devil is in the detail, as the litany of objects within these modern apartments creates a claustrophobic atmosphere designed to produce hysteria in the players, and their relationships with objects around them become illustrative of their vexed psyches. In one revealing moment, Gowan dashes his whiskey tumbler into an ice bowl and then pours himself another drink in a fresh tumbler; Faulkner describes that "at first he makes no sound, but at once it is obvious that he is laughing: laughter which begins normally enough, but almost immediately it is out of hand, just on hysteria, while he still pours whiskey into the glass, which in a moment now will overflow" (*N* 4: 519). It is clear here that the confining bourgeois environment exerts an oppressive influence on the nuclear family, producing violent eruptions and displacements of energy within an enclosed system.

This lack of physical self-control is reflected in the persistent involuntary quality to character movement in the play. Among Temple's gestures, she "makes a convulsive movement, then catches herself" (*N* 4: 599); seems "to stumble slightly, like a sleepwalker" (*N* 4: 615); and stumbles again at the play's conclusion, "slightly and infinitesimally, so infinitesimally and so quickly recovered that the Jailor has barely time to react to it" (*N* 4: 663). These convulsions are quintessentially melodramatic, since they convey a symbolic meaning through repetition and patterning, which remains obscure to the individual character. Taken out of context they appear erratic and excessive, but within the architecture of the whole work the players' bodies present a unified dramatic message, as meaning is conveyed through structural repetition rather than on a direct literal level. In *Requiem*, character movement functions to illustrate a larger sense of unease rather than an individual psychological reality, as gestural excess becomes the measure of social crisis within melodrama's principal aesthetic program of sublimation and transference. We are invited to read the symbolic plane of Faulkner's play contained in his mise-en-scène and stage directions as symptomatic of a wider struggle rather than directly illustrative of character, and therefore as typically melodramatic.

The Hollywood woman's film too, like earlier incarnations of melodrama, responded to social and ideological crises, representing a hidden "moral universe" through the excesses of melodramatic characterization. The genre developed in reaction to female-dominated cinema audiences during World War II. Addressed to women, these films structurally reflected male absence and the redefinition of women's role in society. The extreme neurotic gestures of the characters in a film such as *Mildred Pierce*, however, should also not be read for psychological credibility. When Veda confronts her mother, Mildred, about the latter's job in a restaurant, delivering the outraged and vindictive line "my mother, a waitress" (*Mildred Pierce*), she voices not only individual shame but also the collective social judgment of wartime housewives who entered the world of work, filling the vacuum the men left in American society. The strain on the female performers in this film is that they are required to embody the positions of *all* women in American society, who were reassessing their relationships to work, motherhood, and marriage in an international climate of world war. In this way the characters' extreme behaviors reflect normative gender ideology enforced in relation to a global crisis. Faulkner used similar symbolic excess in *Requiem* to respond to the Cold War. However, he drew on the sacrificial woman's film, where domestic cohesion ultimately triumphs over female transgression, to launch a scathing critique of the drive toward containment in melodramatic Cold War culture and discourse.

Requiem for a Nun's Cold War contexts

In his address when receiving the Nobel Prize in Literature in December 1950, Faulkner described how the Cold War threatened to shape artistic production, asserting that "there are no longer problems of the spirit. There is only the question: When will I be blown up? Because of this, the young man or woman writing today has forgotten the problems of the human heart in conflict with itself which alone can make good writing" (*ESPL* 119). Faulkner described the struggle to reconcile generalized anxiety about the real potential for humanity's extinction with the spiritual life of the artist, whose work requires deep internal contemplation.

Requiem was Faulkner's first major work to emerge after his receipt of the Nobel Prize, which ushered in his years as a literary figure on the global stage. Concomitant to this, as John T. Matthews highlights, Faulkner's work of the 1950s responded to Cold War preoccupations "in years during which global geopolitics were creating an era of apocalypse" ("Cold War Conflicts" 7). Indeed, the language of the Nobel address looms large over *Requiem*, which he was working on in the months before the Nobel ceremony. The first act's prose prologue concludes with the line "the clock . . . shattered the virgin pristine air with the first loud dingdong of time and doom" (*N* 4: 505), echoing Faulkner's words in Stockholm that "when the last ding-dong of doom has clanged and faded . . . there will still be one more sound: that of [man's] puny inexhaustible voice" (*ESPL* 120). Reflecting these words' Cold War context, *Requiem* is a textual manifestation of Faulkner's attempts to find his artistic "voice" despite the creative pressures the threat of nuclear annihilation posed to writing.

The work was a new experiment in form for the author: a prose-drama hybrid. The published three-act play comprises seven dramatic scenes, with each act preceded by an extensive prose prologue. The discourses of Cold War domestic containment circulate between *Requiem*'s prologues and dramatic scenes. The prologues detail the history of the locations that frame the dramatic action—the courthouse, the state capital, and the town jail—while the domestic melodrama presented in the dramatic sections of *Requiem* focuses on Temple Drake from Faulkner's previous novel, *Sanctuary* (1931). In the third prologue, Faulkner describes the GIs "returning no more to inherit the long monotonous endless unendable furrows of Mississippi cotton fields, living now (with now a wife and next year a wife and child and the year after that a wife and children) in automobile trailers or G.I. barracks on the outskirts of liberal arts colleges" (*N* 4: 638). It as if the condensation of space described here—from "unendable furrows" to "automobile trailers"—and the urgency with which these US citizens marry and procreate in makeshift accommodations is effected by the imposition of global concerns on individual behavior. Faulkner observes that in a globalized postwar America—what he calls "one nation, one world" (*N* 4: 638) after "one boom, one peace" (*N* 4: 639)—"young men who had never been further from Yoknapatawpha County than Memphis or New Orleans . . . now talked glibly of street intersections in Asiatic and European capitals" (*N* 4: 638). The global is reflected in the local here as Cold War concerns exert intense pressure on domestic life. Where the prologues describe the GIs' return to the South en masse as global citizens, the dramatic sections trace the impact of atomic domesticity on a single home. Due to the specific repressive domestic focus, although the dramatic sections of *Requiem* are set in 1937, the action of the play more closely reflects the time of its publication in 1951, as the ideological framework that *Requiem* explores is historically linked to the Cold War rather than the Depression.

Exploring the presence of Cold War discourse and its effects in *Requiem*, Spencer Morrison persuasively argues that *Requiem*'s prologues are "extended meditations on macrocosmic social energies that find microcosmic influence in the lives" (313) of the work's dramatic characters. Morrison observes a specifically spatial dynamic to these echoes by tracing a "newly geopolitical inflection to Faulkner's spatial imagination during the Cold War" (305). He shows, first, how developments in Jefferson, Mississippi, described in the prose prologues reflect projects of urban reconstruction and modernization that were exported globally by the United States during the early Cold War and, second, how Temple is seen to transgress against the constrictive Cold War urban space of the home in the dramatic sections (304–08, 313). While Morrison briefly discusses domestic containment ideology in *Requiem*, his focus is on how the penetration of the home by Cold War discourse is reflected through the drama's negotiation of conflicting spaces (313, 316). In contrast, I show how discourses of containment are embedded not only in a Cold War spatial matrix but also in the conventions of the woman's film that Faulkner had learned in Hollywood and which he subverts to expose the impoverished moral melodrama of Cold War discourse. Analyzing *Requiem* as melodrama, I chart the double subversion of the Cold War script that the text performs, simultaneously undermining the hyperbolic neodomestic consensus of Hollywood films *and* public rhetoric.

The Domestic Facade

To launch a critique of Cold War domesticity in *Requiem*, Faulkner uses characters from two of his earlier texts, *Sanctuary* and the short story "That Evening Sun," both published in 1931.[5] These texts are the gritty underbelly to *Requiem*'s depiction of the domestic idyll that the woman's film sought to defend. The protagonist of the dramatic sections, Temple Drake, lives in a smart apartment in a bourgeois area of Jefferson with her husband, the aristocratic Gowan Stevens, and two children, Bucky, eight, and an unnamed six-month-old infant daughter. Temple describes herself and her husband as a socialite couple and depicts their environment as "a new bungalow on the right street to start the Saturday night hangovers in, a country club with a country club younger set of rallying friends to make it a Saturday night hangover worthy the name of Saturday night country club hangover, a pew in the right church to recover from it in" (*N* 4: 579). Temple lists the key structures of 1950s bourgeois conformity: the home in a popular and conventional area, the country club, and the church. Collectively they are intended to have a rehabilitative effect on Temple while also masking alcohol dependency. As I explored in chapter 1, in *Sanctuary* Temple embraces some of the traits of the sexualized New Woman or flapper as a seventeen-year-old and loses the protection of the men around her. This leads to her extreme victimization through assault and rape by a series of bootleggers and gangsters. Gowan attempts to restore Temple to "respectability" subsequent to her forced loss of sexual innocence. After the events that conclude *Sanctuary*, Gowan joins Temple in Paris and marries her, intending to "fumigate an American past" (*N* 4: 577) before returning to Jefferson to place her in the bourgeois space described.

Domestic containment extends to all women in the text, as the same home is also intended to rehabilitate Nancy Mannigoe, the family's Black housemaid. Nancy is a former prostitute and drug addict who, before joining the Stevens household, was viciously beaten in public by one of her johns, a churchgoing bank cashier, after she asked him for the money he owed her. This backstory is given in greater detail in "That Evening Sun," where Nancy works as laundrywoman and cook for the white upper-class Compson family and has a common-law husband named Jesus. After the beating she is jailed and tries to hang herself in her cell. She is pregnant at the time, allegedly with somebody other than Jesus's child, possibly a john's. We learn in *Requiem* that her baby was killed when she was six months pregnant when a man kicked her in the stomach. In light of Nancy's transgressive and traumatic past, Temple argues that she "hired another reformed whore so that [she] would have somebody to talk to" (*N* 4: 575) who has shared the life the home is intended to "fumigate." Nancy's role extends much further than the house, as she becomes for Temple "nurse: guide: mentor, catalyst, glue . . . holding the whole lot of them together . . . in a semblance at least of order and respectability and peace" (*N* 4: 579). According to Temple, Nancy's presence as the "magnetic center" (*N* 4: 579) of the nuclear family ensures cohesion. Nancy is therefore instrumental in maintaining a convincing "semblance" of domestic security. Faulkner's text, however, shatters this superficial image.

The first act of *Requiem* opens with Nancy's trial and her sentencing to death for the murder of Temple's younger child. It becomes clear that Nancy killed Temple's daughter to prevent Temple from running away to pursue an affair with a gangster named Pete, the younger brother of the man to whom Temple is masochistically attracted in *Sanctuary*.[6] Through murder, Nancy forces Temple to stick by her husband and remaining child out of a sense of guilt. Infanticide, as I will show, is central to the ways *Requiem* simultaneously challenges melodramatic conventions and Cold War political discourse. More immediately, the plot builds on Faulkner's work for *The Damned Don't Cry* and *Mildred Pierce,* broadly following the sacrificial strain of the woman's film by exploring the consequences of Temple's desire to leave children, husband, and home for a lover. Faulkner therefore derives energy from questioning how much Temple is prepared to give up in pursuit of a world outside marriage and the family. In the text Temple moves between the role of the flapper or New Woman, more typical of her character in *Sanctuary*, as "Temple Drake," and her bourgeois role as wife and homemaker, "Mrs Gowan Stevens."

In a different fashion, *Sanctuary* also launches a critique of normative gender roles and sexual mores in US culture beyond its interrogation of the flapper figure. In the earlier novel, Faulkner presents Temple as a fallen image of Southern white womanhood: the virginal and innocent belle. As a teenager Temple loses the protection of the men whose putative role is to defend her against violation. Joseph R. Urgo comments that "the myth of sanctified womanhood, created and protected by civil society, is what Temple tragically expects to experience at all times" ("Truthful Perjury" 437–38). Its loss leads to Temple's assault and rape in the Old Frenchman place and Miss Reba's Memphis brothel. In this sense, Diane Roberts argues, Faulkner disables the virgin/whore opposition in Southern culture, as Temple is a virgin forced into sexual knowledge through subjugation (*Southern Womanhood* 129). More widely, Roberts advances, the novel explores "the sexual violence inherent in a society built on a discourse of rape" (*Southern Womanhood* 135). The Southern rape complex was central to the mythic construction of gender and race relations in the antebellum and Reconstruction periods. It holds that the virginal belle has to be protected by white men against the threat of rape posed by Black men, an argument used to justify lynching. In *Sanctuary*, however, as Deborah Barker describes, Faulkner dismantles the stereotypical narrative of the complex through a series of substitutions, which reveal "the hypocrisy and perversion at [its] heart" ("Modern Mammy" 72). Temple is raped not by a Black man but by an impotent white man with a corncob, a fate from which none of the white men in the text rescue her. In addition, to avenge Temple in *Sanctuary*, a group of white men rapes and lynches an innocent white man. This act does not affirm racial domination and therefore, for Barker, "nullifies [the Southern rape complex] as a tool used by whites to commit violence" ("Modern Mammy" 72).

Sanctuary and *Requiem* show us how the respective figures of "Temple Drake" and "Mrs Gowan Stevens" came into being. *Requiem* explores the paradox that although these roles are positioned oppositionally in the text (the belle turned whore versus the self-sacrificing mother), they are in fact related forms of gender performance. Both Gowan and Gavin Stevens, Gowan's uncle, assert that Temple's time in the Memphis brothel led to Stockholm syndrome, through which Temple came perversely to enjoy her sexual subjugation and sympathize with her captors. This is a psychological state that Temple herself later affirms when she claims that the Temple Drake of *Sanctuary* "liked evil" (*N* 4: 564), where "evil" stands in for a forced awakening of female sexuality. For Temple and the men around her, the Memphis underworld of vice in *Sanctuary* is now, in *Requiem*, associated with masochistic desire.

Requiem presents the idea that, in acquiescing to domestic conformity as "Mrs Gowan Stevens," Temple has in fact traded one sexual prison for another, moving from the Memphis brothel to the constrictive bourgeois home. The environment, however, gradually becomes imprisoning. Gowan begins to doubt the paternity of their older child, and Temple has to live under the oppression of his forgiveness, continually forced to recognize how he intends to absolve her of her former "transgressions." Gowan even jokes that his expectation of Temple's thankfulness has turned the domestic space into a prison where she will serve another "eight-year term" (*N* 4: 609).

Temple's past, however, intrudes into the bourgeois prison. Pete blackmails Temple with the sexually explicit love letters she wrote in Memphis to his elder brother Red, which remind Temple of the sexually transgressive self that the bourgeois environment has not managed to "fumigate." She admits that "I not only hadn't forgot about the letters, I hadn't even reformed" (*N* 4: 575). This leads Temple to withhold the money and jewels Pete has requested, in favor of eloping with him. Her affair with Pete is positioned as the sexual alternative to domestic containment and the role of "Mrs Gowan Stevens." The sad reality is that in leaving husband, home, and children, Temple would merely trade one form of sexual and gender imprisonment for another, as it seems highly unlikely that she would be able to revisit sexual trauma as liberating pleasure. In this regard, rather than highlighting the oppositional qualities of the roles of "Mrs Gowan Stevens" and "Temple Drake," Faulkner demonstrates how both roles are enforced through extreme violence and sexual containment. If *Sanctuary* shows us how "Temple Drake" is created through sexual subjugation in a Memphis whorehouse, *Requiem* shows us how "Mrs Gowan Stevens" is created through gender policing in the bourgeois town apartment.

In *Requiem* Temple's oscillation between these two roles results in a divided female subject, a key feature of female character presentation in the woman's film. This is a trope Faulkner encountered in his work on *Mildred Pierce*, in which Mildred is presented as torn between her roles as wife and homemaker, on the one hand, and the masculinized world of work, on the other. Michael Renov discusses the split-female trope in the postwar woman's film, arguing that "a profusion of contradictory cultural messages had produced a confusion, a self-distortion rich with the possibilities of schizophrenia" (28–29) resulting in a destabilized female self-image. Temple appears to be aware of this conflict when she expresses her concern that she represents "two different people begging for the same clemency; if everybody concerned keeps on splitting up into two people, you wont even know who to pardon, will you?" (*N* 4: 578).

Such division partly derives from the fact that Temple is forced to shift between different positions in the account she gives of her child's murder in the drama's second act. Temple returns to Jefferson after spending some time in California with her eldest child. Once home, Gavin, who is a lawyer, takes her to meet with the state governor and intervene in Nancy's trial.

Temple tries to describe her implication in her child's death, explaining how her masochistic desires motivated Nancy's actions. In trying to save Nancy, Temple insists that she must engage with the law in a maternal role, whereas Gavin believes that her former self, Temple Drake, the wayward flapper with a predilection for "evil," is required. Her claim that "Temple Drake is dead" elicits from Gavin the most famous line in the work: "The past is never dead. It's not even past" (*N* 4: 535). Gavin maintains that a revival of Temple's sexualized self is necessary for her to justify the child's sacrifice, which preserved the maternal role. But as Karl F. Zender highlights, Gavin's intentions here are not to "renew her illicit memories" but rather to "purge her of them" ("Imagination" 277). But Gavin also takes this as an opportunity to dominate Temple, since, as Kelly Lynch Reames asserts, he tries to appropriate and control her narrative (35). This frames the conflict between Temple and Gavin in act 2 as essentially a struggle over how her desires should be expressed in narrative. These suppressed desires will erupt into the domestic drama, leading to an act of murder that Faulkner frames within the conventions of filmic melodrama. Yet in a significant departure, Faulkner utilizes these tropes to challenge them. Most trenchantly, he exposes the violent ideological function maternal sacrifice served in Hollywood cinema from the period.

Excessive Violence: Subverting Filmic Melodrama

Nancy's act of murder causes Noel Polk to advance that it is "the most savage and reprehensible act of violence in all of William Faulkner's fiction" (*Critical Study* xiii). Jay Watson observes, however, that despite this excess, "*Requiem* frames Nancy's gesture . . . in ways that strongly suggest that this gesture expresses a nomos, a normative vision, with an integrity and validity of its own" ("Dangerous Return" 114). Watson concedes that this nomos "remains elusive, unclear" ("Dangerous Return" 114), which, I believe, is precisely because the murder needs to be understood not as a psychologically credible action but rather within its wider creative context as a borrowed and exaggerated filmic trope that fuses elements from two strains of melodrama prevalent in the Hollywood of the 1930s and 1940s: the woman's film and race melodrama. This violent plot device, first, amplifies a trope of women's films, where the child's death is implicitly presented as punishment for the mother's transgression. Second, the child's murder distorts a sentimental feature of the race melodrama, where the mammy's utter devotion to the white family leads to attempts to police the white woman's desires. Through its effects (the mother's return to the home), it recalls the woman's film, but in its motivation (the Black housemaid's commitment to domestic cohesion), it recalls the race melodrama. Through hyperbole, Faulkner subverts these tropes and challenges the normative underpinnings of both Hollywood variants of melodrama, questioning through violence the limited presentations of gender and race such melodramas pursued.

Particularly in act 2, *Requiem* reveals its debt to both the woman's film and race melodrama when Temple "confesses" her implication in her child's death. Confession is central to women's films such as *Mildred Pierce*, in which the eponymous heroine frames herself for a murder Veda has committed, giving her account in the chief inspector's office. Similarly, in act 2 of *Requiem* Temple attempts to shift blame for her child's murder from Nancy to herself in the governor's office. Consequently, both Mildred and Temple give their accounts under intense legal scrutiny. The director of *Mildred Pierce*, Michael Curtiz, creates this mood through high-angle shots, which visually position Mildred as a closely observed object under a magnifying glass (see fig. 4). In *Requiem*'s stage directions for the confession scenes, Faulkner instructs that the whole of the bottom of the stage should be in darkness, "so that the visible scene has the effect of being held in the beam of a spotlight" (*N* 4: 548). The effect is one of scrutiny through elevation of the stage, rather than the viewers themselves being elevated above the action, since Faulkner stipulates that the upper left of the stage should be "suspended . . . above the shadow of the stage proper," conveying the symbolism that this is "the ultimate seat of judgment" (*N* 4: 548).

The most striking affinity between *Mildred Pierce* and *Requiem* is structural, since Mildred's and Temple's accounts of the past shape both works. Mildred's account serves as a voice-over that summons a visual narrative of her past. Echoing this narrative structure, in *Requiem* Gavin invites Temple to relay the events that led up to her daughter's murder. Temple's voice generates a flashback scene, propelling the dramatic narrative back to the night six months earlier when the murder took place. The flashback scene, act 2, scene 2, distills the sacrificial theme of the woman's film. It becomes clear that Temple has dispatched her eldest child, Bucky, to her mother's house to allow for an untroubled flight with Pete. Her actions here strongly recall the woman's film *Letter from an Unknown Woman* (1948), in which Lisa Berndle similarly sends her child to her parents in order that she might resume an

FIGURE 4. Mildred Pierce (Joan Crawford) is viewed from a high-angle shot in the inspector's office. (Warner Brothers)

affair with her former lover. Drawing on this conceit of the woman's film, *Requiem* ostensibly suggests that a willingness to pursue erotic impulses and to compromise the family unit is effectively to sacrifice one's children.

The sacrifice is brought about by conflict between Temple and Nancy in act 2, scene 2. Nancy believes she has tried every possible tactic to persuade Temple to stay with her husband and children. Having already hidden Temple's money and diamonds, the financial support for her to run away, she asks Temple whether she would leave, "children or no children" (*N* 4: 601), a challenge Temple affirms.[7] Mary Ann Doane summarizes the affective power of maternal melodrama as deriving from its focus on motherhood in "scenarios of separation and return, or threatened separation" (*Desire to Desire* 73). As such, the mother becomes the site of contradictions in a play of closeness and distance. Temple challenges this closeness, and it takes an act of disproportionate violence to reinstate it. Despairing of another course of action, Nancy kills Temple's infant daughter in the nursery.

Nancy's motivations here should be understood within the conventions of race melodrama. This distinct melodramatic tradition emerged in the mid-nineteenth century to express racial conflict in the United States. Williams defines the "racial melodrama" as a mode in which one racially constituted group is shown to be victimized by another (*Race Card* 4). The virtuous suffering of the victimized party or parties is presented with the aim of gaining rights for the victim(s) "through the recognition of injury" (*Race Card* 4). Williams traces this function of melodrama from the virtuous Black victims in *Uncle Tom's Cabin* (1852) to the reverse image of the white woman endangered by the Black man in the racist "anti-Tom" narratives of Thomas Dixon Jr.'s *The Clansman* (1905) and D. W. Griffith's *The Birth of a Nation* (1915) that Faulkner subverts in *Sanctuary*. Williams argues that "there is a history of mutually informing, perpetually trumping, race cards animating a long tradition of black and white racial melodrama" and that the shared intention of the works in this tradition is, following Brooks's occult, "to give 'moral legibility' to race" (*Race Card* 5). The establishment of the virtue of a body through violence is also explored in *Requiem*. However, Faulkner complicates this relationship by using the white woman and her child's victimization to establish the moral integrity of the Black woman. In stark contrast to classic examples of race melodrama, where victimization and virtue are inseparable, the relationship between the two is disjointed.

Nancy's murderous defense of the coherence of the white Southern family is presented through the racial stereotype of the mammy as "a faithful and loving dependent" (McElya 3). Temple insists that Nancy is not the traditional "ole cradle-rocking black mammy" (*N* 4: 579), due to her past. Barker points out that, despite expressing her socially progressive credentials, Temple's portrayal of Nancy is "characteristic of the most sentimental descriptions of the mammy" ("Modern Mammy" 78). The iconic image of the mammy was developed and solidified in a number of melodramatic works. After the mammy's circulation in the nineteenth century through the sentimental abolitionist literature of *Uncle Tom's Cabin* and the reactionary plantation school of literature, she was most widely promulgated in the twentieth century through Hollywood race melodramas of the South, such as *The Birth of a Nation* and *Gone with the Wind* (1939). Melodrama's enduring focus on domestic spaces suited the presentation of the mammy, for "the scene of black loyalty was almost always the white home" (McElya 9). These films presented the mammy as a faithful servant to her white masters, one who works to ensure the unity of the Southern family during the convulsions of the Civil War and Reconstruction. Most pertinent to the role of Nancy in *Requiem*, the mammy may act to police the deviant desires of the white Southern woman she serves. In *Gone with the Wind*, for example, Scarlett O'Hara's behavior is consistently kept in check by her Black housemaid, who functions as an advocate for Southern upper-class plantation values. Barker highlights that the mammy in films such as these is shown to be "the enforcer of the very rules of ladylike behavior from which she herself is barred" ("Modern Mammy" 77). Faulkner updates this function of the mammy from a Civil to a Cold War context, as Nancy works to ensure 1950s domestic conformity.[8]

The impulse of the mammy to contain potential transgression is, however, grossly exaggerated in *Requiem*, as it is murder, rather than merely disapproving words, that enforces social orthodoxy. It is through such an overblown exaggeration of this role that Faulkner undercuts the mammy's stereotypical unflinching devotion to the white family and the social status quo. Indeed, the text can scarcely contain the ironies of Nancy's actions. Gavin asserts that Nancy is dying to postulate "that little children . . . shall be intact, unanguished, untorn, unterrified" (*N* 4: 615), a sentiment that she brutally violates even as she tries to uphold it. *Requiem* distorts the melodramatic template by offering no clear moral oppositions. Nancy is both perpetrator and victim, since she is executed for her actions. While morally bankrupt in her choice of murder, she nevertheless aligns herself with Christian morality (when her death sentence is pronounced, she simply responds, "Yes, Lord" [*N* 4: 507]) and is held up as a martyr by those around her in her efforts to coerce Temple into maternal devotion. Susan Gillman has argued that race melodramas may challenge moral binaries, suggesting that although they are "narratively organized through the structural polarities dear to the melodramatic imagination . . . the doubling of plots, characters, and events in these texts—formal expressions of polarity—fails notably to provide the sense of order associated with the moral Manichaeism of melodrama" (16–17). Moral disorder reigns in *Requiem*, with both Temple and Nancy simultaneously occupying the positions of perpetrator and victim, thereby blurring the racialized lines of melodramatic moral conflict. These ambiguities reflect the complexities of cinematic spectatorship for minority groups, who were stereotyped and marginalized in melodramatic Hollywood productions. As bell hooks argues, "looking at films with an oppositional gaze, black women were able to critically assess the cinema's construction of white womanhood as object of phallocentric gaze and choose not to identify with either the victim or the perpetrator" (122). Reflecting the disruption of such cinematic binaries on the level of representation in his characterization of the Black housemaid, Faulkner challenges sentimental expectations derived from race melodrama that the virtuous mammy should naturally work to preserve the moral integrity of the white home by presenting Nancy's paradoxical ability to commit righteous infanticide.

Requiem complicates the traditional relationship between victimization and virtue in race melodrama to subvert an essentialist trope of the genre.[9] In contrast, the elements of act 2, scene 2, that draw on the woman's film uphold the genre's linking of female transgression and sacrifice to expose its cruel logic. In contrast to *Mildred Pierce* and *Letter from an Unknown Woman*, where the loss of the child to illness is causally related to the mother's straying (either from the bonds of marriage or domestic work), Faulkner's *Requiem* makes that link literal through an act of vicarious infanticide. In *Mildred Pierce* and *Letter from an Unknown Woman*, the device is highly contrived. In the former, Mildred's younger daughter, Kay, dies from a sudden illness, which suggests that Mildred has fetishized Veda and neglected her other child, the innocent, while in the latter, Lisa's son dies of typhus after they briefly sit in the same train carriage as a dying man before it has been marked for quarantine. In *Mildred Pierce* and *Letter from an Unknown Woman*, the heroine's deviance results in the child's death. Faulkner, however, goes even further than Hollywood, intensifying this feature of the woman's film by linking the threat of a woman's affair to the child's *murder*. In making the warped causation explicit, Faulkner renders the moral judgment of such an equation transparent. Temple elsewhere calls her murdered child the "doomed sacrifice" (*N* 4: 580) for her libidinal errancy. In Faulkner's text we shrink from the violence of the child's sacrificial death when its brutal ideological motivation is laid bare, no longer masked as a sudden twist of fate as is customary in the genre.

Infanticide in *Requiem* simultaneously undercuts gender and racial norms from the woman's film and race melodrama. The text unsettles the sentimental belief that the "mammy" figure will benignly ensure the security of the white home and challenges the punitive logic of the woman's film, in which maternal transgression can lead to incarceration, unbearable dilemmas, stoical separations, or most severely, the deaths of children. In creating a hybrid of these two forms of melodrama, Faulkner challenges both subgenres' overinvestment in perverse fantasies of the cohesive nuclear family that demand either the mammy's utter devotion or the white mother's self-sacrifice. Beyond its subversion of genre conventions, excessive violence in the text critiques Cold War melodramatic political discourses. The child's murder is intended to stave off Temple's transgressive affair, which disregards the sexual and class-based boundaries around female desire in 1950s American society. Written only a few years after the end of World War II, *Requiem* can therefore be seen to manifest the nascent anxieties of the Cold War, demonstrating how postwar fears resulted in the attempted containment of individuals within strict gender and class relations. Murderous excess renders the ideologies of domestic containment absurd by amplifying the acts it takes to enforce gender and sexual conformity, "moral deeds" that cannot conceal their internal contradictions.

The Family Melodrama and the Autocritical Mode

By exaggerating features of the woman's film and the race melodrama, Faulkner made ideology reflect on itself through stylistic excess. His melodrama critiqued Cold War containment by undermining the tropes used to enforce domestic cohesion in earlier filmic examples of the genre. In doing so, he anticipated the autocritical techniques that skilled directors of 1950s family melodramas were beginning to employ and whose films subtly conveyed resistance to Cold War nuclear values. The family melodrama achieved its most sophisticated formal and thematic expression in the work of the directors Vincente Minnelli, Nicholas Ray, and Douglas Sirk. In their films, style is used as a method of undercutting dominant presentations of race, class, gender, and sexuality in American culture while simultaneously displaying them in recognizable fashion. In this way, Thomas Schatz argues, these films appear to be "at once celebrating and severely questioning the basic values and attitudes of the mass audience" (*Hollywood Genres* 223). This brought about a play of both identification and distancing through a self-conscious and exaggerated use of form.

The affinity between *Requiem* and the films that followed later in the same decade parallels the interest Hollywood genre directors of the 1950s had in Faulkner's texts. Three key examples of the family melodrama are in fact adaptations of Faulkner novels: Sirk's *The Tarnished Angels* (1957), which is based on *Pylon* (1935); Martin Ritt's *The Long, Hot Summer* (1958), a loose adaptation of Faulkner's novel *The Hamlet* (1940) and his short stories "Spotted Horses" (1931) and "Barn Burning" (1939); and Ritt's *The Sound and the Fury* (1959), an adaptation of the 1929 novel of the same name. Such adaptations suggest that Hollywood directors were able to excavate melodrama from Faulkner's fiction, even that the inherent melodrama of these texts proved particularly attractive to writers and directors of this period. These films, by divorcing Faulkner's content from his style, reveal how melodramatic many of his plot features and archetypes are. For example, in Faulkner's *The Sound and the Fury,* Caddy pays her brother Jason for a reunion with her teenage daughter, Quentin, whom she has not seen since she was a baby. Jason accepts the money and cruelly drives the young girl past her mother in the street without stopping the car. This scene is milked for full melodramatic potential in the 1959 film adaptation, in which Caddy chases after the car at night dressed completely in black with Quentin screaming, "Jason, stop the car! It's my mother!" (*Sound*). In such moments, the excessive melodramatic features of Faulkner's plots are translated visually but, in addition, the intense psychological excess of a melodramatic modernist novel like *The Sound and the Fury* is approximated by the antipsychological excess of its adaptation as a family melodrama.

E. Ann Kaplan argues that Ritt expressed conflict within 1950s social and ideological codes by "daring to expose the tensions that usually only underlie filmic surfaces . . . to lay bare the dire situation of the modern North American family" (*Motherhood* 179). In *No Down Payment* (1957), Ritt depicts the lives of young lower-middle-class couples in a suburban churchgoing community in postwar California. Behind the motto of Sunrise Hill Estates, "a better place for better living," lies the reality of career disappointment and marital conflict in a claustrophobic network of houses. Indeed, many of the issues Faulkner explores through Gowan in the confining domestic space are represented in the film: alcoholism and men who doubt the paternity of their own children. Also similar to *Requiem*, Ritt presents the idea that violence can intrude suddenly into the domestic realm; in *No Down Payment* the newly arrived middle-class wife in the community is raped by her neighbor, a man embittered by his lack of career opportunities in the US after distinguished service in World War II and his inability to attract what he deems to be a "respectable" woman due to his lack of a formal education (his wife gave a baby up for adoption before they were married, because she was not certain who the father was). Ritt also comments on the fact that these domestic communities are racially exclusive; an Asian shop assistant who also served in the war asks the store manager in Sunrise Hill to petition the subdividers of the estate to make an exception to their policy of only selling to white families. In a similar vein to *Requiem*, Ritt suggests in *No Down Payment* that the domestic idyll of postwar American life is essentially phony, since it conceals harsh realities and cannot defend against violence stimulated by gender and class conflict, in addition to being racially exclusive.

Faulkner uses Rittian exposure in his social critique of Cold War domesticity. He achieves this through using the events of *Sanctuary* and "That Evening Sun"—as well as their ramifications—to serve as the harsh reality underpinning the image of 1950s domesticity in *Requiem*. For example, Temple describes herself and Nancy as "two sisters in sin swapping trade or anyway avocational secrets over coca colas in the quiet kitchen" during "the long afternoons, with the last electric button pressed on the last cooking or washing or sweeping gadget and the baby safely asleep for a while" (*N* 4: 580). Here it is Temple's sense of her and her housemaid's mutual link to prostitution that lies beneath the appearance of domestic serenity. In this sense, the Stevenses' smart town apartment, their membership in the country club, and regular church attendance thinly mask the realities of alcoholism, rape, prostitution, gangland vice, and drug addiction in Temple's, Gowan's, and Nancy's pasts, along with paternal doubt, extramarital affairs, and murder that have caused new conflicts for them in the present.

The director most closely identified with the Hollywood family melodrama of the 1950s is Sirk, who placed Faulkner alongside Herman Melville, Henry James, and Sherwood Anderson as the American writers who had the most profound influence on his film aesthetic (*Sirk on Sirk*). The stylistic excesses of Sirk's films challenge the conventional bourgeois values expressed in the narrative, which means the verbal is often at odds with the visual in his work (Elsaesser 69).[10] This opens up the possibility for subversion not generally present in the woman's film of the 1930s and 1940s. Sirkian excess primarily manifests itself visually, aurally, and symbolically in his films. On a visual level, Sirk suffuses the screen with bold colors and gradations of light, often using brilliant and rich patterns to illuminate the faces of the actors in intense sustained close-ups.[11] This is in addition to the visual opulence of Sirk's films' mise-en-scène and settings, which create a number of improbable hyperrealist tableaus. On the aural plane, Sirk employs overwrought music to underscore heightened emotional states, an intensity reflected in the actors' vehement vocal deliveries, which are anguished, grand, and often strained. Sirk's use of symbolism is also heavy-handed. When an incident should be read metaphorically, the director often presents it within suspended cinematic time. For example, when Cary Scott breaks a vase her lover Ron Kirby has repaired in *All That Heaven Allows*

(1955), symbolic of her destruction of the life Ron wants to fashion with her, Sirk allows twenty seconds to pass after the accident before either of the actors says a word. The aesthetic of the family melodrama is essentially self-ironizing, since stylistics are used to question the attitudes and motivations of the film's characters.

In Sirk's oeuvre the film that most closely resembles *Requiem* is his last Hollywood film, *Imitation of Life* (1959), which similarly examines the perils of maternal sacrifice.[12] Facing dilemmas different from the ones Temple comes up against, the heroine of *Imitation*, Lora Meredith, played by Lana Turner, threatens to sacrifice "healthy" relationships with her daughter and the man she loves for her acting career. In both works the relationship between the bourgeois lady of the house and the Black domestic worker is a key generator of conflict. In *Imitation* the housemaid Annie Johnson's daughter Sarah Jane is able to pass as white and denies her racial identity repeatedly, identifying increasingly with Lora as a white mother figure. Sarah Jane finally runs away to join a chorus line in Hollywood and cuts off contact with Annie completely. These events seem to cause Annie to develop a mysterious condition that leads to her death from what the other characters presume to be a "broken heart." Since *Requiem* ends shortly before Nancy's execution for murder, both Faulkner's novel and Sirk's film conclude with the ideologically questionable sacrifice of the Black housemaid as a contrived resolution to maternal tensions in the white bourgeois home. Nevertheless, the treatment of racial and gender ideology within these parallel plots is rendered autocritically.

From the 1970s there was a resurgence of critical interest in Sirk's films, principally due to their perceived ability to self-consciously reflect on their own narratives. Critics have, however, largely located this strategy in style rather than characterization. Laura Mulvey advances that "characters caught in the world of melodrama are not allowed transcendent awareness or knowledge," and consequently "they do not fully grasp the forces they are up against or their own instinctive behavior" ("Notes on Sirk" 41). For Mulvey, style in the Sirkian melodrama "provide[s] a transcendent, wordless commentary" ("Notes on Sirk" 41). This claim, however, overlooks moments in which the characters *themselves* call attention to their own or each other's excessive self-presentations. In *Imitation* one such moment occurs. Lora is an aspiring stage actress who, after experiencing a career setback when her husband dies, rises to become a Broadway star and the lead in a Felliniesque film. Sirk gives us an actress playing an actress, which immediately lends the role a reflexive quality. Lora moves from humble beginnings, trying to make ends meet as a single mother living in a cold-water apartment in Manhattan, to living in some luxury in the expensive suburbs. Prioritizing her career, Lora neglects her child Susie while spoiling her from a distance, leaving her largely in the care of Annie, with whom they share accommodations and who manages the house. When Susie reaches adolescence, she falls in love with her mother's love interest Steve. After Lora discovers this, she confronts her daughter and resolves that "if Steve is going to come between us—I'll give him up. I'll never see him again" (*Imitation*). These lines are delivered with a faraway stare, quivering lip, and arched eyebrow as a shallow epiphany is seen to flit over the actress's face. Her daughter responds: "Oh, Mama, stop acting! Stop trying to shift people around as if they were pawns on a stage! . . . Oh, don't worry! I'll get over Steve. But please—don't play the martyr!" (*Imitation*; see fig. 5). Susie challenges Lora's overblown performance as a maternal martyr, a stock melodramatic figure, causing her mother to collapse and cover her face as she breaks down in tears. Lora's identity unravels, as she endures forced insight into the gulf between her artificial mask and her authentic self. Judith Butler discusses the way this scene "contests the boundaries" of melodramatic conventions through "the parodic shedding of the grand gesture, the sudden depletion of emotional excess" ("Melodramatic Repetition" 8). Richard Dyer argues that the same scene calls attention to Turner's *own* "poised and posed" acting style, blurring the boundaries between actor and role ("Lana" 424). Both interpretations give credit to Sirk's and Turner's abilities to expose the tension between an "authentic" and an ironically mimetic presentation of the mother. Although Lora may reflect 1950s maternal ideology—the pressure to sacrifice career and love for children—in calling attention to her behavior as an *affectation*, Sirk and Turner subvert the social conformity Lora's behavior might imply.

Imitation of Life emerged at the twilight of both the family melodrama in film—the formula had been largely co-opted by television by the late 1950s—and the classical Hollywood studio system. Faulkner's 1951 work seems to anticipate the decade of melodramas that followed, through his deployment of what became Sirkian self-critical excess. Indeed, Temple most insistently calls attention to the construction of the drama and her own character, fulfilling a function usually placed outside the conscious operation of language in 1950s melodrama. Most directly, we see this in the way she shifts between two roles she narrates in the third person as mutually

FIGURE 5. In a close-up from *Imitation of Life* (1959), the artificiality of the performance by Lora Meredith (Lana Turner) is highlighted by a line of dialogue delivered by Susie (Sandra Dee). (Universal Pictures)

exclusive performances. This places her in the metatextual position of herself being the primary author of the melodrama's social critique through highlighting its structural ironies. Barbara Ladd argues that Temple's ironic function is related to *Requiem*'s Cold War context, since Faulkner "may have felt that the development and use by the United States of an atomic bomb suggested that the destruction of civilization would come from the masculine State itself" (485), a historical reality that Temple's voice critiques. In a more formal sense, however, Temple's adoption of a series of positions lays bare the melodrama's strategy of foregrounding its struggle with itself. Just as Temple is aware of the different roles she plays in the text, so too the melodrama self-consciously questions its own excesses. Temple's excessive performance undercuts the limitations of her situation within bourgeois ideology, challenging the traditional naivety of melodramatic protagonists to the wider social forces that shape their lives.

This form of characterization is advanced in a number of ways. Throughout *Requiem* we see Temple resisting the performance of maternal suffering by insistently calling attention to the construction of her role. We see her self-reflexively adopt the position of the "bereaved mother ... herself *watching* the accomplishment of her revenge; the tigress over the body of her slain club" (*N* 4: 527; emphasis added). Temple's ability to *watch* herself in this maternal role as a melodramatic protagonist is central to the self-critical dynamic of her performance. Indeed, she continually narrates the function of the maternal martyr as if she were watching herself, foregrounding both her knowledge of the requirements of the role ("Let me be bereaved and vindicated, but at least let me do it in privacy" [*N* 4: 510]) and the expectations other characters place on her performance ("If what you came for is to see me weep, I doubt if you'll even get that" [*N* 4: 511]). Temple's use of language is self-conscious throughout, as she is seemingly aware of the need to tailor her verbal performance for staged interactions with the other characters. In her attempted resurrection of her former role as a gangster's moll in *Sanctuary*, Temple tries to shift her language into a hard-boiled register during an exchange with Pete, asking him: "No dough, no snatch. Isn't that how you would say it?" (*N* 4: 591). There are also suggestions of this kind of self-conscious language in Faulkner's delineation of Beryl Sigman in his screenplay for "The Left Hand of God," an adaptation of William E. Barrett's 1951 novel of the same name; both screenplay and novel are set in an American mission in China after World War II during a period of civil war in the country. Faulkner worked on the script between February and April 1951 (Gleeson-White, "Left Hand of God" 755). Beryl is the wife of the mission's doctor, and in her dialogue with the new village priest, she seems to be aware of her language's artificiality, as she delivers a line "almost like a cue, watching him intently while she waits for him to pick it up. Obviously he is not going to. She prompts him again" (*TCF* 803). Such correspondences between the screenplay and *Requiem* are perhaps not surprising, since Faulkner was working on this novel alongside his Hollywood work; he asked his young collaborator Joan Williams to send material for the play's third act to his Hollywood address in February 1951 (*SL* 312). In fact, parts of Faulkner's screenplay appear on the reverse of several manuscript pages of *Requiem*, providing evidence of a highly intimate material relationship between the two works (Gleeson-White, "Left Hand of God" 753–54; Solomon, *Screenwriting* 197–98).[13]

In *Requiem*, the function of the female actor's language is taken further than in Faulkner's version of "The Left Hand of God," since Temple also checks the excesses of the other players' language. When Gavin asserts the necessity of her testimony, he argues that in trying to combat injustice, only "truth" or "love" will be sufficient to the task, to which Temple responds, "Love. Oh, God. Love" (*N* 4: 532), mocking these words' glib inability to contain meaning and the moral absolutes fundamental to melodrama. Most importantly, Temple appears to possess metatextual awareness of the sadistic apparatus of the maternal melodrama itself, questioning whether the action is moving toward the "wanton crucifixion of a bereaved mamma" (*N* 4: 516). In insisting on Temple's identity as a performer, Faulkner, in a method similar to Sirk in *Imitation,* frames maternal suffering as a mask the actress figure assumes, thus exposing the ideological composition of the trope. In highlighting the artificiality of dramatic language, dialogue, and action, Temple strongly contributes to the autocritical program of Faulkner's family melodrama. In *Requiem* it is primarily Temple's ironic verbal commentary on the action that exposes and critiques arbitrary maternal suffering in melodrama, drawing attention to the ways gender ideology shapes genre. In this sense, Temple's dialogue can be considered filmic within a genre framework; indeed Frederick Morgan, a contemporary reviewer of *Requiem,* commented that the language of the play sections more closely resembles a movie scenario than theatrical dialogue. Morgan even suggested that Lauren Bacall would be suitable for the role of Temple (qtd. in Rollyson, *Alarming Paradox* 373), with whom Faulkner had collaborated at Warner's on *To Have and Have Not* (1944) and *The Big Sleep* (1946) and who would also star in one of Sirk's family melodramas directed in a Southern Gothic style, *Written on the Wind* (1955).

However, in concert with the traditional stylistics of the Sirkian family melodrama, where characters are unaware of wider social forces, Faulkner uses the white family's *limits* of knowledge about the Black woman's life to question racial ideology.[14] In *Imitation* Sirk intimates that Annie's sickness and death may not solely result from the loss of her daughter. It is implied that Annie's role as "everybody's Rock of Gibraltar" (*Imitation*), providing support to the white family of which she is a part, has proved an unbearable burden. Even when Annie is bedridden and critically ill, Lora and Susie continue to trouble her with their problems, both of whom, it transpires, know little of Annie's life beyond her role within their home. As Lauren Berlant highlights, "Annie has a secret non-diegetic life in the black community" (132). The audience shares Lora's surprise that the housemaid has a private life, and is embarrassed by what Allison Whitney calls their "internalized acceptance of the mammy stereotype" (7).

In *Requiem* we learn that Temple hired Nancy to act as her "confidante," someone who was able to speak "Temple's Drake's language" (*N* 4: 579). This is essentially an exploitative relationship, since Nancy is "somebody paid by the week just to listen" (*N* 4: 580). As in *Imitation,* it is as if the Black woman cannot exist for the white characters outside the mammy stereotype, as Nancy's role is confined to her domestic utility. In the most extreme example, shortly before Nancy's execution, Gavin speculates that Nancy will not be able to escape the mammy role even in heaven, arguing that "the harp, the raiment, the singing, may not be for Nancy Mannigoe—not now. But there's still the work to be done—the washing and sweeping, maybe even the children to be tended and fed and kept from hurt and harm" (N 4: 659). This excessive description is, as Dorothy Stringer describes, a "hyper-literalization of plantation-tradition celebrations of faithful slaves" (62), and it functions to ironize the white characters' ignorance. Both Faulkner and Sirk frame the "mammy" as a figure created, limited, and preserved by the investments of the white characters around them. While Temple is able to narrate the restrictions of her role within maternal melodrama, she does not possess the same insight into how she constrains Nancy. Nancy's and Annie's service to the white families is therefore presented as willful social containment in narratives that both conclude with the Black woman's death.

In *Requiem*'s final scene, which takes place in jail shortly before Nancy's execution, Gowan's voice calls to Temple offstage, and she follows with the word "coming" (N 4: 664). The conclusion is highly open-ended. Although Temple may appear to be "rehabilitated" through reunion with her husband, one can only speculate how long she will remain with him and her surviving child. This return to the home is overshadowed by the specter of death in the forms of Temple's grief for her child and the ineluctable fact of Nancy's execution. One also wonders whether without Nancy to act as the family's "magnetic center" the Stevenses will be able to hold together. Such ambiguity and irresolution add to our sense that melodramatic endings may be neither entirely affirmative nor entirely subversive of the social order they document. Sirk elaborates that even in the desired conclusion to his Hollywood melodramas, "there is no real solution of the predicament the people in the play are in, just the *deus ex machina*, which is now called the 'happy end' . . . It makes the crowd happy. To the few it makes the aporia more transparent" (*Sirk on Sirk* 157). In similarly aporetic fashion, we sense that Temple may no longer allow herself to be bound to the bourgeois prison, even through violence. This reality is made most apparent through her bizarre metatextual awareness of the arbitrary cruelty of her suffering as a grieving mother in the text. Her self-consciousness suggests potential for her escape from the limitations of the maternal role she has to perform. In a different fashion, the way Nancy's life and suffering are simply appended to the desires of the white family throughout the work critiques a failure or a refusal to contemplate alternative roles for Black women beyond domestic servitude. In both cases, the ironic generic mode invites us to think critically about prescribed roles for Black and white women in melodrama and Cold War society.

Faulkner's *Requiem* recirculates the conventions of melodrama from his 1940s screenwriting projects in an adaptation that challenges the woman's film by advancing a scathing critique of its central sacrificial theme. His use of tropes from earlier forms of melodrama is self-ironizing and therefore typical of the sophisticated 1950s Hollywood melodrama that followed. By locating the primary autocritical presence in a reflexive female character, Faulkner demonstrates how female agents could actively ironize the contemporary ideologies of gender and sexuality that these melodramatic works superficially appeared to enforce. At the same time, Temple's failure to perceive the irony in how her *own* language contains Nancy within a racial stereotype exposes the structures of exploitation that support a normative vision of the nuclear family.

Faulkner's subversion of these tropes was intended as an attack on the moral Manicheism of melodramatic political discourse, specifically the potent Cold War ideology that contained women within the home to help shore up the national front against the rise of a nebulous Communist threat to American security. *Requiem*'s critique of containment highlights the limitations of roles for women in 1950s society. This opens up an additional space in the text that offers the potential for resistance, since the process of imagining new roles would become central to nascent social movements of the age. In 1963 Betty Friedan's *The Feminine Mystique* heralded the beginning of second-wave feminism by exposing the unhappy reality of suburban housewives' lives. In addition, prior to the 1960s the occupational choices of African American women were severely limited, and they were often only able to find work as domestics. With the civil rights movement, K. Sue Jewell explains, African American women "experienced upward mobility against seemingly insurmountable odds, by rejecting [the domestic role] and other cultural images and defining and redefining their roles, capabilities and aspirations in society" (44). Inspired by Hollywood narratives, Faulkner questioned the relative positions of white housewife and Black housemaid in the confining Cold War domestic space, prefiguring the ways women would begin to liberate themselves from postwar containment through an interrogation of the constraints and asymmetries of domestic roles.

6

"Castrate of Sound"

The Mansion and the Silence of Cinematic Archetypes

THE MANSION (1959) WAS Faulkner's penultimate novel, published five years after he had completed work on his last Hollywood screenplay.[1] In the summer of 1957, Faulkner's publisher, Random House, announced that there would be a sequel to the author's previous novel, *The Town* (1957), the second volume of the Snopes trilogy that had begun with *The Hamlet* (1940). In a session as writer-in-residence at the University of Virginia in Charlottesville, Faulkner was asked whether he intended to write the story of Eula Varner Snopes's daughter in the new book, to which he replied, "Yes, sir . . . She's one of the most interesting people I've written about yet, I think. Her story will be in the next book" (Blotner, *Biography* 644). Although Faulkner was now finally at a remove from his Hollywood work, his portrayal of this distinctive heroine, Linda Snopes Kohl, would draw on tropes and conventions from his screenplays across the breadth of his Hollywood career.

Linda's character develops significantly across the three novels in the Snopes trilogy. In *The Hamlet,* she is the unnamed, illegitimate child of Eula Varner and Hoake McCarron, who leaves Eula when he finds out she is pregnant. Eula is quickly married off by her father to Flem Snopes to protect her reputation. Flem, a man who rises from being the son of a tenant farmer to the position of bank president in the trilogy, is representative of "Snopesism," the unscrupulous, money-driven upward mobility of the white working-class family, from Frenchman's Bend to Jefferson, where they rapidly infiltrate and take over the town's institutions of power. In *The Town*, Linda appears as a teenager who is popular with the young men of Jefferson but is mentored and schooled in literature by the much older Gavin Stevens, a highly educated lawyer, who wishes to "save" Linda from Flem by sending her to an educational institution outside the bounds of Yoknapatawpha. Eula's long affair with Manfred de Spain becomes public knowledge towards the end of *The Town*. Due to the pressure Flem puts upon Eula and the widespread scandal about her eighteen-year-long affair, she kills herself, it is speculated out of boredom (*N* 5: 315), although it seems she despairs that this is the only way to liberate Linda from her father. To protect Linda from Flem, Gavin arranges her departure to Greenwich Village, as "a place with a few unimportant boundaries but no limitations where young people of any age go to seek dreams" (*N* 5: 307). The final novel in the trilogy, *The Mansion*, is divided into three books named after three key players in the Snopes saga: "Mink," "Linda," and "Flem." Each book is narrated by a pluralistic mixture of first-person and omniscient narrators. "Mink" covers almost four decades, from Mink's murder of Jack Houston to his release from jail. "Linda" reintroduces the novel's principal female character, now living in Greenwich Village, New York, where she marries a Jewish Communist sculptor named Barton Kohl. The final book, "Flem," follows Mink's journey from the Mississippi state prison farm, Parchman, back to Yoknapatawpha, where he will murder Flem for what Mink sees as Flem's role in his long incarceration. By the end of the novel, it becomes clear that Linda has avenged her mother's suicide and overcome her father through her complicity in this murder.

Similar to his film projects, collaborative processes, both fraught and harmonious, would accompany *The Mansion*'s journey to publication. Faulkner's editor at Random House, Albert Erskine, brought a series of inconsistencies between the different volumes of the trilogy to the author's attention. Faulkner insisted that *The Mansion* was the "definitive" volume, and that *The Hamlet* and *The Town* "can be edited in subsequent editions to conform" (*SL* 426). In a somewhat dismissive response to Erskine, who raised specific discrepancies between the novels, Faulkner proclaimed that he was "a veteran member of a living literature. . . . So if what I write in 1958 aint better than what I wrote in 1938, I should have stopped writing twenty years ago; or, since 'being alive' equals 'motion,' I should be 20 years in the grave" (*SL* 429). Despite such objections, Faulkner would accommodate a number of Erskine's proposed changes. He would, however, defend his position on literature as a living, evolving organism in his short prefatory note to *The Mansion*, arguing that "his entire life's work is a part of a living literature, and since 'living' is motion, and 'motion' is change and alteration and therefore the only alternative to motion is un-motion, stasis, death, there will be found discrepancies and contradictions in the thirty-four-year progress of this particular chronicle" (*N* 5: 331).

Many scholars have commented on Linda's distinctiveness as a well-rounded female character in Faulkner's prose. Theresa M. Towner identifies Linda as having "predecessors in the Faulkner canon but no direct prototype" and finds that she is "Faulkner's most complex female character and the character of either sex whose political sympathies and goals have the strongest resonances for contemporary audiences" (110). Keith Louise Fulton sees Linda as an anti-patriarchal figure who, in meting out revenge against her "father," Flem, succeeds in "achieving what no other female or male character in Faulkner's fiction achieves, an act of justice that settles her conflicts with the past and empowers her move into the future" (425). Evelyn Jaffe Schreiber also views this radical act as a "challenge [to] the dominant social system" that enables Linda "to move from an object position to one of subject" (84). Hee Kang additionally identifies Linda as a character who represents a substantial change in Faulkner's depiction of women, "tracing a trajectory from the space of victimization, betrayal, and death to a newly configured feminine space of desire, autonomy, and freedom" (22). Distinct from the work of these critics, I would like to attribute this new portrayal, in large part, to Faulkner's work in Hollywood and the collaborative practices that had animated his screenwriting and fiction over the previous decades.[2] In the analyses that follow, I demonstrate how Faulkner's depiction of Linda draws on female archetypes he had written for the screen and absorbed into his Hollywood novels, namely the wartime woman, the masculinized Hawksian heroine, the sacrificial woman of melodrama, and the deathly femme fatale. Significantly, through Linda, Faulkner manages to overcome some of the ideological limitations of these genre types. I do not approach these figures chronologically according to Hollywood film history but rather in the order in which these archetypes come into sharper focus within the progression of the novel itself.

Take 1: Linda as Wartime Heroine

The Mansion reintroduces Linda within the cultural ferment of Greenwich Village, where she will marry the sculptor Barton Kohl. Linda is embedded within the modernist communities of the East Coast, and Chick Mallison observes that such is Barton's commitment to artistic abstraction that it resists the comprehension of even the learned classes of Jefferson, since his work is "so advanced and liberal that even Gavin couldn't recognise what he sculpted" (*N* 5: 519). Chick later comments that "the piece of sculpture" Barton eventually bequeaths to Gavin confuses him too, "because I didn't even know what it was, let alone what it was doing" (*N* 5: 539).[3] It is Barton's death, after he is shot down in an old airplane in the Spanish Civil War of the 1930s, that precipitates Linda's return to Jefferson, where she takes up the civil rights cause through her largely unsuccessful interventions in the town's Jim Crow education system.

Linda's role as prodigal child is framed dramatically; Faulkner referred to her return to the South after living in New York and Spain as "the third-act curtain to the whole thing" (Blotner, *Biography* 648). The novel has a classical structure, divided into three books named after the central three players, and the disparate narrators of the text function as a chorus providing a commentary on the motivations of the Snopeses. More than theater, though, *The Mansion* is indebted to Hollywood cinema, and Faulkner describes Linda's return in the "third act" using conventions from the war film, creating a hybrid of tropes he had employed for both male and female characters in his scripts.

Giving an account of Linda's arrival at Memphis airport, where Gavin and Chick pick her up to bring her back to Jefferson, Chick places Linda within a lineage of veterans who returned to Yoknapatawpha as heroes. Chick points out that Linda "wasn't the first wounded war hero to finally struggle back to Jefferson" (*N* 5: 492). He also elaborates that "she was not even the first female hero," as Chick recalls a nurse who served as "an authentic female lieutenant . . . on the staff of a base hospital in France and . . . had actually spent two days at a casualty clearing station within sound of the guns behind Montdidier" (*N* 5: 492). Mallison qualifies, however, that the World War I nurse had not actually been a "citizen of Jefferson" (*N* 5: 492) but was related to a Jefferson family, and therefore Linda will be the town's "first female" war hero of whom they can claim complete ownership (*N* 5: 503).[4] Through Chick's narration, Faulkner positions Linda in relation to the war heroes of his Yoknapatawpha fictions. However, Faulkner also situates Linda as a successor to the characters he had written in his scripts for MGM and Fox, since the mood of her return and the descriptions of her labor on the front appear more closely related to aspects of his screenwriting for the war film genre.

In terms of tone, *The Mansion* presents Linda as a war hero who returns in a state of hopefulness and ambition, a narrative development that recalls one of Faulkner's early MGM screenplays: "War Birds / A Ghost Story" (1932–33). In the script, Faulkner adapted aspects of the story of the brothers John and Bayard Sartoris, who appear in a number of the author's World War I aviation fictions: *Flags in the Dust* [*Sartoris*] (1929),[5] "Ad Astra" (1930), and "All the Dead Pilots" (1931). In "War Birds," after a series of self-destructive flying missions on the front in France, John is shot down by German fliers and dies (*MGM* 375). John's nihilism appears motivated by his sexual guilt about betraying his pregnant wife with a French mistress during war. After the armistice, his brother, Bayard, returns to the widowed Caroline and their young son, Johnny, in the American South. He bizarrely chooses to bring both the German man who killed John and John's French mistress with him, forcing Caroline to forgive them, which she finally achieves with the lines: "I ask you to forgive me. I don't—don't hate . . . he is part of all three of us. Bayard says that in us he is not dead, in the three of us and Johnny" (*MGM* 416). Reflecting Faulkner's title for the work, the screenplay explores how to make peace with the ghosts of the past. Like Bayard, Linda returns to the South after war and her presence has a disruptive effect on her family, but the mood of her return is more of a piece with "War Birds" than Faulkner's Yoknapatawpha fictions that dealt with prodigal war heroes. As Bruce F. Kawin points out, through "War Birds" Faulkner showed that history can "assume a new, positive course—a way of looking both backward and forward, a paradoxical optimism" ("War Birds" 263). Similarly, Linda reappears in Jefferson to settle scores and restore relationships, and she is associated with a challenging modernity rather than clinging to the past and the memory of her deceased aviator husband. Linda is not ravaged by survivor's guilt, and the novel resists the atmosphere of postwar doom that pervades Faulkner's aviation literature of the late 1920s and early 1930s.

The description of the activities of Jefferson's first unnamed female war hero—a character that does not appear in another Faulkner text and from whom Linda is descended—also recalls those of the character Monique from Faulkner's 1936 script for "The Road to Glory." Monique serves as a nurse on the front in support of the French army during World War I; she carries out her work in terrible conditions and is terrified by the explosions of bombs falling at night (*TCF* 61). Advancing his characterization of Monique through *The Mansion*, Faulkner shows how Linda does not shrink from the bombs of warfare; her work as an ambulance driver places her in the midst of the conflict, and her injury from war is the direct consequence of her proximity to an explosion, as she was "blown up by a Franco shell or landmine or whatever it was that went off in or under the ambulance she was driving and left her stone deaf" (*N* 5: 503).

Faulkner gives us a character who is distinctive within modern Yoknapatawpha war narratives of return as a woman but nevertheless has clear antecedents within his Hollywood scripts. Linda reenters Jefferson as an alien figure, and her particularity is met with a muted reception in Jefferson, since she challenges misogynistic preconceptions of what kinds of female achievement should be met with celebration; the people of Jefferson would have turned out for an "elected Miss America" (*N* 5: 503) but are little interested in a returning heroine from the Spanish Civil War. Jefferson's reaction to Linda places her outside of the community, and her marginalization appears to be linked to her atypical portrayal, which is saturated with the tropes of Faulkner's Hollywood screenplays.

Take 2: The Masculinized Hawksian Heroine

Linda's presentation additionally recalls the Hawksian heroines of Faulkner's scripts from the mid-1930s and 1940s in the gender-crossing aspects of her appearance and behavior, particularly through her work as an ambulance driver during the Spanish Civil War and as a shipyard riveter in World War II–era Mississippi. Her portrayal was likely inspired by Faulkner's trip to an aircraft factory for a Warner Brothers war movie script, "The Life and Death of a Bomber," in November 1942, as discussed in chapter 4, in which he observed women operating heavy machinery and welding.[6] Linda, in terms of cinematic history, is very much a post-Code heroine whose sexuality is sublimated into collective labor. Although she evidences some of the frank, sexual assertiveness of the pre-Code bad girl, her words are scrupulously removed from the narrative by Gavin as narrator; Linda says to Gavin, "'But you can me' . . . That's right. She used the explicit word, speaking the hard brutal guttural in the quacking duck's voice" (*N* 5: 546). Gavin acts as censor here, controlling Linda's words, thereby ensuring her portrayal adheres to Hays Code stipulations on profanity.

When Gavin reintroduces Linda to Chick on her return to Jefferson, Chick observes that "she was as tall as Gavin and damn near as tall as me, as well as a nail-biter. . . . when she shook hands she really had driven that ambulance and apparently changed the tires on it too" (*N* 5: 509–10). This masculine image, as a result of labor, is compounded by her job in a Mississippian factory that builds ships to transport airplanes, guns, and tanks to help the Allied war effort in Europe. She takes up the role at the end of 1941 shortly after the United States enters World War II. Similar to Laverne Shumann's work as a mechanic in the early sections of *Pylon* (1935), her work blurs her gender identity, taking up the position of a "tool-checker" while trying to secure a job as riveter, for which her "deafness would be an actual advantage" and donning "overalls again, once more minuscule in that masculine or rather sexless world" (*N* 5: 553). Reflecting the androgynous heroines of Hawks's workplace films, such as *His Girl Friday* (1940), and statements made by Faulkner and his collaborators about Hollywood working practices, cross-gender collaborative labor results in the masculinization of women and the potential emasculation of men. These features of Linda's presentation distinguish her from the community of women in California in which she is situated; when Linda accompanies Gavin to a restaurant, he observes that her overalls, and general masculine quality, mark her out from "the other female customers," adding that "she could have worn anything beyond an ear trumpet and a G string, and even then probably the ear trumpet would have drawn the attention" (*N* 5: 555).

After the end of World War II, Linda returns to Jefferson, but she preserves her aberrant masculine quality during peacetime. The transvestism of the immediate postwar period was also explored by Hawks in his 1949 screwball comedy *I Was a Male War Bride*. In the film, a French army captain, Henri Rochard (Cary Grant), marries a female American lieutenant, Catherine Gates (Ann Sheridan), in Allied-occupied Germany and is only able to enter the United States as an immigrant through a bureaucratic loophole as Catherine's male "war bride," since the regulations do not determine the sex of American military personnel's wives. In a series of madcap scenarios that keep the newlyweds apart and in which Henri learns "what it is to be a soldier's wife"—which makes him wish he could "go some place to turn back into a man"—he is finally able to board the ship to New York with his wife in the improvised drag of a female military uniform and a horsehair wig (*War Bride;* fig. 6). Cross-dressing emerges as a pragmatic response to overcome obstacles between lovers in a world where traditional gender roles have been upended, as Henri is continually surrounded and given orders by women in uniform.

In an inversion of Henri's postwar drag, Linda's masculine attire communicates her refusal to accept the neodomestic imperative that was directed at American women in the Cold War period. As detailed in chapter 5 on *Requiem for a Nun* (1951), women were subjected to "domestic containment" (May 16) during this period, in which their adherence to the home as wives and mothers within the nuclear family unit was championed as an essential national bulwark against Communist infiltration. Despite such Cold War policing of normative gender roles, in fall 1945 the narrator presents Linda as a chivalric figure with "a really splendid dramatic white streak in her hair running along the top of her skull almost like a plume," but now this "knight had run out of tourneys and dragons, war itself had slain them, used them

FIGURE 6. Henri Rochard (Cary Grant), accompanied by Catherine Gates (Ann Sheridan), dresses in female uniform in order to return to the US as a "war bride." (Twentieth Century–Fox)

up, made them obsolete" (*N* 5: 644). Even though she has hung up the overalls of her job as a riveter, she maintains her androgynous dress in postwar Yoknapatawpha, sporting "expensive English brogues scuffed and scarred but always neatly polished each morning, with wool stockings or socks beneath worn flannel trousers or a skirt or sometimes what looked like a khaki boiler-suit under a man's stained burberry" (*N* 5: 655). Linda appears to contest domestic containment as social monolith, since she serves as one of the "precursors of revolution" and "harbingers of change" that would gather force in the US in the 1950s and early 1960s (De Hart 134). As Michael Williams points out, the crossover behavior of Faulkner's women who "display masculine characteristics" is usually related to a particular profession, such as Laverne's work as a mechanic, or is the product of war, but Linda is different since "after her stint working as a riveter, [she] seems to settle comfortably into a fairly masculine lifestyle" (370). Linda therefore resists the conformist domesticity that attended Cold War society, in which gender roles were strictly controlled, through her self-presentation. This depiction situates Linda within a long lineage of Faulknerian-Hawksian masculinized heroines across literature and film from the 1930s and 1940s, including Laverne in *Pylon*, Charlotte in *If I Forget Thee, Jerusalem* (1939), Hildy in *His Girl Friday*, and Marie in *To Have and Have Not* (1944), as Faulkner once again returned to the archetype in the late 1950s.

Take 3: The Sacrificial Woman of Melodrama

Faulkner had previously used the sacrificial conventions of the woman's film in his Warner Brothers scripts for "The Damned Don't Cry" (1941) and "Mildred Pierce" (1944), which he adapted and exaggerated in *Requiem*, and he would make use of them again in *The Mansion*. Carl Rollyson comments that Linda's character "could easily fit into *Mildred Pierce* and other women's films of the 1940s" (*Alarming Paradox* 509). Rather than incorporating tropes from those sacrificial melodramas in which women give up their desires for the sake of their children, as he had done in *Requiem*, Faulkner weaves a different incarnation of this genre into *The Mansion*. A series of scenes from the novel reflect those women's films in which the female protagonist sacrifices, as Molly Haskell defines, "her lover for marriage or for his own welfare" (*Reverence* 163). In the novel, although Linda appears to love Gavin, she insists that he marry someone else for the sake of his own happiness. Towner persuasively argues that this proposition is part of Linda's "manipulation" of Gavin to bring about the downfall of her father, and we should therefore not view the presentation of "the frightened and trusting" Linda in *The Town* as consistent with the "emotional hardness" she embodies in *The Mansion* (111). Despite these discrepancies in character, Linda's language is strikingly consistent across the latter two Snopes novels in its use of sentimental features of melodrama. In fact, Linda employs precisely the same rhetorical strategy in *The Town* when Gavin suggests the two of them could marry; Linda tearfully insists in response, "I dont want to marry anybody!' . . . 'You're all I have, all I can trust. I love you! I love you!" (*N* 5: 170). As she will go on to do again in *The Mansion*, Linda affirms her love for Gavin while refusing marriage. Where in *The Town* Faulkner uses this register as indicative of Linda's cloying, teenage naivety, in *The Mansion* Linda seems to deploy the same language as part a knowing verbal manipulation of Gavin's feelings. Faulkner thereby undercuts the overblown language of the woman's film, since it is used as a cynical mask to conceal Linda's true intentions. Additionally, Faulkner's recurring use of the sacrificial trope demonstrates his continuing immersion in the conventions and registers of sacrificial melodrama across his 1950s fictions. The author appears to recognize that this was a Hollywood genre with significant communicative power in conveying emotional drama.

The scenes from *The Mansion* in which discussions of marriage occur contain many parallels to the sacrificial woman's film that Haskell names as an example of this subgenre: 1939's *Intermezzo*, which was directed by Gregory Ratoff and starred Leslie Howard and Ingrid Bergman. However, Faulkner resists the defeated marginalization of the female figure that typically concluded these films. *Intermezzo* focuses on a virtuoso violinist named Holger Brandt (played by Howard) who returns to his wife, Margit, and children after a period on tour, whereupon he meets his daughter Ann Marie's Danish piano teacher, Anita Hoffman (played by Bergman). Holger and Anita begin an affair, and Holger invites her to accompany him on tour. Once they return, Anita first attempts to sacrifice her lover for the sake of his marriage; Anita tells Margit that she needs to travel to Denmark and will stop working as Ann Marie's teacher, exiling herself for the good of the family. This intended sacrificial act proves to be a false start, since Holger decides to leave his wife and child, taking Anita on tour round Europe as his lover and musical collaborator. While in exile, it becomes clear to Anita that Holger misses his daughter, and Anita gives up on a series of opportunities to advance her musical career. It is here that Anita faces the core sacrificial quandary of the film: should she give up on her own musical career for Holger or make him give up fatherhood for her? When she makes her decision, she states that "we both know where Holger belongs. . . . I have been an intermezzo in his life," and she leaves without telling him (*Intermezzo*).

After making this decision, Anita is never seen nor mentioned again for the remaining duration of the film. Once she has fulfilled her sacrificial function, she is surplus to the narrative trajectory. Holger returns to the family home and is reunited with his wife, but the film has a markedly ambiguous "happy" ending, common in the woman's film, which cannot dispel the audience's fears that "darkness and despair" (Haskell, *Reverence* 124) may await the couple. Margit descends the stairs with tears in her eyes, telling her husband, "welcome home" (*Intermezzo*). The film pointedly never shows any reaction on Holger's face other than blankness, and Margit repeats the line like a discordant incantation. The film's final shot positions the camera behind Holger as he closes the door to the family home behind him, as he and his wife are engulfed in shadows. Within the woman's film template, the family unit is preserved, even in a state of unresolved unhappiness, while the woman who faced the greatest sacrificial dilemma is removed entirely from the film's narrative.

In the scenes from *The Mansion* that recall sacrificial women's films like *Intermezzo*, Gavin visits Linda in Pascagoula on the Mississippi Gulf Coast, where she is working in her wartime riveter job. They go to the beach together, and Linda describes the romance of their reunion in the heightened terms of melodrama: "for the earth to have come all this long way from the beginning of the earth, and the sun to have come all this long way from the beginning of time, for this one day and minute and second out of all the days and minutes and seconds . . . and now [we] are together at last and are desperate because of all the long waiting" (*N* 5: 554). The sentimentality of these exchanges is, however, strongly undermined by the nature of communication between the couple; Linda talks to Gavin in her "quacking duck's voice" (*N* 5: 546), and he responds to her by writing on a tablet with a small golden stylus, as she cannot lipread, rendering these exchanges stilted. The tablet of small, gold-cornered pages mounted on gold rings is a gift from Gavin, and an entirely impractical one at that, since there is only space on each page "to hold three words at a time" (*N* 5: 525). Diane Roberts therefore reads the dainty present as Gavin's attempt to "'feminize' and control" Linda ("Death of Nature" 168), but it is, ironically, Gavin who will use this tool most. Rollyson observes that Linda's characterization also resembles that of a woman's film like *Johnny Belinda* (1948), directed by Jean Negulesco, which similarly featured a deaf character, played by Jane Wyman (*Alarming Paradox* 509). In *Johnny Belinda* too, alternative methods of communication are used as a tool of romance; in the film, Wyman plays Belinda MacDonald, a woman from a Nova Scotian farming family. Belinda has been written off by her family and the wider village as a "Dummy," but a young doctor named Dr. Robert Richardson, who joins the community, teaches her how to lipread and use a distinct form of sign language. Their exchanges are intimate and exclusive; in the film's final melodramatic trial scene, Robert steps in to interpret Belinda's testimony, as the sign-language expert the court has hired cannot understand her. Nonverbal communication is similarly used as spur to romance in the melodramatic scenes of *The Mansion*. Gavin predicts that Linda is going to propose to him; she has arranged for them to stay in adjacent rooms in a hotel, and in an exchange in her room, she tells Gavin that she wants him to marry someone else so he can know the love she has experienced for him and for Barton: "I love you. If it hadn't been for you, I probably wouldn't have got this far. But I'm all right now. So I want you to have that too" (*N* 5: 558). Linda's language and emotional strategy in relation to marriage here are remarkably consistent with her youthful interactions with Gavin in *The Town* and, more broadly, the conventions of the woman's film, but now they are deployed by Linda to involve Gavin as an accomplice in her father's murder.

Linda's seemingly sacrificial act is the culmination of the desires of two generations of the Snopes family, as explored across the trilogy. In Faulkner's previous Snopes novel, *The Town*, Linda's mother, Eula, had repeatedly asked Gavin to marry her teenage daughter to protect her from her putative father, Flem. Gavin makes a promise to Eula that if "nothing else but marrying me can help her, and she will have me" (*N* 5: 292), he will do so, but he would prefer it to be an active decision on Linda's part. In *The Mansion*, Gavin agrees to Linda's unorthodox nonproposal, under her insistence that he needs to "just stop resisting the idea of being married" (*N* 5: 558–59). What Linda is suggesting here, born out of self-interest, is union and intimacy through separation. She first insists that "we can always be together no matter how far apart either one of us happens to be or has to be" (*N* 5: 558) and then tells Gavin to return to his own hotel room and leave the next morning, suggesting that she'll "put [her] hand on the wall and when you're in bed knock on it and if I wake up in the night I can knock and if you're awake or still there you can knock back" (*N* 5: 559). In contrast to a film like *Intermezzo*, however, although Linda at least appears to sacrifice her romance with and potential marriage to Gavin for what she argues is his own welfare, this does not lead to her marginalization from the narrative. On the contrary, Linda will become an even bigger player in the events that conclude the Snopes saga, as she engineers the murder of Flem with the aid of Gavin. In Faulkner's hands, Linda's performance of melodramatic sacrifice—which successfully secures Gavin's involvement in her criminal plotting—does not amount to self-abnegation.

Take 4: The Deathly Femme Fatale

Near the conclusion of the novel, Linda's image finally boldly traffics in the imagery of the femme fatale, particularly in those scenes that reveal her involvement in the events that lead to her father's death. Linda works to secure the release from prison of her cousin Mink, who, after thirty-eight years in Parchman, is intent on murdering Flem. Gavin questions Linda's efforts, asking her, "dont you know what he's going to do the minute he gets back to Jefferson or anywhere else your father is?" (*N* 5: 661). She responds to his question with the line "say it slow and let me try again," wishing to practice lipreading Gavin's expressions of love for her and thereby abruptly shifting the conversational terrain from criminal plotting to romance (*N* 5: 661). News that Linda is trying to arrange for Mink's release begins to spread around Yoknapatawpha, but Gavin refuses to see the murderous nature of her actions, shrinking from V. K. Ratliff's blunt statement that "likely she's jest finished killing her maw's husband" (*N* 5: 668). In such moments, Gavin appears as a noir stock figure, "the doomed man duped by a femme fatale" (Mecholsky 88) through her use of the sentimentalized romantic language of melodrama. Additionally, as Taylor Hagood has observed, despite the limitations Linda experiences in terms of hearing and speech, Faulkner shows that she is able to shape her position among men in a state of "empowering dependency," which "is not one of subservience but equality, in ways even superiority, to the men who help execute her plot" (*Writer of Disability* 138, 86). In keeping with noir tropes, male narrators imply that Linda is complicit in the destruction of the men around her; Chick observes that "Gavin had seen her once when she was thirteen years old, and look what happened to him. Then Barton Kohl saw her once when she was nineteen years old, and look where he was now" (*N* 5: 527), and Ratliff also later pithily comments, "she's jest dangerous" (*N* 5: 654).

Typical of the characterization of the femme fatale, the inscrutability of Linda's actions is emphasized, particularly when she is made the subject of an FBI investigation due to her ties to Communism and her infiltration into Yoknapatawpha's education system (*N* 5: 537). The narrative works to investigate her motives, but her inscrutability is maintained by the novel's structure; among the text's many narrators, Linda is never given the space to give a first-person account of events, and she therefore does not offer a confession. Towner comments that Linda remains an enigma, since "we know . . . what she has done and how, but we never know why" (112). Faulkner maintains this inscrutability through narrative structure: "her inner life . . . matters less than what she does; so [Faulkner] constructs her portrait from the stories other characters know about her, and the core of her personality remains essentially unknowable" (Towner 113). Her actions therefore remain the source of speculation by others.

Linda's inscrutability and fatal quality align her with the criminal female protagonists of Faulkner's mid-1940s noir scripts for "The Big Sleep" (1944), "Mildred Pierce," and "Stallion Road" (1945), which he adapted through his new presentation of Caddy in the Compson "Appendix," as demonstrated in chapter 4. The narrative trajectory of these screenplays, and the films that resulted from them, ultimately led to the "containment" (Doane, *Femmes Fatales* 116) or exposure of the femme fatale. In contrast, Linda as fatale is associated with liberation, avoids punishment, and maintains a degree of mystery around her actions, thereby overcoming many of the ideological limitations of the role. After Mink shoots and kills Flem, he tries to hurriedly leave by the door behind the corpse, but then turns around and sees Linda standing in the hall door to his rear. Mink views Linda as a dangerous engineer of death, observing that "it was the same power had brought her here to catch him that by merely pointing her finger at him could blast, annihilate, vaporise him where he stood" (*N* 5: 703). But she becomes his accomplice; Mink throws the pistol to Linda, which she deftly catches, and then instructs him, "come and take it. That door is a closet. You'll have to come back this way to get out" (*N* 5: 703). Linda assists Mink's escape as a collaborator in crime, and she redirects Mink from a space of containment to one of liberation, which facilitates her own departure from Jefferson unscathed.

Linda is therefore an anomalous femme fatale in Faulkner's work, and in the noir genre more broadly, who metes out murderous revenge and gets away with it, ultimately evading death or imprisonment.

Similar to Caddy in the "Appendix," Linda is associated with glamorous mobility, technological modernity, and transnational exchange; Linda unabashedly displays her getaway vehicle in front of Gavin, allowing him to "discover the new Jaguar and what it implied in the circumstances of her so-called father's death . . . she had ordered the car from New York or London or wherever it came from, the moment she knew for sure he could get Mink the pardon" (*N* 5: 711). Gavin, as a detective figure, does not prevent Linda's departure or try to force a confession; rather than writing "haven't I just finished being accessory before a murder" on the stylus, he inscribes "we have had everything" (*N* 5: 711). He is finally undone by the noir female, as Kristopher Mecholsky points out, "like the femme fatales of noir, Eula and Linda . . . lead Gavin to a kind of destruction by implicating him in his employer's murder" (89). She remains, to the end, inscrutable—her "dark blue eyes" (*N* 5: 711) revealing neither gentleness, tenderness, nor candor to Gavin—mobile, and free, as she exits from the novel with the decisive line: "Yes. It's time" (*N* 5: 712). She thereby controls her own narrative and dictates the circumstances of her departure, rather than outside forces intervening to neutralize the threat the femme fatale poses to the men around her.

Film Sound and Silence

As we have seen, Linda is associated with many of the tropes Faulkner had employed in his screenplays and Hollywood fictions throughout his career in the film industry: she is variously the returning war hero; the masculinized Hawksian laborer; the (deceptively) self-sacrificing lover from the woman's film; and the dangerous, avenging femme fatale. In addition to these tropes, Linda is repeatedly associated with the motif of silence throughout the novel. Due to the Nationalist bomb in the Spanish Civil War, Linda loses her hearing. Faulkner comments that this is the point at which she entered "real silence," making her "forget that everything does not take place in that privacy and solitude" (*N* 5: 510). Linda's association with silence is markedly filmic. When Chick looks back at Linda entering the DeSpain mansion, he notices how much her silent state protects her, as she appears "immured, inviolate in silence, invulnerable, serene" after having been "immobilised by a thunderclap into silence" (*N* 5: 513, 514).⁷ Linda's presentation as a "the inviolate bride of silence ... fixed, forever safe from change and alteration" (*N* 5: 514) echoes André Bazin's description of cinema as "objectivity in time" or "change mummified" (14–15). Linda's image is shrouded in silence, arrested against change within the progression of the narrative, since, Gavin speculates, "maybe to live outside human sound is to live outside human time too" (*N* 5: 544). Linda appears to exist outside sound, embodied mobility, and temporal decay. Consequently, according to the logic of Faulkner's prefatory note to the novel—in which he states that "'motion' is change and alteration" and "the only alternative to motion is un-motion, stasis, death"—Linda is ascribed an unnerving imagistic deathliness.

Through Linda's association with film through silence, Faulkner explores two aspects of his Hollywood writing: the relationship between writing and speech in the studio system and the role of sound in Hollywood cinema. First, Faulkner uses Linda's close association with silence to explore the connections between text, speech, and sound in his screenwriting. In their unusual mode of communication, Linda speaks to Gavin in a "duck voice" (*N* 5: 510), to which he responds by inscribing words on a pad with a gold stylus (*N* 5: 525). The rapid traffic between the textual and the verbal, which are layered on top of one another, and the charged collaborative exchanges between the couple echo Faulkner's intimate working practices in Hollywood.

The efforts of writers to engage in and produce dialogue evoke the competitive environment of the studio system, in which writers struggled to get their words delivered for the camera.⁸ In the transition from silent cinema to the talkies, it was screenwriters who were primarily sacrificed to the change in medium; Kenneth MacGowan points out that few of the silent screenwriters "could handle dialogue," and in the early years of the talking pictures "Hollywood hired playwright after playwright from Broadway. It didn't much matter whether their plays had been successes or flops. They knew how to write lines" (290). Faulkner was of course part of this influx of new writing talent to Hollywood in the early 1930s, and his work equally had to bow to the supremacy of dialogue. The British screenwriter and dramatist Charles Bennett, who frequently collaborated with Alfred Hitchcock and worked for several of the major Hollywood studios, recalls the valorization of dialogue over plot in 1930s American cinema: "It was a strange period, the beginning of sound. Everybody in America believed that the story didn't mean a damned thing; the only thing that mattered was sound—dialogue, dialogue, dialogue. The result was that, in the middle-thirties, in American films, a horrible thing happened; every line had to be a quip of some sort. Every damned line. Like someone would say, 'I won't forget you,' and someone else would reply, 'I've forgotten you already.' . . . That sort of dialogue had nothing to do with story development" (McGilligan, *Backstory 1* 32). Bennett's comments highlight screenwriters' frustrations when faced with the demands of the American studios for rapid-fire dialogue without clear narrative trajectory.

The emphasis on spoken dialogue in classical Hollywood could also upend literary hierarchies outside the studio system. For example, the producer Joseph L. Mankiewicz assigned Edward E. Paramore Jr. to work with F. Scott Fitzgerald on the screenplay for *Three Comrades* (1938), which was set in post–World War I Germany; Fitzgerald was annoyed at being forced to collaborate with a writer he deemed of lesser standing, and incidentally it was the only film on which Fitzgerald would gain a screenwriting credit (Hamilton 146). Mankiewicz made cuts from the Fitzgerald screenplay and polished the dialogue, recalling that "I personally have been attacked as if I had spat on the American flag because it happened once that I rewrote some dialogue by F. Scott Fitzgerald. But indeed it needed it! The actors, among them Margaret Sullavan, absolutely could not read the lines. It was very literary dialogue, novelistic dialogue that lacked all the qualities required for screen dialogue. The latter must be 'spoken'" (Hamilton 148). The emphasis is placed squarely on delivery, and Fitzgerald's literary dialogue was rejected as a result. Faulkner experienced a similar rejection of his garrulous writing by Hollywood studio actors; when working on *To Have and Have Not*, Faulkner would bring new dialogue onto the set for Humphrey Bogart, to which the actor responded on one occasion, "Bill, how am I supposed to say all that?" (Blotner, *Biography* 518).

By introducing a series of obstacles between text and voice in *The Mansion*, Faulkner draws our attention to gaps between the textual and the verbal, and to the differing motivations of writers and speakers, in collaborative modes of dialogue construction. As Gavin writes to Linda when they are reunited at Memphis airport, "this is no place to restore your voice" (*N* 5: 511), meaning that Linda's thoughts do not necessarily match her speech, delivering her lines with what she calls an "ugly sound" (*N* 5: 510). Although Linda has a distinctive, feminine mode of expression in the novel, the individual voice struggles to be heard here, and Faulkner shows how collective modes of communication obscure and mute conflicting voices. Two of the narrators of the novel, Gavin and Chick, compete to control dialogue in these scenes with Linda. Chick tries to intervene in Gavin's hybrid textual-verbal conversation with Linda, but he cannot wrest the pencil and pad from Gavin (*N* 5: 511). Gavin recognizes the crowded scene, and jokes to Chick that "maybe we should each have a pad and pencil . . . Then everybody could hear" (*N* 5: 513).[9]

The community of writers involved in soliciting Linda's voice steadily grows. When Linda meets the school board in her efforts to change the educational program, she comes prepared with the appropriate tools, "armed with no petty ivory tablet and gold stylus this time but with a vast pad of yellow foolscap and enough pencils for everybody" (*N* 5: 533). The network of writers becomes unmanageable, as they struggle with each other to shape dialogue, and therefore the direction of the narrative. In these scenes, Faulkner appears to reflect on several aspects of the screenwriting craft by presenting the relation between text and speech as one of disjuncture.[10] Faulkner shows us how, in the competition between writers, dialogue produced by an individual writer can be marginalized and subordinated. Additionally, textual dialogue may not be delivered as intended when embodied by an actor or performer; we see this in the disconnection between Gavin's carefully crafted lines and the powerfully insistent "duck voice" of Linda's verbal responses. Diane Roberts suggests that Linda's voice in such moments is "an inversion, maybe a parody, of the quiet woman whose real voice is ignored by the world of men . . . writing her story for her as Gavin tries to write words *for* Linda—words she usually rejects" ("Death of Nature" 175). The lines of Linda's interlocutors, who write on tablets and sheets of paper, are also rarely audibly delivered by a character, highlighting a disjuncture between textual form and its verbal presentation. Much of Faulkner's dialogue never reached the screen, as relatively few of his scripts were filmed, and those that were realized were subject to extensive revision. Consequently, whole projects, characters, and exchanges were consigned to text. Through Linda and the community of writers around her, Faulkner comments on the hurdles characters written for film face in the process of coming into audible language tailored to the expectations of mass audiences.

Although Faulkner presents Linda's silence as form of liberation, since she is closed off from the world around her, he also suggests that this state is synonymous with emasculation: "She was free, absolved of mundaneity; who knows, who is not likewise castrate of sound, circumcised from having to hear, of need too" (*N* 5: 520). Linda is a Hollywood-inspired character that Faulkner uses to represent the difficulties of speech and the communicative gap between the textual and verbal. I believe we should read this description allegorically as a reflection on the author's creative emasculation through exclusion from the production of discourse. Building on Laura Mulvey's work, Kaja Silverman has argued that "like the phallus, the speaking subject is a symbolic figuration which always exceeds the individuals defined by it" and that "the exclusion of classic cinema's viewer from the point of discursive origin is thus simultaneously an isolation from the phallus. Every reminder of the foreclosed site of production draws attention to that isolation, revealing the gulf separating the male spectator from the paternal signifier upon which he relies for his cultural identity" (30). In *The Mansion*, the "foreclosed site of production" is that of text as discursive origin of speech, which serves to highlight a masculine lack. Faulkner seems to suggest that the denial of sound to such Hollywood-esque characters as Linda undermines masculinity and leaves both creator and creation "castrate of sound" and "circumcised from having to hear."

To make the filmic qualities of this description of Linda's unmanned silence explicit, Faulkner goes on to use the metaphor of the Hollywood film set during the silent film era: "She had the silence: that thunderclap instant to fix her forever inviolate and private in solitude; let the rest of the world blunder in all the loud directions over its own feet trying to find first base at the edge of abyss like one of the old Chaplin films" (*N* 5: 520). Faulkner references the early silent films of Charlie Chaplin, particularly those from the 1920s and early 1930s, to contrast Linda's quality of emasculated quietude with the "loud" and chaotic production of Hollywood cinema.

This comparison may at first seem paradoxical, differentiating Linda's silence through lack of hearing from silent film. However, it would be wrong to assume that silent cinema is synonymous with a lack of sound. Indeed, as Rick Altman has described, there were many sounds produced in the process of exhibiting a movie beyond the sound that accompanies the film in talking pictures (31).[11] Altman asserts that "the silencing of all sounds not produced as a complement to the image helps us to recognize the stakes involved in the cinema industry's eventual reduction of all theater sounds to the one type that we now think of as film sound" (33); therefore, a 1920s Chaplin film was noisy in both the production and exhibition stages of its realization and transmission.

Equally, it would be incorrect to assert that silence does not play a role in sound film. As Béla Balázs states, "silence, too, is an acoustic effect, but only where sounds can be heard. The presentation of silence is one of the most specific dramatic effects of the sound film. No other art can reproduce silence, neither painting nor sculpture, neither literature nor the silent film could do so" ("Sound" 117). Balázs argues that silence is particular to the sound film, as it enables the audience to differentiate between sounds in the aural landscape to "read the score of life's symphony" and "redeem us from the chaos of shapeless noise" ("Sound" 116). In contrast, silence has a homogenizing effect, and in the silent film, characters "speak a common silent language and we could feel their irrational conversation in the music which was common to them all" (Balázs, "Sound" 118). Silence is, therefore, integral to the sound film, and so too sound encompasses the silent film.[12]

Linda, however, is cut off from the differentiated "tonal milieu" (Balázs, "Sound" 122) of the sound film—Balázs additionally argues that deaf people cannot know the relative silence of the talking pictures ("Sound" 118)—and the noise that envelops silent film. Consequently, Faulkner asserts that Linda has been liberated from the "loud directions" of filmic noise through deafness. She has achieved what Chick wishes for himself when he contemplates a world in which "there were no such thing as sound. If it only took place in silence, no evil man has invented could really harm him: explosion, treachery, the human voice" (*N* 5: 513). Linda exists in a state of serene isolation, impervious to the clamor that surrounds her, experiencing the "solitude of living not enclosed with sound but merely surrounded by gestures" (*N* 5: 531). As Stephen M. Ross points out, Linda's "gain lies in the conversion of necessary communication from sound to writing, a conversion embodied in [her] ivory writing tablet" (63), and Karl F. Zender additionally asserts that "by deafening Linda, Faulkner forces the world to abandon its allegiance to sound and to resume its dependence on reading" ("Faulkner" 105). Faulkner's statements on Linda's silence seem to reveal his attachment to the inaudibility of literature as a textual medium, which includes his Hollywood screenwriting that would never be delivered by the human voice and therefore continues to exist in a world where there was "no such thing as sound."[13] In the competition of Hollywood's collaborative networks, Faulkner had produced textual constructs intended to achieve visual and audible presence. In his late-career work *The Mansion*, through Linda, who is a medley of Hollywood archetypes enveloped by silence, Faulkner appears to lament that many fully developed characters from his scripts never made it onto the screen. A figure representative of the disjuncture between text and speech, Linda is herself marginalized in Yoknapatawpha, perhaps Faulkner's reflection on the marginal status of his own Hollywood screenwriting. However, Faulkner also suggests in this novel that his cinematic legacy is equally traceable through the inaudibility of the written word within both his unproduced screenplays and his displaced Hollywood fictions.

Notes

Introduction

1. With a similar emphasis on the circulation of inherited images and symbols, Diane Roberts focuses on Faulkner's reimagining of female stock characters and stereotypes of the US South in his fiction, such as the confederate woman, the mammy, the belle, and the tragic mulatta, to destabilize the binaries that uphold their images (*Southern Womanhood* xi). However, she does not consider the relation of Faulkner's women to the new cultural types he produced in his screenplays.
2. It is noteworthy from this aggregated data that direct mentions of "Hollywood" do not appear in Faulkner's Yoknapatawpha fictions for a long time after he first worked for the movie industry as a screenwriter in the early 1930s; these allusions do not begin to surface in his work until the mid-1940s, but they then pepper his novels of the 1950s. Such a pattern suggests that Faulkner may indeed have tried to keep explicit references to Hollywood out of the Yoknapatawpha saga for some time.
3. Faulkner refers to this technique on another occasion earlier in *The Mansion*, when V. K. Ratliff says that a man "looked at me and then done what the moving pictures call a double take" (*N* 5: 479). Faulkner clearly endows the characters of Yoknapatawpha with a degree of literacy in the conventions of commercial cinema by this point in his career.

4. Elsewhere in his letters, Faulkner would again associate this process of selling to magazines with feminization, since in tailoring a story for submission to *Cosmopolitan* he was unsure whether he was too "out of touch with the Kotex Age" (*SL* 96)—a reference to an American brand of menstrual hygiene products—to be successful within this contemporary "female" market.
5. For readings of the introduction of *Sanctuary* as ironic and performative, in light of the formal complexity of the novel, see Polk, "Afterword," and Cohen.
6. See also Benstock, Gilbert and Gubar, Felski, and Scott.
7. Joseph R. Urgo additionally proposes that the high-modernist novel *Absalom, Absalom!* (1936) is "about movie-making, and the production of images and moving pictures under strange, forced, and often brutal conditions of an environment foreign to everyone, Hollywood" ("*Absalom*" 56), paying specific attention to the ways in which the collective processes of narration in the text mimic collaborative practices in the studio system. This interpretation follows the standard definition of the Hollywood novel as providing a displaced critique of working conditions in the industry, but Urgo does not consider *Absalom*'s material, dialogic relationship to Faulkner's screenwriting: Faulkner drew on aspects of the plot from a film treatment about the Californian gold rush, titled "Sutter's Gold," that he had penned for Hawks in 1934 when he was also composing *Absalom* (see Gleeson-White, "Auditory Exposures"), and Faulkner would himself adapt the novel into an unproduced screenplay, titled "Revolt in the Earth," produced with Dudley Murphy in 1937 after the publication of *Absalom*.
8. A treatment is a prose description for a film story without the addition of dialogue.
9. Godden and Knights also speculate that *If I Forget Thee, Jerusalem* may have been influenced by Horace McCoy's *They Shoot Horses, Don't They?* (1935), a key work in the emerging Hollywood novel genre that amplifies "the cry of the little man raised against the market's invasion of every aspect of his life" (200).
10. The observation of the use of montage in the American modernist novel gained significant critical attention before Kawin's work (see Bazin; Magny; Spiegel).
11. Other recent articles have allied Faulkner's experimentations in modernist form with silent cinema and early film. For example, Mark Steven has suggested that Faulkner's "presentation of time" in *The Sound and the Fury* "is aesthetically determined by literary prose's media-ecological situation and its perceived relationship to cinema during the 1920s" (197). Pardis Dabashi has explored how Faulkner's *The Sound and the Fury* may have been influenced by the contingencies of early cinema, namely films which "captured moments of life without fitting them into larger narrative frameworks" (530). For Dabashi, the novel stages "a master-allegory for... the encounter between the modern novel and the anti-narrative contingency associated with film" (529). While such approaches are illuminating, they again sidestep

an engagement with the narrative-driven sound films of classical Hollywood that Faulkner was involved in producing, which, I argue, influenced his modernist fiction from the 1930s to the 1950s.

12. Paul Virilio has shown how the use of cinematic techniques was integral to twentieth-century conflict itself; he describes how "film sequences in aerial reconnaissance" were deployed extensively during World War I, since prerecorded images were thought to be more reliable than the observation of battle terrain in real time, since the battleground could be disturbed by weapons of warfare (1). As such, "in industrialized warfare . . . the image was starting to gain sway over the object, time over space" (Virilio 1).

13. Within this transactional emphasis, Gleeson-White has demonstrated how Faulkner redeployed the "auditory experimentalism" ("Auditory Exposures" 87) of his exploration of film sound in "Sutter's Gold" in his high-modernist novel *Absalom*, and she has also highlighted the common exploration of "questions of legitimacy and inheritance" stimulated by "the formation and direction of the American nation" ("Screenwriter" 438) in a series of frontier narratives of various kinds: Faulkner's film treatments for "Sutter's Gold" and "Drums Along the Mohawk" (1937) and his novels *Absalom* and *Go Down, Moses* (1942).

14. In addition to the work of Gleeson-White, Solomon, and Rollyson, a focus on instances of transactional exchange between Faulkner's novels and screenplays has been pursued by other critics in various articles and book chapters: Michael Zeitlin has explored the dialogue between Faulkner's aviation short stories and his early treatment for MGM, "Manservant" (1932) (*Faulkner, Aviation, and Modern War*); a series of scholars have considered the intersections of culture and gender within Faulkner's self-adaptation of his short story "Turnabout" (1932) as a screenplay for the film *Today We Live* (Hulsey; Matthews, "Culture Industry"; Ramsey, "Stars"); Jeff Karem has highlighted the common exploration of the Caribbean and African slave trade in Faulkner's Fox screenplay "The Last Slaver" (1936) and *Absalom;* Robert W. Hamblin has studied Faulkner's use of the Christ story from his screenplay "The De Gaulle Story" (1942) in his novel *A Fable* (1954); Robert H. Brinkmeyer Jr. has shown how Faulkner's work on pro-war propaganda film screenplays, "The De Gaulle Story" and "Battle Cry" (1943), prefigured the author's use of a "national voice" in the perhaps more "straightforward and politically conscious" (188) fiction that succeeded that work, such as *Intruder in the Dust* (1948) and *A Fable;* and Michelle E. Moore has illustrated how the horror script Faulkner wrote for Hawks, "Dreadful Hollow" (c. 1944), drew on the conventions of the vampire narrative that he had also reworked in *Absalom* ("Unsleeping Cabal").

15. Due to my focus on specific instances of dialogue between Faulkner's Hollywood novels and screenplays, I do not discuss all of the author's many film projects. Faulkner

worked across a wide range of commercial genres and produced material for Westerns (*Drums along the Mohawk*, 1939), swashbuckling adventure films (*Adventures of Don Juan*, 1948), and historical epics (*Land of the Pharaohs*, 1955). However, these genres do not stand in close dialogic relationship with the author's fictions in terms of their evolving presentations of women, despite containing distinctive portrayals of female characters in some cases, such as the manipulative and ambitious Princess Nellifer of Cyprus from *Land of the Pharaohs*, who plots the Pharaoh's downfall and was played by Joan Collins in the film. One exception here is Faulkner's 1937 adaptation of *Absalom* as the screenplay "Revolt in the Earth," which uses horror conventions to develop portrayals of Judith and Clytie from the novel. However, Faulkner produced this screenplay outside of the studio system in collaboration with the experimental film director Dudley Murphy for an independent production company, Associated Artists. Therefore, it does not provide an example of dialogic exchange between Faulkner's modernist fictions and commercial Hollywood cinema.

16. After the 1940s, Ford became better known for her work in theater and television; after much wrangling with agents and directors, she finally appeared in Faulkner's *Requiem for a Nun* on the London stage in 1957.
17. The final section of chapter 2 analyzes the genetic development of Faulkner's screenplay revisions for "To Have and Have Not" in terms of female characterization.
18. For qualifications of Mulvey's argument, see Doane, *Desire to Desire*; De Lauretis; and Williams, "Maternal Melodrama." In the decades since the publication of Mulvey's essay, a number of scholars have shown how the psychoanalytic model of film-viewing Mulvey delineates does not sufficiently take into account categories of race, sexuality, and class. Feminist scholars have since pursued more intersectional approaches to cinematic representation of women and to acts of film spectatorship, to take into account the differing experiences of Black women and lesbian women (see hooks and Gaines). For example, bell hooks describes the divergent relationship of Black women to filmic viewing, since they are excluded from processes that objectify the female body as the focus of desire. hooks shows how "black female spectators have had to develop looking relations within a cinematic context that constructs our presence as absence, that denies the 'body' of the black female so as to perpetuate white supremacy and with it a phallocentric spectatorship where the woman to be looked at and desired is 'white'" (118). Instead, Black female spectators have developed an "oppositional gaze" that neither identifies with white womanhood nor adopts "the phallocentric gaze of desire and possession," thereby creating "a critical space where the binary opposition Mulvey posits ... was continually deconstructed" (122–23).
19. "To Have and Have Not," 4–19 April 1944, LDBC 2–3.
20. In his analyses of another Faulkner text published in 1931, *Sanctuary*, Peter Lurie has shown, as part of his broader focus on the critical role played by acts of looking in

Faulkner's 1930s novels, how the character Temple Drake "furnishes the male characters" with "voyeuristic pleasure" (9) and that the text questions this activity by revealing "the painful longing associated with vision, commodities, and fetishism" (40) in which readers of the novel are implicated as observers.

21. See Creed; Doane, *Femmes Fatales;* and Williams, *Hard Core.*
22. For M. J. Burgess, too, Faulkner's "cinematic techniques underscore his own complicity, as an artist, in the very models that his [use of filmic devices] critiques" (100).
23. Although this screenplay was written for the director John Ford, Faulkner built on the nascent Hawksian woman type he had penned for a previous film at Fox for Hawks, the war movie *The Road to Glory.*
24. See chapter 4 for close analyses of Faulkner's noir screenplays.

1. *Sanctuary,* Flapperhood, and the Pre-Code Vice Film

1. In this first period of working for the studios, Bankhead appears to be almost synonymous with Faulkner's general image of Hollywood; when asked by his teenage stepdaughter what Hollywood was like after returning to Mississippi in October 1932, Faulkner shared a salacious anecdote about Bankhead's antics at a Hollywood party as indicative of the film community's licentiousness (Rollyson, *Past* 364).
2. Even Temple's hypothesized gender transformation reflects the conflicted physical attributes of the flapper, what Molly Haskell lists as the "incongruities" of the screen-type's "round cherubic face, wide eyes, and tiny lips, and the slinky satins clinging suggestively to slender, boyish bodies" (*Reverence* 82).
3. William M. Drew has explored how, in the transition from silent to talking films, there were still a number of silent films in production in Hollywood early in 1930 that would be completed and released as silents at the beginning of the new decade to avoid reshooting them with dialogue (1).
4. D. Matthew Ramsey explores how this line from the film was circulated in advertising and publicity and how the idea of Temple's "split personality" reflected contemporary discourses about lesbianism and bisexuality and played into public speculation about the sexuality of the lead actress, Miriam Hopkins ("Lifting the Fog" 26–27).
5. Stefan Solomon has shown that Faulkner's ambiguous relation to the New Woman was carried over into two short story projects he revised in the mid-1930s after he left MGM; he focuses specifically on the stories "Elly" (1934) and "Two Dollar Wife" (1936), which was partly inspired by Faulkner's work on "The College Widow." Similar to his screenwriting projects, Faulkner is unsure whether to celebrate or caution against female sexual libertinism here; as Solomon comments, "While 'Elly' condemns the flapper ethos, 'Two Dollar Wife' revels in it" (*Screenwriting* 38).

6. In contrast to Crawford, Bankhead struggled to have any success in Hollywood beyond the early 1930s. After her work on a series of pre-Code films, she was considered for the role of Scarlett O' Hara in *Gone with the Wind* (1939). However, Bankhead would not return to the screen with a substantial role for over a decade, until she starred in Alfred Hitchcock's 1944 adventure film *Lifeboat*. While her performance was well received, she never secured a studio contract and was therefore considered to be, in her words, "an outlaw" (Bankhead 269). She worked little for Hollywood after this point.
7. Solomon shows that Faulkner's loss of authority over his writing highlights the importance of voice in film in relation to the screenplay, since "Faulkner had to relinquish control over the way in which his writing was expressed, with writing ultimately bowing to speech on this occasion" (*Screenwriting* 40). The way in which Faulkner's dialogue would be delivered by an actress such as Crawford was unpredictably bound up with her distinctive screen persona, which she actively cultivated; Hawks would in fact describe Crawford as "a personality more than an actress" (McCarthy 186).
8. Indicative of the dialogue between the author's screenwriting and fiction at this time, Faulkner asked permission to turn the script into a novel, a project that never materialized (Blotner, *Biography* 314).

2. Collaborative Labor and the Dialogic Construction of the Hawksian Woman

1. Despite the myth, Faulkner could draw on his experience of training with the Royal Canadian Air Force in 1918. Through this he gained "a rigorous education in modern war systems, technologies, mentalities" (Zeitlin, "Royal Air Force" 24), which would influence the aviation stories, novels, and screenplays that he penned between 1919 and the 1950s. Hollywood gave him the opportunity to visualize these experiences for the screen and fashion them within prescribed genre conventions.
2. The reference to the "still" quality of the novel's narration may even hint at the film still photographs that would serve to publicize movies by means of images captured during production.
3. This daredevil activity also featured in Faulkner's treatment for "Flying the Mail" from June 1932 (*MGM* 88).
4. Keith was also a figure who made an impression on Faulkner. In Hollywood in the early 1940s, Faulkner would occasionally go fishing with Hawks, his two children, and Slim. Faulkner said of her: "The way she cleans a fish—it's beautiful" (Blotner, "Hollywood" 285).
5. The model for Jiggs potentially came from another of Faulkner's MGM screenplays, specifically the character of Otto Birdsong in his script for "Mythical

Latin-American Kingdom Story" (1933), who was also an airplane mechanic who abandoned his family (Blotner, *Biography* 339).

6. For this screenplay in the *Faulkner's MGM Screenplays* volume, edited by Kawin, the screenplay source itself does not appear but only Kawin's critical analysis of it.
7. I would like to thank one of the anonymous reviewers of an earlier version of this chapter for pointing this out.
8. As Karl F. Zender succinctly puts it, the novel's portrayal of the barnstormers starkly communicates "the degrading and life-destroying power of the need for money" (*Crossing* 47). John T. Matthews has emphasized how the reporter's "sentimental idealization" of the fliers seeks to sanitize this reality, denying the crushing effects of the economic imperative on their lives ("Autograph of Violence" 250). Taylor Hagood has proposed that the struggle on the reporter's part to narrate the actions of the barnstormers either as "objective" journalism or literature is part of Faulkner's investigation of "the ways that media create and empower narratives for capitalist culture and its consumers" ("Media" 107), communicating the dilemma literature faces as a potentially counterhegemonic force that can challenge dominant capitalistic ideologies. Michael Zeitlin additionally contends that this indictment of modernity extends to the novel's urban setting in the fictional New Valois, advancing that "the novel is unique in Faulkner's oeuvre in defining the city as a great collecting-place of modernity's oppressive, alien, and hostile forces" ("City in the Age" 230).
9. Zeitlin has analyzed how Faulkner's portrayal of the "gathering of large crowds" in *Pylon* recalls not only the mass spectacle of cinema but also fascist displays of aerial dominance in the 1930s across Europe and North America, which were pursued "in celebration of the militarization of flight" ("European Fascism" 109).
10. The gathered cars illuminating the spectacle recall a drive-in cinema, the first of which opened in Los Angeles in 1934, where Faulkner would have most likely first come into contact with the phenomenon.
11. Letter to Hawks and "Morningstar," WFFC 1, 2.
12. "Continuous Performance," WFFC 18.
13. The screenplay was produced at the time Faulkner was finishing the manuscript of *Absalom, Absalom!*, a feat that demonstrates the author's impressive work ethic and his ability to juggle projects across the vertiginous "great divide." Faulkner was clearly able to produce high-modernist prose alongside screenplay work, and the work did not undermine his literary talent.
14. Faulkner had also previously made use of the technique of double exposure in his MGM screenplay "War Birds" (Kawin, "War Birds" 264), which he wrote between November 1932 and January 1933.
15. The reference to "slumming" here echoes Charlotte Rittenmeyer's playful language at the beginning of "The Wild Palms."

16. Faulkner also worked on *The Big Sleep* (1946) during the high period of Hawks's achievement as a director in which Hawks significantly developed his portrayal of women. The character Vivian Sternwood in Faulkner and Leigh Brackett's screenplay for the film bears some of the hallmarks of the Hawksian woman, but her presentation is too bound up with the gender presentations of noir, in which women are positioned as a dangerous threat to the hero, to be typical of that figure (see chapter 4 for more on this screenplay).
17. Letter to Estelle Faulkner, LDBC 2.
18. Kawin states in his introduction that "Furthman remained on the payroll but did no writing after Faulkner was brought on the job" ("No Man Alone" 28). From consulting the revisions to the screenplay, this is evidently not the case, as the first set of revisions attributes pages of new material to both Faulkner and Furthman separately. Furthman can also be seen to edit Faulkner's work by hand in the second collection of revised scenes. From a genetic perspective, the archival holdings actually show work done by Faulkner after the dates of the second revised final, from 25 April to 1 May (LDBC; "To Have and Have Not"). While these documents are labeled "treatments" by those working with the scripts in Hollywood in 1944, a practice carried over into the archival names for the documents, one would better describe them as revised screenplays, additional scenes, or story outlines, since they mostly contain dialogue and were intended to be shot on-set immediately after they were written.
19. "To Have and Have Not," 26 February—19 April 1944, LDBC 80–81. This is the only full-length revised screenplay for "To Have and Have Not" that I cite from in the Brodsky Collection. The other holdings contain drafts and new versions of sections of the full screenplay. All cited excerpts from the revised screenplay and additional scenes for "To Have and Have Not" are attributed solely to Faulkner, whether revisions of previous scenes from Furthman's screenplay or newly inserted. This particular moment is part of a six-page scene headed "William Faulkner" and dated 8 April 1944, while the other scenes are marked "Furthman" or "Mr. Furthman's pages." Page numbers are taken directly from the typescripts.
20. Addie Bundren in Faulkner's *As I Lay Dying* (1930) also emphasizes the value of action over language, or doing over saying, when she states that words are "just a shape to fill a lack," making a contrast between words as deeds and "the other words that are not deeds, that are just the gaps in people's lacks" (*N* 2: 116, 117).
21. "To Have and Have Not," 2–15 March 1944, LDBC 59.
22. "To Have and Have Not," 26 February–19 April 1944, LDBC 81.
23. "To Have and Have Not," 2–15 March 1944, LDBC 78.
24. "To Have and Have Not," 2–15 March 1944, LDBC 83–84.

25. "To Have and Have Not," 2–15 March 1944, 10 March 1944 version, LDBC 91–92. In some cases, there is an overlap between different versions of the same scene within one screenplay file, meaning that page numbers recur. To distinguish between these versions, I have added the date that is attributed to the revised portion of the screenplay.
26. "To Have and Have Not," 2–15 March 1944, 2 March 1944 version, LDBC 74.
27. "To Have and Have Not," 4–19 April 1944, 17 April 1944 version, LDBC 101a.
28. "To Have and Have Not," 2–15 March 1944, 13 March 1944 version, LDBC 95.
29. "To Have and Have Not," 4–19 April 1944, 17 April 1944 version, LDBC 101d.
30. "To Have and Have Not." 4–19 April 1944, LDBC 6. The pages in which this scene appears are labeled "Story line for new ending" and dated 6 April 1944. This particular section is labeled "New scene."

3. *If I Forget Thee, Jerusalem,* Corporate Artists, and Hack Writers

1. Although the novel was first published under the name of one of its parts as *The Wild Palms*, Faulkner's preferred title for the novel was *If I Forget Thee, Jerusalem*, which was reinstated in the 1990 Library of America edition of the novel (see "Note on the Texts" in *N* 3: 1111–12).
2. Jones does connect the text to Hollywood via Meta Carpenter, suggesting that this "was Faulkner's first sustained and intimate encounter with a woman who was both profoundly sexual and increasingly autonomous and his first encounter with an entire world structured around mass culture" (145), which stirred up questions about gender and art for the author. However, she does not consider how specific working practices in Hollywood affected Faulkner's understanding of the creativity of men and women across cultural categories.
3. Charlotte's vision of the deer's motion and speed is also realized in the prose of one of the "Old Man" sections of *Jerusalem*, when the convict sees the "swimming deer" beside the skiff, whose rapturous movement through flight, suspension, and finally, evaporation is described as follows: "watching the deer begin to rise out of the water bodily until it was actually running along upon the surface, rising still, soaring clear of the water altogether, vanishing upward in a dying crescendo of splashings and snapping branches, its damp scut flashing upward, the entire animal vanishing upward as smoke vanishes" (*N* 3: 614).
4. Phil Smith also argues that Faulkner uses Harry to brood on the position of the "hack" writer in the early media age, a figure who is most closely associated in Faulkner's imagination with his Hollywood work. Smith charts the process through which Harry's early confession stories are "redeemed" from their status as derivative

mass cultural trash. This is achieved, for Smith, through the character's increasingly writerly consciousness, ultimately producing a "triumphant" confession narrative in the novel's final scene, where Harry is imprisoned after Charlotte's death; in other words he transforms from a "derived and self-deriding hack" to become a "serious and poetic writer" (P. Smith 172). However, such a reading seems to overlook that Harry's literary imagination never in fact leaves a material trace, and neither are Charlotte's popular cultural products presented as artefacts that have to be "redeemed" from their commercialism.

5. The work Faulkner refers to here is left unidentified. The letter references television, though, and Commins would submit the teleplay of "Old Man" to an agent just four months after this letter was written in April 1953. Faulkner's other television work from the period—*Shall Not Perish* and *The Brooch*—were both written for CBS in March 1953, while Faulkner's version of "Old Man" was never televised.
6. "Story Line on OLD MAN," WFFC 2.
7. "OLD MAN," WFFC 4. The erotically charged visiting days are only mentioned briefly in the novel, when the tall convict discusses the last sexual encounter he had had before the flood, with "a nameless and not young negress, a casual, a straggler whom he had caught more or less by chance on one of the fifth-Sunday visiting days" (*N* 3: 723).
8. "OLD MAN," WFFC 5. Faulkner chooses to transplant the misogynistic line of dialogue that concludes "Old Man" in the novel to this point in the teleplay, suggesting that it is no longer the emphatic, conclusive message of the tale. A fellow inmate questions the convict why he doesn't have a woman on the special and how long it has been since his last encounter; he replies "Women, shit" ("OLD MAN," WFFC 4).
9. "OLD MAN," WFFC 5.
10. "OLD MAN," WFFC 5.
11. "OLD MAN," WFFC 5.
12. "OLD MAN," WFFC 10–11.
13. "OLD MAN," WFFC 14–15.
14. "OLD MAN," WFFC 17–18.
15. "OLD MAN," WFFC 26.
16. Faulkner makes an explicit reference to film in this location, comparing the camp to "a scene like something out of an Eisensteinian Dante" (*N* 3: 621). James D. Bloom comments that Eisenstein's innovative use of cinematic montage reflects Charlotte's own "artistic commitment . . . to evoking fluidity, motion, speed" (87). It is equally significant that Eisenstein came to Hollywood in 1930 after Paramount Pictures offered him the opportunity to make a film there, but none of the Russian director's projects got off the ground, as he was unable to adapt his style to the modes of production in the American studios. This allusion therefore sustains the novel's critique of male labor in the culture industry, as Eisenstein, the experimentalist, fails

to adapt to Hollywood formulas. Stefan Solomon also points out that Faulkner's original reference in the manuscript was to "DeMille," and that the author may have been trying to evoke "the crowd dynamics of a film by Cecil B. De Mille" ("Screen Culture" 204) in his description of the immigrant miners in this passage.
17. Michael Grimwood asserts that Faulkner used a brief period of financial independence in 1937 and 1938 to write the novel in order "to utter a lament for the periods of Babylonian captivity [in Hollywood] he had temporarily left behind" (116).

4. Inscrutable Images and Cultural Migrations

1. The transnational movements that "Snow" traces are somewhat different from those in the "Appendix." The central female character in "Snow" only travels *within* Europe, from Switzerland to Italy and then on to Serbia. However, one of the American tourists, Don, is from California and comments on Hollywood's artificiality in comparison with Europe: "I love snow . . . At home we never have it except in Hollywood" (*US* 666).
2. "Life and Death of a Bomber," LDBC 1.
3. The hazy look of noir films derived in part, as Sheri Chinen Biesen argues, from "wartime constraints on filmmaking practices" necessitating stylistic choices such as "low-lit images, recycled sets (disguised by shadows, smoke, artificial fog, and rain)" (3). Biesen demonstrates how the aesthetic and content of the noir film in early 1940s Hollywood was influenced by material factors of the war such as "city-wide blackouts, enclosed or tarped sound stages, limits on location shooting, censorship of film content, and a severe labor shortage" (6). In his letters, Faulkner evoked the gloomy mood and aesthetic in wartime Hollywood: "The street lamps are hooded from above here, wardens patrol the streets for cracks in window shades . . . There are barrage balloons along the coast, and searchlights . . . in all sorts of unexpected places through the city" (*SL* 165). His description of this environment has particularly noirish overtones when he mentions that the city is populated by "blackmailing private detectives who live on the people who draw motion picture salaries" (*SL* 165). Wartime Los Angeles no doubt had an influence on Faulkner's own noir aesthetic.
4. In Hawks's shooting script, after bringing in Jules Furthman to help with revisions, the presentation of Vivian became much less morally ambiguous, since, Bruce F. Kawin argues, Hawks "had no intention of putting Bogart through the kind of professional crisis and moral self-examination basic to a picture like *The Maltese Falcon* and to Chandler's novel" (*Faulkner and Film* 120). Hawks was also keen to foreground the romance between Bogart and Bacall that had made *To Have and Have Not* a commercial success and inserted additional scenes that were more playfully erotic than aggressive.

5. Faulkner seemingly drew on the wisecracking dialogue of Bacall's roles in *To Have and Have Not* and *The Big Sleep* here, as Daisy similarly demonstrates how wit can be used to mask vulnerability and disarm men whom she genuinely cares for.
6. Faulkner was not working within the discrete genre of the 1940s Gothic woman's film here, in which the male figure is presented as deceptive or inscrutable to the heroine, the opposite relation to that which exists in noir between the male hero and the femme fatale. Murray Smith compares the investigative structures of both genres and concludes that "in the female gothic, female perception is as much scrutinized as enigmatic male behavior, since frequently the woman's perception is proved erroneous" (64). While the Gothic woman's film, like noir, was concerned with the ambiguities of perception, Faulkner made use of Gothic elements in the service of the genre of melodrama. In his screenplay "Mildred Pierce," in place of an enigmatic male, it is an ambiguous Gothic woman who poses a threat to the heroine.
7. *Mildred Pierce* has also been categorized as a noir film due to its framing scenes set in the narrative present, which depict a murder and Mildred's subsequent interrogation in the detective's office. The flashback scenes that show the development of Mildred's family life are, however, written in the vein of the melodramatic woman's film of the 1930s and 1940s, or "weepie," and it was to these scenes that Faulkner primarily added the Gothic elements of Veda's characterization.
8. She is renamed "Kay" in the film.
9. "Mildred Pierce (House on the Sand)," LDBC 113–14.
10. "Mildred Pierce," LDBC 114.
11. "Mildred Pierce," LDBC 114.
12. "Mildred Pierce," LDBC 114.
13. "Mildred Pierce," LDBC 114.
14. "Mildred Pierce," LDBC 114.
15. "Mildred Pierce," LDBC 122.
16. "Mildred Pierce," LDBC 168.
17. "Dreadful Hollow," LDBC 8.
18. "Dreadful Hollow," LDBC 45.
19. "Dreadful Hollow," LDBC 37–38.
20. "Dreadful Hollow," LDBC 17. There is an erotic charge to these scenes, and as Michelle E. Moore argues in her analysis of Faulkner's adaptation of the source text, the author made "significant changes" and "chose to emphasize the vampire's lesbianism to a greater extent than any earlier female vampire text" ("Vampires"). Moore places Faulkner's "Dreadful Hollow" in dialogue with the homoeroticism and tropes of vampirism present in Faulkner's *Absalom, Absalom!* (1936), a text that also draws on Gothic conventions ("Vampires").
21. "To Have and Have Not." 2–15 March 1944, LDBC 83.

22. Only three works contained in *The Portable Faulkner*—"Was," "The Bear," and "Delta Autumn"—appeared in print during the war years, as parts of Faulkner's novel *Go Down, Moses* (1942).
23. Solomon also links the photograph in the "Appendix" to film noir. He makes a comparison between the blackmail photo of a nude Carmen Sternwood in Faulkner and Brackett's screenplay for "The Big Sleep" and the scandalous image of Caddy with a Nazi companion, part of a circulation of the private within the public sphere that was a pattern in noir (*Screenwriting* 183).
24. Pardis Dabashi suggests that in at least part of *The Sound and the Fury*, Caddy can in fact be seen to shape narrative, since she provides her brother Benjy "with rudimentary social frameworks that would allow him to make sense of his observations and experiences" (536). In this instance, Faulkner may momentarily challenge "the dominant techniques of female objectification typical to the cinema" (Dabashi 536), by highlighting how Caddy produces narrative rather than being herself investigated by it.

5. *Requiem for a Nun* and Cold War Hollywood Melodrama

1. After much wrangling with agents and directors, *Requiem for a Nun* received its London premiere in 1957, where it ran into 1958 with "rave notices" (Blotner, *Biography* 651). It finally premiered on Broadway at the end of January 1959 but closed at the end of February after forty-three performances (Blotner, *Biography* 661). Although Ford would star in both these productions, she missed out on other, more lucrative radio and television work because of the delays (*SL* 325).
2. Although Elizabeth R. Anker differentiates between the "public, national, and state-centered register" (3) of melodramatic political discourse, on the one hand, and the domestic concerns of much filmic and literary melodrama, on the other, this overlooks how these works' focus on domesticity was closely related to public discourses of Cold War containment.
3. Faulkner revisited the property in May–June 1944 while under contract at Warner Brothers, although this later version does not draw on his original treatment. The film did not reach the screen until 1950, by which point it retained little of the content found in Faulkner's 1941 story treatment.
4. Peter Brooks traces melodrama's origins to the convulsions of the French Revolution and its aftermath.
5. Faulkner considered a title for a new work, *Requiem for a Nun*, in October 1933, a couple of years after he published *Sanctuary* and "That Evening Sun." He produced about a page and a half of an early draft of the novel in mid-December, before putting it to one side (Blotner, *Biography* 323, 326). When he returned to the work in 1950, he conceived of it as a play.

6. Faulkner describes Pete as looking "exactly like a youthful city detective in a tough moving picture" (*N* 4: 590), recalling the kind of roles he had penned for Humphrey Bogart in noir films at Warner Brothers.
7. The line recalls Charlotte Rittenmeyer's resolve to pursue her affair at the cost of leaving her children behind. After being challenged by Harry Wilbourne, she insists, "I dont need to think of [the children] anymore . . . I settled that a long time ago" (*N* 3: 526).
8. Deborah Barker points out that the 1961 adaptation of parts of *Requiem for a Nun* in the film *Sanctuary* appropriates the text for the civil rights movement by casting Odetta Holmes, an African American protest singer, as Nancy. She argues that "as a political rather than religious act, Nancy's murder of the child can signal the ultimate symbolic rejection of the role of mammy" (Barker, "Modern Mammy" 94).
9. Anker also observes the "delinking [of] virtue and injury" (253) in Douglas Sirk's *All That Heaven Allows* (1955), which, she argues, shows how characters may also be complicit in the social injustices that victimize them.
10. Thomas Elsaesser comments that in a form of "low-brow" melodrama, the German *Bänkellied* (ballad), music is layered over the song's narrative to subvert its content (69), which reflects the ironic relationship between style and language in Sirk's films.
11. *Requiem for a Nun* also uses lighting experimentally to convey psychological disturbances. Temple is forced to hear Gavin relay to the governor how Pete blackmailed her, after which "the lights flicker, grow slightly dimmer, then flare back up and steady again, as though in a signal, a warning" (*N* 4: 581). The lighting thereby highlights Temple's shock, momentary loss of composure, then returning resolve.
12. Fannie Hurst's 1933 novel *Imitation of Life* was also adapted as a woman's film directed by John M. Stahl in 1934. Typical of the differences between melodramas of the 1930s and those of the 1950s, Stahl's version does not treat gender and race autocritically.
13. Considering this close relationship, a number of scholars have identified thematic and formal affinities between "The Left Hand of God" and *Requiem*: Carl Rollyson has approached them as parallel stories of "redemption" (*Alarming Paradox* 366); Sarah Gleeson-White has compared the figures of Dr. Sigman and Gavin Stevens as educated, reason-led, and principled characters ("Left Hand of God" 754); and Stefan Solomon has considered their shared thematic focus on "fugitive characters, corporal punishment, and divine justice" (*Screenwriting* 198), as well as the "nature and meaning of suffering" (*Screenwriting* 209). Solomon also makes a formal link between the two, speculating that Faulkner's insertion of a second-person voice-over into the screenplay may have influenced his change in decision to write "The Jail" prologue to act 3 in the second person rather than the third person (*Screenwriting* 214).

14. Ethel Young-Minor also observes an equivalent technique in "That Evening Sun," one of the "prequels" to *Requiem*, which, she argues, emphasizes "the Compson family's blindness when it comes to the diversity of black culture" (173).

6. "Castrate of Sound"

1. The last script Faulkner worked on from 1953 to 1954, in collaboration with Harry Kurnitz and Harold Jack Bloom, was *Land of the Pharaohs*, a historical epic set in Ancient Egypt, which was directed by Howard Hawks and released in 1955.
2. Carl Rollyson has suggested that the nonsexual bond between Linda and Gavin echoes the friendship between Faulkner and the Hollywood actress Ruth Ford (*Alarming Paradox* 501).
3. In contrast to Gavin, V. K. Ratliff is able to understand the artistic intention behind the sculpture and "knew at once what it was" (*N* 5: 511). Ratliff embodies an unschooled, rural intellectualism that contrasts with the limits or failures of Gavin's educated cosmopolitanism.
4. Chick seems to overlook Drusilla Hawk here, a character from *The Unvanquished* (1938), who joins the Confederate army under John Sartoris and masculinizes herself after the death of her father and fiancé in the Civil War by wearing pants and cutting her hair short (*N* 3: 379–80). Unlike Linda, however, after the war Drusilla bows to pressure from women in Yoknapatawpha to "refeminize" herself when she agrees to return to feminine dress and marry her fellow soldier, John.
5. The novel was first published under the title *Sartoris* in 1929, but Faulkner's original title was *Flags in the Dust*. Revised editions of the novel published since 1973 have restored Faulkner's preferred title.
6. "Life and Death of a Bomber," LDBC 1.
7. The emotional qualities that are attributed to Linda's deafness are quite different to those Richard perceives in Belinda's distance from the world in the trial scene of *Johnny Belinda*, when he begs for the jury's understanding for a woman "living in a world apart, shut off from everyone never hearing the warmth of a human voice. Think of the loneliness and the fear." Instead, Linda's loss of hearing confers advantages upon her, allowing her to transcend her environment.
8. Joseph R. Urgo observes a similar parallel to the struggles of Hollywood screenwriters in chapter 8 of *Absalom, Absalom!* (1936), which, he argues, "culminates in [the] demonstrated ability by Quentin and Shreve to project and produce a Sutpen screenplay—to transfer their collaboration into a single, coherent set of images and dialogue" ("*Absalom*" 71).
9. Interestingly, this appears to be a mode of communication that Linda only needs to pursue with male characters. When Linda talks with Chick's mother, Maggie, about the Spanish Civil War, the two characters seem to ignore what Maggie scribbles on

the pad, and Chick observes that "she and Mother didn't need it" (*N* 5: 526). It appears that communities of female writers and speakers are better able to transcend the gap between text and speech through intuition, a potential nod to the women's angle that worked to target filmic writing at female audiences.

10. Sarah Gleeson-White has also observed the disruptive role of filmic sound in Faulkner's writing. She considers how Faulkner may have been influenced by Eisenstein's presentation of "a radical disjuncture of sound and image" ("Auditory Exposures" 90) when he built on the director's 1930 scenario "Sutter's Gold" to produce his own 1936 treatment. These techniques appear to have influenced Faulkner's work on *Absalom*, a novel in which it is frequently difficult to "align speakers with speech," thereby disrupting "the verisimilitudinous transmission and reception of sound" (Gleeson-White, "Auditory Exposures" 93–4). Rather than focusing on "the non-synchronous relation of sound and image, voice and its source" (Gleeson-White, "Auditory Exposures" 97), I am concerned with disruptions in the relationship between voice and text, in which text is considered as the material origin of filmic dialogue.

11. These included the sounds of the apparatus itself, the audience inside the movie theater, and the historical use of advertising sound for promotions taking place outside of the theater (Altman 32).

12. Jay Watson has argued that Faulkner was influenced by silence as a feature of the sound film, as the advent of the talkies "helped cultivate a new awareness of silence as an active, dynamic element of the cinematic landscape," which Faulkner absorbed into his early modernist works by using silence as "the acoustic scaffolding for scenes of dramatic intensity and immediacy" (*William Faulkner* 160, 165).

13. In making a claim for the "silence" of Faulkner's oeuvre here, I am not reading against studies of literary acoustics that have explored how literature is "a privileged site for the representation of the noises of our acoustic world" (Schweighauser 3) or innovative recent approaches to the "resonances" of Faulkner that draw on sound studies (Napolin). Instead, I am interested in Faulkner's apparent investment in literature as an inaudible medium.

Works Cited

Adorno, Theodor W. "Culture Industry Reconsidered." *The Culture Industry: Selected Essays on Mass Culture,* by Theodor W. Adorno, edited by J. M. Bernstein, Routledge, 1991, pp. 98–106.
All That Heaven Allows. Directed by Douglas Sirk, performances by Jane Wyman and Rock Hudson, Universal Pictures, 1955.
Altman, Rick. "Film Sound—All Of It." *Iris,* vol. 27, 1999, pp. 31–48.
Anker, Elizabeth R. *Orgies of Feeling: Melodrama and the Politics of Freedom.* Duke UP, 2014.
Bachelor Mother. Directed by Garson Kanin, performances by Ginger Rogers and David Niven, RKO Radio Pictures, 1939.
Baker, M. Joyce. *Images of Women in Film: The War Years, 1941–45.* UMI Research Press, 1980.
Balázs, Béla. "Theory of the Film: Sound." *Film Sound: Theory and Practice,* edited by Elisabeth Weis and John Belton, Columbia UP, 1985, pp. 116–25.
———. "Visible Man, or the Culture of Film (1924)." *Screen,* vol. 48, no. 1, 2007, pp. 91–108.
Baldwin, Doug. "Putting Images into Words: Elements of the 'Cinematic' in William Faulkner's Prose." *Faulkner Journal,* vol. 16, nos. 1–2, fall 2000–spring 2001, pp. 35–64.
Bankhead, Tallulah. *My Autobiography.* U of Mississippi P, 2004.
Barker, Deborah. "Demystifying the Modern Mammy in *Requiem for a Nun.*" *Faulkner and Film, Faulkner and Yoknapatawpha, 2010,* edited by Peter Lurie and Ann J. Abadie, UP of Mississippi, 2014, pp. 71–97.

———. "Moonshine and Magnolias: *The Story of Temple Drake* and *The Birth of a Nation*." *Faulkner Journal*, vol. 22, nos. 1–2, fall 2006–spring 2007, pp. 140–75.

Barthes, Roland. "The Face of Garbo." *Film Theory and Criticism*, edited by Leo Braudy and Marshall Cohen, 7th edition, Oxford UP, 2009, pp. 471–73.

Bazin, André. *What Is Cinema?* U of California P, 1967.

Benjamin, Walter. *The Arcades Project*. Belknap Press of Harvard UP, 1999.

———. *The Work of Art in the Age of Its Technological Reproducibility, and Other Writing on Media*. Harvard UP, 2008.

Benstock, Shari. *Women of the Left Bank: Paris, 1900–1940*. U of Texas P, 1986.

Berlant, Lauren. "National Brands / National Body: *Imitation of Life*." *Comparative American Identities: Race, Sex, and Nationality in the Modern Text*, edited by Hortense J. Spillers, Routledge, 1991, pp. 110–40.

Berliner Commins, Dorothy. *What Is an Editor? Saxe Commins at Work*. U of Chicago P, 1978.

The Bible: Authorized King James Version. Oxford UP, 2008.

Biesen, Sheri Chinen. *Blackout: World War II and the Origins of Film Noir*. Johns Hopkins UP, 1995.

The Big Sleep. Directed by Howard Hawks, performances by Humphrey Bogart and Lauren Bacall, Warner Brothers, 1946.

Binggeli, Elizabeth. "Worse than Bad: *Sanctuary*, the Hays Office, and the Genre of Abjection." *Arizona Quarterly*, vol. 65, no. 3, 2009, pp. 87–116.

Bleikasten, André. *The Most Splendid Failure: Faulkner's The Sound and the Fury*. Indiana UP, 1976.

Bloom, James D. "The Hollywood Challenge." *William Faulkner in Context*, edited by John T. Matthews, Cambridge UP, 2015, pp. 79–88.

Blotner, Joseph. "Faulkner in Hollywood." *Man and the Movies*, edited by W. R. Robinson, Penguin, 1969, pp. 261–303.

———. *Faulkner: A Biography. One-Volume Edition*. Vintage Books, 1991.

Bogdanovich, Peter. "Interview with Howard Hawks." *Howard Hawks: American Artist*, edited by Jim Hellier and Peter Wollen, BFI Publishing, 1996, pp. 50–67.

Boon, Kevin Alexander. *Script Culture and the American Screenplay*. Wayne State UP, 2008.

Bordwell, David, Janet Staiger, and Kristin Thompson. *The Classical Hollywood Cinema: Film Style and Mode of Production to 1960*. Routledge, 1988.

Bourdieu, Pierre. *The Field of Cultural Production: Essays on Art and Literature*. Polity Press, 1993.

Brackett, Leigh. "A Comment on 'The Hawksian Woman.'" *Howard Hawks: American Artist*, edited by Jim Hillier and Peter Wollen, BFI Publishing, 1996, pp. 120–28.

Brinkmeyer, Robert H., Jr. *The Fourth Ghost: White Southern Writers and European Fascism, 1930–1950*. Louisiana State UP, 2009.

Brodsky, Louis Daniel. "Glimpses of William Faulkner: An Interview with Stephen Longstreet." *Stallion Road: A Screenplay,* by William Faulkner, edited by Louis Daniel Brodsky and Robert W. Hamblin. UP of Mississippi, 1989, pp. xvii–xxvii.

Brook, Vincent. *Driven to Darkness: Jewish Emigre Directors and the Rise of Film Noir.* Rutgers UP, 2009.

Brooks, Peter. *The Melodramatic Imagination: Balzac, Henry James, Melodrama, and the Mode of Excess.* Yale UP, 1976.

Burgess, M. J. "Watching (Jefferson) Watching: *Light in August* and the Aestheticization of Gender." *Faulkner Journal,* vol. 7, nos. 1–2, fall 1991–spring 1992, pp. 95–114.

Butler, Judith. "Lana's 'Imitation': Melodramatic Repetition and the Gender Performative." *Genders,* vol. 9, 1990, pp. 1–18.

Cantrell, Frank. "An Unpublished Faulkner Short Story: 'Snow.'" *Mississippi Quarterly,* vol. 26, no. 3, 1973, pp. 325–30.

Carpenter Wilde, Meta, and Orin Borsten. *A Loving Gentleman: The Love Story of William Faulkner and Meta Carpenter.* Simon and Schuster, 1976.

The Cheat. Directed by George Abbott, performances by Tallulah Bankhead and Harvey Stephens, Paramount Pictures, 1931.

Christensen, Jerome. *America's Corporate Art: The Studio Authorship of Hollywood Motion Pictures.* Stanford UP, 2012.

Clarke, Deborah. *Robbing the Mother: Women in Faulkner.* UP of Mississippi, 1994.

Cohen, Philip. "'A Cheap Idea . . . Deliberately Conceived to Make Money': The Biographical Context of William Faulkner's Introduction to *Sanctuary.*" *Faulkner Journal,* vol. 3, no. 2, 1998, pp. 54–66.

Coindreau, Maurice Edgar. "William Faulkner in France." *Yale French Studies,* vol. 10, 1952, pp. 85–91.

Cook, Pam. "Melodrama and the Women's Picture." *Imitations of Life: A Reader on Film and Television Melodrama,* edited by Marcia Landy, Wayne State UP, 1991, pp. 248–62.

Cowie, Elizabeth. "Film Noir and Women." *Shades of Noir: A Reader,* edited by Joan Copjec, Verso, 1993, pp. 121–65.

———. *Representing the Woman: Cinema and Psychoanalysis.* Macmillan, 1997.

Cowley, Malcolm. *The Faulkner-Cowley File.* Viking Press, 1966.

Creed, Barbara. "Horror and the Monstrous-Feminine: An Imaginary Abjection." *The Dread of Difference: Gender and the Horror Film,* edited by Barry Keith Grant, U of Texas P, 1996, pp. 35–65.

Crowther, Bosley. "'The Big Sleep,' Warner Film in which Bogart and Bacall Are Paired Again, Opens at Strand." *New York Times,* 24 August 1946, p. 6.

Dabashi, Pardis. "The Compsons Were Here: Indexicality, the Actuality, and the Crisis of Meaning in *The Sound and the Fury.*" *Modernism/Modernity,* vol. 24, no. 3, 2017, pp. 527–48.

The Damned Don't Cry. Directed by Vincent Sherman, Warner Brothers, 1950.

Dardis, Tom. *Some Time in the Sun*. Scribner, 1976.

Davis, Thadious M. "Reading Faulkner's Compson Appendix: Writing History from the Margins." *Faulkner and Ideology, Faulkner and Yoknapatawpha, 1992*, edited by Donald Kartiganer and Ann J. Abadie, UP of Mississippi, 1995, pp. 238–52.

De Hart, Jane Sherron. "Containment at Home: Gender, Sexuality, and National Identity in Cold War America." *Rethinking Cold War Culture*, edited by Peter J. Kuznick and James Gilbert, Smithsonian Institution P, 2001, pp. 124–55.

De Lauretis, Teresa. *Alice Doesn't: Feminism, Semiotics, Cinema*. Macmillan, 1989.

DiBattista, Maria. "Introduction." *High and Low Moderns: Literature and Culture 1889–1959*, edited by Maria DiBattista and Lucy McDiarmid, Oxford UP, 1996, pp. 3–22.

Digital Yoknapatawpha. Created and directed by Stephen Railton. faulkner.iath.virginia.edu.

Doane, Mary Ann. *The Desire to Desire: The Woman's Film of the 1940s*. Indiana UP, 1987.

———. *Femmes Fatales: Feminism, Film Theory, Psychoanalysis*. Routledge, 1991.

Dobbs, Cynthia. "Flooded: The Excesses of Geography, Gender, and Capitalism in Faulkner's *If I Forget Thee, Jerusalem*." *American Literature*, vol. 73, no. 4, 2001, pp. 811–35.

Doherty, Thomas. *Cold War, Cool Medium: Television, McCarthyism, and American Culture*. Columbia UP, 2003.

———. *Pre-Code Hollywood: Sex, Immorality, and Insurrection in American Cinema, 1930–1934*. Columbia UP, 1999.

Dore, Florence W. "Free Speech and Exposure: Obscenity, the Phallus, and William Faulkner's *Sanctuary*." *Narrative*, vol. 9, no. 1, 2001, pp. 78–99.

Duvall, John N. *Faulkner's Marginal Couple: Invisible, Outlaw, and Unspeakable Communities*. U of Texas P, 1990.

Drew, William M. *The Last Silent Picture Show: Silent Films on American Screens in the 1930s*. Scarecrow Press, 2010.

Dyer, Richard. "Lana: Four Films of Lana Turner." *Imitations of Life: A Reader on Film and Television Melodrama*, edited by Marcia Landy, Wayne State UP, 1991, pp. 409–28.

Edington, K. "The Hollywood Novel: American Dream, Apocalyptic Vision." *Literature/Film Quarterly*, vol. 23, no. 1, 1995, pp. 63–67.

Eisenstein, Sergei. *The Film Sense*. Faber and Faber, 1970.

Eliot, T. S. *The Complete Poems and Plays of T. S. Eliot*. Faber and Faber, 2011. E-book.

———. *Notes towards the Definition of Culture*. Faber and Faber, 1948.

Elsaesser, Thomas. "Tales of Sound and Fury: Observations on the Family Melodrama." *Imitations of Life: A Reader on Film and Television Melodrama*, edited by Marcia Landy. Wayne State UP, 1991, pp. 68–91.

Esperdy, Gabrielle. "From Instruction to Consumption: Architecture and Design in Hollywood Movies of the 1930s." *Journal of American Culture*, vol. 30, no. 2, 2007, pp. 198–211.

WORKS CITED

Faulkner, William. "At Washington & Lee University." *Faulkner at Virginia: An Audio Archive,* 15 May 1958, edited by Stephen Railton, faulkner.lib.virginia.edu/display/wfaudio31#wfaudio31.17.

———. *Collected Stories of William Faulkner.* Random House, 1995.

———. "Continuous Performance." February 1946. William Faulkner Foundation Collection 1918–1958, accession number 6074–6074-d, series IV: Writing for Television and Movies, Albert and Shirley Small Special Collections Library, U of Virginia, box 10, item 2, 37 pages.

———. *Country Lawyer and Other Stories for the Screen.* Edited Louis Daniel Brodsky and Robert W. Hamblin, UP of Mississippi, 1987.

———. "Dreadful Hollow." December 1944? Louis Daniel Brodsky Collection, Kent Library, Southeast Missouri State U, series IX, subseries 1, box 1657, folder 1, 159 pages.

———. *Essays, Speeches and Public Letters.* Edited by James B. Meriwether, Random House, 1965.

———. *Faulkner: A Comprehensive Guide to the Brodsky Collection, Battle Cry.* Edited by Louis Daniel Brodsky and Robert W. Hamblin, vol. 4, UP of Mississippi, 1985. 5 vols.

———. *Faulkner: A Comprehensive Guide to the Brodsky Collection, The De Gaulle Story.* Edited by Louis Daniel Brodsky and Robert W. Hamblin, vol. 3, UP of Mississippi, 1984. 5 vols.

———. *Faulkner: A Comprehensive Guide to the Brodsky Collection, The Letters.* Edited by Louis Daniel Brodsky and Robert W. Hamblin, vol. 2, UP of Mississippi, 1984. 5 vols.

———. *Faulkner's MGM Screenplays.* Edited by Bruce F. Kawin, U of Tennessee P, 1982.

———. Letter to Estelle Faulkner. March 1944. Louis Daniel Brodsky Collection, Kent Library, Southeast Missouri State U, series I, subseries 10, box 1694, folder 19, 2 pages.

———. Letter to Howard Hawks and "Morningstar." 29 June 1948. William Faulkner Foundation Collection 1918–1958, accession number 6074–6074-d, series IV: Writing for Television and Movies, Albert and Shirley Small Special Collections Library, U of Virginia, MSS 6074, box 11, folder 7, 3 pages.

———. Letter to Joan Williams. 3 March 1950. Massey-Faulkner Collection, Albert and Shirley Small Special Collections Library, U of Virginia, MSS 9394, box 1, 1 page with envelope.

———. Letter to Joan Williams. 6 November 1952. Massey-Faulkner Collection, Albert and Shirley Small Special Collections Library, U of Virginia, MSS 9394, box 2, 3 pages with envelope.

———. "The Life and Death of a Bomber: Preliminary Notes." Report on visit to Consolidated Aircraft Factory re "LIBERATOR." 14 November 1942. Louis Daniel Brodsky Collection, Kent Library, Southeast Missouri State U, series IX, subseries 1, box 1653, folder 10, 3 pages.

———. *Lion in the Garden: Interviews with William Faulkner, 1926–1962.* Edited by James B. Meriwether and Michael Millgate, U of Nebraska P, 1980.

———. "Mildred Pierce (House on the Sand)." 18 November–2 December 1944. Louis Daniel Brodsky Collection, Kent Library, Southeast Missouri State U, series IX, subseries 1, box 1654, folder 8, 101 pages.

———. *Novels 1926–1929*. Edited by Joseph Blotner and Noel Polk, vol. 1, Library of America, 2006. 5 vols.

———. *Novels 1930–1935*. Edited by Joseph Blotner and Noel Polk, vol. 2, Library of America, 1985. 5 vols.

———. *Novels 1936–1940*. Edited by Joseph Blotner and Noel Polk, vol. 3, Library of America, 1990. 5 vols.

———. *Novels 1942–1954*. Edited by Joseph Blotner and Noel Polk, vol. 4, Library of America, 1994. 5 vols.

———. *Novels 1957–1962*. Edited by Joseph Blotner and Noel Polk, vol. 5, Library of America, 1999. 5 vols.

———. *Selected Letters of William Faulkner*. Scolar Press, 1977.

———. *Stallion Road: A Screenplay*. Edited by Louis Daniel Brodsky and Robert W. Hamblin. UP of Mississippi, 1989.

———. "Story Line on OLD MAN." April 1953. William Faulkner Foundation Collection 1918–1958, accession number 6074–6074-d, series IV: Writing for Television and Movies, Albert and Shirley Small Special Collections Library, U of Virginia, box 10, item 3b, 26 pages.

———. "To Have and Have Not." 4–19 April 1944. Louis Daniel Brodsky Collection, Kent Library, Southeast Missouri State U, series IX, subseries 1, box 1653, folder 18.

———. "To Have and Have Not." 25 April—1 May 1944. Louis Daniel Brodsky Collection, Kent Library, Southeast Missouri State U, series IX, subseries 1, box 1653, folder 19.

———. *Uncollected Stories of William Faulkner*. Random House, 1979.

———. "Undergraduate Writing Class, tape 2." *Faulkner at Virginia: An Audio Archive*, 24 April 1958, edited by Stephen Railton, faulkner.lib.virginia.edu/display/wfaudio23_2 #wfaudio23_2.14.

———. *William Faulkner at Twentieth Century-Fox: The Annotated Screenplays*. Edited by Sarah Gleeson-White, Oxford UP, 2017.

Faulkner, William, and Jules Furthman. "To Have and Have Not." 26 February–19 April 1944. Louis Daniel Brodsky Collection, Kent Library, Southeast Missouri State U, series IX, subseries 1, box 1653, folder 16, 112 pages.

———. "To Have and Have Not." 2–15 March 1944. Louis Daniel Brodsky Collection, Kent Library, Southeast Missouri State U, series IX, subseries 1, box 1653, folder 17.

Faulkner, William, et al. *The Big Sleep*. *Film Scripts One*, edited by George P. Garrett et al., Appleton-Century-Crofts, 1971, pp. 137–329.

Felski, Rita. *The Gender of Modernity*. Harvard UP, 1995.

Fiedler, Leslie. "Pop Goes the Faulkner: In Quest of *Sanctuary*." *Faulkner and Popular Culture, Faulkner and Yoknapatawpha, 1988*, edited by Doreen Fowler and Ann J. Abadie, UP of Mississippi, 1990, pp. 75–92.

Fitzgerald, F. Scott. *The Crack-Up*. New Directions, 1945.

Francke, Lizzie. *Script Girls: Women Screenwriters in Hollywood*. BFI Publishing, 1994.

Friedan, Betty. *The Feminine Mystique*. Norton, 1963.

Fulton, Keith Louise. "Linda Snopes Kohl: Faulkner's Radical Woman." *Modern Fiction Studies*, vol. 34, no. 3, 1988, pp. 425–36.

Gaines, Jane. "White Privilege and Looking Relations: Race and Gender in Feminist Film Theory." *Screen*, vol. 29, no. 4, 1988, pp. 12–27.

Garnier, Caroline. "Temple Drake's Rape and the Myth of the Willing Victim." *Faulkner's Sexualities, Faulkner and Yoknapatawpha, 2007*, edited by Anne Trefzer and Ann J. Abadie, UP of Mississippi, 2010, pp. 164–83.

Gautreau, Justin. *The Last Word: The Hollywood Novel and the Studio System*. Oxford UP, 2020.

Gilbert, Sandra M. and Susan Gubar. *The Madwoman in the Attic: The Woman Writer and the Nineteenth-Century Literary Imagination*. Yale UP, 1979.

Gillman, Susan. *Blood Talk: American Race Melodrama and the Culture of the Occult*. U of Chicago P, 2003.

Gleeson-White, Sarah. "Auditory Exposures: Faulkner, Eisenstein, Film Sound." *PMLA*, vol. 128, no. 1, 2013, pp. 87–100.

———. Introduction. *William Faulkner at Twentieth Century-Fox: The Annotated Screenplays*, by William Faulkner, Oxford UP, 2017, pp. 1–42.

———. Prefatory essay to "The Left Hand of God." *William Faulkner at Twentieth Century-Fox*, by William Faulkner, Oxford UP, 2017, pp. 752–59.

———. Prefatory essay to "The Road to Glory." *William Faulkner at Twentieth Century-Fox*, by William Faulkner, Oxford UP, 2017, pp. 43–49.

———. Prefatory essay to "Splinter Fleet." *William Faulkner at Twentieth Century-Fox*, by William Faulkner, Oxford UP, 2017, pp. 221–25.

———. "William Faulkner, Screenwriter." *Mississippi Quarterly*, vol. 62, nos. 3–4, 2009, pp. 427–42.

Godden, Richard, and Pamela Knights. "'Forget Jerusalem, Go to Hollywood—'To Die. Yes. To Die?'" *Fictions of Labor: William Faulkner and the South's Long Revolution*, by Richard Godden, Cambridge UP, 1997, pp. 179–232.

Gone with the Wind. Directed by Victor Fleming, performances by Vivien Leigh and Hattie McDaniel, Selznick International Pictures and Metro-Goldwyn-Mayer, 1939.

Grayzel, Susan R. *Women and the First World War*. Pearson, 2002.

Greenberg, Clement. "Avant-Garde and Kitsch." *Mass Culture: The Popular Arts in America*, edited by Bernard Rosenberg and David Manning White, Free Press, 1957, pp. 98–107.

Grimwood, Michael. *Heart in Conflict: Faulkner's Struggles With Vocation.* U of Georgia P, 1987.

Gwin, Minrose C. *The Feminine and Faulkner: Reading (Beyond) Sexual Difference.* U of Texas P, 1990.

———. "Feminism and Faulkner: Second Thoughts or, What's a Radical Feminist Doing with a Canonical Male Text Anyway?" *Faulkner Journal,* vol. 4, nos. 1–2, fall 1988, pp. 55–65.

Hackel, Kristina. "Women at Work: Hollywood Screenwriters of the 1940s." *Women Screenwriters: An International Guide,* edited by Jill Nelmes and Julie Selbo, Palgrave Macmillan, 2015, pp. 735–45.

Hagood, Taylor. *Faulkner, Writer of Disability.* Louisiana State UP, 2014.

———. "Media, Ideology, and the Role of Literature in *Pylon.*" *Faulkner Journal,* vol. 21, nos. 1–2, fall 2005–spring 2006, pp. 107–19.

Halberstam, Jack. *Skin Shows: Gothic Horror and the Technology of Monsters.* Duke UP, 1995.

Hamblin, Robert W. "'The Curious Case of Faulkner's 'The De Gaulle Story.'" *Faulkner Journal,* vol. 16, nos. 1–2, fall 2000–spring 2001, pp. 79–86.

Hamblin, Robert W. and Louis Daniel Brodsky. Preface. *Country Lawyer and Other Stories for the Screen,* by William Faulkner, edited by Louis Daniel Brodksy and Robert W. Hamblin, UP of Mississippi, 1987, pp. 7–11.

Hamilton, Ian. *Writers in Hollywood 1915–1951.* Harper and Row, 1990.

Hanley, Lawrence F. "Popular Culture and Crisis: King Kong Meets Edmund Wilson." *Radical Revisions: Rereading 1930s Culture,* edited by Bill Mullen and Sherry Lee Linkon, U of Illinois P, 1996, pp. 242–63.

Hannon, Charles. *Faulkner and the Discourses of Culture.* Louisiana UP, 2005.

Haskell, Molly. *From Reverence to Rape: The Treatment of Women in the Movies.* U of Chicago P, 1987.

———. "Howard Hawks: Masculine Feminine." *Film Comment,* vol. 10, no. 2, 1974, pp. 34–39.

———. "Man's Favorite Sport? (Revisited)." *Howard Hawks: American Artist,* edited by Peter Wollen and Jim Hellier, BFI Publishing, 1996, pp. 107–11.

Hemingway, Ernest. *To Have and Have Not.* Arrow Books, 2004.

Herman, David. "Hypothetical Focalization." *Narrative,* vol. 2, no. 3, 1994, pp. 230–53.

Hickman, Lisa C. *William Faulkner and Joan Williams: The Romance of Two Writers.* McFarland, 2006.

His Girl Friday. Directed by Howard Hawks, performances by Cary Grant and Rosalind Russell, Columbia Pictures, 1940.

Hogue, Peter. "Hawks and Faulkner: *Today We Live.*" *Literature/Film Quarterly,* vol. 9, no. 1, 1981, pp. 51–58.

hooks, bell. *Black Looks: Race and Representation.* Routledge, 2014.

Horkheimer, Max, and Theodor W. Adorno. *Dialectic of Enlightenment.* Translated by John Cumming, Continuum, 1972.

Hulsey, Dallas. "'I Don't Seem to Remember a Girl in the Story': Hollywood's Disruption of Faulkner's All-Male Narrative in *Today We Live*." *Faulkner Journal*, vol. 16, nos. 1–2, 2000–2001, pp. 65–77.

Humm, Maggie. *Feminism and Film*. Edinburgh UP, 1997.

Huyssen, Andreas. *After the Great Divide: Modernism, Mass Culture, Postmodernism*. Indiana UP, 1986.

Imitation of Life. Directed by Douglas Sirk, performances by Lana Turner and Sandra Dee, Universal Pictures, 1959.

Intermezzo. Directed by Gregory Ratoff, performances by Leslie Howard and Ingrid Bergman, United Artists, 1939.

I Was a Male War Bride. Directed by Howard Hawks, performances by Cary Grant and Ann Sheridan, Twentieth Century–Fox, 1949.

Jackson, Robert. "Images of Collaboration: William Faulkner's Motion Picture Communities." *Faulkner and Film, Faulkner and Yoknapatawpha, 2010*, edited by Peter Lurie and Ann J. Abadie, UP of Mississippi, 2014, pp. 62–86.

Jacobs, Lea. *The Wages of Sin: Censorship and the Fallen Woman Film*. U of Wisconsin P, 1991.

Jewell, K. Sue. *From Mammy to Miss America and Beyond: Cultural Images and the Shaping of US Social Policy*. Routledge, 1993.

Johnny Belinda. Directed by Jean Negulesco, performance by Jane Wyman, Warner Brothers, 1948.

John-Steiner, Vera. *Creative Collaboration*. Oxford UP, 2000.

Johnson, Marta Paul. "'I Have Decided Now': Laverne's Transformation in *Pylon*." *Mississippi Quarterly*, vol. 36, no. 3, 1983, pp. 289–300.

Johnston, Claire. "Women's Cinema as Counter-Cinema." *Feminist Film Theory: A Reader*, edited by Sue Thornham, Edinburgh UP, 1999, pp. 31–40.

Jones, Anne Goodwyn. "'The Kotex Age': Women, Popular Culture, and *The Wild Palms*." *Faulkner and Popular Culture, Faulkner and Yoknapatawpha, 1988*, edited by Doreen Fowler and Ann J. Abadie, UP of Mississippi, 1990, pp. 142–62.

Kang, Hee. "A New Configuration of Faulkner's Feminine: Linda Snopes Kohl in *The Mansion*." *Faulkner Journal*, vol. 8, no. 1, 1992, pp. 21–41.

Kaplan, E. Ann. "Introduction to 1978 Edition." *Women in Film Noir*, edited by E. Ann Kaplan, BFI Publishing, 1998, pp. 15–19.

———. *Motherhood and Representation: The Mother in Popular Culture and Melodrama*. Routledge, 2013.

———. "Theories of Melodrama: A Feminist Perspective." *Women and Performance*, vol 1, no. 1, 1983, pp. 40–48.

Karem, Jeff. "Fear of a Black Atlantic? African Passages in *Absalom, Absalom!* and *The Last Slaver*." *Global Faulkner, Faulkner and Yoknapatawpha, 2006*, edited by Annette Trefzer and Ann J. Abadie, UP of Mississippi, 2009, pp. 162–73.

Kawin, Bruce F. *Faulkner and Film*. Frederick Ungar Publishing, 1977.

———. "Faulkner's Film Career: The Years with Hawks." *Faulkner, Modernism and Film, Faulkner and Yoknapatawpha, 1978*, edited by Evans Harrington and Ann J. Abadie, UP of Mississippi, 1979, pp. 163–81.

———. "Howard Hawks." *Selected Essays and Film Interviews*, by Bruce F. Kawin, Anthem Press, 2013, pp. 89–128.

———. "Introduction: No Man Alone." *To Have and Have Not*, by Jules Furthman and William Faulkner, edited by Bruce F. Kawin, U of Wisconsin P, 1980, pp. 9–53.

———. Prefatory essay to "The College Widow." *Faulkner's MGM Screenplays*, by William Faulkner, edited by Bruce F. Kawin, U of Tennessee P, 1982, pp. 29–39.

———. Prefatory essay to "Turn About / Today We Live." *Faulkner's MGM Screenplays*, by William Faulkner, edited by Bruce F. Kawin, U of Tennessee P, 1982, pp. 101–27.

———. Prefatory essay to "War Birds / A Ghost Story." *Faulkner's MGM Screenplays*, by William Faulkner, edited by Bruce F. Kawin, U of Tennessee P, 1982, pp. 257–74.

Keith, Slim. "Howard the Dreamer." *Howard Hawks: American Artist*, edited by Jim Hellier and Peter Wollen, BFI Publishing, 1996, pp. 200–02.

King, Vincent Allen. "The Wages of Pulp: The Uses and Abuses of Fiction in William Faulkner's *The Wild Palms*." *Mississippi Quarterly*, vol. 51, no. 3, 1998, pp. 503–25.

Ladd, Barbara. "'Philosophers and Other Gynaecologists': Women and the Polity in *Requiem for a Nun*." *Mississippi Quarterly*, vol. 52, no. 3, 1999, pp. 483–502.

Laird, Holly A. *Women Coauthors*. U of Illinois P, 2000.

Landay, Lori. "The Flapper Film: Comedy, Dance, and Jazz Age Kinaesthetics." *A Feminist Reader in Early Cinema*, edited by Jennifer M. Bean and Diane Negra, Duke UP, 2002, pp. 221–48.

Langlois, Henri. "The Modernity of Howard Hawks." *Howard Hawks: American Artist*, edited Peter Wollen and Jim Hillier, BFI Publishing, 1996, pp. 72–75.

LaSalle, Mick. *Complicated Women: Sex and Power in Pre Code Hollywood*. St Martin's Publishing Group, 2001. E-book.

LaValley, Albert J. "Introduction: A Troublesome Property to Script." *Mildred Pierce*, by Ranald MacDougall, edited by Albert J. LaValley, U of Wisconsin P, 1980, pp. 9–53.

Lester, Cheryl. "To Market, To Market: *The Portable Faulkner*." *Criticism*, vol. 29, 1987, pp. 371–89.

Letter from an Unknown Woman. Directed by Max Ophüls, Rampart Productions and Universal Studios, 1948.

Lugowski, David M. "Queering the (New) Deal: Lesbian and Gay Representation and the Depression-Era Cultural Politics of Hollywood's Production Code." *Cinema Journal*, vol. 38, no. 2, 1999, pp. 3–35.

Luhr, William. *Film Noir*. Wiley-Blackwell, 2012.

Lurie, Peter. *Vision's Immanence: Faulkner, Film and the Popular Imagination*. Johns Hopkins UP, 2004.

Lyman, Lauren D. "Mrs. Omlie Beats 36 Men in Derby." *New York Times*, 1 September 1931, p. 8.

MacGowan, Kenneth. "When the Talkies Came to Hollywood." *The Quarterly of Film Radio and Television*, vol. 10, no. 3, 1956, pp. 288–301.

Magny, Claude-Edmonde. *The Age of the American Novel: The Film Aesthetic of Fiction Between the Two Wars*. Frederick Ungar Publishing, 1972.

Maltby, Richard. "More Sinned Against than Sinning: The Fabrications of 'Pre-Code Cinema.'" *Senses of Cinema*, vol. 29, December 2003, sensesofcinema.com/2003/feature-articles/pre_code_cinema/.

———. "The Production Code and the Hays Office." *Grand Design: Hollywood as a Modern Business Enterprise, 1930–1939*, edited by Tino Balio, vol. 5, Charles Scribner's Sons, 1993, pp. 37–72.

Mao, Douglas and Rebecca L. Walkowitz. *Bad Modernisms*. Duke UP, 2006.

———. "The New Modernist Studies." *PMLA*, vol. 123, no. 3, 2008, pp. 737–48.

Matthews, John T. "The Autograph of Violence in *Pylon*." *Southern Literature and Literary Theory*, edited by Jefferson Humphries, U of Georgia P, 1990, pp. 247–69.

———. "Faulkner and the Culture Industry." *The Cambridge Companion to William Faulkner*, edited by Philip M. Weinstein, Cambridge UP, 1995, pp. 51–74.

———. "Many Mansions: Faulkner's Cold War Conflicts." *Global Faulkner, Faulkner and Yoknapatawpha, 2006*, edited by Annette Trefzer and Ann J. Abadie, UP of Mississippi, 2009, pp. 3–23.

———. *William Faulkner: Seeing Through the South*. Blackwell, 2009.

May, Elaine Tyler. *Homeward Bound: American Families in the Cold War Era*. Basic Books, 2008.

McCarthy, Todd. *Howard Hawks: The Grey Fox of Hollywood*. Grove Press, 1997.

McElya, Micki. *Clinging to Mammy: The Faithful Slave in Twentieth-Century America*. Harvard UP, 2007.

McGilligan, Patrick, editor. *Backstory 1: Interviews with Screenwriters of Hollywood's Golden Age*. U of California P, 1986.

———. *Backstory 2: Interviews with Screenwriters of the 1940s and 1950s*. U of California P, 1997.

Mecholsky, Kristopher. "*The Mansion* as Soft-Boiled Noir." *Faulkner Journal*, vol. 28, no. 1, 2014, pp. 79–93.

Menand, Louis. "The Promise of Freedom, the Friend of Authority: American Culture in Postwar France." *Americanism: New Perspectives of the History of an Ideal*, edited by Michael Kazin and Joseph A. McCartin, U of North Carolina P, 2006.

Meriwether, James B. "The Novel Faulkner Never Wrote: His Golden Book or Doomsday Book." *American Literature*, vol. 42, no. 1, 1970, pp. 93–96.

Mildred Pierce. Directed by Michael Curtiz, performances by Joan Crawford and Ann Blyth, Warner Brothers, 1945.

Millholland, Ray. *The Splinter Fleet of the Otranto Barrage*. Bobbs-Merrill, 1936.

Moore, Michelle E. "'The Unsleeping Cabal': Faulkner's Fevered Vampires and the Other South." *Faulkner Journal*, vol. 24, no. 2, 2009, pp. 55–76.

———. "Vampires, Detectives, and Hawks: A History and Analysis of William Faulkner's Unpublished Screenplay *Dreadful Hollow*." *Literature/Film Quarterly*, vol. 45, no. 3, summer 2017, 19 pages, lfq.salisbury.edu/_issues/45_3/vampires_detectives_and_hawks.html.

Morrison, Spencer. "*Requiem*'s Ruins: Unmaking and Making in Cold War Faulkner." *American Literature*, vol. 85, no. 2, 2013, pp. 303–31.

Mortimer, Claire. *Romantic Comedy*. Routledge, 2010.

Mulvey, Laura. "Notes on Sirk and Melodrama." *Visual and Other Pleasures*, by Laura Mulvey, Indiana UP, 1989, pp. 39–44.

———. "Visual Pleasure and Narrative Cinema." *Film Theory and Criticism: Introductory Readings*, edited by Leo Braudy and Marshall Cohen, Oxford UP, 1999, pp. 833–44.

Murphet, Julian. *Faulkner's Media Romance*. Oxford UP, 2017.

My Sin. Directed by George Abbott, performances by Tallulah Bankhead and Scott Kolk, Paramount Pictures, 1931.

Napolin, Julie Beth. *The Fact of Resonance: Modernist Acoustics and Narrative Form*. Fordham UP, 2020.

Naremore, James. *More than Night: Film Noir in Its Contexts*. U of California P, 1998.

Nelmes, Jill, and Julie Selbo, editors. *Women Screenwriters: An International Guide*. Palgrave Macmillan, 2015.

No Down Payment. Directed by Martin Ritt, Twentieth Century–Fox, 1957.

Only Angels Have Wings. Directed by Howard Hawks, performances by Jean Arthur and Cary Grant, Columbia Pictures, 1939.

Penner, Erin. "Reading the *Portable Faulkner* through Digital Yoknapatawpha: Recovering the 'Problems' and 'Difficulties' of 'Appendix Compson 1699–1945.'" *Digitizing Faulkner: Yoknapatawpha in the Twenty-First Century*, edited by Theresa M. Towner, U of Virginia P, 2022, pp. 104–24.

The Plastic Age. Directed by Wesley Ruggles, performances by Clara Bow and Donald Keith, Preferred Pictures, 1925.

Polk, Noel. "Afterword." *Sanctuary: The Original Text*, by William Faulkner, edited by Noel Polk, Random House, 1981, pp. 293–306.

———. *Children of the Dark House: Text and Context in Faulkner*. UP Mississippi, 1996.

———. *Faulkner's* Requiem for a Nun: *A Critical Study*. Indiana UP, 1981.

Ramsey, D. Matthew. "'Lifting the Fog': Faulkners, Reputations and *The Story of Temple Drake*." *Faulkner Journal*, vol. 16, nos. 1–2, fall 2000–spring 2001, pp. 7–33.

———. "'Touch Me while You Look at Her': Stars, Fashion and Authorship in *Today We Live*." *Faulkner and Material Culture, Faulkner and Yoknapatawpha, 2004*, edited by Joseph R. Urgo and Ann J. Abadie, UP of Mississippi, 2007, pp. 82–103.

Reames, Kelly Lynch. "'All that Matters Is that I Wrote The Letters': Discourse, Discipline and Difference in *Requiem for a Nun*." *Faulkner Journal*, vol. 15, no. 1, 1998, pp. 31–52.

Renov, Michael. "Leave Her to Heaven: The Double Bind of the Post-War Woman." *Imitations of Life: A Reader on Film and Television Melodrama*, edited by Marcia Landy, Wayne State UP, 1991, pp. 227–36.

Rhodes, Chip. *Politics, Desire, and the Hollywood Novel*. U of Iowa P, 2008.

Rideout, Walter B. and James B. Meriwether. "On the Collaboration of Faulkner and Anderson." *American Literature*, vol. 35, no. 1, 1963, pp. 85–87.

Roberts, Diane. "Eula, Linda, and the Death of Nature." *Faulkner and the Natural World, Faulkner and Yoknapatawpha, 1996*, edited by Donald M. Kartiganer and Ann J. Abadie, UP of Mississippi, 1999, pp. 159–78.

———. *Faulkner and Southern Womanhood*. U of Georgia P, 1994.

Rollyson, Carl. *The Life of William Faulkner: The Past Is Never Dead, 1897–1934*. Vol. 1, U of Virginia P, 2020. 2 vols.

———. *The Life of William Faulkner: This Alarming Paradox, 1935–1962*. Vol. 2, U of Virginia P, 2020. 2 vols.

Ross, Sara. "'Good Little Bad Girls': Controversy and the Flapper Comedienne." *Film History*, vol. 13, 2001, pp. 409–23.

Ross, Stephen M. *Faulkner's Inexhaustible Voice: Speech and Writing in Faulkner*. U of Georgia P, 1989.

Sarris, Andrew. "Notes on the Auteur Theory in 1962." *Film Theory and Criticism: Introductory Readings*, edited by Leo Braudy and Marshall Cohen, 7th edition, Oxford UP, 2009, pp. 451–54.

Sayre, Joel, and William Faulkner. *The Road to Glory: A Screenplay*. Southern Illinois UP, 1981.

Sbardellati, John. *J. Edgar Hoover Goes to the Movies*. Cornell UP, 2012.

Schatz, Thomas. *Hollywood Genres: Formulas, Filmmaking, and the Studio System*. Random House, 1981.

———. *The Genius of the System: Hollywood Filmmaking in the Studio Era*. Pantheon, 1988.

Schrader, Paul. "Notes on Film Noir." *Film Comment*, vol. 8, no. 1, 1972, pp. 8–13.

Schreiber, Evelyn Jaffe. "What's Love Got to Do with It? Desire and Subjectivity in Faulkner's Snopes Trilogy." *Faulkner Journal*, vol. 9, nos. 1–2, fall 1993–spring 1994, pp. 83–98.

Schweighauser, Philipp. *The Noises of American Literature, 1890–1895: Toward a History of Literary Acoustics*. UP of Florida, 2006.

Scott, Bonnie Kime. *The Gender of Modernism*. Indiana UP, 1990.

Sensibar, Judith L. *Faulkner and Love: The Women Who Shaped His Art*. Yale UP, 2009.

Sharot, Stephen. "The 'New Woman,' Star Personas, and Cross-Class Romance Films in 1920s America." *Journal of Gender Studies*, vol. 19, no. 1, 2010, pp. 73–86.

She Done Him Wrong. Directed by Lowell Sherman, performances by Mae West and Cary Grant, Paramount Pictures, 1933.

Silverman, Kaja. *The Acoustic Mirror: The Female Voice in Psychoanalysis and Cinema*. Indiana UP, 1988.
Sirk, Douglas. *Sirk on Sirk: Conversations with Jon Halliday*. Faber and Faber, 1997.
Sklar, Robert. *Movie-Made America: A Cultural History of American Movies*. Chappell and Company, 1978.
Smith, Murray. "Film Noir: The Female Gothic and Deception." *Wide Angle*, vol. 10, no. 1, 1988, pp. 62–75.
Smith, Phil. "Faulkner and 'The Man with the Megaphone': The Redemption of Genre and the Transfiguration of Trash in *If I Forget Thee, Jerusalem*." *Faulkner and Film, Faulkner and Yoknapatawpha, 2010*, edited by Peter Lurie and Ann J. Abadie, UP of Mississippi, 2014.
Solomon, Stefan. "Faulkner and Screen Culture." *The New Faulkner Studies*, edited by Sarah Gleeson-White and Pardis Dabashi, Cambridge UP, 2022, pp. 200–15.
———. *William Faulkner in Hollywood: Screenwriting for the Studios*. U of Georgia P, 2017.
The Sound and the Fury. Directed by Martin Ritt, performances by Yul Brynner and Joanne Woodward, Twentieth Century–Fox, 1959.
Spiegel, Alan. *Fiction and the Camera Eye: Visual Consciousness in Film and the Modern Novel*. UP of Virginia, 1976.
Stella Dallas. Directed by King Vidor, performance by Barbara Stanwyck, United Artists, 1937.
Steven, Mark. "William Faulkner's Mediated Time: Capitalism, Cinema, Syntax." *William Faulkner in the Media Ecology*, edited by Julian Murphet and Stefan Solomon, Louisiana State UP, 2015, pp. 195–215.
Stillinger, Jack. *Multiple Authorship and the Myth of Solitary Genius*. Oxford UP, 1991.
The Story of Temple Drake. Directed by Steven Roberts, performances by Miriam Hopkins and Jack LaRue, Paramount Pictures, 1933.
Stringer, Dorothy. *"Not Even Past": Race, Historical Trauma, and Subjectivity in Faulkner, Larsen, and Van Vechten*. Fordham UP, 2010.
Sundquist, Eric J. *Faulkner: The House Divided*. Johns Hopkins UP, 1983.
Tiger Shark. Directed by Howard Hawks, performance by Edward G. Robinson, First National Pictures, 1932.
Towner, Theresa M. *Faulkner on the Color Line: The Later Novels*. UP of Mississippi, 2000.
Urgo, Joseph R. "*Absalom, Absalom!*: The Movie." *American Literature*, vol. 62, no. 1, 1990, pp. 56–73.
———. *Faulkner's Apocrypha: A Fable, Snopes, and the Spirit of Human Rebellion*. UP of Mississippi, 1989.
———. "Temple Drake's Truthful Perjury: Rethinking Faulkner's *Sanctuary*." *American Literature*, vol. 55, no. 3, 1983, pp. 435–44.
Virilio, Paul. *War and Cinema: The Logistics of Perception*. Translated by Patrick Camillier, Verso, 1989.

Ware, Susan. *Holding Their Own: American Women in the 1930s.* Twayne, 1982.
Watson, Jay. "Dangerous Return: The Narratives of Jurisgenesis in Faulkner's *Requiem for a Nun.*" *Modern Fiction Studies*, vol. 60, no. 1, 2014, pp. 108–37.
———. *William Faulkner and the Faces of Modernity.* Oxford UP, 2019.
Watts, Jill. *Mae West: An Icon in Black and White.* Oxford UP, 2001.
West, Nathanael. *Miss Lonelyhearts and A Cool Million.* Penguin, 1991.
Whitney, Allison. "Race, Class, and the Pressure to Pass in American Maternal Melodrama: The Case of *Stella Dallas.*" *Journal of Film and Video*, vol. 59, no. 1, 2007, pp. 3–18.
Williams, Linda. *Hard Core: Power, Pleasure, and the "Frenzy of the Visible."* U of California P, 1999.
———. *Playing the Race Card: Melodramas of Black and White from Uncle Tom to O. J. Simpson.* Princeton UP, 2001.
———. "'Something Else Besides a Mother': *Stella Dallas* and the Maternal Melodrama." *Imitations of Life: A Reader on Film and Television Melodrama*, edited by Marcia Landy, Wayne State UP, 1991, pp. 307–30.
Williams, Michael. "Cross-Dressing in Yoknapatawpha County." *Mississippi Quarterly*, vol. 47, no. 3, 1994, pp. 369–90.
Wise, Naomi. "The Hawksian Woman." *Howard Hawks: American Artist*, edited by Peter Wollen and Jim Hellier, BFI Publishing, 1996, pp. 111–19.
Wollen, Peter. "Introduction." *Howard Hawks: American Artist*, edited by Peter Wollen and Jim Hellier, BFI Publishing, 1996, pp. 1–11.
———. *Signs and Meaning in the Cinema.* 5th edition, BFI and Palgrave Macmillan, 2013.
Wood, Robin. *Howard Hawks.* Wayne State UP, 2006.
Yarbrough, Scott. "The Dark Lady: Temple Drake as Femme Fatale." *Southern Literary Journal*, vol. 31, no. 2, 1999, pp. 50–64.
Young-Minor, Ethel. "'I Sees de Light, en I Sees de Word': Black Female Transcendence of Racial, Gendered Boundaries in *The Sound and the Fury* and 'That Evening Sun.'" *Faulkner and Formalism: Returns of the Text, Faulkner and Yoknapatawpha, 2008*, edited by Annette Trefzer and Ann J. Abadie, UP of Mississippi, 2012, pp. 163–77.
Zeitlin, Michael. *Faulkner, Aviation, and Modern War.* Bloomsbury Academic, 2022.
———. "Faulkner and the Royal Air Force Canada, 1918." *Faulkner Journal*, vol. 30, no. 1, 2016, pp. 15–38.
———. "Faulkner's *Pylon*: The City in the Age of Mechanical Reproduction." *Canadian Review of American Studies*, vol. 22, no. 2, fall 1991, pp. 229–40.
———. "*Pylon* and the Rise of European Fascism." *Faulkner Journal*, vol. 26, no. 1, spring 2012, pp. 97–114.
Zeitz, Joshua. *Flapper: A Madcap Story of Sex, Style, Celebrity, and the Women who Made America Modern.* Crown, 2006. E-book.
Zender, Karl F. *The Crossing of the Ways: William Faulkner, the South, and the Modern World.* Rutgers UP, 1989.

———. "Faulkner and the Power of Sound." *PMLA*, vol. 99, no. 1, January 1984, pp. 89–108.

———. "*Requiem for a Nun* and the Uses of the Imagination." *Faulkner and Race, Faulkner and Yoknapatawpha, 1986*, edited by Doreen Fowler and Ann J. Abadie, UP of Mississippi, 1987, pp. 272–96.

Index

Abbott, George, 63–64
abjection, 151–52
abortion, 130–31, 148–49, 163–65
abstraction, 5–6, 16–17, 24–25, 39, 114–15, 138–39, 187–88, 231
actor, 29–30, 32–33, 50–51, 73–75, 114–15, 149–50, 197–98, 219–21, 223–24, 244–45
Adam's Rib (1949), 100–101
adaptation, 68–69, 262n12; collaborative, 19, 123–24, 178–79, 197–98; Faulkner and, 12–13, 22–23, 28–30, 48, 50–51, 70–75, 95–96, 130–31, 151–53, 155–56, 178–79, 181, 183–84, 197–98, 201–2, 217–18, 226, 236–37, 241–42, 250n7, 251n14, 258n16, 260n20, 262n8; gender and, 87–91, 111, 178–79, 181, 183–84, 201–2, 217–18, 226, 236–37, 241–42
Adorno, Theodor W., 4–6, 147–48
Adrian (Adrian Adolph Greenburg), 74, 76

adventure film, 12–13, 22–23, 41–42, 46, 77–78, 84, 86–87, 89–91, 148–49
agency: gender and, 63, 99, 103–4, 108–9, 116–18, 127–29, 150, 165–66; language and, 59
Air Force (1943), 185–86, 197–98
All That Heaven Allows (1955), 219–20, 262n9
Altman, Rick, 246
Anderson, Sherwood, 25–26, 219–20
androgyny, 94–95, 98–101, 109, 112–13, 121–22, 129–30, 134, 234–36. *See also* gender
Anker, Elisabeth R., 198, 261n2, 262n9
art (sculpture), 13, 46–47, 109, 133–35, 137–42, 231, 263n3
art deco, 138
Arthur, Jean, 93–94, 116
Associated Artists, 251n15
Association of Motion Picture Producers (AMPP), 70–71, 158–59

auteur theory, 24–25, 86–87, 121, 130–31, 149–50, 190–91
authorship, 25–26, 30–31, 111–12, 121. *See also* collaboration
autocriticism, 217–26, 262n12
autonomy, 23–25, 99–100, 133–36, 138, 141–42, 149–51, 230
aviation, 16–17, 83–84, 94–97, 101, 232, 251n14, 254n1

Baby Face (1933), 62, 115
Bacall, Lauren, 1–3, 29–30, 35, 45, 92–93, 123, 126, 178–79, 223–24, 259–60nn4–5
Bachelor Mother (1939), 85–86
bad girl, 28–29, 45–46, 48, 50–52, 62–72, 80–81, 100–101, 107–9. *See also* vice film
Balázs, Béla, 114–15, 246–48
Baldwin, Doug, 15–16
Ball of Fire (1941), 91–92, 109–10
Banjo on My Knee (1936), 118–19
Bankhead, Tallulah, 2–3, 28–29, 49–51, 63–65, 253n1, 254n7
Barbary Coast (1935), 121
Barker, Deborah, 59–60, 208–9, 214–15, 262n8
Barr, Caroline, 2–3
Barrett, William E., 222–23
Barrymore, John, 73
Barthes, Roland, 149–50
Bazin, André, 184–85, 242–43
Beery, Wallace, 73
Behn, Harry, 95–96
Benjamin, Walter, 37–38, 145–46
Bennett, Charles, 243–44
Bergman, Ingrid, 185–86, 237–38
Berlant, Lauren, 224
Bernard, Raymond, 111
Biesen, Sheri Chinen, 259n3

Big Sleep, The (1946), 1–2, 19, 30–31, 44–45, 47–48, 167, 192–93, 223–24, 256n16, 260n5, 261n23
Binggeli, Elizabeth, 80–81
Birth of a Nation, The (1915), 213–15
Blanchot, Maurice, 184–85
Bleikasten, André, 194
blindness, 56–57, 112–13
blonde bombshell, 108–9
Bloom, Harold Jack, 263n1
Bloom, James D., 140–41, 161, 258n16
Bogart, Humphrey, 1–2, 29–31, 35, 45, 123, 125–26, 167, 178–79, 192–93, 244, 259n4, 262n6
Boon, Kevin Alexander, 33–34
Borde, Raymond, 189–90
Bourdieu, Pierre, 24–25, 142
Bow, Clara, 54–56, 58–60
Brackett, Leigh, 2–3, 19, 30–31, 44–45, 89–91, 178–80, 192–93, 256n16, 261n23
Breen, Joseph I., 50, 71–72, 105
Bringing Up Baby (1938), 109–10, 154
Brinkmeyer, Robert H., Jr., 251n14
Brodsky Collection (Southeast Missouri State University), 125–26
Brook, Vincent, 188–89
Brooks, Peter, 202, 261n4
buddy film, 29–30, 67–68
Burgess, M. J., 35–36, 253n22
Butler, Judith, 220–21

Cabell, James Branch, 196
Cain, James M., 201–2
Caldwell, Erskine, 190–91
capital, symbolic, 24–25
capitalism, 98–99; market, 146–47
Carpenter Wilde, Meta, 2–3, 7–9, 31–33, 118–22, 125–26, 132–33, 162, 257n2
Casablanca (1942), 167, 185–86
Catholic Legion of Decency, 71

INDEX 283

Cendrars, Blaise, 113–14
censorship, 45, 51, 61, 63, 105, 233–34
Cervantes, Miguel de, 140
Chandler, Raymond, 19, 178–79, 192–93
Chaplin, Charlie, 246
characterization: gender and, 22–23, 28–29, 40–47, 52–60, 65–66, 76–77, 85–94, 107–9, 126, 152–54, 168–69, 172–73, 175–85, 193–96, 202–4, 210–11, 220–23, 230–43, 249n1, 253n2, 260nn6–7; hybridity and, 42, 48; identity and, 58–59, 74–75; in melodrama, 220–26, 236–41; post-Code, 85–87, 91–94; race and, 214–17, 224–26, 262n8; stereotypes and, 41–42. *See also individual character types by name*
Chaumeton, Étienne, 189–90
Cheat, The (1931), 63–64
Christensen, Jerome, 121, 137
Cinderella story, 63
Circumstantial Evidence (1945), 197–98
Clansman, The (1905), 213–14
Clarke, Deborah, 2–3, 58
class: domesticity and, 198–200; film and, 252n18; gender and, 52, 55–56, 117–18, 148–49, 163, 214–19, 228–29; race and, 207–8, 214–15; sexuality and, 55–56
Coindreau, Maurice, 190–91
Cold War: art and, 204–5; domesticity and, 205–7, 214–15, 218–19, 225–27, 235–36, 261n2; melodrama and, 198–99, 208, 216–17, 221–22, 225–27, 261n2; television and, 153–54
collaboration, 3, 21; erotics of, 101, 123–24; gender and, 14–15, 23–33, 46, 86–87, 95–96, 123–24, 127, 129–30, 162–63; in Hollywood, 27–33, 75–76, 86–87, 98–99, 111–12, 119–27, 129–30, 162–63, 197–98, 243–45, 250n7; labor and, 86–87, 95–96, 117–18, 127, 129–30; literature and, 26–27, 122; modernism and, 23–27; sexuality and, 27; theatrical, 197–98
Collins, Joan, 251n15
Columbia Pictures, 28–29
Come and Get It (1936), 124–25
comedy, 53–56, 85–86. *See also* screwball comedy
commerce: art and, 12–13, 133–48; film and, 3, 5–11, 13, 16, 33, 36–41, 45–47, 86, 97–98, 100–101, 106, 157–60, 199, 249n3, 251n15; gender and, 3, 6–10, 33, 36–41, 45–47, 81–82, 86, 97–98, 100–101, 106, 140–48, 154–60, 162–63, 168–69, 175–76, 199; literature and, 16, 19–20, 40–41, 42, 86, 154–56, 168–69, 175–76, 199, 249n3, 251n15
Commins, Dorothy Berliner, 25
Commins, Saxe, 25, 152, 258n5
commodification, 3–4, 10, 12–13, 21–22, 36–40, 47–48, 56–57, 133–48, 157–61, 165–66, 172, 195
Communism, 198–99, 226–27, 235–36, 241
community, 92–94, 123. *See also* collaboration
Confessions of a Nazi Spy (1939), 185–86
consumerism, consumption, 4–5, 13, 33–34, 36–39, 56–57, 86, 99–106, 139, 142, 157–58, 195, 255n8
contagion, 3–5, 10, 106–7
Cook, Pam, 199–200
Cooper, Gary, 71
Cowie, Elizabeth, 45, 88–89, 92–95, 102–3
Cowley, Malcolm, 24–25, 169–70, 189–91
Crawford, Joan, 1–3, 29–30, 73–76, 81–82, 134, 254n8
Creed, Barbara, 151–52
crime film, 167
Croix de Bois, Les (1932), 111
cross-dressing. *See also* androgyny; gender; transvestism

Crowd Roars, The (1932), 84–85
Crowther, Bosley, 192–93
Cukor, George, 100–101
Cunningham, Anne, 71–72, 75–76
Curtiz, Michael, 212

Dabashi, Pardis, 157–58, 250n11, 261n24
Damned Don't Cry, The (1941), 208
Dardis, Tom, 83–85
Davis, Thadious M., 173–74, 194–95
Day of the Locust, The (1939), 11
deafness, 234, 238–39, 247–48, 263n7
de Lauretis, Teresa, 33
De Mille, Cecil B., 258n16
Design for Living (1933), 71
desire: art and, 13, 17–18; collaboration and, 25–26, 29–30; gender and, 17–18, 42–43, 45, 54–55, 74–75, 80–81, 89–91, 93–94, 99–101, 103–6, 109, 148–49, 158–60, 199–200, 210–17, 252n18. *See also* sexuality
detective fiction, 179–80, 189–90. *See also* hard-boiled writing
detective film, 1–2, 8–9, 53, 167, 189–90, 192–93. *See also* noir
dialogic exchange, 13–15, 21–23, 40, 42, 45–46, 53, 65–66, 83–87, 101–2, 135–36, 250n7, 251nn14–15
dialogue (speech), 29–33, 68–69, 74, 116–17, 223–24, 243–45, 254n8, 258n8
Diamond Lil (1928), 68–69
DiBattista, Maria, 10
Dietrich, Marlene, 93–94, 126
digital humanities, 4, 9–10
Digital Yoknapatawpha (DY) resource, 4, 9–10
director, 15–17, 41, 72–73, 86–88, 120–24, 127, 162, 188–89, 217–22, 258n16. *See also* Hawks, Howard; Sirk, Douglas

Dixon, Thomas, Jr., 213–14
Doane, Mary Ann, 34–35, 99–101, 150, 177–78
Dobbs, Cynthia, 139, 144–47
Doherty, Thomas, 17–18, 61, 63, 81–82, 153–54
domesticity, 88–89, 93–94, 97–98, 154–56; Cold War and, 198–99, 205–10, 216–19, 225–27, 235–36, 261n2; containment and, 198–99, 205–11, 216–20, 225–27; family and, 197–204, 212–26; race and, 207–9, 211–17, 220, 224–26; violence and, 218–19. *See also* gender; melodrama
Dore, Florence, 80–81
Dorgelès, Roland, 111
Dos Passos, John, 1–2, 190–91
double exposure, 113–14, 255n14
Double Indemnity (1944), 188–89
Drew, William M., 253n3
Duvall, John N., 97–98, 102–4
Dyer, Richard, 220–21

Edington, K., 11–12
Eisenstein, Sergei, 15–16, 113–15, 258n16, 264n10
Eliot, T. S., 140–41, 146–47, 155
Elsaesser, Thomas, 262n10
Erskine, Albert, 25, 229–30
Esperdy, Gabrielle, 138
espionage. *See* spy movie
exclusion, 1–2, 4–5, 9–10, 21–22, 68–69, 150–51, 245–46
experimentalism, 1–3, 13–21, 83, 134–35, 137–38, 142, 147–48, 152, 156, 165–66, 250n11, 258n16

fallen woman, 50, 63–67, 70–71, 77–78, 193–94
Faulkner, Maud, 2–3

INDEX

Faulkner, William: *Absalom, Absalom!* (1936), 31–33, 83, 161–62, 250n7, 251nn13–15, 255n13, 260n20, 263n8, 264n10; "Absolution," (1932), 67–68; "Ad Astra" (1930), 232; "All the Dead Pilots" (1931), 232; "Appendix Compson: 1699–1945" (1946), 9–10, 47–48, 167–96, 241–42, 259n1, 261n23; *As I Lay Dying* (1930), 8–9, 15–16, 49, 256n20; "Barn Burning" (1939), 217–18; "Battle Cry" (1943), 47–48, 168–69, 186–87, 251n14; "The Big Sleep" (1944), 168–69, 175–82, 192–93, 241–42; "The Brooch" (1936), 36; Cold War context of writing, 204–6, 221–22; collaboration and, 23–33, 86–87, 101, 119–22, 134, 197–98, 263n1; "The College Widow" (1932), 17–18, 28–29, 33–35, 50–51, 66–72, 81–82, 253n5; "Continuous Performance" (1946), 109–10; "The Damned Don't Cry" (1941), 43–44, 48, 197–98, 200–201, 208, 236–37; "The De Gaulle Story" (1942), 47–48, 168–69, 186–88, 251n14; "Dreadful Hollow" (c. 1944), 47–48, 168–69, 183–85, 251n14, 260n20; "Drums Along the Mohawk" (1937), 251n13; "Dry September" (1931), 35–36; "Elly" (1934), 25–26, 253n5; *A Fable* (1954), 251n14; *Flags in the Dust* [*Sartoris*] (1929), 232, 263n5; "Flying the Mail" (1932), 83–84, 254n3; *Go Down, Moses* (1942), 251n13, 261n22; "Golden Land" (1935), 5–6, 11, 36–37, 39–40; *The Hamlet* (1940), 217–18, 228–30; on Hollywood, 3–10; "Honor" (1930), 95–96; *If I Forget Thee, Jerusalem* (1939), 12–14, 31–33, 37–40, 46–47, 109, 129–30, 132–66, 235–36, 250n9, 257n1, 257n3; *Intruder in the Dust* (1948), 251n14; "The Last Slaver" (1936), 251n14; "The Left Hand of God" (1951), 222–24, 262n13; "The Life and Death of a Bomber" (1942), 176–77, 233–34; *Light in August* (1932), 8–9; "Manservant" (1932), 67, 251n14, 254n6; *The Mansion* (1959), 4, 6–7, 9–10, 13–14, 22–23, 25, 39–40, 48, 228–48, 249n3; *The Marionettes* (1920), 28–29; "Mildred Pierce" (1944), 168–69, 182–83, 197–98, 201–2, 208, 210, 236–37, 241–42; "Morningstar" (1948), 109–10; *Mosquitoes* (1927), 25–26; "Mythical Latin-American Kingdom Story" (1933), 52, 77–82, 255n5; "Night Bird" (1932), 50–51, 63–64, 66–67; Nobel Prize, 204–5; *The Portable Faulkner* (1946), 167–70, 189–91, 195–96; *Pylon* (1935), 13–14, 38–40, 46, 83–87, 93–110, 129–30, 217–18, 234–36, 255n9; reception (in France), 24, 189; *The Reivers* (1962), 25; relationship with Carpenter, 118–22, 132–33; relationship with Hawks, 83–87; *Requiem for a Nun* (1951), 4, 13–14, 26–29, 31–33, 43–44, 48, 108–9, 197–99, 202–17, 219, 221–27, 235–37, 252n16, 261n1, 261n5, 262n8, 262n11, 262–63nn13–14; "Revolt in the Earth" (1937), 250n7, 251n15; "The Road to Glory" (1936), 111–15, 119–20, 122, 129–30, 232–33; *Sanctuary* (1931), 8–9, 12, 28–29, 45–46, 49–60, 65–67, 70–73, 80–82, 144, 195, 205–9, 213–14, 219, 222–23, 250n5, 252n20, 261n5; scholarship on, 14–23; as screenwriter, 1–2, 7–8, 12–13, 16–25, 27–36, 40–52, 61–82, 108–30, 134–37, 144, 151–56, 167–69, 171, 174–88, 191–93, 195–98, 200–202, 222–23, 231–33, 236–37, 241–45, 247–48, 249n2, 250n7, 251nn14–15, 253n1, 254n6, 254nn8–9, 255n14, 256n16, 256nn18–19, 258n5, 260n6, 261n3,

Faulkner, William (*continued*)
  262n6, 263n1; sexual difference and,
  33–40; "Snow" (1942), 168–69, 174–76,
  195–96, 259n1; *Soldier's Pay* (1926),
  25–26, 72–73; *The Sound and the Fury*
  (1929), 8–10, 15–16, 25–26, 47–49,
  139–40, 157–58, 167–68, 170–74, 191–96,
  217–18, 250n11, 261n24; "Splinter Fleet"
  (1936), 42, 46, 115–20, 122, 129–30;
  "Spotted Horses" (1931), 217–18;
  "Stallion Road" (1945), 44–45, 47–48,
  168–69, 175–76, 181–82, 241–42; "Sutter's Gold" (1934), 16, 113–15, 250n7,
  251n13, 264n10; "That Evening Sun"
  (1931), 207–8, 219, 261n5, 263n14; "To
  Have and Have Not" (1944), 168–69,
  186–88, 256n19; *The Town* (1957), 4, 25,
  228–30, 236–39; "Turn About" (1932),
  29–30, 46, 52, 72–77, 80–84, 251n14;
  "Two Dollar Wife" (1936), 253n5;
  The Unvanquished (1938), 263n4; "War
  Birds / A Ghost Story" (1932–33), 232,
  255n14; women and, 2–3
Female (1933), 115
Feminine Mystique, The (1963), 226–27
feminist criticism, 9, 92–94, 226–27;
  feminist film criticism, 33–35, 38–39,
  41, 56–57, 93–94, 252n18
femme fatale, 22–23, 44–45, 47–48, 58,
  167–69, 171–73, 175–82, 195–96, 230,
  240–43. *See also* noir
fetishization, 33–35, 56–57, 92–94,
  100–101, 105, 143–44
Fiedler, Leslie, 53
Fielding, Henry, 196
Filene, Catherine, 158–59
film: audiences for, 13, 17–18, 29–30, 33–35,
  41–43, 65–66, 74–76, 81–82, 94–95,
  113–14, 156, 158–59, 161, 204; aviation
  and, 16–17, 83–84; change and, 242–43;
  close-up, 71, 113–15, 182, 219–20, 222;
  collaboration and, 23–25, 27–33, 75–76,
  86–87, 101, 111–12, 119–27, 129–30, 134,
  197–98, 234, 243–45, 250n7, 263n1; continuity editing, 6–7, 15–16; as corporate
  art, 137; cross-media exchanges, 2–4,
  6–9, 11–16, 19–23, 28–29, 35–36, 48,
  66–67, 83–85, 93–94, 151–54, 171, 175–76,
  195–96, 231–33, 247–48, 250n11, 251n14;
  gender and, 3, 6–9, 22–23, 33–46, 53–54,
  56–58, 63, 65–66, 71–72, 74–75, 80–82,
  85–86, 99–101, 148–60, 168–69, 172, 230,
  261n24; genre conventions of, 12–14,
  17–19, 22–23, 40–48, 63, 65–66, 81–82,
  143, 148–56, 158–59, 260nn6–7; high-angle shot, 212–13; indecipherability
  and, 192–93; lighting, 188–89, 219–20;
  mise-en-scène, 106–7, 202–4, 219–20;
  modernism and, 15–17, 19, 250n11;
  morality and, 61–66, 71–72, 80–81;
  180-degree rule, 6–7; pornography
  and, 9–10; race and, 211–17, 262n8; set
  design and, 138–39; sexuality in, 17–18,
  29–30, 45–46, 50–52, 62, 66–72, 76–77,
  80–81, 85–86, 100–105, 123–24, 128–29,
  148–51, 153–56, 181–84, 186–89, 193–94;
  shot/reverse shots, 6–7; sound and,
  219–20, 246–48, 264n10, 264n12; space
  and, 33–34; spectatorship and, 17–18,
  33–40, 56–58, 136, 149–56, 252n18; style
  and, 219–20; technique and, 113–14;
  time and, 33–34, 242–43; transnational
  exchange and, 168–69, 188–91, 195–96;
  violence and, 50–51; visual language of,
  114–15; voice and, 254n8; voice-over,
  177–78, 212–13, 262n13; war and, 83–84,
  113–18, 251n12, 259n3
Fitzgerald, Edith, 75–76
Fitzgerald, F. Scott, 1–2, 11, 23–25, 53, 62,
  75–76, 143–44, 244

Fitzgerald, Zelda, 59–60
flâneur, 145–46
flapper, 28–29, 45–46, 50–60, 62, 65–67, 70–72, 80–82, 207–8, 253n2
Flaubert, Gustave, 38
focalization, 59
Ford, John, 1–2, 86, 115–16, 253n23
Ford, Ruth, 2–3, 28–29, 197–98, 252n16, 261n1, 263n2
Forsaking All Others (1934), 71–72
Francke, Lizzie, 150–51, 158–60, 162–63
Frankfurt School, 4–5
Friedan, Betty, 226–27
Fulton, Keith Louise, 230
Furthman, Jules, 93–96, 124–26, 128–30, 256nn18–19, 259n4

Gable, Clark, 73
gangster (genre), 53, 58, 70–71
Garbo, Greta, 68–69, 73, 148–51
Garnier, Caroline, 58–59
Gautreau, Justin, 11–12
gaze, 33–34, 38–39, 56–57, 74–75, 86, 92–93, 97, 151–52, 154, 157–58
gender: agency and, 63, 99, 103–4, 108–9, 116–18, 127–29, 150, 165–66; androgyny and, 94–101, 109, 112–13, 121–22, 129–30, 134, 234–36; authority and, 79–81; body and, 163–66; characterization and, 22–23, 40–47, 52–60, 65–66, 74–77, 85–94, 107–9, 126, 152–54, 168–69, 172–73, 175–85, 193–96, 202–4, 210–11, 220–23, 230–43, 249n1, 253n2, 260nn6–7; class and, 55–56; collaboration and, 14–15, 23–33, 46, 75–76, 95–96, 101, 123–24, 127, 134, 162–63, 234; commodification and, 36–40, 47–48, 56–57, 142–48, 157–61, 165–66, 172, 195; community and, 92–94, 97, 263n9; consumption and, 37–38, 86, 99–101, 103–5; contagion and, 10; cross-dressing and, 88, 112–13, 234–36, 263n4; desire and, 17–18, 42–43, 45, 54–55, 74–75, 80–81, 89–91, 93–94, 97, 99–101, 103–6, 109, 148–49, 158–60, 199–200, 210–17, 252n18; domesticity and, 88–94, 97–98, 108–9, 154–56, 199–204, 207–13, 216–17, 220–27, 235–36; genre and, 2–3, 6–9, 14–15, 22–23, 28–29, 40–48, 63, 65–66, 81–82, 143, 148–59, 168–69, 172–73, 176–82, 223–24, 230, 236–38, 240–42, 256n16, 260nn6–7; high/low divide and, 46–47; indecipherability and, 175–80, 182–85, 187–88, 191–96, 241–42; labor and, 87–88, 91–99, 101–3, 105–6, 111–14, 117–22, 127, 129–30, 134–36, 139–48, 160–63, 165–66, 233–36, 242–43, 250n4, 258n16; market and, 140–48; marriage and, 9–10, 43–44, 62, 69–70, 85–88, 97–98, 172, 198–202, 208, 216, 236–40; mediation and, 2–3, 6–9, 36–37, 194–95; mobility and, 56–57, 145–46, 242–43; modernism and, 9–10, 14–15, 22–23, 38, 45–46, 134–42, 146–48, 168–69; morality and, 61, 63–66, 71–72, 80–81; motherhood and, 106–9, 197–202, 210–13, 220–23, 225–26; popular culture and, 6–10, 14–15, 22–23, 46–47, 51–53, 56–57, 134–51, 157–61, 165–66, 172; race and, 207–9, 211–17, 224–27, 252n18; screenwriting and, 7–9, 22–25, 27–31, 42, 45–46, 52, 62, 65–66, 75–76, 79–82, 93–96, 111, 120–26, 130–31, 134–36, 150–51, 158–62, 178–79, 183–84, 199–202, 226, 230; sexual difference and, 33–40, 168–69; sexuality and, 17–18, 42–43, 45–46, 50–52, 66–72, 76–82, 85–86, 93–94, 100–106, 119–20, 123–24, 128–29, 148–51, 153–54, 157–60,

gender (*continued*)
163, 172–73, 176–79, 181–84, 186–89, 193–94, 198–99, 208–11, 233–34, 252n18, 253nn4–5, 260n20; spectatorship and, 56–59, 92–94, 97, 99–100, 105–6, 136, 149–58, 184–85, 252n20; transgression and, 70–72, 76–82, 89, 93–94, 96–97, 101–2, 105–6, 117–18, 121–23, 127–30, 134, 144, 197–202, 209–11, 214–17, 234–36, 263n4; transnational exchange and, 172, 193–94, 242, 259n1; violence and, 58–59, 63–64, 179–82, 207–19; visual culture and, 3, 14–15, 22–23, 33–40, 47–48, 50–51, 53–54, 56–57, 59, 86, 92–93, 97–109, 113–15, 136, 148–63, 168–69, 173–78, 182, 184–85, 191–96, 212; voice and, 244–46; warfare and, 111–18, 176–77, 185–89, 195–96, 199–200, 230–36, 242–43, 263n4; womanhood and, 85–86, 108–9, 119–20

genre: conventions of, 1–5, 11–14, 17–19, 22–23, 40–48, 63, 65–66, 81–82, 143, 148–56, 158–59, 260nn6–7; gender and, 2–3, 6–9, 14–15, 22–23, 28–29, 40–48, 63, 65–66, 81–82, 143, 148–59, 168–69, 172–73, 176–82, 223–24, 230, 236–38, 240–42, 256n16, 260nn6–7; hybridity and, 84; as ideological, 40–48; regional, 11–12

Gentlemen Prefer Blondes (1925), 62
German Expressionism, 188–89
Gilbert, John, 73
Gillman, Susan, 215–16
Gleeson-White, Sarah, 16, 21–22, 24–25, 112, 115–16, 251n13, 262n13, 264n10
Godden, Richard, 12–13, 250n9
Goldman, Morton, 8–9
Gone with the Wind (1939), 48, 214–15, 254n7

Gorilla Man, The (1943), 197–98
Gothic, 47–48, 168–69, 172–73, 175–76, 182–85, 201–2, 260nn6–7, 260n20
Grand Hotel (1932), 73
Grant, Cary, 69–70, 87–91, 109–10, 234–35
Grayzel, Susan R., 76–77
Greenberg, Clement, 106–7
Griffith, D. W., 213–14
Grimwood, Michael, 12–13, 259n17
Gwin, Minrose C., 2–3, 164, 173–74

Hackel, Kristina, 178–79
hack writer, 7–8, 136, 142–44, 147–48, 165–66, 257n4
Hagood, Taylor, 97–98, 255n8
Halberstam, Jack, 183–84
Hamblin, Robert W., 251n14
Hannon, Charles, 161–62
hard-boiled writing, 30–31, 55–56, 58, 178–82, 189–91, 201–2, 222–23
Harlow, Jean, 38–39, 68–69, 100–101
Haskell, Molly, 41–43, 50, 59–60, 85, 93–94, 200, 236–38, 253n2
Hawks, Howard, 1–2, 7–8, 12–13, 15–17, 19, 21–22, 29–31, 72–74, 81–92, 95–96, 111, 121, 123–26, 129–30, 134, 137, 178–79, 183–84, 192–93, 234–35, 253n8, 254n4, 256n16, 259n4, 263n1
Hawksian woman, 42, 46, 48, 86–95, 108–10, 112–19, 122–24, 126–27, 129–30, 230, 233–34, 242–43, 253n23, 256n16
Hays Code. *See* Motion Picture Production Code
Hecht, Ben, 88
Hélion, Jean, 24–25
Hemingway, Ernest, 16–17, 123–25, 190–91
Hepburn, Katherine, 109–10
Herman, David, 59
Hervey, Harry C., 200–201
Hickman, Lisa C., 26–27

high/low divide, 4–6, 9–10, 19–22, 46–47, 133–48, 250n7, 251n13, 255n13
His Girl Friday (1940), 85–89, 234–36
Hitchcock, Alfred, 243–44, 254n7
Hollywood novel, 3, 11–14, 33, 38–40, 48, 133–34, 230, 250n7, 250n9, 251n15
Holmes, Odetta, 262n8
hooks, bell, 215–16, 252n18
Hopkins, Miriam, 71, 253n4
Horkheimer, Max, 4–6, 147–48
horror, 38–39, 151–52, 156, 168–69, 197–98, 251nn14–15
Howard, Leslie, 237–38
Hulsey, Dallas, 74
Humm, Maggie, 41
Hurst, Fannie, 262n12
Huston, John, 120–21
Huyssen, Andreas, 9, 38, 134–35, 146
hybridity, 13–14, 42, 51–52, 84, 88, 205–6, 216–17, 231, 244–45
hypothesis, 58–59, 253n2

illusion, 3–6, 10
Imitation of Life (1959), 220–24
improvisation, 29–33, 104, 124–27, 234–35
In a Lonely Place (1950), 13
indeterminacy, 16–19
infanticide, 207–8, 211–17
inscrutability, 38–39, 47–48, 145–46, 158, 168–69, 172, 175–79, 182–83, 185–88, 192–96, 241–42, 260n6
interiority, 114–15, 160
Intermezzo (1939), 237–40
International Alliance of Theatrical Stage Employees (IA), 161–62
Isherwood, Christopher, 24–25
I Was a Male War Bride (1949), 234–35

Jackson, Robert, 24–25, 27–28, 101
Jacobs, Lea, 63

James, Henry, 219–20
Jazz Age, 53–54, 62
Jewell, K. Sue, 226–27
Johnny Belinda (1948), 238–39, 263n7
John-Steiner, Vera, 23–24
Johnston, Claire, 41, 100–101
Jones, Anne Goodwyn, 135, 141–42, 257n2
journalism, 87–89, 255n8

Kang, Hee, 230
Kaplan, E. Ann, 177, 218–19
Karem, Jeff, 251n14
Karlova, Irina (Helen Mary Elizabeth Clamp), 183–84
Kawin, Bruce F., 15–16, 66–69, 95–96, 123, 125–26, 129–30, 232, 255n6, 256n18, 259n4
Keaton, Buster, 73
Keith, Nancy "Slim," 88, 254n4
King, Vincent Allen, 148–49
kitsch, 106–7
Knights, Pamela, 12–13, 250n9
Kristeva, Julia, 151–52
Kurnitz, Harry, 263n1

labor, 93–95; art and, 139–48; collaborative, 95–99, 101–3, 117–22, 127, 129–30, 243–45, 250n7; erotic, 105–6; gender and, 96–99, 101–2, 111–14, 117–22, 127, 134–36, 139–48, 160–63, 165–66, 233–36, 242–43, 250n4, 258n16; modernism and, 139–42; of screenwriting, 97–99, 101–2, 243–45; wage, 133–34
Ladd, Barbara, 221–22
Laird, Holly A., 25–26
Landay, Lori, 56
Land of the Pharaohs (1955), 251n15, 263n1
Lang, Fritz, 188–89
Langlois, Henri, 16–17
LaSalle, Mick, 62

Last Slaver, The (1937), 118–19
Laughing Sinners (1931), 75–76
LaValley, Albert J., 182
Left Hand of God, The (1955), 118–19
Lester, Cheryl, 170–71
Letter from an Unknown Woman (1948), 212–13, 216
Levien, Sonya, 158–59
Lifeboat (1944), 254n7
literature: collaboration and, 86–87; cross-media exchanges, 2–4, 6–9, 11–16, 19–23, 28–29, 35–36, 48, 66–67, 83–85, 93–94, 151–54, 171, 175–76, 195–96, 231–33, 247–48, 250n11, 251n14; gender and, 6–9, 22–23, 45–46, 66–67; genre and, 11; popular culture and, 97; sound and, 247–48, 264n13; transnational exchange and, 190–91, 195–96. *See also* film; popular culture
Long, Hot Summer, The (1958), 217–18
Longstreet, Stephen, 181
Loos, Anita, 62, 75–76, 158–59
Lord, Father Daniel, 51, 61
Loved One, The (1948), 11–12
Lugowski, David M., 61
Luhr, William, 192–93
Lurie, Peter, 19–21, 97, 143, 148–49, 161, 252n20

M (1931), 188–89
MacArthur, Charles, 88
MacGowan, Kenneth, 243–44
magazines, 8–9, 38–40, 46–47, 133–35, 140–44, 147–48, 157–58, 167–68, 172–73, 183–86, 195–96, 250n4
Maltby, Richard, 17–18, 62
Maltese Falcon, The (1941), 120–21, 167
mammy, 211–17, 224–26, 262n8
Mankiewicz, Joseph L., 244
Mao, Douglas, 21–22

March, Frederic, 71
Marion, Frances, 75–76, 159–60, 162
market, 12–13, 46–47, 133–48
Markey, Gene, 115
Marx, Sam, 75–76
masquerade, 38–39, 86, 101–4
mass culture. *See* popular culture
materialism, 121, 146–47
Matthews, John T., 9, 19–21, 74–76, 97–99, 101–2, 119–20, 148–49, 205, 255n8
May, Elaine Tyler, 198–99
McCall, Mary, Jr., 162
McCarthy, Todd, 29–30, 87
McCoy, Horace, 250n9
Mecholsky, Kristopher, 242
mediation, 3, 20–21, 34–38, 41–42, 44–45, 93–95, 97–99, 123, 146–47, 151–54, 156–58, 172–73, 175–78, 194–96
melodrama, 22–23, 38–39, 42–44, 48, 63, 84, 108–9, 143, 160–61, 167, 261n4, 262n10; characterization and, 202–4, 210–11, 220–26, 230, 236–43, 260nn6–7; Cold War and, 198–99, 205–8, 216–19, 221–22, 225–27, 261n2; domesticity and, 143, 198–211, 214–15, 217–20, 224–27, 261n2; family and, 199–200, 208, 217–26; maternal, 197–98, 200–202; race and, 48, 211–20, 224–27; sacrificial, 236–40, 242–43; style and, 217–26, 262n12; themes of, 199–200; violence and, 211–17
Melville, Herman, 219–20
Mercury Theatre group, 28–29
Meriwether, James B., 169–70
Metro-Goldwyn-Mayer (MGM), 1–2, 12, 28–30, 33–34, 45–46, 50–52, 61–62, 65–66, 71–82, 115, 137, 144, 150–51, 153–54, 158–60, 254n6
Midnight Mary (1933), 115
migration, 168–69, 188–91, 195–96

INDEX

Mildred Pierce (1945), 1–2, 19, 44–45, 47–48, 167, 201–4, 208, 210, 212–13, 216, 260n7
Millholland, Ray, 115–16
Minnelli, Vincente, 217
misogyny, 29–30, 36–37, 60, 123–24, 129–30, 154–55, 233, 258n8
Miss Lonelyhearts (1933), 144
mobility, 56–57, 145–46, 242–43
modernism, 86–87, 231; collaboration and, 23–27; film and, 15–17, 19; gender and, 8–10, 14–15, 38, 45–46, 134–42, 146–48, 168–69; inscrutability and, 194–96; labor and, 139–42; motion and, 139; popular culture and, 2–11, 14–16, 19–22, 46–47, 134–42, 146–48, 165–66, 168–69, 189–91, 194–96, 250n11; transnational exchange and, 190–91, 195–96
modernity, 16–17, 57–58, 98–99, 242
moll (gangster's girlfriend), 58
montage, 15–16, 113–14, 160–61, 250n10
Montgomery, Robert, 73
Moore, Michelle E., 183–84, 251n14, 260n20
Morgan, Frederick, 223–24
Morocco (1930), 93–94
Morrison, Spencer, 206
Motion Picture Producers and Distributors of America (MPPDA), 61
Motion Picture Production Code, 17–18, 45–46, 50–51, 58, 61–63, 70–72, 85–86, 91–92, 101–2, 104–6, 181, 233–34
movie theater, 36, 246, 264n11
Mulvey, Laura, 33–36, 56–57, 92–93, 220–21, 245–46, 252n18
Murphet, Julian, 19–21
Murphy, Dudley, 250n7, 251n15
My Sin (1931), 64–65

Naremore, James, 19, 189–91
Negulesco, Jean, 238–39

network, 23–25, 46, 50–51, 75–76, 86–87, 102, 124, 130–31, 149–51, 162–63, 171, 245
New Modernist Studies, 21–22
newspaper, 38–40, 87–91, 97–99, 140, 174–75
New Woman, 51–53, 59–60, 65–66, 207–8, 253n5
Nobel Prize, 204–5
No Down Payment (1957), 218–19
noir, 17–19, 22–23, 30–31, 38–39, 41–45, 47–48, 58, 167–69, 188–93, 195–98, 240–42, 256n16, 259n3, 260n7, 261n23; gender and, 168–69, 172–73, 175–82. See also femme fatale

Ober, Harold, 174–75
objectification, 9–10, 39–40, 195, 252n18, 261n24
Oldham, Estelle, 2–3, 25–26, 28–29
Omlie, Phoebe, 96–97
Omlie, Vernon, 96–97
Only Angels Have Wings (1939), 87, 89–96, 116, 124–25

Paramore, Edward E., Jr., 244
Paramount Pictures, 49–51, 68–69, 70–71, 158–59
Parker, Dorothy, 158–59
patriarchy, 2–3, 45, 58, 60, 92–93, 97–98, 101–2, 108–9, 193–94, 201–2, 230
Penner, Erin, 171, 191–92
performance, performativity, 57–59, 103–4, 220–23
Plastic Age, The (1925), 54–55
Polk, Noel, 25, 211–12
popular culture: body and, 114–15; colonization of, 106–7; commerce and, 3–4, 7–10, 12–13, 133–48; critique of, 14–15, 19–21; gender and, 7–10, 14–15,

popular culture (*continued*)
22–23, 46–47, 51–52, 53, 56–57, 91–92, 134–51, 157–61, 165–66, 172; illusion and, 3–4, 7–10, 12–13; inscrutability and, 194–96; literature and, 97; modernism and, 2–11, 14–16, 19–23, 46–47, 134–42, 146–48, 165–66, 168–69, 189–91, 194–96; sexuality and, 9–10, 13, 104–5, 148–51; technology and, 106–7; transnational exchange and, 188–91. *See also* film; visual culture
pornography, 9–10, 104, 146–47, 158
prestige, 24–25
Production Code Administration, 50, 61, 71–72, 85, 105–6
prostitution, 8–9, 63, 68–69, 107–8, 185–88, 193–94, 207–8, 219
psychoanalysis, 33–35, 56–57, 252n18
pulp fiction, 8–9, 38, 146–49, 165–66

queerness, 61
Quigley, Martin, 51

race, racism, 35–36; in film, 262n8; gender and, 207–9, 211–17, 224–27, 252n18; melodrama and, 48, 211–20, 224–27; stereotypes and, 213–17, 224–27. *See also* mammy
Radio-Keith-Orpheum (RKO), 1–2, 118–19, 137
Ramsey, D. Matthew, 29–30, 74–75, 253n4
Random House, 25
rape, 57–59, 63–64, 152–54, 186–87, 207–9, 218–19. *See also* violence
Ratoff, Gregory, 237–38
Ray, Nicholas, 217
realism, 137–39, 188–89
Reames, Kelly Lynch, 210–11
Rebner, Wolfgang, 132–33
Red-Headed Woman (1932), 62, 68–69, 75–76, 100–101

Red River (1948), 87
Renov, Michael, 210
repetition, 21–22
repulsion, 38–39
resemblance (formal), 14–17
Rhodes, Chip, 13
Ritt, Martin, 217–19
Rivera, Diego, 137
RKO. *See* Radio-Keith-Orpheum
Road to Glory, The (1936), 7–8, 31, 46, 118–19, 121, 253n23
Roberts, Diane, 104, 193–94, 208–9, 238–39, 245, 249n1
Rogers, Ginger, 85–86
Rollyson, Carl, 21–22, 76–77, 236–37, 262n13, 263n2
romance, 19–21, 85–86, 143, 148–52, 154–56
Rosen, Marjorie, 41
Ross, Sara, 53–54, 56–58
Ross, Stephen M., 247–48
Rostand, Edmond, 140
Ruggles, Wesley, 54–55
Russell, Rosalind, 85–91, 93–94

sacrificial woman, 108–9, 200–204, 208, 211–13, 216–17, 220–21, 226, 230, 236–40. *See also* melodrama
Sartre, Jean-Paul, 190–91
Sayre, Joel, 111–15
Sbardellati, John, 198
Scarface (1932), 137
Scarlet Street (1945), 188–89
Schatz, Thomas, 40–41, 137, 217
Schrader, Paul, 188–89
Schreiber, Evelyn Jaffe, 230
Schulberg, B. P., 11–12, 158–59
Scola, Kathryn, 2–3, 30–31, 115–18
Screen Directors Guild, 162
screenplay (form), 15–23, 33–35, 42, 74–82, 93–94, 111–18, 125–26, 134–35, 168–69,

171, 174–76, 178–85, 195–96, 200–201, 222–23, 232–33, 241–42, 251nn14–15, 254n8, 255nn13–14, 256nn18–19
Screen Writers Guild (SWG), 162
screwball comedy, 12–13, 22–23, 38–39, 42, 46, 85–88, 91, 109–10, 154, 234–35
Scribner's, 25–26
Script Clerks Guild, 162
script supervisor, 7–8, 31, 118–19, 121, 162. *See also* Carpenter Wilde, Meta
secret agent, 22–23, 47–48, 167–69, 186
Sensibar, Judith L., 2–3, 25–26
sentimentality, 42–43, 48, 75–76, 120–21, 143, 211–12, 214–15, 236–37, 240–41
set design, 135–39
sexuality: agency and, 103–4; class and, 55–56; collaboration and, 27; domesticity and, 198–99; in film, 17–18, 29–30, 33–36, 45–46, 50–52, 62, 66–72, 76–81, 85–86, 100–105, 123–24, 128–29, 149–51, 153–56; gender and, 17–18, 42–43, 45–46, 50–52, 66–72, 76–82, 85–86, 93–94, 100–106, 119–20, 123–24, 128–29, 148–51, 153–54, 157–60, 163, 172–73, 176–79, 181–84, 186–89, 193–94, 198–99, 208–11, 233–34, 252n18, 253nn4–5, 260n20; popular culture and, 9–10, 13; race and, 35–36; technology and, 102–3; wartime and, 76–79
Shakespeare, William, 140
Shanghai Express (1932), 93–94
Sharot, Stephen, 52
She Done Him Wrong (1933), 68–70
Sheridan, Ann, 234–35
Sherman, Lowell, 68–69
silence, 242–48, 264nn12–13
silent film, 51–53, 59, 61, 73, 114–15, 161, 243–48, 250n11, 253n3
Silverman, Kaja, 245–46
Sirk, Douglas, 48, 217, 219–26, 262nn9–10

Sklar, Robert, 51, 69–70
Smith, Harrison, 8–9
Smith, Murray, 260n6
Smith, Phil, 257n4
Solomon, Stefan, 21–22, 65–66, 68–69, 174–75, 185–86, 253n5, 254n8, 258n16, 261n23, 262n13
Sound and the Fury, The (1959), 217–18
source text, 21–22
Southern imaginary: gender and, 3, 25–26, 65–66, 119–20, 185–86, 193–94, 208–9, 249n1; Hollywood and, 3, 50–51, 175; race and, 214–15
spectacle, 33–36, 38–40, 59, 91–92, 103–6, 150–52, 156–58
spectatorship, 56–57, 92–94, 97, 99–100, 105–6, 136, 149–58, 184–85, 215–16, 252n18
Spiegel, Alan, 12
Splinter Fleet of the Otranto Barrage, The (1936), 115–16
spy movie, 167, 185–86, 197–98
Stahl, John M., 262n12
Stanwyck, Barbara, 93–94
Steinbeck, John, 190–91
Stella Dallas (1937), 201
Sternberg, Josef von, 126
Steven, Mark, 250n11
Stillinger, Jack, 25
Stoker, Bram, 183–84
storyboarding, 136, 160–61
Story of Temple Drake, The (1933), 70–71
Stringer, Dorothy, 224–25
studio system: collaboration and, 121–22, 250n7, 263n1; corporate, 121; dialogue and, 243–46; end of, 221–22; gender and, 39–40, 52, 101–2, 121–22, 135–36, 158–61; genre and, 41–42; labor and, 101–2, 138, 158–59, 161–63, 250n7, 258n16; stars and, 1–2, 73, 75, 121

Submarine Patrol (1938), 30–31
suffering woman. *See* sacrificial woman
suicide, 67–68, 228–29
Sullavan, Margaret, 244
Sundquist, Eric J., 194
Sunset Boulevard (1950), 13
superwoman, 110
surface/depth distinction, 3–7, 202
Susan Lennox (Her Fall and Rise) (1931), 68–69

Tarnished Angels, The (1957), 217–18
Taylor, Dwight, 75–76
television, 136, 151–56, 221–22, 252n16, 258n5
Thalberg, Irving, 29–30, 73, 75–76, 159–60
theater, 28–29, 143, 197–98, 223–24, 231, 252n16
Three Comrades (1938), 244
thriller, 167, 185–86
Tiger Shark (1932), 84–85
Today We Live (1933), 1–2, 16–17, 19–21, 73, 83–84, 95–96, 134, 251n14
To Have and Have Not (1944), 1–2, 19–21, 29–31, 35, 45–48, 86, 88, 91–96, 123–30, 167, 223–24, 235–36, 244, 259n4, 260n5
Towner, Theresa M., 230, 241
transgression. *See under* gender
transnationalism, 168–69, 172, 193–96, 242, 259n1. *See also under* film; gender; literature; modernism; popular culture
transvestism, 38–39, 86, 88–91, 93–94, 97, 99–101, 112–13, 234–36, 263n4. *See also* androgyny; gender
treatment, 12, 15–18, 28–29, 34–35, 45–46, 50–51, 66–72, 75–76, 79–81, 85, 110, 113–14, 144, 197–98, 200–202, 250n8, 256n18
Tunberg, Karl, 115–16
Turner, Lana, 220–21

Twentieth Century-Fox, 1–2, 7–8, 46, 81–82, 86, 111, 118–19, 132–33, 137

Uncle Tom's Cabin (1852), 213–14
unionization, 161–62
Universal Studios, 1–2, 137
Urgo, Joseph R., 31–33, 173–74, 208–9, 250n7, 263n8

vampires, 168–69, 183–85, 251n14
vamps, 65–66
Variety (magazine), 62
vice film, 12, 17–18, 22–23, 28–29, 41–42, 45–46, 50–51, 62, 65–66, 69–71, 80–81, 144, 151–52. *See also* bad girl
Viertel, Salka, 150–51
violence: in film, 50–51; gender and, 58–59; in melodrama, 211–19; sexual, 57–59, 63–64, 152–54, 186–87, 207–11, 218–19
Virilio, Paul, 251n12
vision, 3, 13–14, 36, 38–39, 47–48, 136, 139, 168–69, 177–78, 194–95
visual culture: body and, 114–15; gender and, 3, 14–15, 22–23, 33–40, 47–48, 50–51, 53–54, 56–57, 59, 86, 92–93, 97–109, 113–15, 136, 148–63, 168–69, 173–78, 182, 184–85, 191–96, 212; mediation and, 3, 114–15; sexuality and, 103–6, 153–54, 157–58; style and, 15–16, 19–21, 50–51, 53–54, 138–39, 212–13, 219–20
voyeurism, 33, 36, 38, 52, 56–57, 92–93, 99, 104–5, 252n20

Wagner, Vivian, 102–3
Wald, Jerry, 4–5
Walkowitz, Rebecca L., 21–22
war film, 22–23, 30–31, 47–48, 74, 83–84, 86–87, 111–18, 167–69, 176–77, 185–88, 195–96, 231–34, 242–43, 251n14

Warner Brothers, 1–2, 28–30, 42–43, 46–48, 62, 81–82, 86, 108–9, 115, 120–21, 123, 167, 174–78, 181, 185–86, 191, 197–98, 200–201, 233–34, 236–37, 261n3, 262n6
Waste Land, The (1922), 140–41
Watson, Jay, 16–17, 211–12, 264n12
Waugh, Evelyn, 11–12
Welles, Orson, 28–29
West, Mae, 68–70
West, Nathanael, 1–2, 11, 144
Western film, 28–29, 163–64, 178–79, 251n15
What Makes Sammy Run? (1941), 11–12
Whitney, Allison, 224
Wilder, Billy, 188–89
William Morris Agency, 152
Williams, Joan, 26–27, 222–23
Williams, Linda, 158, 201–2, 213–14
Williams, Michael, 235–36
Winchester Pictures, 118–19
Wise, Naomi, 91
wisecrack, 116–18

Wister, Owen, 163–64
Wizard of Oz, The (1939), 74
Wollen, Peter, 16–17, 88–89, 92–93
woman's film. *See* melodrama
Woman Who Came Back, The (1945), 197–98
Wood, Robin, 92–93, 123–24
working woman, 46, 65–66, 85–86, 109
workplace film, 234
World War II, 44–45, 47–48, 91–92, 130–31, 168–70, 176–77, 185–90, 197–98, 204, 216–19, 233–36
Wright Brothers, 16–17
Written on the Wind (1955), 223–24
Wyman, Jane, 238–39

Yarbrough, Scott, 58
Young-Minor, Ethel, 263n14

Zanuck, Darryl F., 112, 115
Zeitlin, Michael, 16–17, 83–84, 251n14, 255nn8–9
Zender, Karl F., 12–13, 97–98, 146–47, 163, 210–11, 247–48, 255n8

www.ingramcontent.com/pod-product-compliance
Lightning Source LLC
Chambersburg PA
CBHW030609230426
43661CB00053B/1903